THE BELARUSIAN SHTETL

JEWS IN EASTERN EUROPE

Jeffrey Veidlinger
Mikhail Krutikov
Geneviève Zubrzycki
Editors

THE BELARUSIAN SHTETL

HISTORY AND MEMORY

EDITED BY
Irina Kopchenova and Mikhail Krutikov

TRANSLATED BY
Bela Shayevich and Sebastian Z. Schulman

INDIANA UNIVERSITY PRESS

This book is a publication of

Indiana University Press
Office of Scholarly Publishing
Herman B Wells Library 350
1320 East 10th Street
Bloomington, Indiana 47405 USA

iupress.org

© 2023 by Indiana University Press

All rights reserved
No part of this book may be reproduced or utilized in any form or by any means, electronic or mechanical, including photocopying and recording, or by any information storage and retrieval system, without permission in writing from the publisher. The paper used in this publication meets the minimum requirements of the American National Standard for Information Sciences—Permanence of Paper for Printed Library Materials, ANSI Z39.48-1992.

Manufactured in the United States of America

First printing 2023

Cataloging information is available from the Library of Congress.

ISBN 978-0-253-06730-2 (cloth)
ISBN 978-0-253-06731-9 (paperback)
ISBN 978-0-253-06732-6 (ebook)

CONTENTS

Acknowledgments vii
Note on Geographical Names, Transliteration, and Maps ix
Maps x

Introduction *by Samuel D. Kassow, Irina Kopchenova, and Mikhail Krutikov* 1

History, Folklore, Ethnography

1. Between Miastechka and Shtetl: *Ethnicity and Religion in Small Belarusian Towns, 1800s–1930s, by Ina Sorkina* 27

2. The Soviet Belarusian Shtetl: *Between Tradition and Modernization in the 1920s and 1930s, by Arkadi Zeltser* 50

3. Days of Remembrance for Jews of the Russo-Belarusian Borderlands, *by Svetlana Amosova* 76

4. Why Hitler Did Not Like the Jews: *The Folklore Version of the Reasons behind the Holocaust, by Andrei B. Moroz* 95

Hlybokaye: Memories of the Shtetl

5. The Death of the Shtetl of Hlybokaye through the Eyes of Its Teenagers, *by Julia Bernstein* 115

6. A Family between the Ghetto and Red Army Partisans: *Two Holocaust Testimonies from Hlybokaye, by Julia Bernstein* 146

7. Daily Life in the Hlybokaye Ghetto: *Photographs from the United States Holocaust Memorial Museum, by Irina Kopchenova* 159

8. Representations of the Jewish Past in Today's Hlybokaye: *Memory on Demand?, by Mikhail Lurie and Natalia Savina* 171

Appendix: *The Shtetl of Zhaludok: A Memoir,
by Miron Mordukhovich*   199

Bibliography   247
Editors and Contributors   267
Index   269

ACKNOWLEDGMENTS

This book would not be possible without the dedicated help and support of many individuals and organizations. The ethnographic expeditions that produced field materials were conducted by the Sefer Center for University Teaching of Jewish Civilization (Moscow), and we are grateful to their academic leaders—Olga Belova, Aleksandra Fishel, Motl Gordon, Andrei Moroz, Michael Nosonovsky, Tamara Solomatina, and Mikhail Vasilyev—as well as to the Sefer's research director, Victoria Mochalova, and director, Anna Shayevich. We want to express our thanks to Margarita Kozhenevskaya for suggesting her native town of Hlybokaye as an expedition site and managing many of the organizational aspects, and to Sergey Pivovarchik for the idea of exploring the Belarusian-Jewish heritage of the town of Zhaludok. In Hlybokaye, Iurii Kolbasich, a teacher at the local art school, generously shared with us his expert knowledge of his native town and helped collect valuable materials.

Our thanks go to Margarita Trofimova for her permission to publish the memoirs and drawings of her late father, Miron Mordukhovich, about his childhood in prewar Zhaludok, and to Iakov Sukhovolskii (Kaliningrad) for sharing fragments of his memoirs.

Bela Shayevich bravely tackled the challenge of rendering the scholarly Russian, heavy with subordinate clauses, into clear English, and Sebastian Shulman contributed to the translation of Mordukhovich's memoirs. Abbey Roelofs meticulously created historical maps of Belarus. Deirdre Casey spent numerous hours putting the entire manuscript in order. We are grateful to the series' coeditors, Jeffrey Veidlinger and Geneviève Zubrzycki, for their encouragement and helpful suggestions, and to two anonymous reviewers for their careful reading and critical comments.

In the United States, the most enthusiastic supporter of this project was Deborah Rothman (Rochester, NY), whose family comes from Hlybokaye. She shared unique family photographs and put us in touch with the sons of Hlybokaye survivors Zalman and Don Feigelson (Felson). We are indebted to Leonard Felson and the Felson family for sharing their documents and photographs. The translation and publication of this book have been supported by the Stan and Pearl Felson Philanthropic Fund, the Don and Ada Felson Donor Advised Fund, Miriam Engel and Family, Leah Wolf and Lisa Ratté, and Deborah and Robert Rothman.

We express our thanks to the institutional partners of our expeditions: the Institute of Slavic Studies of the Russian Academy of Sciences, Yanka Kupala State University (Hrodna), and Polatsk State University. We are grateful to the US Holocaust Memorial Museum for the permission to reproduce photographs from the Hlybokaye ghetto, and to the YIVO Institute for Jewish Research for the permission to reproduce a prewar image of the synagogue in Zhaludok. We gratefully acknowledge the support of Sefer's expeditions and publications by the Avi Chai Foundation, the Chaise Family Foundation, the Genesis Philanthropy Group, the Jewish Agency for Israel, the Joint Distribution Committee, the Russian Science Foundation, the UJA Foundation of New York, and the Yad Hanadiv Rothschild Foundation.

The production team at Indiana University Press worked hard on bringing this manuscript to print. We thank Gary Dunham, Anna Francis, and Nancy Lightfoot for their enthusiastic support, as well as Pete Feely from Amnet Systems for taking good care of the production process and Cyndy Brown for compiling the index.

NOTE ON GEOGRAPHICAL NAMES, TRANSLITERATION, AND MAPS

As far as possible, we have tried to use the Library of Congress system of transliteration from Belarusian, including geographical names. Exceptions were made for the names of administrative regions in the Russian Empire, such as Grodno or Mogilev *guberniia*, where the Russian place-names are used, as well as for the few cities that have well-known English versions, such as Minsk and Vitebsk. We have used the Library of Congress system for Russian and the YIVO system for the transliteration from Yiddish. We used both Belarusian and Russian variants for the miastechka/mestechko. The geographical names on the four historical maps are given in the form that was official during the respective period: in Polish, Russian, or Belarusian.

MAPS

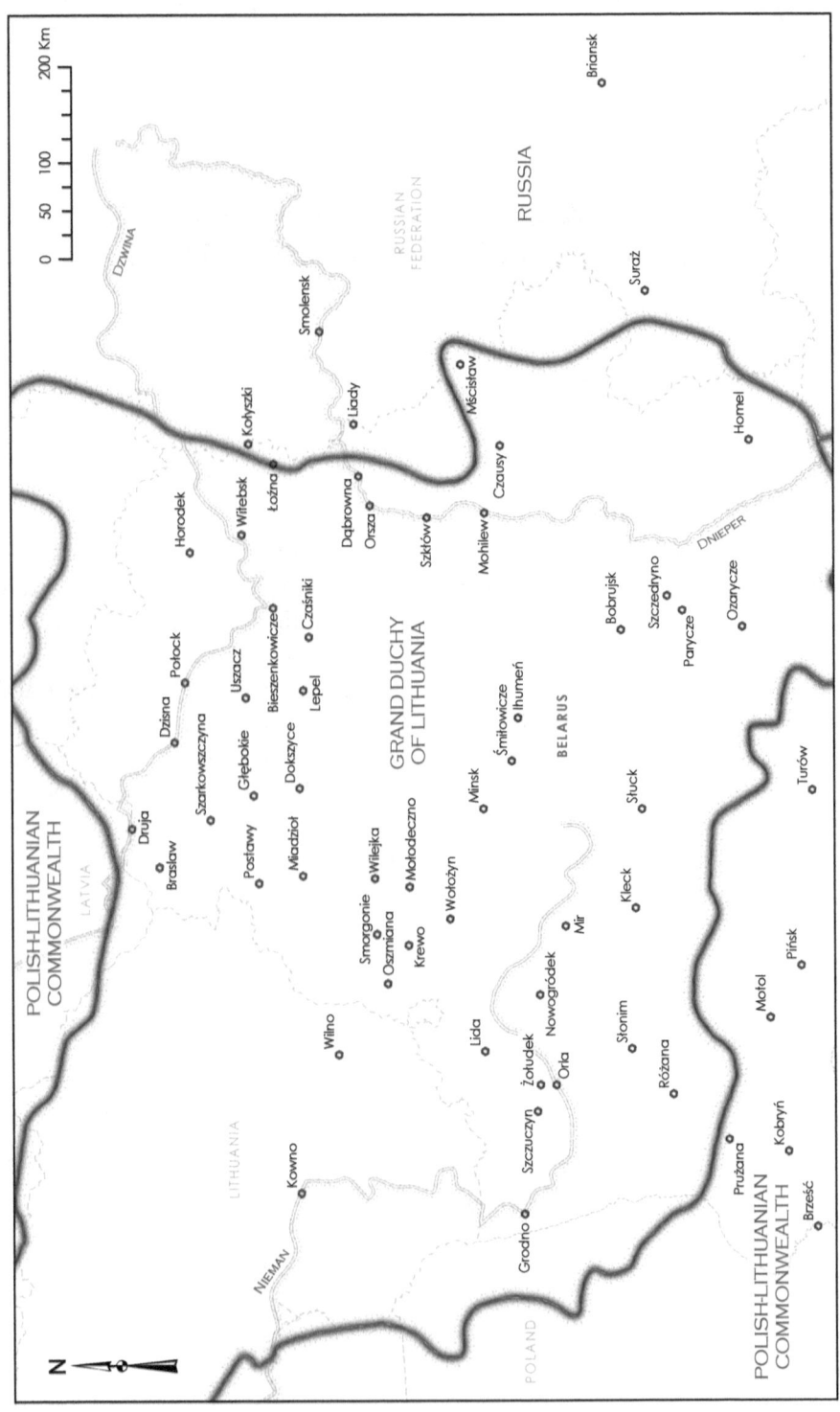

Belarus in 1757.

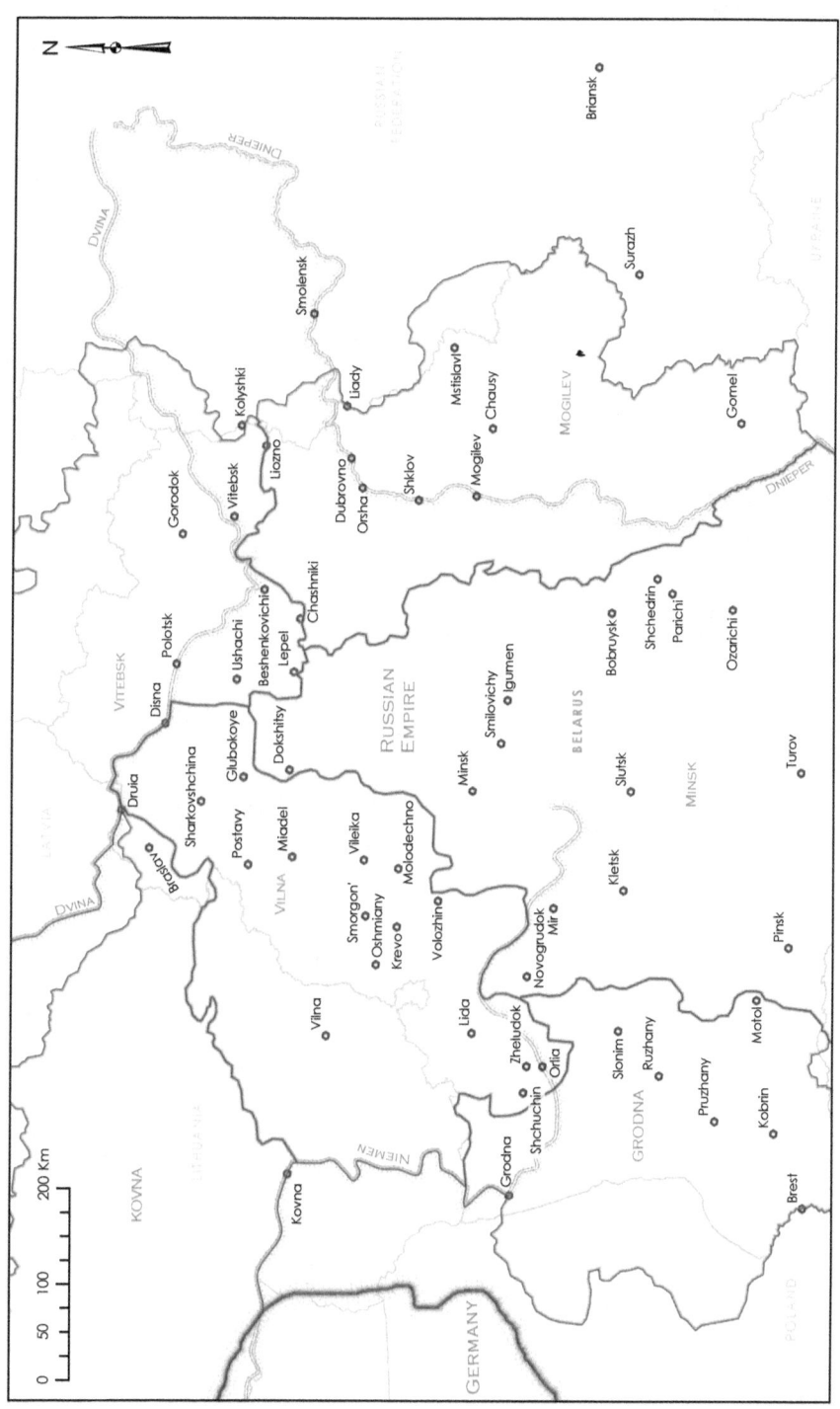

Belarus in the 19th century.

Belarus between 1921 and 1939.

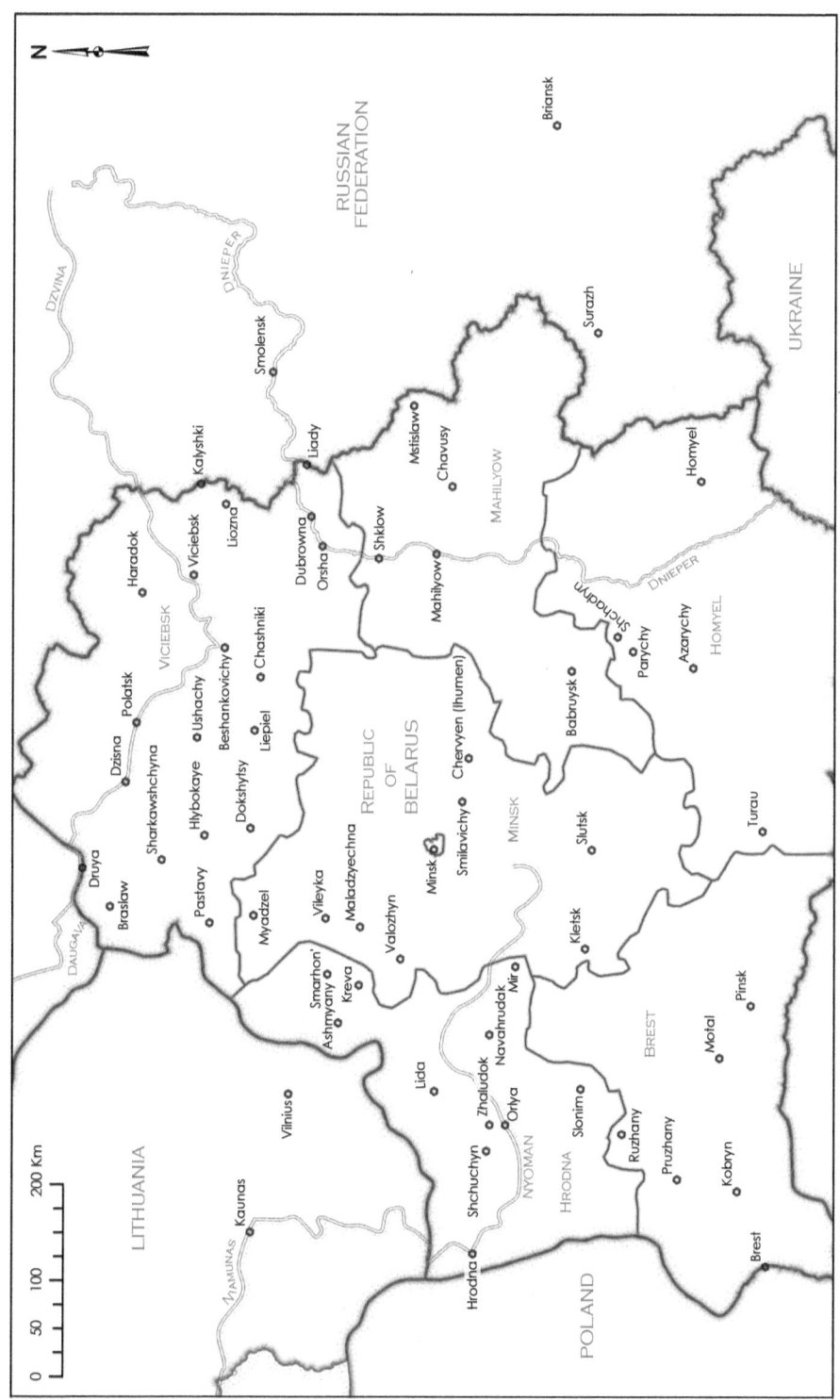

Republic of Belarus after 1991.

THE BELARUSIAN SHTETL

Introduction

SAMUEL D. KASSOW, IRINA KOPCHENOVA, AND
MIKHAIL KRUTIKOV

In the Jewish geography of Eastern Europe, Belarus was understood in two different ways. On the one hand, it was an integral part of Jewish Lithuania or *Lite*, the lands that had belonged to the Grand Duchy of Lithuania and that include, besides present-day Belarus, present-day Lithuania, northeast Poland, and part of northern Ukraine. Lite was home to the Litvaks, a Jewish "tribe" distinguished by the Yiddish language spoken by its people; its specific religious and cultural history; its cuisine; and, if one credits Jewish folklore, a certain propensity to skepticism, rational thought, and learning.[1] After the Grand Duchy became part of the Polish Commonwealth in 1569, the landowning nobility in this vast region adopted Polish culture, while the peasants, Catholic and Orthodox by religion, spoke various dialects that eventually became Lithuanian, Polish, and Belarusian.[2] On the other hand, Jews also saw Belarus as a distinct region of its own. Journeying east in Lite, one would pass into the region of Raysn, today's Belarus. In this immense region, covered by huge forests, lakes, and swamps, settlements were more spread out. While the landowning nobility still spoke Polish, the peasant dialects were closer to today's Belarusian, and more Orthodox churches appeared alongside the Catholic ones. One would observe subtle but unmistakable differences between the Jews in Raysn and their Litvak brothers to the West. While the Hasidic movement gained little traction among the western Litvaks, many shtetls in Raysn, such as Hlybokaye, embraced the Chabad sect and, to a lesser extent, the Stolin, Slonim, and Karlin sects.[3]

The Jewish toponym Raysn, a Jewish adaptation of the historic name Rus', appears in Jewish documents in the seventeenth century as a designation of eastern regions of the Grand Duchy of Lithuania and has a Polish equivalent in Kahały Białoruskie (Belarusian Jewish communities). According to Vladimir

Levin and Darius Staliunas, "Traditionally, the name Raysn had never been applied to the areas west of the River Biarezina (Barisau = Babruisk line)."[4] In the nineteenth century, Raysn became associated with the area of the Chabad Hasidism that originated in what is today Belarusian-Russian borderlands. After World War I, as Levin and Staliunas observe, "the meaning of the words *Lite* and *Raysn* changed again. While Lite became reserved for the independent Lithuanian Republic, Raysn began to be used as a name for Belarus within its political borders."[5] During the nineteenth and early twentieth centuries, the shtetl Jews of Raysn faced many challenges: the fallout from two failed insurrections against Russian rule; rapid population growth; economic development spurred by railroad building; the rise of Haskalah, Bundism, and Zionism; and the disruptions of World War I and the Russian Revolution, which resulted in the Belarusian Jewry being divided, in the interwar years, between an ethnocentric Polish Republic and a Belarusian Soviet Republic where Yiddish was one of four official languages.

Belarusian nationalism had not developed as much as Polish or Ukrainian nationalism, and relations between Jews and the Belarusian peasantry were not as fraught. Industrialization was not as intense as in Poland or Ukraine; therefore, there was little in-migration. This might help explain why the pogroms that swept through Ukraine in 1905 and particularly in 1918–21 largely, though not completely, spared Raysn (if one does not count the Polish military pogroms of 1918–20). Compared with Poland or Ukraine, a larger proportion of Belarusian Jewry lived in small shtetls and rural settings (well described in Moshe Kulbak's poem *Raysn*), and even in the few cities—Minsk, Pinsk, or Babruisk—the Jews who moved from elsewhere were Litvaks from nearby shtetls. Thus, unlike Warsaw or Lodz, which were roiling mosaics of different Jewish tribes and cultures, the cities and towns of Belarus were homogenously Litvak.

This was reflected in the cultural features of Belarusian Jewry. After the failed anti-Russian insurrections of 1830–31 and 1863–64, Russian culture, not Polish, became the "high" culture for the Jewish intelligentsia of this region. But since there were few native Russians in the area, apart from military officers and government officials, the Jewish intelligentsia in Belarus had no ready assimilationist option, nor, on the whole, did it seek one. This made the region particularly hospitable to specifically Jewish responses to modernity, such as the development of Hebrew and Yiddish literature and distinctively Jewish political movements such as Zionism and the Bund. In interwar Poland, the Jews living in Belarusian lands were the most likely to resist acculturation to Polish: the region was a stronghold of Jewish education in Hebrew and Yiddish. Likewise, in the Soviet Union, the Jews in the Belarusian Soviet Socialist

Republic (BSSR) were most likely to speak Yiddish and marry other Jews. The Jews of Polish Belarus got a temporary reprieve from Nazi rule after the outbreak of World War II when the Soviet Union invaded Poland and annexed its eastern territories in September 1939, implementing the Molotov–Ribbentrop Pact. But when Hitler attacked the USSR in June 1941, the Germans advanced so swiftly that very few Jews from the formerly Polish areas of Belarus were able to escape. Those who tried were cut off by the panzer divisions or, as happened in many cases, stopped by Soviet border guards from crossing the pre-1939 Polish-Soviet border.

Julia Bernstein's chapter "The Death of the Shtetl of Hlybokaye through the Eyes of Its Teenagers," based on the eyewitness accounts of survivors who had been teenagers in the Hlybokaye ghetto, offers important insights into the horrible experiences of the Jews under German occupation as well as important observations about the act of testimony and the inevitable guilt felt by survivors who could not rescue their loved ones and who often felt they had contributed to their deaths.[6] As in other ghettos in the area, the Germans established a Judenrat (Jewish council), which from the outset was torn between its position as an intermediary for German orders and its valiant but ultimately doomed attempt to allay Jewish suffering and save Jewish lives. Unlike in central Poland, the growing presence of a Soviet partisan movement by the second half of 1942 offered some Jews a small ray of hope, despite the indifference and even antisemitism of many partisan commanders.[7] But as Bernstein's chapter also shows, all choices were fraught. To escape the ghetto often meant to bring down German reprisals against one's family. And while these survivors' recollections of their Polish and Belarusian neighbors are largely negative, they also recall many instances when help was given.

In eastern Belarus, which was Soviet before 1939, more Jews were able to evacuate, but even so, most were captured by the Germans. It had taken the Germans four years to reach Minsk in World War I; in 1941, it took them only six days. While Soviet Jews had been told that they were equal citizens in a country that offered opportunity and outlawed antisemitism, most who fell under German rule experienced indifference and betrayal from their non-Jewish neighbors.[8] Compounding these feelings of betrayal was the callous postwar reception that many returning Jews were given by local officials, who often denied them their rights to their former homes.[9] Few areas of the Soviet Union suffered more destruction and bloodshed than Belarus. Not only did the Germans massacre virtually the entire Jewish population; they also murdered or deported a large proportion of the non-Jews. Yet with the end of the war, survivors made valiant efforts to rebuild some form of Jewish life. They tried to reopen synagogues or held services in private homes. The actors from the Minsk Yiddish Theater returned from Central Asia and resumed their activities. Perhaps most important, Jewish survivors lost no time in trying to build memorials on the sites where their loved ones had been murdered, even in the face of outright obstructionism and threats from Soviet officials. But official antisemitism in the Soviet Union, particularly severe between 1948 and 1953, made these efforts to maintain a semblance of Jewish life all the more difficult.[10]

The Shtetl as a Jewish Home

The first chapter in this volume, by Ina Sorkina, discusses the origins and development of shtetls in Belarus. This is an invaluable contribution to the growing number of studies about a form of Jewish settlement, the shtetl, that was enshrined in Jewish collective memory as the true home of Eastern European Jewry. Just as the *derevnya* (village) became the symbol of the "real" Russia for many Russian writers and intellectuals, the shtetl became a substitute for the consolidated territory that Eastern European Jewry lacked, a focus of memory and a symbol of a Jewish civilization simultaneously rooted in the expanses of Eastern Europe and the Land of Israel. Sorkina joins the ever-growing number of scholars who propose various definitions of what a shtetl actually is—not an easy task.

In terms of their numbers, their language, and the occupational diversity of their Jewish residents, shtetls have a unique place among the different types of settlements in the Jewish diaspora.[11] In other key Jewish centers—Spain, Babylonia, Germany, Italy—Jews, usually fewer in number, lived scattered among the general population or clustered together in one special section of town. In the shtetl, Jews were often a majority, usually dominating the central streets around the market, with Gentiles tending to live along the periphery. In Spain or Germany, Jews and Gentiles basically spoke the same language. In the shtetl, however, Yiddish was an important marker of difference. Although Yiddish incorporated many Slavic terms, it was inextricably linked to Jewish tradition and Jewish texts, full of idioms and expressions that reflected a vibrant folk culture.

Another difference between the Eastern European shtetls and other kinds of Jewish diaspora settlements was the former's occupational diversity. In Iraq, Spain, or Germany, most Jews worked in a limited number of occupations, but in the shtetl, the Jews' economic activities ran the gamut from wealthy contractors, entrepreneurs, and merchants to shopkeepers, tailors, shoemakers, and—at the bottom of the pecking order—water carriers and teamsters. These differences in occupation and status were reflected in social divisions and conflict, even as they contributed to the development of shtetl humor and folklore. But for the most part, whatever occupations the Jews engaged in complemented rather than overlapped with those of the surrounding peasantry, further underscoring their differences.

The shtetl was also defined by interlocking sets of economic and social relationships: Jews and peasants in the market; Jews coming together to maintain a network of religious and communal institutions; and, beginning in the early twentieth century, the increasingly important ties between the shtetl and its residents' kinfolk abroad organized in *landsmanshaftn*. Each shtetl was also part of a local and regional ecosystem that included other shtetls and nearby cities.

The origins of the shtetl date back to the Polish Commonwealth, where Jews, often fleeing persecution elsewhere, were invited to settle and help develop the Polish economy.[12] Although most shtetls began as the private market towns of the Polish nobility in the old Rzeczpospolita, over time, the term *shtetl* came to describe any town in Eastern Europe with a large Jewish population, including areas that had not been part of the old Commonwealth: Bukovina, Bessarabia, and Hungary, regions that attracted a great deal of southward Jewish migration from Poland over the centuries.

Over time, even as tensions escalated between Jews and Christians in nonnoble towns, the Polish nobility, the most powerful group in the Commonwealth, increasingly relied on Jews to settle in their private towns and help develop their lands. The eastern expansion of the Commonwealth into present-day Lithuania, Belarus, and much of Ukraine after the signing of the Union of Lublin in 1569 coincided with a sharp increase in European demand for Polish grain, furs, salt, timber, and honey. Polish nobles needed not only Jewish entrepreneurial and managerial skills but also Jewish market towns that would stimulate the economy of the surrounding villages. The nobility also liked the fact that Jews, unlike Christian merchants, could never become potential political rivals. The touchstone of this emerging relationship between Jews and landowners was the *arenda* or lease-holding. Nobles gave Jews long-term leases on forests, mills, and distilleries, and the latter in turned subcontracted parts of the enterprise to other Jews and thus stimulated more Jewish migration eastward. Particularly important in this emerging economic ecosystem was the distillation and sale of alcohol. Taverns became a major locus of contact between Jews and peasants, and the sale of alcohol gave landlords fat profits and also provided an important hedge against falling grain prices in the late seventeenth and eighteenth centuries.

How to attract Jews to settle in these vast, underpopulated eastern territories, including present-day Belarus? The answer was to build private towns where noble charters promised them security, the right to establish their own institutions, and the chance to make a living. The extensive rights enjoyed by the nobility in the Commonwealth offered Jews a higher degree of protection from the chicaneries of the Church and Christian rivals found in non-noble towns. The very layout of these towns underscored the triangular nexus between noble, Jew, and peasant. The marketplace at the center of the town; the church at one end of the market square, signifying noble ownership and presence; the surrounding peasant villages, close enough for peasants to easily make the journey to the shtetl on market days; the synagogues, ritual baths, Jewish schools and businesses—these all reflected the roles and relationships that characterized the shtetl. The shtetl also served as a base from which Jewish peddlers, handymen, tailors, and shoemakers would fan out to the surrounding villages during the week, sleep in peasant barns, do business, and then return in time for the Sabbath. There were, of course, many Jews who lived lonely lives outside the shtetl running taverns or inns. But they would return to the shtetl for the major holidays.

While many shtetls emerged as early as the sixteenth century, their Jewish population, particularly in Belarus, saw peak growth between 1675 and 1800. Despite the heavy losses caused by the wars and massacres of the seventeenth and eighteenth centuries, the Jewish population of the Commonwealth increased rapidly, from thirty thousand in 1500 to more than eight hundred thousand in the census of 1764. On the eve of the First Partition of Poland in 1772, more than half of Polish Jews lived in the private towns, and a further third lived in villages where a large number ran taverns and inns. During the course of the eighteenth century, the center of gravity of Jewish settlement in the Commonwealth continued to shift eastward, into present-day Belarus and Ukraine.

After the devastation of Poland's wars with the Cossacks, the Swedes, and the Muscovites between 1648 and 1656, and the Great Northern War of 1700–21, landlords needed Jews more than ever to rebuild, particularly in light of a serious decline in the Gentile population. But, as Sorkina shows, not all these Belarusian shtetls initially conformed to one model. A shtetl like Hlybokaye was for a long time divided between a private town on one side, where Jews could live, and a Carmelite town on the other, where they could not. Some arose not as market towns but as adjuncts to nearby castles or as service points along roads to provide inns and provisioning for horses. But in time, they all tended to evolve into market towns.

One of the most significant events in modern Jewish history was the collapse of the Polish Commonwealth, which was partitioned between the Russian Empire, Prussia, and Austria between 1772 and 1795. All the shtetls of present-day Belarus became part of Russia. Before Russia acquired six hundred thousand Jewish inhabitants from the former Commonwealth, its rulers had virtually no experience with Jews and certainly not with the heavily Jewish private market towns of the Polish nobility. Russian military officers and government officials saw the shtetl as a sinister base for Jewish exploitation of the peasantry through loan-sharking and alcohol.[13] The last thing they would have wanted was for these masses of shtetl Jews to migrate into the prepartition Russian interior. On the other hand, the Russian government did have to figure out how to deal with the hundreds of thousands of Jews who were suddenly part of the empire. Beginning with Catherine II, Russian policy veered between two primary and conflicting goals: transforming the Jews into productive subjects of the empire and limiting their contacts with the ethnic Russians. In 1791, Catherine decreed that with few exceptions, Russia's Jews could only live in the former Polish provinces. By 1835, this principle of Jewish confinement to a specific territory was legally codified as the Pale of Settlement, which included the former areas of the Commonwealth and new lands in Ukraine. (Congress Poland, while under Russian rule and open to Jewish settlement, had a separate legal status.) Under Alexander II, the restrictions on Jewish settlement outside the Pale were relaxed, and more categories of Jews—graduates, wealthy merchants, skilled artisans—would be allowed to leave the Pale and settle in the Russian interior.[14] Nonetheless, the Pale would remain in legal force until 1917 (although it was abolished de facto in 1915). This meant that 95 percent of Russian Jewry would continue to live there, usually in cities and towns with very large Jewish populations. Clearly, the kind of rapid assimilation and acculturation that took place in Germany and France or the United States would affect only small segments of the Russian Jewish population.

The term *shtetl* did not exist in Russian legal and political discourse. Jews had no say in the formulation of Russian laws, and their representation in local governing bodies was limited, even in places where they formed an absolute majority of the town. Under Russian law, what Jews commonly referred to as a shtetl might be a city, a town, a settlement, or a village. In 1875, the Russian senate established the legal category of *mestechko*, a small town, as distinguished from a city (*gorod*). Unlike a village, however, a mestechko had a council of town dwellers called the *meshchanskoe obshchestvo*; its inhabitants were classified as *meshchane* (townsmen) rather than *krestian'e* (peasants) These seemingly arcane distinctions between village and small town suddenly assumed decisive importance for the Jews of the Pale in 1882 when a set of anti-Jewish decrees known as the May Laws expelled Jews from "villages" but allowed them to live in "towns." Jews who had lived in a shtetl for generations were suddenly faced with brutal expulsion, which might be averted by liberal bribes to the police or extended litigation in the Russian courts in an effort to reclassify a "village" as a "town." The Russian census of 1897 had about a third of Russian Jewry living in these "towns" (mestechki), although the real shtetl population was probably much higher since many shtetls were also classified as "cities."

While the idea of the shtetl was absent from Russian, it certainly was prominent in Yiddish. Jews distinguished between a shtetl (small town), a *shtot* (city), a *dorf* (village), and a *yishev* (tiny rural settlement), although there were no hard-and-fast distinctions between a shtetl and a shtot. Various scholars have tried to define a shtetl. Kassow defines the shtetl as a face-to-face community that was big enough to support the basic network of institutions essential to Jewish life—at least one synagogue and probably more, a mikvah (ritual bath), a cemetery, schools, and a network of voluntary associations (*khevres*) that performed basic religious and communal functions. In this way, a shtetl differed most clearly from a village, and shtetl Jews spared no effort to poke good-natured (and not-so-good-natured) fun at their country cousins. But the shtetl, unlike the city, was small enough for Jews to be familiar with their fellow residents. Yiddish author Yisroel Aksenfeld, in his *Dos shterntikhl* (*The Headband*), a biting satire of the shtetl, wrote that in a city, unlike a shtetl, "everyone boasts that they greeted someone from the next street because they mistook him for an out-of-towner." Of course, these definitions were fluid. A new railroad line could suddenly turn a sleepy shtetl into a bustling city. The reverse was also true. The Ukrainian town of Berdichev, bypassed by the mainline railroad, became, in the words of the writer Sholem Yankev Abramovitsh, known as Mendele Moykher-Sforim, an "overgrown shtetl."[15]

In the days of the Commonwealth, a great deal of power over the Jews in the shtetl was vested in the hands of the kahal, a governing body elected by the Jewish elite—those with wealth, status, and learning—which oversaw education; social welfare; legal disputes between Jews; and, unofficially, local problems that might arise with non-Jews. The various kahals elected district councils, which in turn elected the touchstone of Jewish autonomy in the old Commonwealth, the Council of the Four Lands (Va'ad Arba Aratsot), which was established around 1580 and abolished in 1764. Quite often, when Jews sought to turn their settlement into a full-fledged shtetl, one of their first steps was to dispute the jurisdiction of the nearby kahal and assert their rights to their own local council. When the Commonwealth collapsed, the new absolute monarchies had little interest in maintaining these structures of Jewish autonomy. In the Pale, kahals were formally abolished by Tsar Nicholas I in 1844. In practice, however, kahal-like structures continued to exist in some form as bodies that oversaw local charity, ritual slaughter, and synagogues.

While these forms of Jewish communal governance in the shtetl were largely abolished in Soviet Belarus soon after the Civil War, in Polish Belarus, they remained quite important right up to the beginning of the Holocaust. The status of these kehillot (*kehiles* in the Ashkenazi pronunciation used in Yiddish), as they were known in Poland, was defined in Polish law in 1928. This law regulated elections, allowed kehillot to impose taxes, and specified their jurisdiction, which was primarily to supervise and finance various religious institutions, but their activities also included social welfare, particularly in the large cities. Despite many internal conflicts and disagreements, these kehillot gave Jews in the shtetls of Polish Belarus a forum for communal debate and for making decisions about the allocation of resources, something that did not exist across the border.[16]

Over the nineteenth century, the traditional shtetls in the Pale, and particularly in Belarus, suffered many abrupt political and socioeconomic changes. Many Polish nobles who had participated in the anti-Russian revolts of 1830–31 and 1863 lost their estates, and this dealt a hard blow to many shtetls that had depended on the traditional economic symbiosis with the Polish landowners. The abolition of serfdom—which hurt many nobles who could not adjust to the challenges of a new economy without serf labor and rents—also encouraged agricultural modernization. This in turn changed the relationship between the Jews and the Belarusian peasants, undermining the traditional role of the shtetl. The rapid spread of railroads in the second half of the nineteenth century heightened divisions between shtetls that were bypassed by the new lines and shtetls that suddenly saw new economic growth. The railroads also facilitated the introduction of cheaper factory-made goods that undercut the livelihoods of many shtetl craftspeople.

Beginning in the last third of the nineteenth century, an ever-increasing number of shtetl Jews emigrated from Belarus and Lithuania. Between 1880 and 1924, as many as 2.5 million Jews left Eastern Europe for the United States, Argentina, South Africa, and Western Europe.[17] A few hundred thousand more left the lands of Belarus for the burgeoning cities of Congress Poland and Ukraine—Lodz, Warsaw, Odessa—which offered better economic opportunities. And in the 1920s and 1930s, many young Jews left the shtetls of Soviet Belarus for Moscow and Leningrad.

But while the cultural and political center of gravity of Russian Jewry shifted to the big cities, rapid natural increase alone ensured that, despite out-migration, the absolute numbers of Jews living in shtetls either did not decline or declined very slowly. At the same time, contacts between the local Jews and their relatives who had left became an ever more important lifeline for Polish Belarusian shtetls such as Zhaludok, described in Miron Mordukhovich's memoir. Between the wars, in Polish Belarus, the smaller the shtetl, the larger the role of help from abroad. Landsmanshaftn supported local institutions, while relatives sent money that helped keep many families afloat. The same was true for Jews living across the Soviet border, where the foreign currency sent from abroad, accepted in special Torgsin stores, assured many dispossessed Jews—at least until the 1930s—of a basic livelihood.[18]

The geographical and economic center of the shtetl was the market square. Before dawn on market days, peasants from an area of up to one hundred square miles would hitch their horse-drawn carts and journey to the shtetl. Once in town, they would often meet up with "their" Jews, who had arranged to buy their produce. With money in their pockets, the peasants then went into the Jewish shops and taverns. Market day was a cacophony of shouting, bargaining, and hustling. Often after the sale of a horse or a cow, peasants and Jews would shake hands and share a drink. Sometimes fights would break out, and everyone would run for cover. Especially on a hot summer day, with hundreds of horses standing around, the shtetl would have an unforgettable stench. But market day was the lifeblood of the shtetl and illustrated how Jews and Gentiles, though belonging to different religious and cultural universes, could also be drawn together by personal bonds that were often lacking in the big cities.

If market day was all noise and bustle, the Sabbath was the only real leisure time for the shtetl Jew. During the interwar years in Poland, the shtetl Sabbath began to reflect the major changes coming in from the outside world, and synagogue attendance began slipping. A visiting Yiddish writer from a big city might lecture to a large audience at the fireman's hall. Young people from Zionist or Bundist youth movements would go on hikes or perform amateur theater—much to the dismay of their religious parents, who saw this as a desecration of the holy day. Miron Mordukhovich gives a good description of the large-scale involvement of the Jews of Zhaludok in political parties, youth movements, and amateur theater. Yet these secular Sabbaths preserved the concept of a special day set aside as a break in time and a period dedicated to the spirit.

Although the trauma of the Holocaust led many descendants of Eastern European Jews to embrace the memory of the shtetl as a harmonious community suffused with religious spirit and Jewish solidarity, the reality was somewhat different. Status—*yikhes*—meant a lot in the shtetl. *Sheyne yidn* (the well-to-do) and *balebatim* (the middle class) did not encourage their children to mix with the children of tailors and shoemakers. Those who had little education and little money occupied lower rungs on the social ladder, as did women from poor families.

One key feature of this face-to-face community was the pervasive use of nicknames, which signaled the place of each Jew in the social universe of the shtetl. One woman recalled that in her shtetl, Pruzhany, located in Polish Belarus in the 1930s,

> many Jews had nicknames that were derived either from their occupation, physical appearance, or deformities, such as Chaim the Redhead, Moishe the Icon, Faivel Parch (Favus), Eli Puz (big belly), Avrum the Hernia, Meishl Pick (the stutterer), Berl the Copperbeard, Henoch the Tin Collar (his garment shone like metal, for it had not been cleaned since he put it on twenty years earlier). There was Libitchke the Maiden. Although she had been married and had children, the townsfolk could not forget that Libitchke had married late in life. We had in our shtetl Crutch the Tailor, who lost a leg and walked with one crutch; Yankl the Hunchback; Yosl the Latrine, because he had a disagreeable body odor; and so on.[19]

Sanitary conditions were often appalling: oceans of mud in the spring and fall, the terrible stench of raw sewage, outhouses, and piles of horse manure on market days. Frequently, the Gentile farms that ringed many shtetls limited the space available for building new houses, and thus many shtetls had serious overcrowding. In Belarus, most shtetl buildings were made of wood, although the wealthy could afford a brick building (a *moyer*) near the marketplace. Few shtetls in Belarus were lucky enough to escape the frequent fires that often leveled whole towns, and that became a staple of Yiddish literature. (The local volunteer fire brigade usually saw an atypical degree of Jewish-Gentile cooperation.) Before 1914, educational facilities in Belarusian shtetls often left much to be desired, particularly for poor children who attended overcrowded, squalid heders where they were often taught by a hapless melamed who was regarded with contempt by most of the shtetl Jews. After World War I, compulsory elementary education was introduced in both Polish and Soviet Belarus, transforming the lives of the younger generation. In Soviet Belarus, state-sponsored Yiddish schools educated the majority of Jewish children until the late 1930s, even though, as Arkadi Zeltser shows, many of their parents would have preferred Russian schools. And while in theory the communists banned religious education in Soviet Belarus, underground heders continued, some right up to the Second World War.

A key pillar of shtetl communal life, dominant until World War I and still important up to the Holocaust, at least in Polish Belarus, was the so-called *khevres*, or associations. No matter where Jews lived in the diaspora, their communal affairs were determined in large part by key commandments from the Torah and the Oral Law, which governed the following: marriage and procreation, the education of sons, how to enjoy the Sabbath and the complex Passover dietary laws, ritual purity laws for women, prayer in a quorum, a proper burial, and spare time given over to study. The network of khevres tried to meet all these needs.

The most prestigious and most powerful of these khevres was the *khevra kadisha*, the burial society, which arranged the religious rituals associated with washing the deceased, watching over the body until burial, and then determining where in the cemetery the burial would take place. While some plots were sought after, others were not, and families who had run afoul of shtetl norms might be forced to pay hefty burial fees to give their loved ones a proper send-off. While in most shtetls the khevra kadisha was controlled by the well-to-do, between the wars in some shtetls artisans and poorer Jews managed to join the society as well.

Other key khevres included those that provided dowries for poor brides, visited the sick, or collected and distributed funds to help the poor observe the Sabbath and Passover. Also central to shtetl life were khevres devoted to study, which embraced Jews of all social classes and levels of learning, from *Eyn Yaakov* (Talmudic legends) to Mishnah study to the study of Talmud at an advanced level. Another important form of associational life was the synagogues. Most shtetls in Belarus had a main synagogue maintained by the town and also many smaller synagogues supported by tailors and shoemakers, where they could enjoy the honors in religious services—such as being called to read from the Torah—that might have been denied them in the larger, more upscale synagogues. Belarus was less of a Hasidic center than Podolia, Ukraine, Congress Poland, or Galicia, but some Belarusian shtetls did become Hasidic hotbeds. The most popular Hasidic sect in Belarus was Chabad, but Karlin, Slonim, and Stolin also had their *shtibls* (synagogues). Indeed, in some shtetls like Hlybokaye, up to half of the Jewish population might have been followers of the Lubavitcher Rebbe, the spiritual leader of the Chabad Hasidism.

In theory, traditional Jewish society frowned on social activities—parties, card playing, or banquets—that were not connected to an ostensible religious purpose.[20] But in fact, there was a great deal of social life, much of it linked to the khevres or to rites of passage: weddings and holidays like Purim or Simkhas Toyre, which provided occasions for drinking and public merrymaking. Each khevre had a traditional banquet, often scheduled for the week when a particular portion of the Bible was read. The banquet of the khevra kadisha, known for its extravagant consumption of delicacies, usually took pride of place. But these honors and banquets also extended to Jews at the bottom of the social ladder. In one Jewish town, the water carriers would meet on Saturday afternoons to study *Eyn Yaakov*. Their yearly banquet took place during the week when the parashah Emor (Lev. 21:1–24:23) was read. This was because *Emor* resembled *emer*, the Yiddish word for water pail.[21] This pun might seem forced, but it reflected the determination to anchor life in religious tradition.

Gender roles in the shtetl seemed fairly straightforward. Men held the positions of power: they formed the prayer quorums and ran the *kehilles*, the synagogue, and most of the khevres. Women played a secondary role: they were exempt from most time-bound commandments and had no formal role in the running of communal affairs. But the increasing space allotted to the women's sections of synagogues built after 1650 reflected a growing need for women to be present in synagogues and have some kind of communal religious experience. Behind the scenes, women—particularly from well-to-do families—often played key roles in the communal and economic life of the shtetl. They clearly had some opportunities to learn how to read and write. Religious and secular literature in Yiddish for them (and for poorer, less-educated men) included such mainstays as the *Tsene-rene* (figurative translations of and legends based on the Pentateuch), private individual prayers called *tkhines*, and romances.[22] Ayzik Meyer Dik, a bestselling Jewish writer in nineteenth-century Eastern Europe, wrote didactic Yiddish novels that were largely read by women. But girls from poor families faced bleak prospects in the shtetl, especially if they could not find a husband. As the Jewish population skyrocketed in the last half of the nineteenth century, the social safety net that had helped the poor in the past was hard-pressed to cope, and many of the shtetl poor, including women, migrated to cities such as Bialystok, Hrodna, Warsaw, and others, where they worked for low wages in tobacco and apparel factories. In time, some of these women would be among the earliest activists in the nascent Jewish labor movement.

After the collapse of tsarist Russia and the Russian Revolution, Belarusian Jewry in the interwar years was divided between Poland and the Belarusian Soviet Republic, a division that, as reflected in the chapters by Miron Mordukhovich and Arkadi Zeltser, led to markedly different experiences.

Interwar Polish Jewry was a story of contrasts. It was the most culturally creative community, the most aware of its distinctive identity, in the entire Jewish world, a veritable laboratory for new experiments in Jewish life. At the same time, it was a community in ferment, undergoing rapid urbanization, cultural change, political division, and intergenerational conflict, all exacerbated by the widespread poverty that was the legacy of wartime destruction and state-sponsored policies to encourage Jews to emigrate. Although one in four Polish Jews lived in the five largest cities by 1939, half of Polish Jewry still lived in shtetls, and in Polish Belarus, they were still home to the majority of the Jewish population.

The rich associational life of the traditional shtetl now became more diverse. The most remote shtetl felt the impact of the city through newspapers, visiting lecturers, and films. Dances, sporting events, and even beauty contests all became common features of shtetl life. Nevertheless, despite secularization, the interwar shtetl was a place where even nonreligious Jews were more likely to go to synagogue on the Sabbath and holidays—if only to "keep up appearances." New organizations were established alongside the traditional khevres: youth movements and artisans' associations that challenged the traditional power structure of the shtetl, as well as libraries and amateur theater groups. One of the most striking changes in the interwar shtetl in Polish Belarus was the establishment of new schools alongside the traditional heder: Polish public schools; left-wing Central Yiddish School Organization (CYSHO) schools in Yiddish; and Zionist Tarbut schools, which were particularly popular in that region.[23]

Polish taxes, economic boycotts, and the loss of traditional Russian markets pushed many former sheyne yidn and balebatim to the brink of poverty, and this downward mobility radicalized and politicized their children. But the shtetl also mobilized to defend itself. One effective weapon was the free loan societies, sponsored by the Joint Distribution Committee, which not only extended microcredit but also gave beleaguered Jews crucial moral support. There was also expanded vocational training. And, as Mordukhovich points out, Belarusian-Jewish relations were for the most part better than Jewish relations with Poles and Ukrainians, in part because, as we have seen, Belarusian nationalism was less fierce, and in part because both Jews and Belarusians felt persecuted by the Poles. The fewer Poles in a shtetl, the more likely that it would be spared the wave of pogroms that occurred between 1936 and 1939.

Across the Soviet border, as Arkadi Zeltser shows, shtetl Jews faced a very different reality. Soviet Jewish policy was very much in flux. By 1921, once the turmoil and the bloodshed of war and revolution subsided, about 2.5 million

Jews found themselves under Soviet rule, where they presented their new rulers with a whole array of knotty problems—social, economic, and ideological. Ideologically, the Jews were an anomaly: without a territory of their own, their claim to recognition as a Soviet nationality was tenuous. Before the revolution, both Lenin and Stalin had questioned whether the Jews were really a people. But some facts could not be ignored: in places like Belarus and Ukraine, Jews were thick on the ground, they mostly spoke Yiddish, and a great many lived in shtetls.

Belarusian shtetls were largely spared the carnage that decimated many Ukrainian shtetls during the Civil War of 1918–20. However, they suffered greatly from the war's devastation and from new Soviet policies that turned many shtetl Jews into legal pariahs and unemployed paupers. Soviet legislation deprived former traders, property owners, religious functionaries, and merchants of their political and civil rights, turning many shtetl Jews into *lishentsy*, disenfranchised people whose children were barred from educational institutions. In theory, the shtetl as a market town that linked the peasants with the wider urban economy lost most of its previous economic foundation in the new Soviet state. Although shtetl Jews saw some relief during the years of the New Economic Policy, high taxes ruined many shtetl businesses, and collectivization further undercut the traditional shtetl economy.

Despite migration to the big cities, particularly by young people, and despite attempts to "productivize" Jews by settling them in agricultural colonies and, later, in Birobidzhan, a great many Jews remained in their former shtetls, especially the very old and the very young. And somehow, many shtetl Jews in Belarus continued to get by: by trading on the black market, by working in artisans' cooperatives (artels), or by becoming lower-level white-collar workers in Soviet enterprises or service workers for nearby collective farms. Many still got help from relatives abroad.

The rich associational life of Zhaludok described by Miron Mordukhovich did not exist in the shtetls of Soviet Belarus. The Jewish sections of the Communist Party, the Evsektsiia, were often more intolerant than non-Jewish Communists and spearheaded a crusade against religion, Zionism, and Hebrew culture. The regime severely restricted religious instruction, closed down synagogues, and banned all political activity not sanctioned by the Communist Party. Still, Zionist groups and religious schools continued to exist illegally well into the 1930s. Many Jews managed to attend religious services, circumcise their newborn sons, eat matzo on Passover, and buy kosher meat.

Despite persecution, many shtetls still preserved a large measure of their Jewish character. In Ukraine and Belarus, local Communist authorities supported the Evsektsiia's policy of promoting Yiddish schools for Jewish children, and until the mid-1930s, Jewish children in these small towns were not only speaking Yiddish at home; they were also receiving their primary education in that language. Whatever the shortcomings of the Communist Yiddish schools, they did provide a counterforce to assimilation, but parents understood that the path to higher education and advancement favored graduates of Russian schools.

After inaugurating the Five-Year Plans in 1928, the Soviet regime began offering Jews more social mobility and educational opportunities. New legislation modified many of the restrictions on the lishentsy. Many Jews, particularly young people, began leaving the shtetls for work or to study in the bigger cities, including Moscow and Leningrad. By the mid-1930s, many former shtetls had begun to adapt to the new socioeconomic reality created by collectivization and the Five-Year Plans. They became centers for local artisan production or served nearby collective farms. Despite the momentous changes that transformed these shtetls, Jews who lived in them were more likely to speak Yiddish and much less likely to intermarry than their counterparts in the larger cities. It was the Holocaust that finally destroyed the Belarusian shtetl and changed the sociocultural character of Soviet Jewry by eliminating its least acculturated and most consciously Jewish elements.

One has to treat with caution the charges leveled by a wide variety of critics—maskilim, Zionists, socialists, Soviet Jewish scholars—that the shtetl was a dying community riven by hypocrisy, stultifying tradition, and bitter class conflict, just as one has to reject the view of the shtetl as an island of Jewish harmony and devotion in a sea of Gentile hostility. The reality is much more complex and demands close attention to historical context, economic developments, and regional variations.

The Shtetl as an Object of Memory and Research

For political reasons, few Western scholars were able to visit the Soviet countryside until the late 1980s, and it was even more difficult for those working in Jewish studies, since the discipline of Jewish studies did not exist in the Soviet Union. As a result, the post–World War II Soviet shtetl remained terra incognita to Westerns. After the Holocaust, the study of the shtetl focused on the memory of the lost shtetl, largely under the influence of the popular book *Life Is with People: The Culture of the Shtetl*, by Mark Zborowski and Elizabeth Herzog, which effectively introduced the term *shtetl* into the English language.[24] As many critics have noted, this book painted an idealized and composite portrait of the shtetl as an exterritorial Jewish island in the Gentile sea. It largely disregarded two key aspects of the historical phenomenon of the shtetl: its geographical variability and the close interaction between Jews and non-Jews. And even with the growth of scholarly and popular interest in the shtetl, the study of the phenomenon has remained largely conducted from afar, focusing on the pre–World War II period and the Holocaust. Individual visits by foreign scholars and former residents to former shtetls have produced mostly impressionistic accounts colored by nostalgia, which tend to ignore the broader social and cultural contexts of life in the shtetl. Among the few exceptions are the web-based research project AHEYM (Archives of Historical and Ethnographic Yiddish Memories), conducted by Indiana University, and the book *In the Shadow of the Shtetl: Small-Town Jewish Life in Soviet Ukraine*, by Jeffrey Veidlinger, one of the project participants.[25] The primary goal of this project is to document the language, culture, and oral history of the remaining Yiddish speakers in Ukraine, Moldova, Romania, Hungary, and Slovakia. But Belarus, with the exception of the ongoing linguistic research by Dovid Katz, has so far remained beyond its purview. In the past decade, Poland has emerged as the major European center for the study of East European Jewry. Polish scholars such as Alina Cała, Anna Engelking, Magdalena Waligórska, and others are conducting anthropological, sociological, folkloristic, and historical fieldwork in former shtetls, including in the Polish-Belarusian borderlands. Their work focuses on Polish-Jewish relations, antisemitism, and the memories of local residents of their Jewish neighbors before the Holocaust.

The Moscow Sefer Center and Its Research Projects

Following the fall of the USSR and the mass emigration of more than 1.5 million Jews from the former Soviet Union, the Jewish population of Belarus dropped precipitously. Nonetheless, the collapse of communism has allowed the establishment of significant centers of academic Jewish studies. Especially important has been the interdisciplinary fieldwork in former shtetls carried out by the Judaica Interdepartmental Center of the European International University in St. Petersburg and, above all, the Moscow Center for University Teaching of Jewish Civilization (Sefer). Hearkening back to the legacy of the legendary Ansky expeditions of 1912–14, teams of scholars and students from many different disciplines have returned to the sites of former Jewish shtetls to interview Jews and non-Jews, seeking to elicit information as well as insights into memory, to discover surviving markers of identity and ethnic affiliation, and to unearth not only evidence from old cemeteries and prewar houses but also the backstories of memorials erected for Holocaust victims.[26]

Most of the scholarship and memoir literature that has appeared on Soviet Jewry tends to focus on Moscow- and Leningrad-based intellectuals and accomplished professionals who were highly educated Russian speakers. By contrast, the shtetl studies carried out by the Sefer are a reminder that not all Soviet Jews moved to the capitals and went to universities, nor did they become Russian speakers or go on to become scientists, physicians, and engineers.[27] The main directions of fieldwork in the Sefer expeditions are the study of ethnography and folklore and epigraphic examination of the cemeteries. The team of ethnographers and folklorists conducts interviews with local residents using the specially designed questionnaire "Ethno-Cultural Stereotypes in the Folk Tradition: Slavs and Their Neighbors," which contains over one hundred questions. Based on these interviews, the expedition members can construct a collective "portrait" of the town. It comprises materials from oral history, local toponymy, local legends and folklore, and memories about former Jewish neighbors, their lifestyle, language, customs, religious practices, and places of worship. These expeditions to former shtetls have raised new questions about how to understand Jewish identity in the former Soviet Union. Is it to be measured by adherence to or deviation from a normative model of religious observance and textual knowledge? Or is it to be understood by other criteria: culinary traditions, folk memory, rituals of remembrance, subtle differences in routine and custom that distinguished Jews from their neighbors?[28] For example, Svetlana Amosova's chapter on rituals of remembrance encourages us to balance Zvi Gitelman's point about the "thin" Jewish identity of most Soviet Jews against the ways that Soviet Jews devised new customs and rituals that served to set themselves apart from non-Jews. By the same token, chapters such as Andrei Moroz's "Why Hitler Did Not Like the Jews: The Folklore Version of the Reasons behind the Holocaust" offer revealing insights into how Jews were remembered in these small towns decades after they had vanished from the shtetl landscape. Today, as Michael Lurie and Natalia Savina show, some Belarusian towns are trying to reintroduce markers of their Jewish past into public space to promote tourism and reconnect with the children and grandchildren of their former Jewish residents. The extent to which this new interest in the Jewish past will impact the current residents of these towns remains to be seen.

The Sefer has been conducting field research in the territory of the former Russian Pale of Settlement for nearly twenty years. It has organized over forty expeditions, which have explored nearly fifty former shtetls in Belarus, Latvia, Lithuania, Moldova, Ukraine, and Russia. These expeditions combine research and teaching activities, operating as field schools for training the new generation of researchers in Jewish studies. Jointly with the Institute of Slavic Studies at the Russian Academy of Sciences and the researchers from the Belarusian Academy of Sciences, Belarusian State University, and the Yanka Kupala State University of Hrodna, the Sefer has been conducting research expeditions in the former shtetls of Belarus since 2012. Some of those towns still have a small Jewish population, while others have only the personal recollections of current residents about their former Jewish neighbors and/or whatever written records have been preserved. The purpose of this ongoing and wide-ranging project is to collect new data about the history, traditions, and folklore of former Jewish shtetls; discover new archival documents; make those documents available for the scholarly community and the general public; and draw public attention to the problem of preserving the Jewish cultural legacy. A key feature of the Sefer expeditions is their interdisciplinary methodology and complex approach to the study of the phenomenon of the shtetl. They combine ethnographic field research, epigraphic study of Jewish cemeteries, and the examination of archival and testimonial sources. Focusing on the social, cultural, and demographic dynamics of the shtetl from the early years of Jewish settlement, this approach helps identify characteristic elements of local traditions while exploring the historical aspects of the interactions among Jews, between Jews and Christians, and between Jews and the authorities. The choice of a particular location for each expedition is determined by several factors, such as the richness of its local Jewish history, the condition and size of its Jewish cemetery, whether a sizeable and well-preserved historic Jewish area exists, and whether the population was ethnically and religiously diverse. No less important is the receptiveness of the local authorities and the availability of volunteers.

The first expedition, in 2012, explored the town of Zhaludok, in the Hrodna Region, one of the oldest Jewish settlements in the Neman area, with a rich multicultural history. A Jewish community emerged in Zhaludok around the late seventeenth century, and before World War II, about 70 percent of the population was Jewish. The town still has a well-preserved former Jewish area and a large Jewish cemetery with about three hundred tombstones, mostly from the nineteenth and twentieth centuries. In 2015, there was a Sefer expedition to the town of Hlybokaye, in the Vitebsk Region. Historically, the population of Hlybokaye was ethnically and religiously diverse and included Jews, Belarusians, Poles, Tatars, and Roma. The residents there practiced Judaism, Christianity (Greek Orthodox, Greek Catholic, and Roman Catholic), and Islam. The local Jewish cemetery has one of the oldest preserved Jewish tombstones in Belarus, which is dated 1708. The Jewish population of Hlybokaye grew over three centuries, reaching nearly four thousand people (over 70 percent of the total population), according to the Russian census of 1897. Located in the western part of Belarus, which belonged to Poland up to 1939, Hlybokaye and Zhaludok largely preserved the traditional Jewish way of life up to World War II. By contrast, the small towns of Liepiel, Ushachy, Chashniki, and Beshankovichy located in the eastern part of the Vitebsk Region were subject to the aggressive policy of Sovietization during the 1920s and 1930s. The presence of Jewish communities in these towns reaches back to the first half of the eighteenth century. Everywhere in Belarus, close contact between Jews and their neighbors left a strong impression on local Slavic residents' perception of the Jewish way of life and religion, but the memory of Jewish religious traditions and customs is much weaker in eastern than in western Belarus.

The ethnographic and epigraphic studies along with archival and testimonial sources were published in a collection of volumes on particular Belarusian towns: *Zhaludok: Memory of a Jewish Shtetl* (ed. Irina Kopchenova, 2013); *Liepiel: Memory of a Jewish Shtetl* (ed. Svetlana Amosova, 2015), and *Hlybokaye: Memory of a Jewish Shtetl* (ed. Irina Kopchenova, 2017), published by the Sefer Center. They are available online at https://sefer.ru/rus/publications/field-materials.php. Materials from field expeditions and archival sources are also available in the online database Sefer Field Research Archive (SFIRA, www.sfira.org).

Memory is a shared theme and concern in all the case studies in this volume. They draw their materials from a wide range of sources such as archival documents, memoirs, material objects, and personal interviews that were either conducted and collected during the expeditions or recorded by other archival projects such as that organized by the USC Shoah Foundation. Combined, these materials present a complex and sometimes contradictory picture of the workings of individual and collective memory and imagination. This volume presents the findings of many years of interdisciplinary research on the Belarusian shtetl before, during, and after the Holocaust. It includes works by historians and anthropologists, focusing on the ways Jews and their neighbors interacted. Some of the chapters have been specially commissioned for this publication, while others have been substantially revised for the English edition. A significant translation challenge was the term *mestechko*, which can be translated as town, small town, or shtetl. Depending on the context, we decided to use all these options, and in some cases, we leave the term untranslated. Another editorial choice is the use of the toponym Belarus transhistorically. Although Belarus as an ethnolinguistic concept emerged only in the late nineteenth century, its historical variants such as Belaya Rus', Belorussia, or Białoruś (or, in translation, White Russia) were used since the thirteenth century in Russian and Polish political discourse to designate territories that

Fig Intro.1 Members of the Sefer expedition in Zhaludok, July 2012. In the background is the building of the former synagogue. *Courtesy SEFER Center for University Teaching of Jewish Civilization.*

Fig Intro.2 Members of the Sefer expedition in Hlybokaye, July 2015. *Courtesy SEFER Center for University Teaching of Jewish Civilization.*

Fig Intro.3 Interviewing a local resident in Hlybokaye, July 2015. *Courtesy SEFER Center for University Teaching of Jewish Civilization.*

largely coincide with today's Republic of Belarus.[29] For geographical names, we use contemporary Belarusian versions with a few exceptions if there is a widely accepted English spelling such as Minsk or Vitebsk.

The first section includes two chapters, the first written by Belarusian historian Ina Sorkina and the second by Israeli scholar Arkadi Zeltser, which provide historical overviews of the Jewish shtetl in Belarus under the Russian Empire and the Soviet Union up to 1939. They are followed by chapters by Moscow scholars Svetlana Amosova and Andrei Moroz, which focus on local folkloric beliefs and practices related to remembering and commemorating the dead. The second section presents the case study of Hlybokaye. It opens with two chapters by Julia Bernstein, who reconstructs the story of the Hlybokaye ghetto as it is narrated by its survivors in their interviews in the Visual History Archive of the USC Shoah Foundation and closely analyzes the different narrative strategies in two closely related testimonies. Irina Kopchenova introduces a series of photographs of the Hlybokaye ghetto from the collection of the US Holocaust Memorial Museum. Saint Petersburg anthropologists Mikhail Lurie and Natalia Savina use Hlybokaye as a case study to examine the formation of memory about Jews as an interactive process with diverse sets of local and external actors by drawing on historical sources and ethnographic research. As an appendix, the collection includes a memoir about prewar Jewish life in Zhaludok by a former resident, Miron Mordukhovich.

Chapters 1–8 are translated by Bela Shayevich. The appendix is translated by Sebastian Schulman and Bela Shayevich.

Notes

1. Much has been written about the Litvaks and Jewish Lite. A few important sources include Levin and Staliunas, "Lite on the Jewish Mental Maps"; Katz, *Lithuanian Jewish Culture*; Katsenelenbogen, "Litvakes."

2. Among the many good treatments of this topic is Snyder, *The Reconstruction of Nations*.

3. On Hasidism in Belarus, see Biale et al., *Hasidism: A New History*, 118–40; Wodzinski, *A Historical Atlas of Hasidism*; Rabinowitsch, *Lithuanian Hasidism*.

4. Levin and Staliunas, "Lite on the Jewish Mental Maps," 336.

5. Levin and Staliunas, "Lite on the Jewish Mental Maps," 335–36.

6. The most detailed treatment of the murder of the Jews of Hlybokaye and the surrounding towns is Rayak and Rayak, *Hurbn Glubok, Sharkoystene, Dunilovitsh, Postov, Kazan*.

7. See, for example, Slepyan, "The Soviet Partisan Movement and the Holocaust"; Smilovitsky, "Antisemitism in the Soviet Partisan Movement"; Kaganovitch, *Der yidisher onteyl in der partizaner bavegung fun Sovet Rusland*.

8. Romanovsky, "The Soviet Person as a Bystander of the Holocaust." For an original analysis of the interplay between the development of the Soviet economy in Belarus and antisemitism, see Sloin, *The Jewish Revolution in Belorussia*.

9. Smilovitsky, *Jewish Life in Belarus*.

10. Smilovitsky, *Jewish Life in Belarus*. See also Kaganovich, *The Long Life and Swift Death of Jewish Rechitsa*.

11. There is an enormous and growing literature on the shtetl. A few recent titles include Veidlinger, "Everyday Life and the Shtetl"; Shandler, *Shtetl: A Vernacular Intellectual History*; Kassow, "Shtetl"; Klier, "What Exactly Was a Shtetl?"

12. On the shtetl in the Polish Commonwealth, see Rosman, *The Lords' Jews*; Hundert, *Jews in a Private Polish Town*; Teller, *Money, Power and Influence in Eighteenth-Century Lithuania*.

13. On this general topic, see Klier, *Russia Gathers Her Jews*.

14. The Jewish community in St. Petersburg was by far the most important concentration of Jews who were allowed to live outside the Pale. See Nathans, *Beyond the Pale*.

15. See Kassow, "Shtetl."

16. On this point see Kassow, "Community and Identity in the Interwar Shtetl."

17. Stampfer, "East European Jewish Migration to the United States"; Stampfer, "Patterns of Internal Jewish Migration in the Russian Empire"; Stampfer, "Gidul ha'okhlusiyah ve'hagira be-Yahadut Poli-Lita be'et ha'hadasha"; Alroi, *Ha-mahpekha ha-shkeyta:ha-hagira ha-yehudit me-ha'imperiyah ha-rusit 1875–1942*.

18. See Estraikh, "The Soviet Shtetl in the 1920s"; Shkolnikova, "Transformatsiia evreiskogo mestechka v SSSR v 1930e gody"; Zeltser, *Evrei sovetskoi provintsii*.

19. Bat, *Through Tears and Laughter*.

20. Katz, *Tradition and Crisis*.

21. Roskies and Roskies, *The Shtetl Book*.

22. Weissler, *Voices of the Matriarchs*.

23. Kassow, "Community and Identity in the Interwar Shtetl."

24. The first edition of that book was titled *Life Is with People: The Jewish Little-Town of Eastern Europe* (New York: International Universities Press, 1952). The word *shtetl* appeared in the title of the second, 1962 edition.

25. https://libraries.indiana.edu/aheym-project.

26. See, for example, Dymshits, Lvov, and Sokolova, *Shtetl, XXI vek*; Kopchenova, *Zheludok: Pamiat' o evreiskom mestechke*; Amosova, *Lepel': Pamiat' o evreiskom mestechke*; Kopchenova, *Glubokoe: Pamiat' o evreiskom mestechke*; Veidlinger, *In the Shadow of the Shtetl*.

27. See Deborah Yalen's insightful review of *Shtetl, XXI vek*.

28. On this point, see Lvov, "Shtetl v XXIv. i etnografiya postsovetskogo evreistva."

29. On the emergence of this term, see Olga Mastianica, "Between Ethnographic Belarus and the Reestablishment of the Grand Duchy of Lithuania."

HISTORY, FOLKLORE, ETHNOGRAPHY

1

Between Miastechka and Shtetl

Ethnicity and Religion in Small Belarusian Towns, 1800s–1930s

INA SORKINA

The Belarusian word *miastechka* (Polish *miasteczko*, Russian *mestechko*) comes from the pan-Slavic word *mesta*, meaning place, town, or city, so a *miastechka* is a small town. *Miastechki* were settlements falling somewhere between town and village that organically melded urban and rural ways of life and the day-to-day practices of the villager and the city dweller. People of different ethnicities and religions participated in the historical development of these settlements. This created unique forms of domestic and sociocultural activity and special patterns of interaction among different groups. Because of their large number and their economic importance, miastechki exercised an enormous influence on the economic, cultural, and political configuration of the Belarusian lands for the duration of their existence, from the fifteenth century through the middle of the twentieth.

When and why did this dense network of miastechki emerge in Belarusian lands? How did they become plurireligious and multiethnic settlements dominated by Jewish populations? What is a shtetl? Did all miastechki across Belarusian lands become shtetls? The search for the answers to these questions will shed light on the evolution of the ethnoreligious situation in the miastechki and define the main stages of their history.[1]

The Genesis of the Miastechki in Belarusian Lands

Miastechki were actively established between the fifteenth and the first half of the seventeenth century. Because of the economic and political situation in the Grand Duchy of Lithuania (GDL), the number of town-type settlements was increasing, and living conditions in them were improving: by the middle of the seventeenth century, there were 37 cities and 425 miastechki in the Belarusian lands.² The majority of the cities were established before the sixteenth century. Thus, the period from the sixteenth century through the second half of the seventeenth century saw the rapid development of miastechki, primarily those that were privately owned. This was made possible by the enactment of the GDL Statute of 1588, which provided for the inviolability of property owned by the *szlachta* (Polish Lithuanian nobility) (Articles 3 and 5, Section 3) and the right of private citizens to establish miastechki (Article 29, Section 1).³

The expansion of the network of miastechki between the sixteenth and the first half of the seventeenth centuries was a result of the economic modernization and westernization of the Belarusian lands within the GDL and the Polish-Lithuanian Commonwealth. This was brought about by the commodification of agricultural products, which in turn followed from the institution of the export-oriented *falvark* system of management. Under this system, peasants were obliged to work without pay for the landlord to produce surplus grain for Western European markets and to develop more efficient distribution systems to provide the local population with manufactured and traded goods. The economies of the miastechki were based on the activities of itinerant merchants and craftspeople who mediated between town and country. To establish a miastechka was to set up a marketplace, which increased landowners' profits. Miastechki had weekly markets, annual market fairs, and inns. The specific circumstances leading to the establishment of any given miastechka remain unknown. Occasionally, this process was accompanied by the issuance of a specific document—for instance, a royal *pryvilei* (a charter of privileges). Based on these documents and other sources, researchers have outlined several paths by which miastechki were established.⁴ The oldest miastechki were settlements that developed next to grand ducal castles or large feudal estates. In the middle of the sixteenth century, out of the 210 miastechki in Belarus, 86 were located next to castles.⁵

Miastechki developed in part due to the expansion of the system of cash rent. To pay the *chynsh* (cash tax), peasants had to exchange some of their goods for cash. Markets thus emerged next to grand ducal and private estates in the fifteenth century, making it possible for peasants to exchange agricultural products for money as well as to obtain necessary goods that could not be produced on a farm. These markets attracted not only peasants, who would visit them sporadically, but also craftspeople and merchants, who began to take up permanent residence near them. As a result, these settlements developed into centers of trade and artisanal production, essentially becoming miastechki, though they were only granted the legal status of a "mesto" (town or city) upon receiving a charter.

A number of miastechki were established with the 1557 Agrarian Reform (*Valochnaia pamera*). Some were established next to or in already existing communities, and others sprang up in undeveloped territories (*na surovym karaniu*), sometimes in the middle of deep forests. Miastechki emerged in response to the demand for various roadside services, including lodging, storing merchandise, repairing wagons and harnesses, and so on. When miastechki were established, the charter would clearly state that residents were responsible for maintaining the roads and building inns and taverns. Thus, in a tax assessor's document establishing the foundation of the miastechka Sokółka in the location of a village of the same name, on the road between Hrodna and Knyzhyn, in addition to organizing trade, residents were also tasked with building inns to facilitate travel by coach.[6]

A number of miastechki were established to support religious institutions, as documented in a 1642 pryvilei for the foundation of a miastechka near Zhyrovichy to "increase[e] the income of the Basilian [Greek Catholic] Monastery."[7] Others were established in connection with new commercial enterprises. For instance, in the Polatsk voivodeship, around 1620, a mine and the miastechka Slabada were founded at the same time.[8]

Some miastechki were established next to preexisting towns and cities or other miastechki, and this was reflected in their names (in prefixes like *Novy* and *Stary* [new, old]). For instance, before the twentieth century, Miadziel had been divided into Stary Miadziel, its northern half (a privately owned miastechka), and Novy Miadziel in the south (a "royal miastechka," which belonged to the treasury). Stary Miadziel was first mentioned in 1454 (on the occasion of the construction of the Roman Catholic Church of St. John the Baptist), and Novy Miadziel in 1463.[9]

Hlybokaye also had a *dwupanskosc*, or dual genesis.[10] Today's town occupies an area that is made up of two miastechki named Hlybokaye, which were established on the border between two estates named Hlybokaye: a privately owned miastechka (belonging to the Zenovich family before 1622; then the Radziwill family; and, finally, beginning in 1832, the Wittgenstein family) and a miaestechka owned by the Carmelite monastery (to which it was bequeathed by Jozef Korsak and that later became the property of the treasury after it was seized from the monastery). During the GDL and Polish-Lithuanian Commonwealth periods, the two parts of Hlybokaye were subject to different administrative units: the estate and the privately owned miastechka belonged to the Ashmianski pavet of the Vilna voivodeship, while the monastery's miastechka was part of the Polack voivodeship. Hlybokaye eventually grew from a rural settlement into a town. As a result of the construction of the Catholic chapel and Carmelite monastery, it became the regional religious center and then, because of its market, a trade center for agricultural products and artisanal goods. Both the church and the market played a role in Hlybokaye's development. Its two halves looked different and would meet different fates according to their distinct characters and the passions and pursuits of the two families they belonged to, the Zenovich and the Korsak.[11]

Thus, the genesis of miastechki was a varied affair. Often, several factors were at work. As a rule, miastechki established next to castles were also located on busy roads. The choice of a village to serve as the site for a new miaestechka was based on the presence of a manor house, convenient roads, an Orthodox or Catholic church, and other such factors. The population of a miastechka was usually a combination of peasants and craftspeople from the feudal holdings where the miastechka was established, fugitives running from other landowners, burghers from big cities or other miastechki, and Jews from the West. The populations grew with the incorporation of new suburban areas and further immigration. To attract people to new miastechki, feudal lords offered new residents temporary tax exemptions.

After Belarusian lands were incorporated into the Russian Empire as a result of Commonwealth's partitions in 1772–95, a new system of municipal administrative centers was established, changing the status of many settlements. A number of miastechki became the administrative center of the *uyezd*, or so-called *zashtatny* town (without administrative function). These included Babinavichy, Vileyka, Haradok, Dokshytsy, Ihumen, Kopys, Liepiel, Stary Bykhaw, Syanno, Chavusy, and others. At the same time, long-established GDL towns such as Beshankovichy, Braslaw, Davyd-Haradok, Dubrowna, Kletsk, Kapyl, Krychaw, Lyakhavichy, Ushachy, Sharashova, and Shklow were demoted to the status of miastechki because they were found to be administratively useless to the empire. Some small miastechki that previously had the status of *mesta* and possessed royal charters giving them Magdeburg rights (rights of municipal self-government) lost their rights as towns under the Russian Empire. Their residents lost their status as urban residents and were reclassified as serfs. This set off a long and difficult battle on the part of the residents of these miastechki to regain personal freedoms and land rights gained during the GDL period when miastechki had received land from the state that their residents considered their property.[12]

New miastechki, transformed from villages, also appeared. To curry the favor of local landowners, the tsarist government bestowed the title of *miastechka* on all settlements that claimed the right to it. According to the 1785 Charter to the Gentry, the right to establish a miastechka was extended to all members of the noble estate. The Senate Decree of October 26, 1810, allowed landowners to reclassify their villages as miastechki for the purpose of selling liquor, which was otherwise forbidden in villages. Special permission from the governor was sufficient for reclassification.[13] New miastechki were founded more and more frequently due to the Russian government's policy of forcing Jews out of rural settlements. To retain the services of Jewish middlemen, many landowners reclassified rural settlements as miastechki and thereby multiplied their number, particularly in the 1820s.[14]

As the nineteenth century progressed, however, the number of miastechki began to dwindle. In an 1863 audit, the Ministry of Internal Affairs found a total of 418 miastechki across the Belarusian region. In 1870–71, data on miastechki was collected by governors, who counted 360 such settlements within the borders of what is today Belarus. At the beginning of the twentieth century, there were only 322. The growth of industry and transportation, the expansion of economic networks between cities, and the increasing size of urban centers and their surrounding areas all diminished the miastechka's functional significance. The need for a large number of intermediaries between town and country, a role formerly played by miastechki, was disappearing. Another factor leading to their declining number was the tsarist government's hostile attitude toward them. The smallest settlements were eliminated, while the number of larger miastechki (with populations over two thousand people) grew.[15]

A characteristic of the network of miastechki in Belarusian lands was the fact that so many of these settlements were privately owned. Beginning in the sixteenth century and lasting until the establishment of the Soviet state, the majority of miastechki belonged to private individuals. Thus, in the second half of the eighteenth century, out of the 276 miastechki in Belarus whose form of ownership is known, 212 (77 percent) were privately owned.[16] Data from 1807 shows that in the Hrodna gubernia, out of eighty-six miastechki, seventy-four were owned privately, nine by the government, and three by religious institutions.[17]

There are more than a few examples of miastechki flourishing thanks to their owners. For instance, the wealthy and influential magnate Sapieha family, whose representatives occupied the highest state, administrative, and military positions in the GDL, developed Ruzhany, Dziarechyn, Halshany, Zelva, Beshankovichy, and others. It was only after Vilna voivode (governor) Cazimir Lev Sapieha took ownership of Beshankovichy in 1630 that it began to develop rapidly, and soon thereafter it attained the status of a miastechka. On October

4, 1634, king of Poland and grand duke of Lithuania Ladislaus IV Vasa bestowed Magdeburg rights on the residents of Beshankovichy and gave his permission for weekly markets and two annual fairs to be held. The Petropavlovsk Fair in Beshankovichy became one of the biggest markets in Belarus from the seventeenth through the nineteenth century, taking on international significance. There are also many examples of miastechki that were successfully developed by the richest and most influential aristocratic family in the GDL—the Radziwills—such as Liubcha, Urechcha, Hlybokaye, Kapyl, Kletsk, and others.

Among the characteristics shared by both cities and miastechki in the GDL were ethnic and religious diversity. In Hlybokaye, for example, historical sources document the presence of various Christian denominations, including Roman Catholics, Calvinists, Lutherans, Greek Catholics (after 1839 - Eastern Orthodox), and Baptists. There were also Jews (Misnagdim and Hasidim) and Muslims. Ethnically, Hlybokaye residents were (at various times and in various proportions) Belarusian, Jewish, Polish, Tatar, Roma, and Lithuanian.[18]

The mosaic of ethnoreligious diversity in these cities and miastechki came together gradually. The main ethnicities in urban centers were Belarusian and Jewish. From the sixteenth through the middle of the seventeenth centuries, no fewer than 80 percent of all urban residents were Belarusian, with Jews comprising from 2 to 10 percent.[19] But from the eighteenth through the nineteenth centuries, the Belarusian region became the land of Jewish miastechki.

The Formation and Development of the Shtetl in Belarusian Lands

The religious and cultural insularity and socioreligious autonomy of Jewish communities in miastechki require the use of the term *shtetl*. The shtetl, localized within a privately owned city or town, was the longest-standing legal, social, and economic form of Jewish settlement in Eastern Europe; however, the concept of the shtetl remains hard to define.[20] This phenomenon has been studied in literature, art, historiography, ethnography, anthropology, and interdisciplinary studies, and there is a vast literature devoted to the topic.[21]

In the multifarious attempts to define the term *shtetl*, the following criteria have been suggested:

- A shtetl could be any kind of settlement in Eastern Europe inhabited by Jews.

- A shtetl was a settlement where the majority of residents were Jews and that had a Jewish character.

- A shtetl was a separate community, clearly different from the surrounding population in terms of language, domestic activity, religion, and culture.
- A shtetl could be a part of a city with a dense Jewish population (a Jewish quarter).

John Klier's definition of the shtetl is particularly interesting. He defines it as an economic and cultural zone that united a group of Jews while also creating connections between Jews and other ethnic and religious groups.[22]

In the present study, a *shtetl* is defined as a Jewish physical and spiritual space in a Belarusian (that is, in the territory of contemporary Belarus), Lithuanian, Ukrainian, or Polish miastechka. The primary assumption is that the shtetl and the miastechka are not one and the same. The miastechka is a broader concept of which a shtetl can be a component. Most often, especially from the nineteenth century through the early twentieth centuries, this component is dominant, but that is not always the case. There were miastechki with few or even no Jews. According to data from the end of the 1860s, there were no Jews in Survylyshki (Ashmiany uyezd), Venzovets, Rahotna, and Staryja Dziaviatavichy (Slonim uyezd). At the same time, some miastechki were wholly Jewish, including Shcherbina (Velizh uyezd), Malta (Rezhitsa uyezd), Mariengauz (Liutsin uyezd), and Birshtany (Troki uyezd). Only Jews lived in Zakharina (Mstislav uyezd): according to official data from 1880, the population consisted of 311 Jewish men and 390 Jewish women.[23] However, these cases where the miastechka was the shtetl and the two concepts completely coincided were rare.

In written sources, information about Jews in miastechki almost always begins to appear in the late sixteenth century. At first, their numbers were insignificant, limited to one or two individuals, usually lease-holders on inns. Beginning in the middle of the seventeenth century, numerous wars (Khmelnitsky's Cossack War of 1648–51, the war between Russia and the Polish-Lithuanian Commonwealth from 1654 to 1667, and the Great Northern War of 1700–21) led to economic and population declines in the Belarusian region. The thirteen-year-long war with Russia was particularly disastrous: 52 percent of the population of Belarus was lost, and 55 percent of its cities and towns were destroyed.[24] The northeast—namely, the Vitebsk, Polatsk, and Mstsislaw voivodeships—was hardest hit, losing over two-thirds of its population. The number of households in Vitebsk was reduced by 94 percent, in Polatsk by 93 percent, and in Chashniki by 74 percent.[25] These military conflicts devastated cities, miastechki, and villages and unleashed a great deal of violence against civilians, often indiscriminate of gender, age, or religion.

Muscovy instituted repressive policies on the occupied eastern territories of the GDL, targeting all those who were not Eastern Orthodox. Jews, like the rest of the GDL population, suffered greatly at the hands of the Muscovite troops. Pogroms were frequent. In 1654, after the bloodless surrender of Mahilyow, Konstantin Poklonsky's Cossacks organized a pogrom in the city and murdered many of the szlachta and the majority of the Jewish population. The Muscovites also implemented a policy of resettling urban residents in the Russian hinterland, including many Jews. As defenders of their cities, they would be taken prisoner and transported to Russia along with the others.[26]

As a result of these battles, famines, epidemics, and mass resettlement in Russia, Belarusian cities, towns, and miastechki became deserted. After the wars, this demographic, socioeconomic, and cultural void was eventually filled by Jews, a process actively facilitated by local magnates invested in rebuilding their cities and miastechki, as well as government authorities eager to reestablish the country's economy.

Thus, after the wars spanning the period from the mid-seventeenth century to the early eighteenth, the number of Jews in miastechki grew significantly. Local aristocrats who wanted to reestablish the economy on their lands and to increase trade and artisanal production invited Jews to live in their settlements in exchange for guarantees of safety, free trade, and freedom to practice their religion, as well as autonomous community governance. Moshe Rosman has convincingly demonstrated that there was a deep, mutual commonality and interdependence between the economic interests of the magnates and the Jews.[27] In 1539, Jews officially came under the jurisdiction of landowners. The landowners were granted significant freedoms to act and regulate the legal status of their subjects and could grant them various privileges. A large number of such privileis were bestowed on Jewish communities from the end of the seventeenth through the eighteenth centuries. This practice corresponded with the overall program of the postwar reconstruction of the Polish-Lithuanian Commonwealth. The system of privilei meant that these Jewish communities were legally acknowledged corporate bodies.[28]

The materials examined for this study of Belarusian mestechki confirm Adam Teller's conclusion that one of the defining characteristics of Jewish life under the Polish-Lithuanian government, which ruled over the Belarusian lands, was the Jews' interest in living on privately owned estates, particularly those owned by major magnates, which offered them greater security, better living conditions, and improved economic prospects.[29] Magnates employed Jews to organize and run their feudal holdings. Studying the economic role of Jews in the Belarusian holdings of the Radziwills from the end of the eighteenth century to the beginning of the nineteenth, Olga Sobolevskaia arrived at the thesis that Jews participated actively in areas such as supply chains, lease-holding, rent collection, and other financial operations.[30] The most common relationship between Jews and landowners on whose land they lived was through lease-holding. In this way, the Radziwills received something that people in their social circles particularly valued: free time to pursue their social lives and careers in the military and at the royal court. According to the notions of that time, it was beneath an aristocrat's dignity to get too involved with running his estate.

Miastechki owners would only deal with the community leadership, the kahal, which collected taxes, organized religious life, provided social assistance, and maintained order in the mestechko, while also presiding over the court and carrying out punitive measures (corporal punishment or herem, banishment from the community). This system allowed Jews to live in their own social, religious, and cultural sphere, while their connection to the outside world remained chiefly economic.[31]

Landowners took advantage of traditional Jewish social structures, using them as sources of revenue and administrative levers for controlling the Jews' economic activities. Often, magnates would interfere with the internal affairs of the Jewish community.[32] This drove cultural changes, particularly when it came to markers of social and political status. Learning and wealth, which had once been the most important markers of success, began to be replaced by one's proximity to the magnate. Naturally, this also weakened the power of the rabbis.

Even after the incorporation of the lands of the former Polish-Lithuanian Commonwealth into the Russian Empire, the majority of landowners, finding themselves in the same socioeconomic situation under the new political leadership as before, continued to rely heavily on Jews to act as middlemen for a wide variety of purposes, as well as to serve other functions. There are many contemporary accounts of this relationship. According to one report, "A large number of landowners seem to be incapable of not only acting but even thinking without a Jew. In a landowner's home and in his affairs, the Jew is equal to if not greater than his master. A landowner almost never makes a decision without his trusted Jew, while that trusted Jew will always make a deal with you without his client."[33]

However, it became more frequent in the nineteenth century for owners to violate the initial terms on which the Jews came to settle in the miastechka. Many Jewish communities began to dispute with landowners over their previously inviolable, established rights to live and make a living off local sources of revenue. Documents establishing Jews' former rights were cited in complaints to various government agencies and in defense of these interests in the courts, sometimes with success.[34]

After the partitions of the Polish-Lithuanian Commonwealth, from the late eighteenth through the beginning of the twentieth centuries, there was a final crystallization of the sociocultural model of the miastechka. These settlements became majority Jewish as a result of the restrictive policies of the Russian government—namely, the establishment of the Pale of Jewish Settlement and the forced resettlement of Jews from villages into towns and miastechki.[35] In addition to this, the anti-imperial uprisings of 1830–31 and 1863–64, which were put down by the tsarist government, forced landowners who had supported rebels to leave their estates. After the abolition of serfdom in 1861, some landowners were unable to adjust to the new capitalist economic conditions and went bankrupt, therefore no longer needing the mediating services of Jews. As a result, the Jewish lease-holders lost their sources of income and were forced to move to towns and miastechki.

The increase in the proportion of Jews in the general population during the nineteenth century was also related to demographic processes: in this period, the Jewish population was growing significantly faster than it had in the past and much more rapidly than other groups. Shaul Stampfer explains this as a case of "demographic transition," a shift from a high birth rate with low life expectancy to a low birth rate with higher life expectancy. In the intermediate period between these two end points, the birth rate remains high while the mortality rate falls. Jews in Eastern Europe experienced this kind of transition during the nineteenth century.[36]

The following representative figures illustrate the growth of the Jewish population in miastechki during the eighteenth and nineteenth centuries, which occurred under the influence of the factors described above. The miastechka of Kletsk was gravely affected by the war between Russia and the Polish-Lithuanian Commonwealth from 1654 to 1667. Before the war, there were 490 households; afterward, there were only 238 (a decrease of 51.4 percent). After the miastechka was devastated in 1706, during the Great Northern War, only 152 households remained (in 1713).[37] Prince Radziwill oversaw the repopulation of Kletsk with Jews in the eighteenth century. In 1766, the kahal was composed of twenty-nine souls. In 1796, a stone synagogue was built with Radziwill money.[38] By the end of the 1860s, Jews made up 94.4 percent of the population of the miastechka (1,836 out of 1,944 people).[39]

Undeniably, the rapid growth of the Jewish population in the Radziwill-owned part of Hlybokaye was also the result of the processes described above, which is well illustrated by data from inventories from the eighteenth through the first half of the nineteenth centuries. Between 1704 and 1820, the population changed radically: while there was an overall tendency toward growth, the number of peasant households decreased from 250 to 89, while the number of Jewish ones rose from 13 to 234.[40] The growth of the Jewish population in Zhaludok is reflected in the following data: in 1829, out of 369 men in the mestechko, 139 were Jewish (37.6 percent); in 1880, among 1,175 people of both genders, 795 were Jewish (nearly 68 percent); and in 1897, there were 1,860 residents, 1,372 of whom were Jews (73.5 percent).[41] In 1861, Jews made up nearly 30 percent of the population in Liepiel (873 out of 2,781 residents); by 1905, the proportion of Jews rose to nearly 60 percent (almost four thousand of seven thousand residents).[42] These examples illustrate a general trend: in the majority of miastechki in the Belarusian-Lithuanian region, Jews became the dominant part of the population. In addition, Ben-Cion Pinchuk has presented numerical data demonstrating that in 1897, Jews were dominant in 462 miastechki across the entire Pale of Settlement and made up over 80 percent of the population in 25 percent of them.[43]

According to tallies from the data collected in the first census of the Russian Empire, in 1897, including military men, the proportion of Jews among the urban population of the Vilna, Hrodna (Grodno), Minsk, Mahilyow (Mogilev), and Vitebsk gubernias was 41.5 percent, and among the miastechka population, 59.8 percent.[44] In the total population of these gubernias, Jews made up 14.1 percent (approximately 1.2 million people), making them the second-largest group after Belarusians (who made up 63.5 percent, nearly 5.4 million people) in the multiethnic Belarusian and Lithuanian region of the Russian Empire.[45]

Thus, in towns and miastechki, Jews were often the majority, while on the national level, they remained the minority. Historically, Jews identified much more strongly with their specific shtetls than with their regions or countries. This was because local structures—the rabbinate, *bes-medresh* (synagogue), or *bikur kholim* (society for caring for the ill)—had much more influence on their communities than regional or national entities.[46] In 1897, only 40 percent of Jews lived in settlements where they composed the majority.[47] A significant portion of Jews were in the minority in their towns, cities, and miastechki. In any case, both in miastechki with Jewish majorities and in those where Jews were a minority, the Jews' involvement in commerce and the trades led to constant contact between a significant portion of them and the surrounding non-Jewish population. Jews were always open to outside influences.

According to my calculations, based on statistical data on miastechki collected in the late 1860s by governors in the northwest region—Belarusian-Lithuanian lands—Jews were dominant (composing over 50 percent of the population) in 271 of 527 miastechki.[48] If a shtetl is defined as a small town with a Jewish majority, then only half of all miastechki had become shtetls by the middle of the nineteenth century. But Jewish communities, with all of their accompanying institutions, also existed in miastechki where Jews were the minority. If the shtetl is defined as a physical and spiritual Jewish space in a Belarusian, Ukrainian, Polish, or Lithuanian miastechka, it can be said that all mestechki with Jewish communities also had shtetls within them.

The important role played by Jews in the reconstruction of cities, towns, and miastechki across Belarus, in shaping municipal construction, in organizing and developing local production, and in establishing manufacturing and commercial concerns is indisputable. Experience with urban living, knowledge of economic realia, business and personal connections, entrepreneurial spirit, and established mutual support structures all rendered the Jewish community a self-organizing core for an urban economy. Even when it did not make up the overall majority of a miaestechka population, the Jewish community is what made miastechka life urban. The Jews were the consolidating factor in Belarusian lands, perhaps even more so than in other regions of the former Polish-Lithuanian Commonwealth. Jews united the miastechka and gave it its character, both its physical appearance and its atmosphere.[49] This is well documented in historical accounts, including Abram Paperna's description of the centrality of Jewish homes in Kapyl in the mid-nineteenth century: "Considering the visibility of the place taken up by Jews, as well as their relatively large numbers and the mobility inherent to trading peoples in general and Jews especially, on first glance, Kapyl gave the impression of being a purely Jewish town."[50]

Thus, from the eighteenth through the nineteenth centuries, Belarus became the land of Jewish miastechki or shtetls, small towns whose way of life was determined by the Jewish majority. In each of these, a community was organized with its own traditional institutions regulating its everyday life. The policies that had been implemented by the Russian government to restrict where Jews could settle led to a concentration of Jews in cities and miastechki, which then facilitated the preservation of traditional Jewish culture and ways of life. For Jews, the miastechka played the same kind of role in preserving traditional culture as the village did for Belarusians. The miastechka or shtetl became the Jews' natural habitat. Eventually, miastechki came to be seen as a form of Jewish homeland, or Israel in exile. The miastechka became the historical center of Jewish life, the sphere of Jews' economic and political activity, and the context of their intensive contacts and conflicts with non-Jews.[51]

Researchers have pointed out the dynamic nature of the shtetl, which went through a series of stages. Historians Gershon David Hundert, Moshe Rossman, and Adam Teller see the period of the Polish-Lithuanian Commonwealth as a time when Jews enjoyed legal protections, guarantees of safety, and an important role in the economy. Antony Polonsky concludes that Jews experienced true flourishing in the Polish-Lithuanian Commonwealth.[52] Ilia Lurie notes that in the Polish-Lithuanian Commonwealth, the system of self-governance in the Jewish community reached the pinnacle of its development, melding organically with the corporate structure of the feudal administration.[53] According to Yohanan Petrovsky-Shtern, the golden age of the shtetl lasted from the 1790s to the 1840s, as evidenced by its economic success, stability, and domestic and cultural vitality. During this stage, the shtetl provided the Russian Empire with a way to integrate the Jews with the rest of the region's population, while it was a chance for Jews to adapt to living in Russia. In pursuing policies shaped by its chauvinist ideology, the Russian government squandered this opportunity.[54]

Beginning in the late nineteenth century and continuing into the early twentieth century, four major trends—emigration, assimilation, socialism, and Zionism—alongside factors such as the emergence of bourgeois society after the abolition of serfdom in 1861, industrialization, urbanization, and the expansion of the railroads destabilized the miastechka. Though the view that the shtetl collapsed as a result of modernization is widely held, it is also controversial. Pinchuk claims that the shtetl did not begin falling apart at the end of the nineteenth century; indeed, it enjoyed a revival. The most common explanation for the disappearance of the shtetl is based on the theory that the traditional Jewish orthodox way of life and its social structures were in decline. However, the population was stable, and the Jewish component of the miastechka remained a community fixture because it "consisted of many elements, the majority of which were not tied to religion (for instance, language, social structure, appearance, etc.) but was overall independent and separate from the surrounding society."[55]

Regional Characteristics of Shtetls on Belarusian Lands

The chronology of the emergence of miastechki in Belarus was not the same everywhere, and the geographic distribution was not uniform. Urbanization, which led to the formation of miastechki, spread from west to east, so that eastern miastechki developed later. The network of miastechki was denser in the more economically developed regions of Belarus due to geographic and geopolitical factors. In the middle of the sixteenth century, the 210 miastechki across Belarus were at the intersections of every land and water route. The Nyoman region had the largest number with 67; the central region, from Budslau to Hlusk and from Byerazino to Snou, had 43; and the Lake region had 40. There were 31 miastechki in the Dnieper region and 27 in Palesie, although the eastern part of Palesie (from Mazyr to Davyd-Haradok) had only 3.[56]

Of the 272 miastechki on Tomasz Makowski's 1613 map of the GDL, 109 were in the Nyoman River basin, 62 in the Dnieper River basin, 55 in the Dvina, 42 in the Prypyat, and 4 in the Bug. On the 1665 map of the GDL, out of 315 miastechki in Belarus, 147 were located in the Nyoman River basin.[57] In the second half of the eighteenth century, of the 398 miastechki on Belarusian lands, 81 were in the eastern part (before 1772), and 317 in the west and center (in the early 1790s).[58]

Most miastechki in Belarus had small populations. At the end of the eighteenth century, an average of 630 people lived in miastechka—around 620 in the western and central regions and around 670 in the east. The average population of a Belarusian miastechka in 1859 was 1,000.[59] Though miastechki in the east were farther apart from one another, they were larger than those in the western and central regions.

Statistical data from the late 1860s illustrate the settlement of miastechki across individual Belarusian gubernias. Vilna gubernia had a large number of small miastechki; the average population was 350. The miastechki in the Vitebsk gubernia were not very large, with an average population of 570. The average population of miastechki in the Mahilyow gubernia was 1,285; in the Hrodna gubernia, 1,210; and in the Minsk gubernia, 1,083.[60]

Statistics gathered by governors in the northwestern region in the late 1860s show that in the Minsk gubernia, Jews composed 45.3 percent of the total mestechki population; in the Vilna gubernia, 50.7 percent; in Hrodna, 57.7 percent; in Vitebsk, 58.3 percent; in Kovna, 59.9 percent; and in Mahilyow, 67 percent.[61] Across the six guberniias, there were 527 miastechki, with Jews making up the majority of the population in 271 (more than half of miastechki were majority Jewish). Among these 271, there were 94 in which Jews made up over 80 percent of the population. Across the gubernias, the proportions were as follows:

According to this data, the highest concentration of miastechki with majority-Jewish populations was in the Mahilyow gubernia, and the lowest, in the Vilna gubernia. Vilna, however, had the densest network of miastechki, which allowed the Jewish population to disperse among numerous individual settlements. In each case, specific circumstances account for the proportion of Jewish residents. Jews were forbidden to settle in Zhyrovichy, a large center of the Uniate Basilian Order, at the start of the reign of John II Casimir Vasa

Table 1.1

Guberniia	Number of Miastechki	Miastechki with a Jewish Majority (over 50% Jews)	Miastechki with over 80% Jews
Vitebsk	46	28 (61%)	13 (28%)
Vilna	185	68 (37%)	25 (14%)
Hrodna	66	42 (64%)	10 (15%)
Kovna	62	36 (58%)	23 (37%)
Mahilyow	73	52 (71%)	13 (18%)
Minsk	95	45 (47%)	10 (11%)
Total	527 (100%)	271 (51%)	94 (18%)

(1648–68). They were not even allowed to spend the night; in fact, even while passing through, they were forced to walk barefoot and with their heads uncovered.[62] By the nineteenth century, however, Jews began settling in Zhyrovichy in small numbers: in 1829, there were three Jewish households there.[63] In 1864, the head of the Zhyrovichy Monastery (which was by then Eastern Orthodox) petitioned the authorities to remove nine Jewish families from the miastechka. Interestingly, local peasants came to these Jews' defense: in an appeal to the governor-general of Vilna, they said that the Jews "provide us significant help and we wish for them to remain our neighbors."[64] Jews did not have the right to live in the Carmelite part of Hlybokaye, while the growth of the Jewish population in the Radziwill-owned section led nineteenth-century researchers to state that "Hlybokaye is inhabited by practically all Jews and does major trade with Riga."[65]

In addition to differences in when they were established, in the density of their networks, and in their population density—particularly of Jews—miastechki exhibited regional characteristics, notably in the ethnoreligious makeup of their overall populations. Miastechki in western and central Belarus often had substantial Tatar Muslim populations (as in Iwye, Lyakhavichy, Kletsk, Kapyl, Mir, Miadziel, Smilavichy, Smarhon, and Hlybokaye). In eastern Belarus, mestechki with a significant Catholic population were more rare than in the west.

Jewish communities were neither ideologically nor ethnoculturally homogenous. Three main trends shaped the character of a shtetl: Hasidism (in the Lithuanian-Belarusian region, Northern Hasidism was more widespread; it was known for being spiritual, elitist, and learning-centric compared with the Southern Hasidism of Ukraine and Bessarabia, which was practical and populist in nature); the Misnagdim movement, which was oriented toward traditional Talmudic learning; and the Haskalah movement of Jewish enlightenment.[66]

In Belarus, Jewish communities with a strong Hasidic presence were concentrated around the Minsk and Vitebsk gubernias, where Hasidism took on the particular local form of *Chabad*. Well-known centers of this branch of Hasidim were Liozna, Lyady, Kopys, and Lyubavichi. The spread of Hasidism slowed in the historical territory of Palesie (the Hrodna gubernia and the western part of Minsk). The Indura dynasty of zaddiks came to an end in two generations under Misnagdim pressure. The most famous center of Hasidism in Palesie was Karlin, a suburb of Pinsk. The Karlin-Stolin dynasty's sphere of influence was thought to extend to the branches of Hasidism in Lyakhavichy, Koidanava (present-day Dzyarshynsk), Kobryn, and Slonim.[67] In the Vilna and Kovna gubernias, the number of Hasidim was insignificant, due to the Misnagdim majority.

In the nineteenth century, when historical Lithuania became famous as a center of Jewish religious learning, the study of the Torah flourished in an unprecedented way. In a number of miastechki and cities across Belarus, chiefly in the Minsk and Vilna gubernias, prestigious institutions for the study of the Torah were founded on a new educational model; these were the so-called Lithuanian yeshivas. "The mother of the Lithuanian yeshivas" was the Valozhyn Yeshiva, founded in 1802 by a student of the Vilna Gaon Rabbi Chaim of Valozhyn. The Valozhyn tradition was carried on by yeshivas in Mir, Radun, Navahrudak, Slutsk, and Lida, and others.

Individual miastechki across Belarus became widely known as centers of Haskalah. An important example is Shklow, which Empress Catherine II had gifted to her favorite, Semyon Zorich, in 1772, after Russia's annexation of eastern Belarusian lands. Zorich founded a magnificent court, modeled after St. Petersburg, with a theater and a school for the children of the local nobility. Almost ten manufacturing enterprises were functioning in the town. Without a doubt, the overall cultural atmosphere in Shklow under Zorich, in addition to the development of trade and manufacturing and the burgeoning connections with Europe, had a powerful effect on the Shklow Jewry. Shklow became a center of rabbinical study and a locus for the dissemination of the ideas and scholarship of the Haskalah movement in Russia. According to historian David Fishman, "The period between the annexation by Russia and Napoleon's conquest (1772–1812) was a golden age in the life of the town/city, when it was a metropolis of the Russian Jewry."[68]

The decline of the miastechka across Eastern Europe—its residents' gradual departure from traditional ways of life—was not simply the result of economic modernization; it was also expedited by anti-Jewish repression, economic restrictions, and pogroms.[69] The Belarusian region fared better than most; its miastechki were spared massive pogroms against the Jews like the ones that had taken place in Ukraine in the early 1880s. Minor (as compared to Ukraine) instances of anti-Jewish violence included the pogroms in the miastechki of Voranava (1883), Dauhinava (1886), and Dokshytsy (1887) in the Vilna gubernia, and the miastechka of Zelva (1885) in the Hrodna gubernia.[70]

At the beginning of the twentieth century, when another wave of pogroms rolled across the Pale of Settlement, the relative infrequency of violent eruptions in the Belarusian region once again distinguished it from other regions. In October 1905, there were twenty-three known pogroms in Belarus, but 292 across the entire Pale of Settlement. Considering that by size and number of Jews the Belarusian gubernias made up a large part of the Pale of Settlement, this disproportion is significant. Studies of pogroms in Belarus between 1903 and 1906 show that the main impetus for these outbreaks of violence came from local representatives of the Russian government and the gendarme and police agencies.[71]

The much lower level of anti-Jewish violence in Belarus can be explained by several factors: the absence of "Cossack traditions," the slow pace of modernization, the lack of strong nationalist feelings and ideology in Belarus, certain characteristics of Belarusian socioeconomic development (each ethnoreligious group had a niche in terms of social and economic roles, which meant that competition between the groups was minimal), and the absence of aggressive antisemitism among Belarusians.[72] Additionally, Belarusian miastechki tended to be small, so their residents were well acquainted with one another.

After the tragic events of World War I, the October Revolution, the Russian Civil War, and the Soviet-Polish war, miastechki entered their final stage of development. The fates of miastechki and their residents in the eastern and western regions of Belarus broadly diverged in the interwar period due to geopolitical circumstances—namely, because of the Treaty of Riga of March 18, 1921, in accordance with which western Belarus was incorporated into Poland.

The term *miasteczko* continued to officially exist across voivodeships in northwestern Poland until 1939, designating a type of settlement that was distinct from a city or a village. Polish authorities in miastechki saw them as special zones of exchange (primarily economic) between the city and the country and did not block their economic development. The integration of miastechki economies into the overall economy of Poland happened quickly, thanks to the participation of the Jews, who turned many miastechki into the trade and manufacturing centers of *gminas*, *povets*, and voivodeships. Even though the level of development in the eastern *kresy* (borderlands) was much lower than in the other voivodeships across the reborn Polish Republic, the economic situation of the Polish miastechki was less dire than in their Soviet counterparts.[73]

The miastechka retained its traditional image as the center of Jewish history and culture. At the same time, miastechki continued to be characterized by ethnic diversity and religious pluralism. This had a positive effect on their continued development and allowed for the self-preservation of minority cultures even under the Polonizing policies instituted by central Polish authorities. Even though the Polish government had restrictive policies targeting minorities in the eastern *kresy*, exceptions were made for Jews, who were granted some degree of autonomy. Jewish communities in hundreds of miastechki became autonomous administrative and territorial entities, allowing them to preserve Yiddish traditions.[74]

According to Antony Polonsky, the most pressing problem facing Jews in interwar Poland was their pauperization.[75] Antisemitism was on the rise. To a certain extent, interwar Poland was a unique state: in no other country in Central or Eastern Europe was the Jewish population so widely represented across various kinds of political and social organizations; yet in no other country were there such widespread manifestations of antisemitism.[76] Field research conducted by the Sefer Center and the RAN Institute of Slavic Studies Center for Slavo-Judaica in the western Belarusian miastechki of Zhaludok and Hlybokaye documented changes in the previously tolerant attitude toward Jews during that period. These changes were most vividly demonstrated in the increasing discrimination against Jewish students in Polish gymnasia: they were admitted less frequently and, in 1938, some were openly beaten. One of the old residents of today's Hlybokaye, Vera Stepanovna Perepechko, born in 1926, recalled the Polish school that was attended by children of all nationalities who lived in the miastechka. She spoke of several antisemitic outbursts and people making fun of the Jewish students. When a rabbi was teaching a religion class, "the children would open the doors, cry 'Aius!' (pig), give up and start over." Sometimes, they would write antisemitic slogans on the board in Polish, such as "Beat up the Yid! To Palestine!"[77]

Another dimension of public opinion on "the Jewish question" among the non-Jewish population of western Belarus can be seen in a 1935 survey of Catholic priests conducted by the curiate of the Vilna metropolitan. The responses of the priests from the Hlybokaye deanery demonstrate antisemitic bias in their calls to "push the Jews out of the labor market and trade in general so that they'll emigrate," "self-defense against the Jews in all respect, cut off all ties and contacts with them," and "leave them to their fates."[78]

East of the Soviet-Polish border, in the 1920s and 1930s, the miastechki in the Belarusian Soviet Socialist Republic (BSSR) and their residents felt the effects of all the Bolsheviks' experiments and every twist and turn in their policies. Having lost their traditional socioeconomic and cultural function, miastechki were slowly transforming, attempting to adapt to the new way of life and fit in as one of its parts, striving to become either collective farm communities or towns.[79] In the end, however, these settlements and their (petit bourgeois) residents were incompatible with the structure of the new socialist society. Private business ownership was eliminated by the end of the 1930s, with many former proprietors sharing the bitter fate of well-off rural landowners. And because miastechki were associated with private ownership, the very concept of the miastechka needed to be eradicated to clear the way for the enshrinement of collective labor. The September 27, 1938, decree of the Presidium of the Supreme Soviet of the BSSR on the classification of settlements in the BSSR eliminated miastechki as administrative entities. In western Belarus, they continued to exist until the fateful events of September 1939.

Over the quarter century from 1917 to 1941, the Jews' traditional way of life in towns, cities, and miastechki across the former Pale of Settlement changed radically. These changes affected Jews' occupations and their social, religious, and family life. A heightened visibility of Jews, due to their unusual social mobility, led to an outburst of antisemitism. At the same time, Jews' departure from tradition was the result not only of Bolshevik policies but also of general processes of modernization. But in places where Jews made up a significant portion of the population, they were more inclined to preserve elements of their traditional way of life. The Jewish miastechka as a locus of traditional life and a sociocultural phenomenon did not entirely disappear, along with its inhabitants, until the Holocaust.[80]

There was great diversity among miastechki and shtetls that makes it difficult to generalize from the studies analyzed for this chapter; there was no such thing as a typical mestechko, and no two shtetls were alike. Each had a unique character. Throughout their historical development, Jewish communities never became a homogeneous unity; instead, they preserved their local specificity. Regional variations were reflected in the institutional, educational, and political spheres, as well as the human factor, since shtetls were primarily shaped by small groups of people who devoted themselves to developing social institutions and youth organizations and to organizing cultural events.[81]

That said, an indisputable general characteristic of all miastechki was their multicultural nature. It is a deep loss that the cities, towns, and miastechki of Belarus, and the country in general, have undergone a dramatic ethnocultural transformation over the past century. Having lost the shtetl forever and having undergone Russification and Sovietization, today's Belarus has preserved only traces of its former multiculturalism. Recovering the memory of the past of the Belarusian people as well as other ethnic communities (including Jews) that for centuries cohabitated with them on Belarusian soil is one of the most important tasks for preserving the true historical, cultural, and linguistic character of Belarus.

After World War II, large former miastechki became regular settlements with unique histories. The difference among the fates of the inhabitants of western and eastern Belarusian miastechki left contrasting impressions on the historical memories of their present-day residents. This can be seen in the interviews recorded during the field studies conducted by the Sefer Center and the RAN Institute of Slavic Studies Center for Slavo-Judaica in Zhaludok, Hlybokaye, Liepiel, and Beshakovichy. In Hlybokaye, where Jewish cultural and religious traditions were preserved until World War II, respondents (Belarusians, Poles, and Tatars) put special emphasis on how Jewish culture dominated the urban landscape, evidence that the character of everyday life in the town was, to a great extent, determined by contacts with the Jewish population.[82] When describing the town, Hlybokaye residents tended to bring up Jews and Jewish culture without being prompted by researchers.[83] Compared with the volume and diversity of reports about Jews provided by informants in western Belarus, oral histories collected in eastern Belarus seem scant. Because Belarusians there lost contact with Jews who adhered to tradition much earlier on, memories of the Jews have been, to a large extent, erased. In Beshankovichy, informants were reluctant to answer questions about Jews; some of them were even surprised that researchers were interested in this topic. Some said that they could say nothing of Jews, their religion, or customs.[84]

Notes

1. Various aspects of the history and culture of the Belarusian miastechki are examined in the works of Stanislaw Alexandrowicz, Yury Bokhan, Zinovii Kopysskii, Afroim Karpachev, Anatol Liuty, Zakhar Shybeka, Olga Sobolevskaia, Aliaksandr Lakotka, John D. Klier, Adam Teller, Moshe Rossman, Ben-Cion Pinchuk, David Fishman, Shaul Stampfer, Yohanan Petrovsky-Stern, Claire Le Foll, Samuel D. Kassow, Antony Polonsky, Darius Staliunas, Olga Belova, Mikhail Krutikov, Leonid Smilovitsky, Arkadi Zeltser, Valentin Mikhedko, Andrei Zamoiskii, Anna Boyteshik, and other scholars. Foundational sources included materials from various statistical collections published in the Russian

Empire (most important among these, the data on miastechki in "Materialy, otnosiashchiesia do novogo obshchestvennogo ustroistva v gorodakh imperii"); archival documents "Svedeniia kantseliarii gubernatorov" from the National Historical Archive of Belarus (NIAB) in Minsk and Hrodna; the Lithuanian State Historical Archives (LGIA); and other collections; and, finally, memoirs. Especially valuable among these sources were books published following expeditions and field research organized by the Sefer Center, which brought together oral history, folklore, ethnography, epigraphy, and archival materials about the lives of Jews in Zhaludok, Hlybokaye, and Liepiel.

2. Kopysskii, *Sotsialno-politicheskoe razvitie gorodov Belorussii*, 10.

3. The twenty-ninth article of the first section stated, "a khto b z abyvatseliaŭ taho panstva nashaha i͡akoha kol'vek stanu i narodu shli͡akhetskaha dli͡a prymnazhénni͡a sabe pazhytku khatseŭ na hruntse svaim miastéchka novae sadzitsi, to i͡amu vol'na budze ŭchynitsi, i tarhovae ŭ im pavodle daŭni͡aha zvychai͡u . . . ustanavits'" (*Statut Vi͡alikaha kni͡astva Litoŭskaha 1588 hoda*, 98–99).

4. Alexandrowicz, *Studia z dziejów miasteczek Wielkiego Księstwa Litewskiego*; Bokhan, "Miastéchki vi͡arkhoŭi͡aŭ Vilii i ni͡omanskaĭ Bi͡arėziny; Lakotka, *Natsyi͡anal'nyi͡a rysy belaruskaĭ arkhitėktury*.

5. Lakotka, *Natsyi͡anal'nyi͡a rysy belaruskaĭ arkhitėktury*, 15.

6. Alexandrowicz, *Studia z dziejów miasteczek Wielkiego Księstwa Litewskiego*, 87.

7. Alexandrowicz, *Studia z dziejów miasteczek Wielkiego Księstwa Litewskiego*, 88.

8. Alexandrowicz, *Studia z dziejów miasteczek Wielkiego Księstwa Litewskiego*, 88.

9. Kni͡azeva, "Mi͡adzel," 246.

10. Hedemann, *Głębokie: Szkic dziejów*, 7.

11. Mochalova, "Glubokoe—stranitsy istorii," 25.

12. See also Sorkina, "The Revolt in the Name of Freedom."

13. Liuty, "Sotsialno-ekonomicheskoe razvitie gorodov Belorussii," 18–19.

14. Sorkina, *Mi͡astéchki Belarusi*, 53.

15. Shybeka, *Harady Belarusi*, 79.

16. Karpachev, *Sotsialno-ekonomicheskoe razvitie gorodov Belorussii*, 91.

17. Hrodna, NIAB, fond 1, opis 1, delo 100, ll. 28–30.

18. Kopchenova, ed., *Glubokoe: Pamiat' o evreiskom mestechke*, pp. 24, 52–54.

19. Confirmation of this can be found in studies by Belarusian historians Anatoly Gritskevich, Zinovii Kopysskii, Yuri Gordeev, and others.

20. Krutikov, "Shtetl mezhdu fantaziei i realnostiu"; Kassow, "Community and Identity in the Interwar Shtetl."

21. The most important among these include Zborowski and Herzog, *Life Is with People*; Roskies and Roskies, *The Shtetl Book*; Miron, *The Image of the Shtetl*; Klier, "What Exactly Was a Shtetl?"; Więcławska, *Zmartwychwstałe miasteczko . . . Literackie oblicza sztetl*; Dymshits, Lvov, and Sokolova, *Shtetl, v XXI v.*; Veidlinger, *In the Shadow of the Shtetl*; Petrovsky-Shtern, *The Golden Age Shtetl*.

22. Klier, "What Exactly Was a Shtetl?," 26.
23. Mstislavsky,"Evrei v Mogilevskoi gubernii," 3.
24. Sahanovich, *Neviadomaia voina*, 130, 139.
25. Sahanovich, *Neviadomaia voina*, 139.
26. Shprit, "Mogilevsky pogrom 1654," 122, 132–33.
27. Rosman, *The Lords' Jews*.
28. Teller, "The Legal Status of the Jews," 41.
29. Teller, "The Legal Status of the Jews," 41–63.
30. Sobolevskaia, "Iudei v belorusskikh vladeniiakh Radzivillov."
31. Roskies and Roskies, *The Shtetl Book*, 181–84, 187–88.
32. Teller, "The Legal Status of the Jews," 57.
33. S. L., "Aktsiznyy otkup i evrei-posredniki v Minskoi gubernii."
34. See also Sorkina, "Evrei i vladeltsy mestechkek Belarusi."
35. See also Sorkina, "Pereseleniia evreiskogo naseleniia."
36. Lurie, *Istoriia evreiskogo naroda v Rossii*, 2:280.
37. Pazdniakoŭ, "Kletsk," 194.
38. Jelski, "Kleck," 123.
39. "Materialy, otnosiashchiesia," 5:101.
40. Sorkina, "Mestechko Glubokoe," 52.
41. Sorkina, *Miastėchki Belarusi*, 413; Pivovarchik and Sorkina, "Istoricheskii ocherk evreiskoi obshchiny Zheludka," 20.
42. Kaperkin, "'Oni zhili v etom gorode . . .,'" 15.
43. Pinchuk, "How Jewish Was the Shtetl?," 112.
44. Numbers based on *Statistika evreiskogo naseleniia*; see appendix.
45. *Belarusy*, 221.
46. Kassow, "Community and Identity in the Interwar Shtetl."
47. Lurie, *Istoriia evreiskogo naroda v Rossii*, 2:279.
48. "Materialy, otnosiashchiesia do novogo obshchestvennogo ustroistva v gorodakh imperii," 82–102.
49. Metelskakia, "Mir evreiskikh mestechek Belarusi," 130.
50. Paperna, "Iz Nikolaevskoi epokhi," 6.
51. Sorkina, "'Ours' or 'Foreign'?"
52. Polonsky, *Dzieje Żydów w Polsce i Rosji*, 72.
53. Lurie, *Istoriia evreiskogo naroda v Rossii*, 2:5.
54. Petrovsky-Shtern, *The Golden Age Shtetl*, 3.
55. Pinchuk, "The Eastern European Shtetl and Its Place in Jewish History," 196.
56. Lakotka, *Natsyianal'nyia rysy belaruskaĭ arkhitėktury*, 15.
57. Kopysskii, *Ekonomicheskoe razvitie gorodov Belorussii*, 206.
58. Karpachev, *Sotsialno-ekonomicheskoe razvitie gorodov Belarussii*, 108.
59. Karpachev, *Sotsialno-ekonomicheskoe razvitie gorodov Belarussii*, 58.

60. "Materialy, otnosiashchiesia do novogo obshchestvennogo ustroistva v gorodakh imperii," 82–102.

61. "Materialy, otnosiashchiesia do novogo obshchestvennogo ustroistva v gorodakh imperii," 82–102.

62. *Słownik geograficzny Królestwa Polskiego*, 14:897.

63. Hrodna, NIAB, fond 1, opis 4, delo 646, l. 56.

64. Vilnius, LGIA, fond 378, General Department, 1864, delo 1612, l. 20 rev.

65. Mochalova, "Glubokoe—stranitsy istorii," 37.

66. Lurie, *Istoriia evreiskogo naroda v Rossii*, 2:103.

67. Lurie, *Istoriia evreiskogo naroda v Rossii*, 120–22.

68. Fishman, *Russia's First Modern Jews*.

69. "Mestechko."

70. On Voranava, see Staliunas, "Anti-Jewish Disturbances," 123. On Dauhinava and Dokshytsy, see Sorkina, "Mestechko Glubokoe," 69. On Zelva, see Sabaleŭskai͡a, "Habrëĭska-khrystsii͡anski dyi͡aloh u Harodni," 148.

71. Mikhedko, "Vlast, revoliutsiia i pogromy v Belarusi," 20, 32.

72. Klier, "The Pogrom Paradigm in Russian History," 14; Le Foll, "The Missing Pogroms of Belorussia"; Mikhedko, "Vlast, revoliutsiia i pogromy v Belarusi," 21, 32.

73. Voiteshchik, "Shtetl kak sotsiokulturnyi fenomen," 11–12.

74. Voiteshchik, "Shtetl kak sotsiokulturnyi fenomen," 11–12.

75. Polonsky, *Dzieje Żydów w Polsce i Rosji*, 309.

76. Moshchuk, "Bor'ba s antisemitizmom," 111.

77. Sorkina, "Mestechko Glubokoe," 71.

78. Sorkina, "Mestechko Glubokoe," 72.

79. Studies on the transformation of mestechki under Soviet rule during the interwar period include Shkolnikova, *Transformatsiia evreiskogo mestechka*; Zeltser, *Evrei sovetskoi provintsii*; Shternshis, *Soviet and Kosher*; Zamoiskii, *Transformatsiia mestechek Sovetskoi Belorussii*; Smilovitsky, *Evrei v Turove*, 255–593; and others.

80. Zeltser, *Evrei sovetskoi provintsii*," 317, 323, 325.

81. Kassow, "Community and Identity in the Interwar Shtetl," 220.

82. Belova, "Byt i povsednevnost," 178.

83. Savina, "Zametki o lokalnom meste Glubokogo," 166.

84. Yasinskaia, "Obraz inoetnicheskogo i inokonfessionalnogo soseda," 317.

2

The Soviet Belarusian Shtetl

Between Tradition and Modernization in the 1920s and 1930s

ARKADI ZELTSER

Introduction

Changes in the social and cultural spheres taking place in the USSR in the 1920s and 1930s had a substantial effect on all Jewish shtetls, including those in Belarus. The most important force was intensive modernization, which impacted both public and private life. The fact that a large number of Soviet Jews were eager to participate in these processes and even be leaders in them was significant, although this was much more common in cities than in shtetls. Also important were Soviet policies aimed at eliminating the shtetl as if it were a historical phenomenon that had outlived its functions as an intermediary between town and country. In Soviet society, these functions were supposed to have been transferred to the state.[1] Shtetls themselves were slated to disappear, to become manufacturing towns or villages. Their inhabitants were supposed to become workers, Soviet civil servants, craftspeople in cooperatives, or peasants. The general idea of the "productivization" of Jewish life, which first appeared in the Jewish world in the nineteenth century with the Haskalah (Enlightenment) movement, complemented the Marxist idea of reshaping society based on class.

The early Soviet period saw the beginning of the end of the shtetl. The traditional shtetl was a unique social and cultural phenomenon, a place where Jews were and knew themselves to be in the majority, where they spoke Yiddish, and where their lives were governed by annual cycles and rites of passage. They had their own religious festivals and rituals, a particular worldview, and a hierarchy of values and notions of prestige. The shtetl was never totally insular; the movement of Jews from one place to another was an essential feature of shtetl life. The concentration of Jews in shtetls was a result of both Jewish tradition and tsarist policy, both of which kept them from engaging in agricultural labor. At the same time, big cities, as centers of contemporary culture, were unattractive to shtetl dwellers whose daily lives were suffused with tradition and who were skeptical of change. Naturally, demographic pressures, which intensified over the nineteenth century due to rapid population growth coupled with weak infrastructure development in the countryside, and general processes of urbanization, industrialization, and improved communications—including the appearance and spread of the railways—all left their mark on shtetl life long before the 1917 Russian Revolution. The percentage of Jewish merchants decreased in the shtetls, while more and more inhabitants found themselves forced to make a living in less prestigious ways, such as working as coachmen. Secularization, a shift in perceptions of proper behavior, the emergence of Jewish and all-Russian political movements and parties, and an increase in Russian-language literacy—all these forces were bound to affect the worldview of shtetl Jews. The changes brought by rapid modernization in the USSR, actively bolstered by the Bolshevist myth of building a new society and creating a "new man," accelerated the transformation of the shtetl. Meanwhile, Soviet social and antireligious policies also created novel conditions for Jews.[2]

The Soviet era also brought an unprecedented examination of what defined the shtetl. Was it necessary for the majority of the population to be Jews, did it need to have common structures like a legally functioning synagogue, a mikvah (ritual bath), religious and charitable societies, and so on? Or were another set of characteristics related to social psychology and everyday customs equally important? The history of Soviet shtetls, including those in Belarus, demonstrates that in the early Soviet period, it is these latter characteristics that became the shtetl's defining traits, albeit in ostensibly new forms. The radical nature of the changes in Jewish shtetl life was itself a product of the times and of social and cultural policy reform.

At the beginning of the Soviet period, an increase in taxes on the urban bourgeoisie, including shtetl inhabitants, from 1923 to 1924, was followed by a comparatively lenient period in 1925–26, and then another steep tax hike from 1928 to 1929. A little later, at the beginning of the 1930s, repression intensified with the imposition of Stalin's ruthless system of governance. However, these processes did not take place in the same way in every sphere. Measures directed at peasants could not mechanically be applied to urban (shtetl) dwellers. Moreover, in the 1930s, a noticeable increase in restrictions in one area was sometimes accompanied by more reasonable, liberal policies in another. In this way, while private licensed trade was forbidden in the early 1930s, the initial plan for the complete cooperativization of artisans was never brought to fruition. Small private enterprises existed in shtetls throughout the 1930s, alternately growing and shrinking depending on evolving tax policy.[3]

This chapter discusses changes in the everyday life of Jews in the shtetls of Soviet Belarus. We will look at these changes in the context of migration, Soviet ethnic policy, social and economic transformation, and the clash between traditional values and modernization.

Migration as a Factor in Change

Mass migrations during the interwar period heavily influenced the social makeup and ethnic composition of the Belarusian shtetl.[4] Although migration had been impacting the shtetl for decades, the reasons for it changed. If in the Russian Empire financial considerations were the deciding factor, with shtetl inhabitants being lured away by opportunities to earn higher wages, in the Soviet period, waves of migration were a response to the processes of urbanization and modernization. Of course, the economic factor, including unemployment, remained an important underlying cause of migration. The difference was that now, all social strata were migrating, including those with relatively stable incomes. Apparently, a large number of young shtetl inhabitants preferred unemployment in the city to muddling along in a shtetl.

Another impetus for migration was the conviction held by many at the time, including some shtetl inhabitants, that shtetls were stagnant.[5] Time seemed to plod along in the shtetl. It is no wonder that Yiddish Belarusian author Moyshe Kulbak used an old wall clock as a symbol for this temporal monotony in his saga *The Zelmenyaners*.[6] In the 1920s and 1930s, the number of people bored by the changelessness of shtetl life and attuned to new ideas about social status grew significantly. Signs of condescension toward the shtetl way of life in the Soviet Union during this period include common Yiddish terms like *kleynshtetldikayt* (*mestechkovost'* in Russian or shtetlness); *hekdeishim* (literally, people who live in alms houses, understood as people of low social status); and, in the economic sphere, the Russian words *kustarnost'* (amateurish work, as in made by hand) and *khalturnost'* (hack work). These words, associated with shtetl culture, became synonyms for backwardness and unprofessionalism.

While the shtetl bore the stamp of mustiness, the city was seen as the pinnacle of modernity (Izi Kharik wrote, "I feel the city down to my tears, to my blood, / Down to the limit and the tremulous breath. / I now bless the happy minute / When I first set foot in it").[7] Jews were drawn to the city by the opportunity to integrate into contemporary culture and establish new norms for everyday life. The indoor plumbing available in urban apartments, which was, in those years, a symbol of technological progress, became one of the main points of difference between the city and the shtetl. The allure of the ideal superurban city—forged in stone, with sidewalks, trams, and, starting in the mid-1930s, a subway system—became an important impetus for migration, as compelling as the attraction of higher education and prestigious modern professions, which symbolized high social status and success.

The new, urban Soviet way of life provided a sharp contrast with the alternate reality of the shtetl, where the main streets were covered in wooden planks, and horses were the only form of transportation. In spring and autumn, because of the clay soil, the streets in Belarusian shtetls turned impassible, effectively cutting smaller shtetls off from civilization. These conditions were reflected in every aspect of life in the shtetls including behavior, clothing, and footwear. It was next to impossible to walk down the crudely assembled wooden planks in fashionable women's shoes, even if a comparatively well-off local fashionista were to allow herself such an indulgence. A young shtetl dweller who wanted to feel "the pulse of the era" was met with disappointment. When it came to information, if a shtetl was not on a train line, by the time the news arrived, it was old: newspapers from Minsk took a week to arrive; from Moscow, ten days.[8] It was not until the radio appeared in many shtetls in the early 1930s that their inhabitants finally found themselves in the stream of current events. At the same time, however, the radio only intensified the draw of life outside the shtetl. Former shtetl dwellers who regularly came back to visit, particularly university students and schoolchildren who returned on holidays, also served as propagandists for urban civilization. Even in a large shtetl, the evening promenade of the young people down the wooden planks would inevitably end in a movie theater, where they always played the same movies; it is no wonder that the city dazzled shtetl inhabitants with its promise of varied and ever-changing entertainments.

Shtetl-to-city migration often moved like an avalanche: when one person left, he or she would soon be followed by friends and relatives. The peak of these migrations came in the second half of the 1920s, and the torrent only abated following the 1932 institution of passports and the introduction of a system of registration at place of residence. By then, however, many of the people who wanted to leave had already left, and the stream of migrants was later replenished mostly by those who had been children during the exodus and who had meanwhile come of age.[9] Migration led to a notable decrease in the Jewish population in Belarusian shtetls. The 1926 census data for 63 shtetls (for ease of analysis, shtetls are defined as small towns with a Jewish population of less than 5,000) showed a total of 99,084 Jews; by 1939, there were only 74,846, a

24.5 percent decrease. The number of Jews in the average Belarusian shtetl at that time had fallen from 1,600 to 1,200.[10]

This raises the question of the difference between those who stayed in the shtetls and those who left them. Clearly, migration to the city was more common among young people interested in prestige and eager for changes in their everyday routines. Being a revolutionary in the shtetl meant turning against not only one's neighbors but also one's parents, which was not easy. People like this inevitably became the targets of censure. Moving to the city granted anonymity, which contrasted sharply with the intense interest that shtetl dwellers took in each other's affairs, believing firmly that they had a right to information such as the details of the personal lives of their relatives and neighbors. In addition to this, dreams of belonging to a cultured social stratum, albeit somewhat naive dreams, were deeply embedded in the shtetl consciousness. One Jewish woman from Dryssa, in the Vitebsk Region, expressed this need to be exposed to and involved in culture at a propaganda meeting in 1938: "My children go to school, my son plays every musical instrument, and the road to education is open to him just as it is to the rest of the children in the Soviet state."[11] The city embodied this high contemporary culture.

To make the move, people needed enough money, at least for the time it would take to adapt, find housing and work, or begin their studies. At the same time, in the best-case scenario, children from poor families had no more than a fourth-grade education, and their opportunities for getting ahead in a big city were significantly limited by this fact. In the second half of the 1920s, the Jews categorized as *lishentsy* had a strong motive for leaving their shtetls. This characteristically Soviet category of "individuals deprived of voting rights" (disenfranchised) was codified in the Soviet constitution of 1918 and enforced until the passage of the 1936 constitution. Lishentsy were members of what had been "non-laboring" groups—that is, they had been involved in the free market, belonged to the privileged estates in the past, held positions in the prerevolutionary government apparatus, or belonged to the clergy.

Although the restrictions applied to lishentsy were not based on ethnicity, the implementation of social policy by categorizing people as belonging to potentially disloyal groups (which included present and former merchants) affected many Jews, particularly between 1926 and 1929. These groups were forced to pay especially high taxes and fees, their children were no longer accepted into institutions of higher education, and they were forbidden from buying groceries and commodities at the state distribution centers introduced in 1929. A significant portion of Jews from Belarusian shtetls found themselves in this category of social pariahs, or, as one shtetl Jew put it, "treyfene."[12] On average, the percentage of lishentsy in a shtetl ranged between 30 and 40, but in some places, it was significantly higher.[13] A number of lishentsy and their children attempted to solve this problem by moving to the city, where they might be lost in the crowd, hiding their unfortunate status from the people around them. Another solution—this one legal—was to move to a Jewish agricultural artel (cooperative) in Crimea or, later, to Birobidzhan, designated in 1934 as the Jewish Autonomous Region, where, in a relatively short amount of time, one could officially regain the right to vote. Migrations like these deprived the shtetls of a portion of the socially and economically active population.

The mass migration of young adults led to major demographic changes: shtetls began to be overrun with children and the elderly. A 1935 study of fifteen Belarusian shtetls shows that in a large number of them, Jews of working age had become the minority.[14] In Shchadryn,[15] a former Jewish agricultural colony not far from Babruysk, Jews between the ages of seventeen and forty-nine made up only 37 percent of the population; in Chavusy, which was closer to Mahilyow, they made up 36.6 percent; in Syanno, near Vitebsk, 38.2 percent. For comparison, even in the medium-sized Belarusian cities of the time, the proportion of Jews in this age bracket was higher: 50.8 percent in Babruysk, and 49.1 percent in Slutsk.[16] This trend of a declining proportion of people of working age in shtetls is even more apparent when comparing the data for Moscow in 1939 and the "shtetled" Palesie Region in Belarus, which had no major cities.

At the same time, both the 1939 census and the 1935 statistics show a comparatively large percentage of children in shtetls. Given the mass migration of people of childbearing age, one would expect a significantly lowered birth rate in the shtetls. However, this trend toward a lower birth rate was seen less among those young people who stayed in the shtetls. That said, the liberal Soviet marriage laws that legalized abortion from 1920 to 1936 also affected even relatively conservative people in the provinces. So, while children made up a larger percentage of the population in shtetls than they did in cities, family size in shtetls was still decreasing over time. At the beginning of the 1920s, a family of five or more was not rare in the shtetls, but by the end of the 1930s, according to partial accounts, the average family size had decreased.[17]

Demographic changes must have affected the number of ethnically mixed families, though Belarusian shtetls probably had a low number of mixed marriages as compared to major cities. Data on analogous "shtetled" regions in Ukraine for 1938 shows that 10 percent of Jewish women and 11 percent of Jewish men were in mixed marriages there.[18] This demonstrates a high adherence to ethnic values among shtetl Jews compared to their counterparts living in cities, especially considering the gender imbalance. In the Palesie Region,

Table 2.1 Proportion of Jews in Moscow and the Palesie Region by Age Range, 1939, in percentages

Age Range	Moscow	Paliessie Region
0–8	10.78	18.01
9–19	14.76	25.63
20–49	58.54	37.14
50+	15.92	19.22

Source: Altshuler, *Soviet Jewry on the Eve of the Holocaust*, 251, 253.

the number of women aged 20–29 was 39 percent higher than the number of men in the same age group, and there were 40 percent more women than men aged 30–39.[19] This means that men were migrating more than women, and, therefore, many women would have had difficulty finding a Jewish spouse. It is possible that the shortage of young men also pushed young women to relocate to the city.

Changes in demographics—young people leaving and a decrease in the number of children—led to the aging of the shtetl. As of 1935, the proportion of people aged fifty and over had risen significantly.[20] This trend is also very clear when comparing Moscow and the Palesie Region (Table 2.1). At the same time, since many of the young people who were actively participating in Soviet social life, who tended to accept new rules, were among those who left the shtetl, the population that remained was comparatively conservative, which allowed for religious and ethnic traditions to be preserved.

The Ethnic Aspect of Social Transformations

Except for small mestechki where Jews were the absolute majority, shtetls were generally not predominantly Jewish. Jewish migration, the decline in the birth rate, and the mass influx of non-Jewish peasants significantly altered the ethnic composition of mestechki. In 1926, Jews made up more than half of the population in 19 out of 63 mestechki, and between 30 and 50 percent in 37 of them. In 1939, of those same 63 towns, only one, Parychy, in the Palesie Region, was still more than 50 percent Jewish, while only 13 were between 30 and 50 percent Jewish.[21] At the same time, the mosaic of dispersion was growing more complex. Often, entire Jewish families would move to the city—on getting settled and establishing careers, young people would resettle their parents. In cases like these, non-Jewish peasants would move to the shtetls and buy up their homes. The image of the shtetl as a place where Jews were concentrated at the center of town and the non-Jewish peasants lived on the outskirts, closer to the farmland, was no longer the reality.

The policy of Belarusization, which aimed to improve the social position of Belarusians and develop Belarusian culture, also supported other minorities, including Jews. This policy entailed seeing to the proportional representation of all ethnic groups in the political and social spheres. A revisal of the Belarusization policies in the early 1930s led to a weakening of this ethnicity-based distribution of positions. Since Jews made up a large part of the population in shtetls, they were entitled to significant representation in the shtetls' political bodies and social institutions. However, as their numbers decreased due to out-migration in the 1920s and 1930s, Jews became overrepresented, since a significant number continued to serve in local government agencies and among party leaders and government workers.

The Stalinist terror of 1936–38 affected all groups, including shtetl inhabitants. Arrests of the elite, including District Party (*raikom*) secretaries, as well as Soviet policies for advancing the careers of certain "titular nationalities" (Belarusians, Russians) beginning in 1937 led to a decline in the social status of the Jews. Meanwhile, by the end of the 1930s, a whole new generation of ambitious, young, and educated representatives of the major ethnicities—Russians and Belarusians—had emerged, ready to push Jews out of their leadership positions. Although new staffing policy did not entail the intentional removal of the previous cohort of leaders, it nonetheless led to the drop in the number of Jews in positions of power.

The two main agencies implementing Soviet nationality policies in the shtetls were the local Jewish national soviets (councils) and Yiddish schools. To create a Jewish soviet, a shtetl had to be at least 60 percent Jewish. As a result, in 1934, there were twenty such soviets in Belarus.[22] Some of them were called *mestechkovye* soviets, and others village soviets, depending on the shtetl's official settlement classification. In terms of the number of Jews involved and their lifestyles, the majority of Jewish village soviets in Belarus were not much different from the shtetl soviets. Officially, it was of great importance for Soviet ethnic policy that soviets enlisted representatives from the entire population, regardless of nationality. The creation of two separate soviets in a single shtetl, one for Jewish citizens and the other for non-Jewish ones, would have been considered a gross violation of Soviet nationality policy. In actuality, the Jewish soviets were symbolic of how the issue of ethnic minorities was dealt with in the USSR: they had their meetings in Yiddish and were allowed to document all of their activities in Yiddish, as well.[23] A number of Jews who had inherited a heightened sensitivity to issues related to ethnic equality from prerevolutionary times sincerely believed that it was these Jewish soviets that would finally defend their interests. The idea that Belarusian soviets and the Belarusian bureaucracy were geared toward specifically Belarusian interests was widespread among Jews during the 1920s and 1930s.

In Belarus, special attention was paid to language, including Yiddish. In the BSSR constitution that was in effect from 1927 to 1938, Yiddish held the status of an official language alongside Russian, Polish, and Belarusian. For Jews, there was an important question of cultural identification, either with Jewish culture (in Yiddish and, more rarely, Hebrew) or non-Jewish culture (in Russian or Belarusian). From the very first days of the Revolution, the issue of Yiddish schools was significant for shtetls; they usually emerged as a result of a grassroots initiative. By the mid-1920s, because of the transition toward the policy of Belarusization, support for Yiddish schools became an important government objective. Yiddish schools grew after a measure was imposed to send children to schools in strict accordance with their native language. This approach meant that children who demonstrated an understanding of Yiddish were automatically enrolled in Yiddish school, regardless of parents' wishes. The measure frustrated parents as well as some Jewish functionaries, since children who attended primary school in Yiddish would be at a disadvantage in high school or the university where instruction was most often in Russian.[24] As a result, in 1927, in the shtetls in the Vitebsk district (*okrug*), 79.3 percent of Jewish children attended Yiddish schools.[25] Apparently, an absolute majority of children in shtetls understood Yiddish, and it would require much effort for them to be placed in any other type of school. For a certain segment of the shtetl residents, avoiding Yiddish-language school thus became a status symbol, setting them apart from the lower classes, which had no other choice.

Belarusian schools grew even faster as a result of the ethnic policies of the 1920s, almost entirely replacing Russian schools in shtetls. This occurred even though many Jews clearly preferred the Russian language, a more prestigious symbol of high, urban culture, to Belarusian, which was seen as the language of the peasantry. Jewish parents in shtetls found themselves faced with a difficult dilemma: they had the choice of sending their child either to an unprestigious Yiddish-language school (*in yidishn hekdesh*; literally, in a Jewish alm-house) or to a school taught in another language lacking prestige, Belarusian. One shtetl Jew expresses a rather typical opinion: "If there were a Russian school, I wouldn't send my son to a Yiddish school, but since there isn't, I'd rather have him go to a Yiddish school than a Belarusian one."[26] Moreover, this choice between two evils came at a time of mass migrations, when speaking Russian became an important factor in one's subsequent educational and career opportunities in the major Russian cities of Moscow or Leningrad. Perhaps the difficult choice regarding schools was an additional reason that Belarusian Jews left their shtetls.

Some shtetl parents made the conscious decision in favor of the *mameloshn* (literally, mother tongue—here, Yiddish), but others were simply going with the flow. The total number of students in Yiddish-language schools grew until 1933, after which there was a precipitous decline.[27] The breaking point came with changes in ethnic policy. Now, the official Soviet position considered forcing Jewish children to attend Yiddish schools to be an expression of Jewish nationalism on the part of local authorities. The data on where Jewish children went to school in fifteen shtetls in 1935 can be seen as a measure of how loyal the inhabitants were to ethnic schools. On average, across these shtetls, 68 percent of the children attended school in Yiddish, and the rest went to Belarusian schools. As with other indices, the situation varied from place to place. While 96.6 percent of the children in Shchadryn went to Yiddish school, only 34.2 percent did so in Kasciukovichy near Mahilyow. The number of Jewish children in these schools continued to decline until, in accordance with a special decree of the Belarusian Central Committee and the Council of People's Commissars from July 3, 1938, all Yiddish-language schools were simultaneously shut down. In Chavusy, over the course of these few years, the number of children in Yiddish schools fell from 149 to 89; in Krasnapolie, also in the Mahilyow Region, the number dropped from 160 to 116. In a number of other shtetls around the Mahilyow Region about which there is data—including Shamava, Klimavichy, Charnewka, Kruhlaye, Klichaw, and others—in 1938, there were fewer than 30 students in each of their respective Yiddish-language schools.[28]

Nonetheless, after the Yiddish schools were shuttered, a number of shtetl parents and, naturally, teachers were very upset, seeing this as a serious error in Soviet nationality policy. In addition to this, the preference of shtetl Jews for Russian culture (there were occasional demands for special Russian classes for Jews in Belarusian schools) remained strong throughout this period.[29] In 1938, there were requests to turn former Yiddish schools into Russian schools as opposed to Belarusian schools, as was happening throughout the region, including in Chashniki, Liepiel, Dubrowna, Haradok (all shtetls in the Vitebsk Region), and other places.[30] In some shtetls, authorities acquiesced to such demands and opened Russian-language schools.[31]

Many Jews did not see the choice of a non-Yiddish school as a conscious rejection of Jewish values or a path toward assimilation. Parents were quite successful in separating their traditional ways of life from their dreams for their children's future. Most parents wanted their children to receive higher education and advance to prestigious careers as doctors, engineers, lawyers, military officers, and so on. Two very different considerations—the ethnic and the pragmatic—were comfortably held at the same time by shtetl Jews.

The 1938 liquidation of Yiddish schools in Belarus came as part of the general policy of "internationalization" aimed at erasing symbols of equal rights for minorities that the authorities and Jews had previously been so proud of. In that same summer of 1938, Yiddish, along with Polish, lost its status as an official state language of Belarus. Another example of the contraction of support for minorities on the symbolic level was the elimination of the ethnic soviets. As previously stated, by the end of the 1930s, there were few shtetls left with a Jewish majority. The Jewish soviets in Belarus were a reflection of the predominance Jews had had in the past rather than the present. Most Jewish soviets were liquidated based on population statistics in 1939, each soviet being shut down with a separate government order. Still, the deciding factor was that ethnic policy had changed: in places where Jews remained the majority, such as Kalyshki, in the Vitebsk Region, a financial justification was found for the reorganization of the Jewish soviet.[32] Another argument for reorganizing the soviets cited the need to root out Jewish nationalism. Essentially, local authorities were extending to Jews the approach that the national organs were using with all minorities that had their ethnic territories outside of the USSR (Poles, Latvians, Greeks, etc.), who were seen as disloyal.[33] This was striking because, officially, Jews did not fall into this category. The typical outcome was for Jewish schools and soviets to be renamed Belarusian.

In general, the "internationalization" of administrative and economic entities was an important part of ethnic policy in Belarus beginning in the late 1920s. The authorities strove to diversify occupations that had traditionally been dominated by a single ethnicity. The justification given for this policy was the need to fight ethnic stereotypes by facilitating regular contacts among different ethnic groups and breaking down traditional ethnic preferences for particular occupations, such as Jews working as tailors, shoemakers, and builders, Poles as workers at glass factories, Tatars as leatherworkers, and so on. Of course, people of different ethnicities interacted in many spheres, without any government encouragement, but intentional policies significantly expedited the integration process. The changes this led to were very apparent at, for example, Dnyaprowskaya Manufaktura, a textile factory that was relatively large for Belarus. Located in Dubrowna, a remote shtetl in the Mogilev *guberniia*—which had become part of the Vitebsk Region before World War II—this textile plant had been established by the ORT (Society for Handicraft and Agricultural Work among the Jews in Russia) in 1902 as a model modern factory aimed at making the Jewish shtetl population more productive. However, by the end of the 1920s, 35 percent of the workers were already non-Jews, and at the end of the 1930s, Jews were in the minority at the plant.[34] Belarusian officials were very systematic when it came to changing the names of ethnic institutions to be consistent with the new situation. The most prominent example of internationalization was what happened to the Jewish collective farms, the majority of which maintained their connection to shtetls. Initially conceived as purely Jewish—agriculture was the only field where creating monoethnic economic entities was legally feasible—by the mid-1930s, most collective farms had not only ceased to be majority Jewish but also stopped being called Jewish, as well.[35]

The changes in ethnic policy had the greatest impact on shtetls. After the liquidation of the schools and soviets, there were no more specifically Jewish official organizations left in the shtetls. The only exception might have been libraries for Yiddish books, but their collections were significantly diminished during the Great Terror, when the books of arrested writers were seized (a great number of Yiddish writers, including Kulbak and Kharik, were targeted in the repressions in Belarus).

The most important remaining indicator of the Jewishness of the shtetls was the inhabitants' way of life, including its economic features.

Economic Factors in Shtetl Life

Despite the authorities' push for uniformity, the average shtetl, as such, did not exist. For the most part, a combination of local factors determined the extent of the transformation of economic activity. These local variations were most prominent in the mid-1920s, a comparatively liberal period in Soviet history. An illustrative example is provided by the comparison of two shtetls, Uzda and Smalyavichy. Both shtetls were located near Minsk and had approximately the same number of Jews in 1926: 1,564 and 1,566, respectively. Although the percentage of Jews in the overall population differed—62.5 and 50.2 percent, respectively—it is unlikely that this was a determining factor in their development.[36] More importantly, Smalyavichy was on a railway line connecting Minsk and Moscow, while Uzda was far from the railroad.

As a result, Smalyavichy was in a much better position to provide badly needed raw materials and manufactured goods from Minsk or Moscow. However, the proximity to the railway station lowered the wages of local craftspeople, who were unable to compete with readily available factory-made goods.

The combination of these factors led to a rise in unemployment among young people, which was higher in Smalyavichy than in the more remote Uzda.[37] The important factor in Uzda was its proximity to the border, which enabled trade in contraband goods, a widespread practice in the early 1920s that slowed down only with the strengthening of border patrols in the second half of the decade.[38]

Geography had less of an impact on common Jewish trades like those of the tailor and shoemaker. As before, these kinds of craftspeople did not work for the market at large but for private clients. The direct relationship between client and maker was maintained, thus preserving a shtetl tradition in which clothes and shoes were custom ordered, and deviations from this tradition might have been seen as low-status. The negative perception of factory-made goods, which were considered generic, can be heard in the bitter exclamation made by Moyshe Kulbak's character Itshe Zelmenyaner when he is forced to go work at the factory: "A lady's coat calls for vision!"[39] For independent tailors and shoemakers, the most important business problems, aside from chronically low demand, were credit and the shortage of raw materials. They could only buy scarce materials such as fabric or leather on receiving cash, and only then could they work. Credit cooperatives were insufficiently developed in shtetls. In Smalyavichy, craftspeople were forced to borrow from private creditors, sometimes at an annual rate of 60 percent, and buy their goods from private merchants. For this reason, many shtetls saw the appearance of credit cooperatives in the form of savings and loan bureaus and artisanal guilds, which provided credit and aided in obtaining scarce materials under favorable terms. Their establishment was initially the result of a grassroots effort. However, the authorities quickly decided to turn these cooperative enterprises into economic and ideological tools to exert influence over local craftspeople. Credit cooperatives ceased being a part of everyday life in the shtetls by the mid-1930s.

The prerevolutionary model whereby the same person might have several occupations was preserved in the Soviet years. In addition to this, there were the numerous and highly visible *luftmentshn* (people of air), living "as though they simply floated along in the ether with nothing under their feet," that is, without any official occupation.[40] Many of these people engaged in unsanctioned forms of economic activity: nonlicensed trade, making and selling liquor, the black market, living on dollars sent by relatives in America, and so on.[41] On top of all this, the abuses perpetrated by tax inspectors undermined the viability of many official businesses. It was often the case that tax inspectors operated on the principle that "if there was no income . . . you wouldn't have done business" and significantly raised the taxes on private businesses, forcing craftspeople and merchants to have to prove the unfairness of the amounts they were charged in local executive committee headquarters.[42] Thus, in Klimavichy, a tax inspector's assessment of income in 1923–24 might be eight or even ten times what a merchant had declared.[43] Moreover, state taxes were accompanied by numerous local fines and fees: for careless bookkeeping, for closing down shop before 7 p.m. or keeping it open during the lunch break, for family members working at the register instead of the merchant himself, and many other minor violations.[44]

A direct consequence of the underdeveloped labor market was unemployment, which was particularly high among young people and women. These groups found themselves in difficult economic circumstances and were thus willing to change occupations. However, it would be wrong to seek a linear correlation between particular occupations and a willingness to change them. The wholesale disappearance of any profession from shtetls in the name of modernization as part of slow, long-term changes was rare. Esther, a penmanship teacher in Kulbak's *Zelmenyaners* who "taught a generation of housewives the elegant art of stylish writing" and whose importance in her community was a thing of the past, was most likely created by the author to highlight the disappearance of the old way of life overall rather than as a specific indicator of real changes in occupations.[45] Much more powerful stimuli for economic changes were government measures aimed at shrinking the private sector, such as eliminating licensed trade and forcing craftspeople to join production cooperatives, the kind of cooperatives closest to factory manufacturing. Nonetheless, the private sector remained a strong factor in shtetl life for the entire interwar period.

The late 1920s and early 1930s saw a redistribution of occupations among shtetl inhabitants. Some former official merchants or those who had been earlier categorized as "without an official occupation" had either left the shtetl or officially become craftspeople, clerks, or workers. Because there was not much of a choice for how to make money in the shtetl, the number of craftspeople grew steadily as former merchants joined their ranks. At the same time, the Soviet bureaucracy had become a viable career path for those seeking social status. Practicing traditional trades was considered lower status than being a merchant, while being a business owner, even as a tailor or shoemaker, was more prestigious than being a hired worker. Under these conditions, joining the Soviet administration—a rather abstract but comparatively privileged category that included all work outside of direct physical labor—became a way to save face. Despite the general trends in the distribution of occupations, there were significant variations between different shtetls. In the mid-1930s, in the comparatively large shtetl of Kascyukovichy, administrative officials made up 62.1 percent of all working Jews, while in Shchadryn, a former agricultural colony, there was only 11.6 percent; craftspeople made up 22.8 and 9 percent, respectively. The majority of the Jews in Shchadryn were peasants—65.2 percent. In Uzda, which was far from any railway line, officials made up 42 percent; craftspeople, 46 percent; and workers, only 2.4 percent.[46] This low percentage for workers was quite typical; even in more-developed Belarusian shtetls, hired workers remained the minority and came from the least-skilled and least-educated strata of the population. An exception to this was Dubrowna, with its aforementioned textile factory.

Officially, in the mid-1930s, the majority of shtetl inhabitants of working age, particularly men, were employed. The reality, however, was more complicated. As part of the "economy of shortages," a significant portion of Jews continued to participate in the black market in conjunction with their official jobs. Thus, members of artels whose official purpose was collecting salvaged materials took advantage of their need to travel to engage in illegal trade.[47] Even the situation with the official occupations statistics was not so clear. According to a governmental committee working in Kalyshki (Kolyshki in Russian) in 1939, nearly sixty Jewish households were involved neither in collective farming nor in traditional trades but survived off unsanctioned income—reselling livestock, including pigs (either directly or through middlemen, first keeping the livestock for a while then selling them off later), agricultural products, and unofficially obtained manufactured goods. Meanwhile, only four Jewish families were part of the local collective farm.[48]

The repression of the 1930s did not spare the average shtetl dweller. An important factor in the increasingly stringent enforcement of repressive policies was the long border with Poland and Latvia. In the 1920s, being located on this border was an advantage, since it allowed access to contraband goods, but in the 1930s, the state became obsessively suspicious, and proximity to the border became a liability. Access was cut off to a significant number of shtetls located in the border zone, which had an impact on their economic and social life. Additionally, in the mid-1930s, there was an intensive campaign to resettle "disloyal groups" from these regions into the interior of the country. Although the primary targets of these policies were ethnic Poles, a number of Jews considered disloyal were also deported.[49] Along with their psychological effects, these measures also had an impact on shtetl economies. The resettlement of comparatively well-off groups led to a general decrease in income across the entire population. Overall, it was characteristic of the 1930s for harsh restrictions based on the law (for example, the laws against lishentsy) to open the door to repressive policies outside of the strictly legal sphere. An example of this that affected a number of shtetl Jews and that, judging by their memoirs, became one of the most traumatic episodes in the interwar years was the mass seizure of gold and valuables that took place in the early 1930s. The government needed currency for industrialization and was eager to obtain it by any means possible, from seizing gold rings from shtetl dwellers to selling off museum collections abroad. Many shtetl Jews who were considered well-off by the authorities, regardless of their actual economic situation, became the targets of these policies. They were arrested, held for weeks at a time in jails, and sometimes subjected to torture—for example, some were fed herring and not given anything to drink. People were often held until they declared that they were willing to give up their gold or currency to the government, or until their relatives brought the demanded "bail" (sometimes these valuables had to be purchased from other Jews). These actions, which took place in the early 1930s and were carried out more or less publicly, were openly talked about in shtetls. They were markedly different from the repressive measures that came later, at the end of the 1930s, when very little information about the arrested people ever reached the outside. The Great Terror affected shtetl Jews in the same way it touched everyone else in the country. Among those who were arrested, there were Soviet and party functionaries, former Jewish activists accused of Trotskyism and spying (and often of Bundism or Zionism as well), rabbis, and ordinary Jews.

It is also apparent that in the 1930s, there was a marked decrease in the number of Jews in the shtetls and therefore, automatically, less participation from Jews in local government agencies. The arrests of the shtetl elite, where Jews were a visible force, and finally the liquidation of Jewish ethnic institutions (soviets and schools) made non-Jews feel that Jewish influence was in decline and thus that social and historical justice was being reinstated. In Kalyshki, in 1939, non-Jews believed that they did not need to buy houses from Jews because they would soon be given away for free.[50] As a result, many houses abandoned by Jews were either moved by them to different shtetls or dismantled by locals for raw materials. The example of Kalyshki also demonstrates how quickly ethnic stereotypes like "all Jews are speculators," which had receded into the background, came back into prominence.[51] This happened even though under the conditions created by the economy of shortages, speculation was widespread among all groups, both Jewish and non-Jewish. Still, there were differences. For shtetl Jews, the combination of unofficial work and official occupations coincided with traditional models. For the non-Jews in the shtetls, particularly former peasants, unsanctioned trade was a new phenomenon; previously, their economic specialization had been more pronounced.

Naturally, many Jews, even those who found themselves in modern occupations—workers and administrators—continued to adhere to shtetl modes of behavior. Their work activities were quite compatible with traditional mores. It would be hard to believe that in the traditional climate preserved in Belarusian shtetls even at the end of the 1930s, the majority of people would have completely changed their ways. It is more likely that they had become more careful in their conversations and public behavior, just as many other Soviet people had. In the 1930s, many shtetl Jews had taken on complex modes of behavior: while they continued to lead relatively traditional lives at home, abiding by many of the rules they had learned in childhood, outside of the home, they were much more modern, combining sincere adherence to some Soviet norms with a degree of opportunism. Undoubtedly, in most cases, Jews' tendency to adhere to traditional ways of life was stronger in the shtetls than in the cities.

Tradition and Modernization

The hollowing out of the independent social realm in the 1930s inevitably led to an increase in the importance of the private sphere. Meanwhile, Jews' behavior in the private sphere had not changed in many everyday matters. For example, Yiddish continued to be used for conversation both within the home and outside, including in social situations with people of different generations. The notable decrease in the percentage of Jews who declared Yiddish as their native language (between the 1926 and the 1939 census, across Belarus, this fell from 90.7 to 55 percent) did not directly correlate with a noticeable decline in the use of Yiddish for everyday purposes in the shtetl.[52] Rather, the census served as an indicator of how part of the adult population felt about their literacy and the literacy of their children.[53] To demonstrate, we may once again look at the Palesie Region, with its absence of major cities and, consequently, Russian language schools. There, in the 1937 census, 15.5 percent of Jews called Belarusian their native language (the highest percentage of any region), with a relatively high 64.7 percent citing Yiddish, and a modest number, Russian (19.8 percent).[54] It seems unlikely that in such an isolated region as Palesie a seventh of the Jews really spoke Belarusian at home.

Alongside outward manifestations of identity such as language, there were a number of other characteristics inherited from earlier times that were not widely acknowledged as markers of traditionalism. One of these was the unchanging furnishing of Jewish homes. Even in the late 1930s, one could still find the portraits of Moses Montefiore that had been sold in huge numbers in the prerevolutionary years.[55] Many shtetl homes also had other traditional accoutrements of Jewish life: mizrah wall plaques, *yortsayt* sheets (lists of memorial calendars), Shabbat candleholders, Hanukkah menorahs, and copper Passover dishware. The traditional way of life was broader than just religious customs. It might include local Yiddish nicknames, the obligatory boiled hen for the woman giving birth, or normative marriages among cousins, as in Kulbak's *Zelmenyaners*. Their practice might be as much an essential part of Jewish life then as they had been in the nineteenth century. At the same time, such rules were excluded from the norms of their non-Jewish neighbors.[56]

One of the biggest signs of the shtetl's transformation was the waning of the system of religious education for children. Along with attending synagogue and celebrating holidays, religious schooling was the most formative influence on Jewish children, shaping everyday behavioral norms and familiarizing children with their traditions. In the 1920s, in many shtetls, children attended unsanctioned heders as well as Soviet schools. According to the Yevsektsiya, a special division of the Communist Party working with the Jewish population from 1918 to 1930, even in the beginning of 1929, 60 percent of the children in Chashniki attended heders, and the number was as high as 85 percent in Sirotino (both shtetls were relatively close to Vitebsk).[57] The heders became more active during summer vacations, when they were relied on as much for education as for childcare.[58] The stricter antireligious policies of the 1930s led to most heders being shut down, although even at the end of the decade, authorities documented instances of their illegal operation, for instance, in Klimavichy in 1937.[59]

Unlike education, other manifestations of traditional Jewish life, including the observance of religious holidays, were much less likely to change. The most important annual event in shtetl life was preparation for Passover and community-wide participation in the baking of matzo. In the 1920s, baking matzo was a part of official shtetl life, and permits for baking matzo could be given out to fire brigades, cooperatives, trade unions, private operators, and even the *khevra kadisha* (funerary society).[60] Matzo was sold in most private and cooperative stores. After the banning of private trade and the simultaneous acceleration of the antireligious campaign, baking matzo in shtetls was relegated to the home or restricted to groups of families or neighbors. This work was hard, and these groups often hired workers under the counter to help. Still, traditional roles were maintained: women rolled out the dough and men baked it. Often, young people and schoolchildren would participate in this makeshift production. Matzo was still eaten during Passover at the end of the 1930s by the majority of shtetl Jews.[61]

Through the 1920s, the rabbinical monopoly on yeast also remained in place. In Smalyavichy, the rabbinical surcharge for yeast in stores was 100 percent as compared with the cooperative prices; there was also a herem (religious ban) against buying yeast in other places. In Uzda, the sale of yeast took on a more legal form: the rabbi ran the official store, after obtaining a license and displaying an official sign required for such cases.[62] Another important financial element of religious life was the special additional fee for the kosher slaughter of livestock, which Yevsektsiya officials, following the traditional, prerevolutionary term, called the "Soviet korobka" (extra tax for kosher meat). In Smalyavichy, for example, the rabbi earned 30 percent from a kosher slaughter.[63] Traditional charitable funds such as the ones providing the poor with matzo for Passover (*moes-khitin*) and interest-free credit (*gmiles-khasodim*) also operated in the financial-religious sphere. The most influential organizations in shtetls were funerary societies (*khevra kadisha*), which buried Jews with the permission of the regional executive committees, receiving money for their services from individuals. The life of the Belarusian shtetl in the 1920s was, for the most part, suffused with religion. Kosher meat was available at most butchers; on Saturdays and Jewish religious holidays, many stores and craftspeople's workshops were closed. Until 1929, even the textile factory in Dubrowna, despite being ethnically mixed, was closed on Saturdays.[64]

The rise of antireligious fervor (i.e., the creation of antireligious societies with their various bureaus in different cities and antireligious magazines) notwithstanding, in the 1920s, the authorities did not impose any serious, repressive, antireligious measures that would have reached all the way down to the shtetls. The atmosphere was relatively liberal, but compared with prerevolutionary times, many elements of religious life had nonetheless gone underground. This did not necessarily mean they existed in secret; many shtetl inhabitants, including Soviet activists, were well aware of local unofficial religious life. Thus, on the level of their everyday lives—except for Communists and Komsomol members and, to a certain extent, teachers—Jews had every opportunity to maintain their adherence to religious rules, including attending synagogue and using the mikvah. On the main religious holidays, it was possible to officially miss work. To an even greater extent, insofar as everyday customs adhered to tradition, they were directly or obliquely tied to religion. Examples of this include prohibitions related to the commemoration of the dead, keeping kashruth and using separate dishware for meat and dairy, observing Sabbath and holidays, children being raised according to certain rules, and so on.

The strong antireligious campaign of 1929 and the early 1930s hit the Jews with full force. There was a mass closure of synagogues, and increased pressure—up to and including arrest—was applied to rabbis and religious slaughterers; many of them were forced to renounce their religious calling publicly (in newspapers). These changes had a particularly notable effect on working people. By the mid-1930s, the majority of workers in the government and cooperatives were no longer able to miss work on Saturdays and Jewish holidays. The disciplinary decree of 1940 authorized that anyone who missed work without an official excuse could be arrested. This contributed to the preference many Jews had for independent craft labor, which allowed them to make their own schedules, especially after the introduction of the continuous-week calendar in the early 1930s, which assigned each worker an individual fixed schedule.

Harsh antireligious regulations led to a further reduction of public religious practice and relegated many of the rites governing Jewish religious life (circumcision, funerals, keeping kosher, etc.) strictly to the home. This transformation took place over a relatively long period, however. In the early 1930s, many Jews who were members of craftspeople cooperatives continued to refuse to work on religious holidays. In Shchadryn (which had its own Jewish soviet), during the 1933 celebration of the October Revolution anniversary—the foundational event of Soviet history—there were two banquet tables, one each for kosher and nonkosher food. Six months later, when a kosher table could not be arranged for the celebration of International Women's Day on March 8, there was strong disapproval among activist women who saw this as discrimination.[65] At the end of the 1930s, in Kalyshki Jews attempted, through the local soviet, to relegalize the activity of the khevra kadisha, which had continued its existence unofficially.[66] Throughout the 1930s, the production and distribution of kosher products took place through unauthorized channels, often within direct client-producer relationships.

Despite the obvious reduction in the number of Jews prepared to openly demonstrate their loyalty to religious traditions, there were people in many shtetls who publicly defended their religious rights in appeals against local authorities who had shut down their last synagogue or mikvah or confiscated Torah scrolls.

This was the case with the synagogue in Liepiel. In 1921, seven of the eleven synagogues there burnt down during a great fire.[67] Residents were able to collect the money to build one new synagogue (a part of this money was obtained through their American *landsmanshaft*, or hometown society). This new synagogue opened in 1923. Then, in 1933, the Liepiel municipal soviet seized the synagogue (as well as the local church), justifying the act with the need to store grain. According to the Jews' petition, when the synagogue was taken over, "religious items, Torah scrolls and religious books were literally thrown out on the street. One Torah scroll was cut into pieces, and the covers were torn off the religious books."[68] In 1936, as a wave of religious activity was cresting in anticipation of changes that would come with the ratification of the new constitution, the Jews of Liepiel implored the authorities to open a new synagogue. This was an extremely unusual request for those times: the most common interaction between believers and the authorities was requests for the return of religious buildings that the state had requisitioned. The exceptional nature of the situation puzzled the Republic administration, and after the People's Commissariat for Internal Affairs (NKVD) exerted some pressure, the Liepiel Jews reverted to the more common practice of petitioning for the return of the synagogue that had been taken away.[69] No less surprising was that the Jews of Beshankovichy, near Liepiel, cited the new Soviet Constitution of 1936 in their arguments, claiming that "Stalin has permitted us to pray."[70] In all of these cases, what is important is the Jews' efforts to organize themselves and the unwavering determination expressed in their letters to the authorities. This courage can be explained in large part by the fact that at the end of the 1930s, these letters were signed mostly by the elderly. These appeals were probably supported by a good portion of the Jewish shtetl population, but public disagreement with the authorities' antireligious policies, such as were made in the early 1920s, was no longer possible for most shtetl Jews. This kind of behavior might easily have been classified as organized anti-Soviet activity. The shtetl population was learning to play by the rules.

Like all other facets of life, religious practices in the shtetl had undergone great changes. This was the result of Soviet antireligious policy as well as the processes of modernization, inescapable even among the conservative populations of the shtetls. Even religious circles were forced to adapt to new social conditions. In shtetls, there was a generation of young rabbis versed in Soviet law and prepared to talk about Marx and socialism in the Talmud and communism in the Torah.[71] In the mid-1920s, religious circles in Liepiel had been troubled when a student home for vacation had suggested holding a concert of religious songs to raise money for building a synagogue in the shtetl. After some vacillation, they agreed to his suggestion, even though a day earlier, he had been seen in the shtetl hatless and in shorts—a crude violation of religious tradition.[72] According to official accounts, in one Belarusian shtetl, in 1937, a woman was even nominated the sexton of a synagogue.[73]

Changes were most apparent in institutional or semi-institutional settings (at synagogues, unsanctioned minyans in private apartments, during holidays and the customs associated with them, circumcisions, etc.). Less formalized realms of activity, which fell under the general Soviet category of "vestiges of the past," proved more resilient. Thus, new forms for the dissemination of information like newspapers or the radio did not replace the old ones. Rumors and gossip among neighbors, relatives, and acquaintances remained an inextricable part of shtetl life, especially when it came to unusual events. Traditional society had spent decades developing the rules for dealing with dissenters. Izi Kharik conveys shtetl dwellers' characteristic thoughts about a new teacher in the following way: "When she walks down the street / everyone points with a finger / as she passes / They blink: — 'Look at her: / 'Her hair is cut short, like a boy! / She might be just as short on brains.'"[74]

Any violation of the established norms inspired intense discussion and judgment. Such are the endless conversations among the Zelmenyaners in Kulbak's novel about Tonka, who had a baby out of wedlock, probably with a non-Jewish man; any deviation from the norms inspired this kind of gossiping. In 1924, in the shtetl of Haradok, a young Komsomol member was buried in a Christian cemetery by his comrades. Rumors started circulating around the shtetl that the departed had appeared in his parents' dreams complaining of how unhappy he was at the Russian cemetery and asking to be reburied according to Jewish tradition.[75] No less controversial was the grandson of the late shtetl rabbi who had moved to Azarychy from Rostov-on-Don at the beginning of the 1920s and who was willing to write in a Russian school on Saturdays, which shtetl Jews disapproved of. The very need to have to consider the possible reaction of the shtetl to one's actions ("What will I tell people?" "What will people think?"), just like the tendency to pronounce a curse and immediately be seized with the superstitious fear that the curse might come true, remained an intricate part of traditional behavior.[76]

The traditional realm resisted in the only way it knew how. While there was a general trend in Soviet society toward trying to make all aspects of life uniform, the situation varied greatly from shtetl to shtetl. "Do you know what?" asked one shtetl Jew. "Give me a job for 10 rubles a month and I'll show you an exemplary Bolshevik. I'll be an honest worker and devote myself to Bolshevism body and soul."[77] This is a formula for loyalty to the regime that does not entail making changes in everyday norms for its sake.

Conclusion

On the eve of the war with Nazi Germany, the Soviet shtetl was already much different than it had been in 1917, having witnessed dramatic changes in its ethnic and demographic composition. Jewish occupational distribution, education, religiosity, and even the very conception of being Jewish had also been transformed. Through all of their paradoxical twists and turns, modernization, urbanization, technological changes, secularization, and Soviet policies for the unification of cultures left their mark on those who lived in shtetls.

If we think of shtetls as small settlements where the majority of inhabitants have town-type occupations, are Jews, and play a special economic role in the life of the country at large, then we can say that by the end of the 1930s, shtetls as such ceased to exist. From this, the disappearance of the term *mestechko* from the administrative dictionary of Soviet Belarus can be seen as justified.

However, if we think of the shtetl as a way of life with special models for behavior and a special linguistic and cultural environment, then this unique Jewish space was indeed preserved in many ways. For the interwar period, it would be wrong to reduce these models merely to folk religiosity. A large number of Jews who lived in shtetls on the eve of the war had gone through the system of Jewish religious education, in the heders or at home, and understood the meaning of Jewish rituals and religious rules. These still held meaning for them and remained an important part of their identity, which combined the past and the present. This new identity could even incorporate knowledge of Soviet Yiddish culture and ideas about prestigious occupations and the secular education needed to attain these occupations. The importance of these factors grew with the strengthening of the connections between shtetls and big cities, where many shtetl inhabitants resettled along with their neighbors and relatives.

Harsh Soviet policies aimed at pushing religion out of the public sphere and liquidating religious institutions had a significant effect on the behavior of shtetl Jews. Although some of these institutions continued to exist in illegal social forms—the ritual slaughter of kosher meat, unregistered minyans, heders, funeral societies, and so on—by the end of the 1930s, Jews' ethnic and religious life was by and large relegated to the home. However, the very fact that many shtetl residents did not even bother to conceal their observance of religious rules from their neighbors turned these Jewish values into an important factor in their public life regardless. And thus, the Jewish shtetl in Soviet Belarus as a sociocultural phenomenon can only be said to have disappeared along with the majority of its inhabitants during the Holocaust.

Notes

1. On Soviet attitudes toward the shtetl, see Yalen, "On the Social-Economic Front."
2. On the shtetl, see Kassow, "Shtetl"; Petrovsky-Shtern, *The Golden Age Shtetl*; Veidlinger, *In the Shadow of the Shtetl*; Katz, *The Shtetl: New Evaluations*; Dymshits, Lvov, and Sokolova, *Shtetl, XXI vek*; Estraikh and Krutikov, *The Shtetl: Image and Reality*.

3. Zeltser, *Evrei sovetskoi provintsii*.

4. On migration out of Belarusian shtetls, see Shmeruk, *Hakibuts hayehudi*, 22–58; Chkolnikova, "The Transformation of the Shtetl in the USSR," 93–100; Altshuler, *Soviet Jewry on the Eve of the Holocaust*, 34–46; Zeltser, "Shinuim demografiim vehevratiim-kalkaliim bekerev hayehudim"; Rozenblat and Elenskaia, "Dinamika chislennosti i rasseleniia belorusskikh evreev," 30–36.

5. Kharik, *Mit layb un lebn*, 53–56. On the poetry of Izi Kharik, see Shneer, *Yiddish and the Creation of Jewish Culture*, 179–228.

6. Kulbak, *The Zelmenyaners*, 175. See also Senderovich's introduction to *The Zelmenyaners*.

7. Kharik, "Lider," *Zamlbikher*, 8 (1952), p. 35.

8. *Der Veker*, December 14, 1924, p. 4.

9. Chkolnikova, "The Transformation of the Shtetl in the USSR," 100; *Di shtetlekh fun vssr in rekonstruktivn period*, 10–15; Altshuler, *Soviet Jewry on the Eve of the Holocaust*, 34–46.

10. Numbers based on Altshuler, *Soviet Jewry on the Eve of the Holocaust*, 232–34.

11. Dzyarzhawny arkhiw Viciebskai voblasti [Vitebsk, The State Archives of the Vitebsk Region] (GAVO or DAVV), fond 1966, opis 1, delo 18, l. 74.

12. Sirotiner, "Iz zhizni 'Vozdukhotresta,'" 113.

13. Natsyyanalny arkhiw Respubliki Belarus [Minsk, The National Archive of the Republic of Belarus] (NARB), fond 4, opis 3, delo 34, l. 35.

14. Chkolnikova, "The Transformation of the Shtetl in the USSR," 101–104.

15. Hershnboym, *Shtshedrin: A shtetl in rekonstruktivn period*.

16. Chkolnikova, "The Transformation of the Shtetl in the USSR," 101–104.

17. Zamoiskii, *Transformatsiia mestechek Sovetskoi Belorussii*, 209. Gosudarstvennyi arkhiv Rossiiskoi Federatsii [Moscow, The State Archive of the Russian Federation] (GARF), fond 7021, opis 82, delo. 6, ll. 46–80.

18. Numbers based on Altshuler, *Soviet Jewry on the Eve of the Holocaust*, 271.

19. Altshuler, *Soviet Jewry on the Eve of the Holocaust*, 258.

20. Chkolnikova, "The Transformation of the Shtetl in the USSR," 102; Zamoiskii, *Transformatsiia mestechek Sovetskoi Belorussii*, 205–206.

21. Altshuler, *Soviet Jewry on the Eve of the Holocaust*, 232–34.

22. Kantor, *Natsionalnoe stroitelstvo sredi evreev v SSSR*, 197–99.

23. Pinkus, *The Jews of the Soviet Union*, 66–71; Zeltser, *Evrei sovetskoi provintsii*, 136–38, 197–99.

24. Gatagova, Kosheleva, and Rogovaya, *TsK RKP(b) i natsionalnyi vopros*, 341; *Der Veker*, March 20, 1925.

25. *Oktyabr*, February 20, 1929, p. 3.

26. NARB, fond 4, opis 10, delo 30.

27. Zeltser, *Evrei sovetskoi provintsii*, 277–98.

28. Selemenev and Zeltser, "The Liquidation of Yiddish Schools in Belorussia," 97–99; GARF, fond 7541, opis 1, delo 875, l. 52.

29. *Oktyabr*, February 20, 1929, p. 3.

30. Selemenev and Zeltser, "The Liquidation of Yiddish Schools in Belorussia," 90.

31. Smilovitsky, *Evrei v Turove*, 336.

32. GAVO or DAVV, fond 1966, opis 12, delo 2, l. 285.

33. Martin, *The Affirmative Action Empire*, 339–40.

34. *Der Emes*, June 5, 1929.

35. Shmeruk, *Hakibuts hayehudi*, 125–77; Chkolnikova, "The Transformation of the Shtetl in the USSR," 114.

36. Altshuler, *Soviet Jewry on the Eve of the Holocaust*, 232.

37. NARB, fond 255, opis 2, delo 130, ll. 21–22.

38. On contraband, see Kotler, "Yaureiskiya myastechki w Belarusi," 103–104; Smilovitsky, *Evrei v Turove*, 345–47.

39. Kulbak, *The Zelmenyaners*, 173.

40. Sirotiner, "Iz zhizni 'Vozdukhotresta,'" 89.

41. On the role of unofficial occupations and how they were treated by the state, see Sloin, *The Jewish Revolution in Belorussia*, 55–82.

42. Sirotiner, "Iz zhizni 'Vozdukhotresta,'" 112.

43. NARB, fond 30, opis 2, delo 3080.

44. NARB, fond 4, opis 3, delo 34, ll. 39–40.

45. Kulbak, *The Zelmenyaners*, 176.

46. GARF, fond 7541, opis 1, delo 875, l. 16.

47. GARF, fond 7541, opis 1, delo 875, l. 38.

48. Selemenev and Zeltser, "Kolyshki—A Shtetl in the Late 1930s," 63.

49. Smilovitsky, "A Belorussian Border Shtetl in the 1920s and 1930s," 116–18.

50. Selemenev and Zeltser, "Kolyshki—A Shtetl in the Late 1930s," 60.

51. Selemenev and Zeltser, "Kolyshki—A Shtetl in the Late 1930s," 56, 60.

52. Konstantinov, *Evreiskoe naselenie byvshego SSSR v XX veke*, 40.

53. For comparison, in Uzda, 9 percent of the Jews enrolled in school had Belorussian as their sole language of literacy at the end of the 1920s. It is consistent that by the end of the 1930s, the percentage of Jews who had gone through Belarusian school had risen (I. L. Zalesskii, "'M-ko Uzda,' Materialy po demografii i ekonomicheskomu polozheniiu evreiskogo naseleniia SSSR" ['The Town of Uzda,' Materials on the demographics and economic situation among the Jewish population of the USSR], no. 8 (June 1930), 64.

54. Altshuler, *Soviet Jews on the Eve of the Holocaust*, 276.

55. *Der emes*, April 5, 1935, p. 3.

56. Kulbak, *The Zelmenyaners*, 188; Reles, *Evreiskie sovetskie pisateli Belorussii*, 218.

57. NARB, fond 42, opis 1, delo 1714, ll. 55–56, copy CAHJP HMF 485.5. For more about the Yevsektsiya, see Gitelman, *Jewish Nationality and Soviet Politics*; Altshuler, *Hayevsektsiya bivrit hamo'atsot*.

58. *Oktyabr*, June 9, 1926, p. 3.
59. *Der emes*, September 16, 1937, p. 3.
60. *Der apikoyres*, no. 3, 1931, p. 17.
61. Selemenev and Zeltser, "Kolyshki—A Shtetl in the Late 1930s," 63.
62. NARB, fond 255, opis 2, delo 130, l. 27.
63. NARB, fond 255, opis 2, delo 130, l. 27.
64. *Oktyabr*, April 13, 1929, p. 2.
65. *Der emes*, March 28, 1934, p. 3.
66. Selemenev and Zeltser, "Kolyshki—A Shtetl in the Late 1930s," 64.
67. Karpekin, "'Oni zhili v etom gorode...,'" 24.
68. Karpekin, "'Oni zhili v etom gorode...,'" 26.
69. Zeltser, *Evrei sovetskoi provintsii*, 261–62, 268.
70. NARB, fond 4, opis 21, delo 1053, l. 28.
71. *Der emes*, August 19, 1927, p. 4; *Oktyabr*, February 10, 1929.
72. Zeltser, *Evrei sovetskoi provintsii*, 273.
73. NARB, fond 4, opis 21, delo 1053, l. 28.
74. Kharik, *Mit layb un lebn*, 12.
75. *Der veker*, June 28, 1924, p. 3.
76. Gindin, "Detstvo v Ozarichakh," 226–29, 238–39, 241.
77. Sirotiner, "Iz zhizni 'Vozdukhotresta,'" 112.

3

Days of Remembrance for Jews of the Russo-Belarusian Borderlands

SVETLANA AMOSOVA

During a 2014 field expedition organized by the Sefer Center, in the town of Liepiel in the Vitebsk Region of Belarus, one of the most colorful and detailed narratives we heard was the description of Jewish burial rituals and days of remembrance.[1] Liepiel is where the term *Jewish Radunitsa* (a description used by both Jews and non-Jews) was first documented in reference to a Jewish day of remembrance.[2] The first theory about the term used in this context was that it was evidence that Jewish traditions had been radically transformed and that Jews had borrowed and integrated cultural practices from neighbors of other ethnicities and integrated them on various levels (particularly the linguistic and ritualistic). However, further research showed that this hypothesis was not correct. The vernacular term *Jewish Radunitsa* is not unique to the Vitebsk Region, and in fact it is fairly widespread. The Jewish Radunitsa is an important day for visiting the cemetery in the Russo-Belarusian borderlands, in the Vitebsk and Mahilyow Regions of Belarus and the Smolensk and Bryansk Regions of Russia.

This chapter's main objective is to describe Jewish commemorative practices on the Russo-Belarusian border. I will not discuss rituals commemorating anniversaries of deaths (*yortsayt*), although all our informants spoke of how important these rituals are for the personal remembrance of the dead, and all of them performed those rituals, which included lighting candles at home and visiting the synagogue or cemetery. Often, the date of these anniversaries is determined by the Gregorian and not the Jewish calendar.

In traditional Slavic culture, there are several important commemorative days: Radunitsa, Troitsa (Trinity Sunday), and what is known as Parents' Saturdays. Depending on the region, one of these days may be more important than the others. For the Russo-Belarusian borderlands, the most important day of remembrance is Radunitsa, the ninth day after Easter Sunday, which falls on a Tuesday. In today's Republic of Belarus and sometimes in the neighboring Briansk and Smolensk Regions of the Russian Federation, Radunitsa is a national holiday that allows people time to visit the graves of their dead relatives. It is one of the key dates in the Orthodox calendar that is specifically associated with remembrance.

None of the Jews in Liepiel could correlate their celebration of Radunitsa to any Jewish holiday. It seemed to be an invention that has nothing to do with Jewish traditions. In the materials collected in the town of Nevel (Pskov Region, Russia) in February 2008, as well as in a number of literary sources, the day of remembrance when it is customary for Jews to visit the cemetery in this region is the fast day Tisha be-Av (the ninth day of the Jewish month Av). Yiddish and Hebrew writer Zalman Shneour describes such a Tisha be-Av ritual in his collection of stories *Shklover yidn* (*Jews of Shklow*) in the town of Shklow in the Mogilev *guberniia*: "This year, Tisha be-Av fell on an especially hot day. The heat was excruciating; steam rose off the lake.... Jews, weakened and tired from their fast, wandered through the streets in their wool stockings, sluggish and speechless, like autumn flies. The stronger ones among them walked in just their stocking feet, as the Law says they must, headed to the cemetery in Ryzhkovichy."[3]

In August 2015, studying the Belarusian-Russian border region on the Russian side, our expedition entered the town of Roslavl, in the Smolensk Region. By a lucky coincidence, our visit to the town fell on August 9, the day of remembrance at the Roslavl Jewish cemetery. We found members of the town's Jewish community, as well as many former residents and their descendants, gathered at the cemetery.

We were a bit surprised to learn that the ninth of Av was the day for remembrance and visiting the cemetery for the entire community because we had previously worked with the Podolian and Bessarabian traditions, where the remembrance period comes in the month of Elul, and every community member independently chooses a day to visit the cemetery (usually a Monday or Thursday).[4] In Podolia, people either do not observe Tisha be-Av, or they know it only as a fasting day and a day of remembrance of the destruction of the temple. Some people told us that on this day, the men fasted and did not wear shoes, and the boys collected burdock and threw it at adults.[5] We knew from various memoirs and literary works that in some communities the ninth of Av was not only a fasting day in memory of the destruction of the temple in certain Belarusian mestechki but also a day for visiting the cemetery. It was these observations and our interviews that day at the cemetery, as well as fragmentary accounts from Liepiel, that led us to continue our research on days of remembrance here and in neighboring regions. As time went on, we saw that in addition to the ninth of Av, the Jews in the Smolensk Region had a second day of remembrance that is consistently called the Jewish Radunitsa. As a result of all our interviews and observations, we learned that Jewish Radunitsa is not a random day, nor is it a new (Soviet) tradition or a borrowing from other ethnicities. It is what the Jews and non-Jews of this region call *Lag ba-Omer*.

Materials used for this article include the observations and interviews collected in the Russo-Belarusian borderlands among the communities of the Bryansk and Smolensk Regions during days of remembrance as well as interviews with members of these Jewish communities. We analyzed a total of 140 interviews, with materials from neighboring regions—the towns of Liepiel (Vitebsk Region) and Klimavichy (Mahilyow Region) in Belarus and the town of Nevel (Pskov Region) in Russia—brought in for comparison.

The Case of Roslavl

The cemetery in Roslavl, like the community itself, is relatively new in comparison with other mestechki in the region (the majority of which date to the middle of the nineteenth century). We knew the name of the founder of the town's Jewish cemetery, a local glassblowing factory owner Iakov Markovich Magidson, and that it was founded in 1913. The oldest part of the cemetery has not been preserved, but there is a part with grave markers from as far back as 1934. Regular burials date back to the beginning of the 1950s. Until recently, the cemetery was strictly divided into men's and women's rows. Beginning in the 2000s, however, the tradition changed slightly, and side-by-side burials of husbands and wives were permitted. Many of the elderly view this negatively and see it as a result of the influence of mixed marriages and the Russian Orthodox tradition. Behind the cemetery, in a ravine, is the mass grave of Holocaust victims. There is a monument and, guarding the descent to it from the side of the cemetery, a gate that is usually locked.

In Roslavl, as noted above, the two main days of remembrance are Tisha be-Av and Lag ba-Omer. It is important to note that none of our informants remembered the Jewish names for these holidays and that almost nobody correlated the dates of the days accepted in the community with any Jewish holidays. Many members of the Roslavl community said that this date (August 9) had been established recently and chosen randomly by the community; that analogous practices were not common among Jews in other places; and that the second day, in the spring, is, in their opinion, related to May 9, the traditional

Soviet day of remembrance.⁶ According to one informant, "We established it, although there is no such Jewish tradition. Everyone goes and remembers their dead."⁷

Some community members did remember that both of these days, in the spring and in the summer, are related to Jewish holidays, that this tradition has existed for a long time, and that the choice of Sunday is based on modern-day circumstances (it is forbidden among the Jews to visit the cemetery on Saturday, while Christians traditionally observe their day of remembrance on Saturday).

> Before, people here in Roslavl and Bryansk would go for Lag ba-Omer. I recently read that it's supposed to be a joyous occasion, they remember some kind of saint, I don't recall who, and they go to his grave over there in Israel. Maybe that's why, probably, people didn't really know why. It was customary to go on Lag ba-Omer. And that's how it used to be here. And then for the past five or six years, we've been going on May 9. It's already a holiday, there are lots of people buried there from the war. And then this year, we did it May 8 for some reason. And then in August, sometimes at the end of July, it was also the ninth of Av, and then we changed it so that it'd be on a weekend, on Sunday, so that everyone could come. People come from Smolensk and other places. But the biggest number of people come in May. In August there's less.⁸

When we visited the cemetery on May 7, 2017, and August 9, 2015, there were a number of similar ceremonial actions. In August 2015, there were about ninety people at the cemetery, and there were over one hundred on May 7, 2017. On both occasions, in addition to the members of the Roslavl Jewish community in attendance, there were people who had moved away—returning from Smolensk, Israel, and other places—and there were non-Jews visiting the graves of their colleagues, neighbors, and friends. In the winter of 2017, Russian language and literature teacher Serafima Kozlova had passed away, and on May 7 her former students came to the cemetery. On the eve of the days of remembrance, community activists ask that the graves be cleaned and the cemetery be put in order by mowing the grass, trimming the bushes, and cutting down dead trees. On days of remembrance, there is a small flower and wreath sale at the cemetery entrance, and a table is placed there with a donation box for cemetery upkeep.

People come with their families or on their own, put flowers on graves, and spend some time near them. There is no assembly or collective prayer on either day of remembrance. Elders say that before the 1970s, there was a person in Roslavl who knew the Kaddish, and he would come to the cemetery on this day and walk from grave to grave, reciting the Kaddish, and be paid for this service by the families of the deceased. There is no such person in the community anymore, neither is anyone specially invited to serve this purpose, nor do people attempt to recite any prayers themselves.[9]

In present-day Roslavl, as in many other places, there is a debate over what should be brought to the graves: flowers or stones. In traditional Jewish practice, one brings a stone to the grave as a sign that there has been a visitor. However, under the strong influence of ethnic neighbors, Jews have begun to bring flowers to their graves. This has prompted debate about the contemporary tradition. Stones are perceived as a new Israeli practice that is a complete departure from the customs among Jews in that region. Even though some people say they have seen or learned that in Israel people bring stones and light candles and that placing memorial wreaths on graves is not part of Jewish tradition, everyone still brings flowers (most often, artificial ones) and, rarely, some stones and candles.

> INTERVIEWER: Can anything be brought to the cemetery?
> INFORMANT: Those are Russian customs. I don't live nearby; I'm a teacher and need to travel here. I found out that in Israel, people bring stones. So that's what I do. Because I don't know the traditional customs well, I'd bring flowers but you have to take care of them, and I can't, so I'd be sad. This way, I'm just telling them that I've been to see them.[10]

In addition to this, some St. George ribbons were sighted on the gates around several graves, most likely belonging to those who had served in World War II.[11] This practice was seen in many other cemeteries, too, not just Jewish ones.

All of this can be thought of as part of a set of general memorial practices, but there are also personal ones that arise out of particular circumstances. We observed a handful of these in Roslavl. For instance, all our informants emphasized that food and drink should not be brought into the Jewish cemetery, but there were oranges on one of the graves, which the wife of the deceased explained:

> INTERVIEWER: Can you tell us why there are oranges and mandarins here?
> INFORMANT: He really wanted oranges, but at that time, it was an ordeal to get them. Then a man went and got them through his connections, but by the time he brought them, it was too late. And so, every year he comes and brings him oranges.[12]

It is not customary in the Jewish tradition to bring food to the cemetery and have a commemorative meal or leave food for the deceased, but in Slavic traditions, such practices are important and continue to be observed. On Radunitsa, people always bring food to the cemetery and leave it at the grave. Of particular importance are special commemorative types of food, such as blini, eggs, and so on. Some people bring objects that the deceased particularly liked or wished to have before death, as if executing his or her last will. This is not a customary Jewish practice, but it is widespread in the Slavic tradition. Russian Orthodox family members may bring food for the dead (usually sweets like candies and chocolates). There is no strict ban on such practices, but it is emphasized that this is not part of traditional Jewish commemorative practices: "He has two sons, and their girlfriends are Russian, so they came and put chocolates on the grave. Orthodox relatives put sweets on graves. Our father was a Jew and we're Jewish. In their Jewish family, it's not customary to do that with sweets, so we never put anything."[13]

Some rules for visiting the cemetery were mentioned in a handful of individual interviews: after visiting the cemetery, people were supposed to wash their hands but not wipe them, and when people left the cemetery, they were to rip up the grass and throw it over their shoulder. We did not see any of the cemetery visitors performing these rituals. Few people from Roslavl mentioned these traditions in interviews. By comparison, researchers who visited Liepiel (Vitebsk Region, Belarus) noted that people did perform these rituals as they exited the Jewish cemetery.[14] Likewise, several interviews from Nevel (Pskov Region) contain detailed descriptions of these customs: "I know that you're supposed to take another route back from the cemetery. And that before leaving, you're supposed to throw grass over your shoulder three times and wash your hands. When I can, I do this."[15]

Overall, the days of remembrance held in May and August in Roslavl are very similar to each other. However, on August 9, the gates to the mass grave were open and most of the cemetery visitors went to the Holocaust memorial and put flowers on it, whereas on May 7, the gates were closed and no one went to the memorial. It is unclear if it is the case every year that the ninth of Av is also the day of remembrance for Holocaust victims, and the day of remembrance in May is only for those buried at the cemetery. Israeli historian Leonid Smilovitsky describes memorial practices connected to the Holocaust from the end of the 1940s and beginning of the 1950s in Belarus and writes that Holocaust victims were usually remembered on May 9 and June 22 (and if these days did not work, then the nearest Sunday). All members of the Jewish community—men, women, and children—would participate in these Holocaust remembrance days by going to the sites of the mass executions, and veterans and partisans would wear their medals. The eighth or ninth of May became a traditional day of remembrance for Holocaust victims in numerous places across Belarus. Many people who escaped during the war would return with their children and grandchildren on those days, saving up for the trip all year.[16] This tradition is somewhat different from what we observe today in Roslavl and other places throughout the Smolensk Region. For instance, in Monastyrshchina, it is customary to go to the mass grave on January 9 (the day of the mass execution there) and May 9, but the traditional day for visiting the cemetery, remembered by the elderly but no longer commemorated, is Lag ba-Omer.[17]

Overall, we see that in Roslavl and other former Jewish mestechki in the Smolensk Region, unlike in many other places in the former USSR, only a minimal number of traditional practices have been preserved. In other places near Roslavl where there are still fewer Jews today (Monastyrshchina, Pochinok, Shumiachi), there is no tradition of going to the cemetery on Jewish days of remembrance. A small number of people in Monastyrshchina remembered that people used to go in the spring and that there was a holiday at the beginning of summer, but people no longer observe it. Certain attachments to traditional Jewish days of remembrance typical of this region remain, but no new customs—for example, collective prayer at the cemetery or an assembly—have emerged.

The days of remembrance still honored in Smolensk mestechki such as Roslavl are perhaps the only times when entire Jewish communities and former residents who emigrated all gather together, and the cemetery becomes a meeting place. Jewish communities in many former Jewish shtetls have designated locations (owned or rented) for communal gatherings on Jewish holidays and Shabbat and for the deliveries of Passover matzo or charity packages. The same location can be also used for a Jewish school or a club for children or elderly people. Although Roslavl has a significant Jewish population, the community has no building that could be used as a gathering place, and community members do not get together for Jewish holidays or other events. Currently, they only have the cemetery, which they visit twice a year. During these gatherings, people share news and solve various problems (difficulties finding a job, finding marriage partners for children, and so on), and money is collected for cemetery upkeep. Participating in these days of remembrance is practically the only thing that unifies the Jewish community of Roslavl today.

The Case of Surazh

For our descriptions of customs in Surazh, the Sefer expedition team used interviews from a summer 2016 expedition and observations at the cemetery in May 2017. For comparison, we will use materials from a neighboring mestechko, Unech. From the beginning of the nineteenth century until 1919, Surazh was part of the Chernigov guberniia. Today, it is the district center of the Bryansk Region. The Surazh Jewish cemetery is on the bank of the Iput River and covers a large area. The oldest part we were able to find dates back to the late nineteenth century, where the oldest tombstone is dated 1882. There are several plots in the cemetery with graves and a large amount of free space in the center and on the steep bank of the river. In the central part, facing the entrance, is the mass grave where the remains of people executed during the Holocaust were brought, along with two memorials standing next to it: a small one, erected during Soviet times, and a wall with the names of the dead built in the 2000s. Unlike Roslavl and many other places, Surazh has an active Jewish community. There is a building where the townspeople gather for all the Jewish holidays and for Shabbat (depending on community members' availability). There is usually prayer and a communal meal on these days.

In Surazh, people usually visit the cemetery once a year, on Lag ba-Omer (*Lagbeymer*, in the local pronunciation), although most often this day is called Jewish Radunitsa, a name that is characteristic beyond this region as well. Lag ba-Omer is referred to as Jewish Radunitsa in the Smolensk Region and also in Liepiel, in the Vitebsk Region of Belarus, as has been mentioned.[18]

In Surazh in the summer of 2016, our informants told us that they always go to the cemetery on the day as it appears on the Jewish calendar; they never move it to a Sunday or any other day. In 2017, Lag ba-Omer fell on Sunday, May 15. Over 150 people came to the cemetery that day, mostly locals, but some had come from Bryansk, Ivanovo, and Odessa. The cemetery had been spruced up at the beginning of May for the celebration of Victory Day (May 9), and some of the graves had been cleaned more recently than that (tombstones washed, branches cleared, etc.), but some people were still cleaning graves on the morning of the ceremony. A wreath had been placed at the memorial to Holocaust victims, and, as a community leader later explained, on the eve of May 9, community members had brought wreaths to the cemetery and to the memorial where the executions had occurred. They did not go to the cemetery on May 9. Most people coming to the cemetery would approach one grave, then walk around to others. Most people came in family groups. Interestingly, some families came with children, and no one in Surazh said anything about how tradition forbids bringing children to the cemetery while their parents are alive (such a prohibition is common in many Jewish communities across the former USSR[19]). Unlike the Roslavl Jewish cemetery, some of the graves at the cemetery in Surazh have little tables on them, like in Russian Orthodox cemeteries. The majority of people did not eat or drink anything, but some did have tea and left candy by the graves or gave sweets to those who visited a grave "to remember the soul" (*na pomin dushi*). The majority of those gathered said it is not customary for Jews to bring food to the cemetery and picnic on the graves, unlike Christians.

At eleven o'clock in the morning, when most people had already visited the graves of their relatives, a ceremony began by the mass grave. Before the ceremony, candles and a box for donations (*tzedakah*) and two piles of stones were laid out, although most people gravitated toward the real or artificial flowers available to put on the graves. The stones had been brought by community activists, and the man who acted as the rabbi said that most people do not know what they are for, but that this is how it is supposed to be according to Jewish tradition. A group of ten men gathered near the mass grave and donned head coverings. The rest of the visitors stood to the side. The acting community leader made a short speech, and then the man acting as rabbi read a prayer in Russian. Candles were lit, and more was said about this traditional day of remembrance and the custom of coming to the cemetery in Surazh on that day.[20] After the ceremony, most people left money in the donation box. Some went to the new memorial to Holocaust victims (some had done this before the gathering) and left stones or flowers (or, rarely, candy) in the niche with their last names (likely their relatives or those otherwise close to them); a number of people went to the memorial but did not put anything on it. No one pronounced the Kaddish by the graves, and none of our informants remembered any traditional formulaic speeches that were said when visiting the cemetery.

After the official part of the ceremony, everyone was invited to eat. The table was set on the riverbank, away from the graves. Women, traditionally the ones who cook for the community on Jewish holidays (Shabbat, Pesach, and others), were in charge of the banquet. Most of the food had been prepared ahead of time and brought from home: salads (egg and onion), sandwiches (with butter, onion, shredded carrot, and garlic), hard-boiled eggs, sausage (boiled and smoked), fruit (bananas, apples, and oranges), cucumbers, candy, compote, and alcoholic beverages (home-brewed vodka). Not all of the cemetery visitors came to the banquet; perhaps only twenty or thirty people. Before the meal, everyone washed their hands (the water had been brought out ahead of time). This part of the ceremony lasted about an hour, and people had casual conversations, discussed news, and paid a lot of attention to us (as guests who had come especially for this occasion). Most of the men did not drink alcohol because they had driven.

All the community members we spoke to that day said that this kind of banquet is traditional. In Soviet times, according to our informants, it had not been customary to have an all-community banquet, but people would still go to the river after visiting the cemetery that day (approximately the same place where the communal table now stood) and would sit down either with friends or just family to have a picnic. Since the 1990s, after the Jewish community in Surazh took its present form, there has been a group meal offering drinks and sandwiches with the table set up in various places—sometimes on the riverbank (as in 2016 and 2017) and sometimes at the cemetery entrance next to the mass grave. Everyone told us that they light bonfires on this day, although it is unclear how old this custom is. The day we visited in 2017 was very windy, so although they had permission from the fire department, they decided not to have a bonfire.

It is important to note that the traditional prohibition against bringing children to the cemetery if their parents are alive, which we documented among some informants in Podolia, Nevel, and a few other places, is unknown in Surazh. There were children present that day, and many adults told us of visiting the cemetery on this day when they were children. However, in neighboring Unech, one of our informants told us that it was specifically on Lag ba-Omer when children should not be brought to the cemetery and that there is a ban on bringing them there if their parents are alive. On other days, however, children could come, and he had done so with his grandmother and grandfather. He also said that on this day, you do not greet people at the cemetery, because they are there to see the dead, and "they are the ones who need to be greeted."[21]

Jews settled in Unech later than they did in Surazh, at the end of the nineteenth and beginning of the twentieth centuries. With the construction of the railroads, Unech had become a major railroad hub. The town's Jewish cemetery is on a plot of land within the general town cemetery, and today there are Christian burials there due to the many mixed marriages resulting in side-by-side burials. Here, Lag ba-Omer is also the day of remembrance, but there are no communal events on that day, not even a box for collecting donations at the cemetery. Everyone comes at a time convenient to them, bringing real or artificial flowers (although we heard talk of how they should have brought stones). People we interviewed on our visit said it is not customary to hold a banquet on the graves but that most people do this symbolically (with compote, etc.). Iakov Kheyfets, one of the oldest community members, had installed a table and bench in the corner of the cemetery some time back to discourage people from eating on the graves and held a picnic there himself (with bacon sandwiches, dyed eggs, onion, and vodka).

> INTERVIEWER: We've been told that people dye eggs for this day.
> Kheyfets: I have some with me. I brought them.
> INTERVIEWER: What do you do with them? How do you eat them?
> Kheyfets: You drink a hundred grams and chase it with an egg.
> INTERVIEWER: How do you dye them?
> Kheyfets: In onion. Jews dye them in onion.
> INTERVIEWER: Where do you do this? At the general table?
> Kheyfets: Yes. I did it here. Jews don't eat at the graves. I made a table.... So, you're supposed to, here you go, my grandfather taught me, that you must drink on this day [Lag ba-Omer] and remember the dead, but not at the cemetery, you leave the cemetery and put a table over there. There used to be another one, but it broke, then I restored it.[22]

Kheyfets also said that in the past, after visiting their relatives at the cemetery, everyone would get on buses and go to the site of the mass execution, meaning that people would also visit the mass grave on that day:

> INTERVIEWER: Do Jews go to the execution site memorial on May 9 or any other day?
> Kheyfets: Of course they do.
> INTERVIEWER: What day do they go?
> Kheyfets: To which memorial? On May 9, we put wreaths there. Before, when my parents were still alive, my grandparents, it was standing room only, so many Jews would come for Lagbeymer, for Radunitsa. Two buses would come. People came out and got on these buses and went to the pit. There would be a service, prayers.[23]

Everyone we interviewed told us that, in addition to Lagbeymer, it was customary to go to the cemetery on May 9 because many of the people buried there had taken part in the war, and the graves were all cleaned before the holiday. This process is part of the general tidying up of the whole cemetery. Local residents can see that the Jewish graves are being taken care of, which promotes communal unity and the preservation of the tradition.

In our interviews, Jews from both Unech and Surazh said they know that it is not traditional for all communities to go to the cemetery on

Lag ba-Omer and that the rabbis who had come there in the 1990s, whom they see in Bryansk today, told them that it is supposed to be a "happy" holiday. Nevertheless, the visit to the cemetery on Lag ba-Omer is still the most important and most Jewish tradition for these *mestechki* in the present day: visiting the cemetery is what marks belonging and inclusion in the Jewish community.

Ritual Food: Dyed Eggs

In most of the communities where we conducted research, our informants told us—and we saw for ourselves on many occasions—that the traditional food for *yortsayt* (the anniversary of a loved one's death) includes *lekekh un bronfen* (sweet cake and vodka). In Unech, our informant Iakov Kheyfets told us that people always dye eggs for Lag ba-Omer and bring them to the cemetery, and so he asked his sister-in-law to make some before the holiday, and he really did eat them at the cemetery. He claimed that this is a longstanding tradition:

> INTERVIEWER: Did your grandfather do this?
> Kheyfets: For Lagbeymer? He'd pray and lay down stones.
> INTERVIEWER: Did people dye eggs when he was alive?
> Kheyfets: Of course. My grandma always dyed them with onion. And yesterday my brother's wife dyed them with onion for me.[24]

Many of our informants in Roslavl (particularly the elderly) had also told us that people really did dye eggs for Radunitsa, but no one said that they would bring them to the cemetery. But in Monastyrshchina and Pochinka, in the Smolensk Region, one person described the timing and the celebration of Lag ba-Omer as follows:

> INFORMANT: Yes, [it occurs] after Jewish Easter.
> INTERVIEWER: What is this called?
> INFORMANT: Well, in Russian it's Radunitsa, and in Jewish, I don't know, either.
> INTERVIEWER: Would the Jews go?
> INFORMANT: Yes, yes, they'd go, they'd go. They'd get together and all go. They'd dye eggs, they would, I know. And go. Yes. They'd roll them on the graves. This I am sure of.
> INTERVIEWER: What color were the eggs, how would they dye them?
> INFORMANT: They'd dye the eggs with onion skin.

INTERVIEWER: And then go to the cemetery that day and roll them on the graves?
INFORMANT: Yes.[25]

The fact that people dye eggs for this holiday was documented in other mestechki as well, including those where it was not customary to go to the cemetery on Lag ba-Omer. For instance, similar games with dyed eggs are described by Shmarya Levin about his native mestechko, Svisloch (near Bobruyisk, Belarus).[26] The custom was also documented in many mestechki around Latgale.[27] For Roslavl and Surazh, the memorial food is now somewhat different: *lekekh un bronfen* is not customary there, and it is unclear whether it had been in the past. If one marks on a map the places where Lag ba-Omer is a day of remembrance, and also the mestechki where it is customary to dye eggs on that day, there is a partial overlap. The Russo-Belarusian borderland, which includes parts of the Mahilyow, Smolensk, and Bryansk Regions, is one of these overlap zones. For instance, none of the native inhabitants of Surazh had ever heard of painting eggs for Lag ba-Omer, but in the summer of 2016, we found the shell of a painted egg on a grave. It is difficult to say whether it was left behind by non-Jewish friends or relatives, or if this tradition is known, after all, in some form (our only informant who told us about this tradition in Surazh, saying that her mother and grandmother would do this, was actually from Smolensk and had moved to Surazh with her family in 1948).

Unfortunately, the Jewish traditions we found in Belarus today are radically curtailed. Our fragmentary evidence does not permit us to fully reconstruct the calendar of memorial rituals or the map where they are observed. We have learned from a number of memoirs that people dyed eggs on Lag ba-Omer, but these memoirs do not mention that this was also a day to visit the cemetery.

Formulaic Texts

As was previously mentioned, the practice of reciting the Kaddish is almost entirely lost across all Jewish communities in the Russo-Belarusian borderlands. Instead of the Kaddish, which is usually recited by a special figure, most of our informants from Podolia themselves recite a special formula in Yiddish at the graves they are visiting: *loif in bet* (run and plead). The following is an example of such a text: "Papa, I beseech you, run and plead for blessings for the children. Let us be healthy, let everything be alright with them, let us have earnings, let things be quiet in the world."[28]

In Podolia, there is also a practice for when there are unpleasant circumstances or events at home, such as an illness. When visiting relatives' graves, people ask them to ask God for help and recite this same kind of text in Yiddish.[29] Visiting the cemetery during difficult times, as a means of dealing with problems or tragedy, is completely unknown in the Russo-Belarusian border region. A woman in Smolensk, who had been born in Roslavl, said that when she had a problem at home, she would make a special trip to visit the cemetery in her hometown, but she had learned of this practice from an article in a Jewish magazine, and no one had ever told her about it:

> INFORMANT: Eight years ago, I was struck by tragedy, and I went to the Jewish cemetery. I have a *tefillin*, there are prayers in it that you say at the cemetery. I remember I was there on a weekday, then I saw some men walking toward me, I hid behind a tree, I was scared. But, in any case, it helped me.
> INTERVIEWER: You said that if you're having some kind of difficulties, you're supposed to go to the cemetery. Did you read that somewhere or did someone tell you?
> INFORMANT: Yes. I think I read it somewhere.
> INTERVIEWER: It's not something your mother did?
> INFORMANT: My mother, no. But I read about it in a magazine. I read somewhere about the prayers you're supposed to say at the cemetery. There are a lot of them.[30]

Some of our informants said that when praying at the cemetery, they said their prayers "internally": "It's two times a year: it was May 10, and then today. We try to tidy up the graves, and come and be with them. I have inner monologues with them. I put my hand on the memorial and ask."[31]

We were, however, able to document one traditional formulaic text that is said in Yiddish, *zay a guter beter*, which means "plead for me, for my wife, and for my children."[32] The sense is similar to what is said in Podolia, but the formula is different; the text from Podolia is much more elaborate. It is also important that this text and the tradition itself are well known among Jews in Podolia, which underlines the great significance of this practice in that region and the complete absence of it among the Belarusian Jews.

Conclusions

The choice of the month of Elul for cemetery visits, which is the usual time for the Jews of Podolia and Bessarabia, is obvious because this is the time preceding Yom Kippur. Sylvie Anne Goldberg writes about how the times before

Rosh Hashanah and Yom Kippur and Tisha be-Av are consistently linked with visiting the cemetery, even in the Talmud and other midrashim. The choice of these days is explained by two factors. The period before Rosh Hashanah and Yom Kippur is the time of "supreme judgement" and the determination of fates, when one can turn to the dead for help and ask them for protection. Tisha be-Av is the day of the destruction of the temple and the day of "confronting death."[33]

Tisha be-Av was typically a day of mourning and commemoration not only among Ashkenazi Jews but also among other Jewish groups. American anthropologist Sascha Goluboff's research describes the memorial practices of the mountain Jews of Krasnaya Sloboda in Azerbaijan, who commemorate the ninth of Av in this way. Goluboff demonstrates that a number of researchers conceptualize memorial practices performed on the ninth day of Av across the diaspora through its connection with Jewish history and the mourning of the destroyed temple and lost homeland of Israel.[34] She explains that these connections with devastation and loss are why, in a number of communities across the diaspora, Tisha be-Av is not only a fast day and a day to remember the destroyed temple but also a memorial day for deceased relatives and other community members.

The case of Lag ba-Omer becoming a day of remembrance among Belarusian Jews is a little more complicated. According to Jewish tradition, this is not a day of mourning like Tisha be-Av, but it does have symbolic significance as a moment when a particular fate is fulfilled because it is in the period approaching Yom Kippur and Rosh Hashanah. Accounting for the choice of this day as a day of remembrance is a rather difficult task. However, in a number of Belarusian towns (for instance, Brest), this was one of only three days when the *khevra kadisha* (burial association) organized banquets for its members (the other two days were in the autumn and winter, Shemini Atzeret and the fifteenth of Kislev, when visiting the cemetery is difficult).[35] It is possible that the khevra kadisha tradition (first practiced by a small, elite group that goes to the cemetery on this day and holds a banquet) is the source of this custom, which has since become a mass phenomenon. However, the khevra kadisha banquet on Lag ba-Omer is not typical throughout Belarus but rather is a localized custom.

It is also possible that the Jews' neighbors of other ethnicities influenced the choice of the day of remembrance, because Radunitsa, which falls close to Lag ba-Omer, is an important holiday of remembrance. As a holiday, Lag ba-Omer does not have any kind of colorful, expressive symbolism of its own, and because of this, it can take on the significance of a day of remembrance, even when this actually contradicts the general meaning of this day in Jewish tradition.[36]

In general, these kinds of ethnographic and folkloric details (including formulaic memorial texts or the tradition of dyeing eggs on Lag ba-Omer), as well as the dates for visiting the cemetery, which, as we have seen, vary across regions, are quite important markers for defining different Jewish groups' cultural and historical boundaries. A similar kind of mapping has already been done for Yiddish dialects and gastronomic differences (such as different gefilte fish recipes).[37] It will likewise be useful to establish which mestechki in this region celebrate both days of remembrance (Lag ba-Omer and Tisha be-Av), and which ones only celebrate one or the other, thus establishing the borders of these traditions. The fact that there are two days of remembrance in this region—Lag ba-Omer and Tisha be-Av—may be due to the influence of Slavic traditions, since in Belarus, there are two important days when one is supposed to visit the cemetery: spring and fall *dziady*.

The commemorative customs among the Jews of this region, their special practices relating to remembering the dead, are among the few traditions that have unified these groups and constituted a core practice of Jewishness during the Soviet period and today. This is the kind of preservation of tradition that Zvi Gitelman, a researcher of Soviet Judaism, called "thin culture": a phenomenon in which only discrete elements are preserved to form an identity against the backdrop of another, more important cultural tradition (in this case, Soviet or Russian).[38] However, thin as this culture may be, the preservation of special days for visiting the cemetery in accordance with Jewish tradition (albeit with some departures from that tradition), eating matzo for Passover, and participation in the memorialization of Holocaust victims are what have formed and maintained Jewish identity—both private and public—in the mestechki of the Russo-Belarusian borderlands in Soviet times and today.[39]

Notes

1. For more, see Belova, "Evreiskoe kladbishche v rasskazakh zhitelei Lepelia i okrestnostei."

2. Belova, "Evreiskoe kladbishche v rasskazakh zhitelei Lepelia i okrestnostei," 108–109.

3. Shneour, *Shklover yidn*, 311–12. All translations, unless otherwise noted, are by Bela Shayevich.

4. For more on this, see Dymshits, "Evreiskoe kladbishche," 137–38.

5. Veidlinger, *In the Shadow of the Shtetl*, 153.

6. The fusion of Lag ba-Omer and May 9 is typical for other places in the region. For instance, an informant from Pochink told us that they go on May 9 and the "day after Passover."

7. Ros_15_02_Kozlova. SEFER Field Research Archive (SFIRA). Interview recorded in Roslavl.

8. Ros_16_07_Ryklich. SEFER Field Research Archive (SFIRA). Interview recorded in Roslavl.

9. In 2008, there was a person like this in Nevel (Pskov Region), and many community members said that on the day of remembrance (the ninth of Av), he is asked to come and recite the Kaddish.

> Inf.: That's our regional pronunciation of Tishebov.
> Int.: What do people do at the cemetery?
> Inf.: They just stand there, ask Berezin to recite the Kaddish for their parents, he has it written out in Russian letters (Nev_08_027_Monosov) SEFER Field Research Archive (SFIRA). Interview recorded in Nevel.

10. Ros_15_02_Kozlova. SEFER Field Research Archive (SFIRA). Interview recorded in Roslavl

11. A St. George's ribbon is a small piece of brown and yellow cloth resembling the ribbon on the "For Victory over Germany in the Great Patriotic War 1941–1945" medal. Since 2005, these ribbons have been distributed among the public in commemoration of the victory in World War II.

12. Ros_15_01_Gamburg. SEFER Field Research Archive (SFIRA). Interview recorded in Roslavl.

13. Ros_15_05_Mirkina. SEFER Field Research Archive (SFIRA). Interview recorded in Roslavl.

14. See Belova, "Evreiskoe kladbishche v rasskazakh zhitelei Lepelia i okrestnostei," 109.

15. Nev_08_027_Monosov. SEFER Field Research Archive (SFIRA). Interview recorded in Nevel.

16. Smilovitsky, *Jewish Life in Belarus*, 166.

17. Inf. 2: In the summer, people go to the cemetery on Radunitsa, but in our tradition, it's a different day. For Russians, it's 9 days after Easter.
> Inf. 1: Sometimes it happens off the date.
> Inf. 2: Yes, for us, it's later, in June. This year, it was June 4th.
> Inf. 1: It just depends on the calendar for us.
> Inf. 1: We have a calendar, the Smolensk community sends us a calendar.
> Int.: Do you go to the execution site?
> Inf. 2: Yes.... They were shot January 9, and then on Victory Day (Mon_15_02_Cherniny) SEFER Field Research Archive (SFIRA). Interview recorded in Monastyrshchina.

18. See Belova, "Evreiskoe kladbishche v rasskazakh zhitelei Lepelia i okrestnostei," 108.

19. See Dymshits, "Evreiskoe kladbishche," 137.
20. This man is an engineer at a cardboard factory who was born and raised in Lviv and was sent to work in Surazh after finishing college.
21. Unech_17_01_Heifec_1. SEFER Field Research Archive (SFIRA). Interview recorded in Unecha.
22. Unech_17_01_Heifec_1, 2. SEFER Field Research Archive (SFIRA). Interview recorded in Unecha.
23. Unech_17_01_Heifec_2. SEFER Field Research Archive (SFIRA). Interview recorded in Unecha.
24. Unech_17_01_Heifec_2. SEFER Field Research Archive (SFIRA). Interview recorded in Unecha.
25. Poch_16_01_Medvednikova. To compare, from Monastyrshchina:

Inf.: Mama knew that Russian Radunitsa was a memorial day for us, and she'd dye eggs for it; she knew, but I didn't know anything. It was around August.
Int.: Would she give the eggs to anyone or anything?
Inf.: No. We'd eat the eggs ourselves and go to the cemetery.
Int.: Is this an egg for the grave?
Inf.: We went, our Jewish cemetery is separate from the Orthodox one.
Int.: What would the eggs be dyed with?
Inf.: Onion skins, what else could they be dyed with?
Int.: Did you play any games with the eggs?
Inf.: We'd knock them together, like in the Russian tradition (Mon_15_05_Lejtes). SEFER Field Research Archive (SFIRA). Interview recorded in Monastyrshchina.

26. Levin wrote that boys brought dyed eggs to the heder on Lag ba-Omer. Poor boys would bring two eggs—one for themselves and one for the rabbi—and rich ones brought more. The eggs were dyed with either onion skins or nettles. He also described a game with the eggs that has simple rules: one player lays down an egg with the pointed end out, and the second player has to hit it with the rounded end. Whoever egg cracks is the loser, and he must give his egg to the winner. Levin noted that this game was taken from Christians. See Levin, *Childhood in Exile*, 64–65.
27. See Amosova, "Nekotorye osobennosti kalendarnykh prazdnikov u evreev v Latgalii," 32–34.
28. "Papochka, tote, ekh beyt dekh, loyf in beyt in di kinde. Lomir zayt gezint, loz zey firn af der velt, lomir 'obm parnuse, loz zayn shtil af derr velt." Dymshits, "Evreiskoe kladbishche," 145.
29. Dymshits, "Evreiskoe kladbishche," 145.
30. Smol_16_07_Saksonova. SEFER Field Research Archive (SFIRA). Interview recorded in Smolensk.

31. Ros_15_02_Kozlova. SEFER Field Research Archive (SFIRA). Interview recorded in Roslavl.

32. Unech_17_01_Heifets_1. SEFER Field Research Archive (SFIRA), Interview recorded in Unecha.

33. Goldberg, *Crossing the Jabbok*, 139.

34. Guboff, "Obshchiny traura," 34.

35. Gavrilenko, "Blagotvoritel'nost' v evreiskoi pogrebal'noi obriadnosti," 137.

36. The author wants to thank Valeri Dymshits for this idea, which was expressed during a discussion of a paper at the 26th Annual International Conference on Judaica, in Moscow.

37. See, for example, Katz, *Litvish: An Atlas of Northeastern Yiddish*; Herzog, *The Yiddish Language*; for more on this, see Levin and Staliunas, "Lite on the Jewish Mental Maps."

38. Gitelman, "Thinking about Being Jewish in Russia and Ukraine."

39. For more on this, see Zeltser, *Unwelcome Memory*.

4

Why Hitler Did Not Like the Jews
The Folklore Version of the Reasons behind the Holocaust*

ANDREI B. MOROZ

In intercultural and interethnic relations, ethnic stereotypes play a decisive role in painting a portrait of the Other (the neighbor) and, through this characterization of the Other, in creating a self-image and a self-definition. Here, we define a stereotype as a "conviction about a social group or individual members of this group, which takes a logical form of judgment and ascribes certain classes of individuals specific characteristics or modes of behavior (or denies the presence of such specific features); it has a tendency toward emotional assessments and expresses itself in a peremptory, simplified, and generalized form."[1] In light of this definition, we may say that the ethnic (or even ethnoreligious) stereotypes of Jews in the western part of the Eastern European ethnocultural region are significantly fixed and functionally loaded. Studies of ethnic stereotypes conducted by Princeton psychologists Daniel Katz and Kenneth Braly in 1933; G. M. Gilbert in 1951; and Marvin Karlins, Thomas L. Coffman, and Gary Walters in 1969—the so-called Princeton Trilogy—demonstrated the fixedness of ethnic stereotypes and their capacity to change under the influence of the cultural milieu, independently of individuals' personal experience.[2] Students were asked to look at a list of characteristics and choose those that, in their opinion, applied to various nationalities and ethnicities. Many of the students made the same choices, and these decisions were not based on personal experiences of interethnic relations so much as their cultural background, including information from mass media. A group of researchers conducted a follow-up study using the same approach but a larger list of characteristics and saw a noticeable change in the nature of these stereotypes that was influenced by the changes in the structure of communications between ethnic groups as well as a number of other factors such as level of education and personal perceptions (accuracy of perception).³ Crises in interethnic relations, such as wars, produce changes in ethnic stereotypes as well.⁴

Among the Slavic population of the former Pale of Jewish Settlement, one of the most widespread and long-standing ethnic stereotypes is the stereotype of the Jew. Living close to Jews but differing from them in many areas fundamental to establishing personal identity—such as religion, customs, clothing, food, and occupations—facilitated the formation of a fixed stereotype of the Jew; the Christian Church also played a role. This stereotype, as described by Olga Belova, comprises the following important characteristics:

Jews:

- are born blind;
- are born in an unusual manner after an anomalous pregnancy;
- have no souls;
- have distinctive physical characteristics (including zoomorphic ones such as tails and horns);
- have a distinctive scent;
- follow "wrong" or awkward, from the Slavs' perspective, customs (such as getting married on piles of garbage);
- die at the hands of others and are buried sitting down;
- are associated with unclean animals (e.g., the legend of the Jewish woman who turned into a pig);
- associate with evil forces (Jews are kidnapped by a demon called *khapun* [catcher]; various demons take on the form of a Jew);
- have supernatural properties, can do magic and witchcraft;
- use blood in their customs and rituals;
- can bring luck and prosperity (the symbolism of encountering a Jew, the symbolism of dreams).⁵

The above stereotypes developed in Europe during the last thousand years due to a number of factors. The earliest accusations against Jews of murdering Christian children for the purpose of making matzos were recorded in the twelfth century.⁶ Rumors about those accusations as well as about the cases of Jews defiling the host undoubtedly contributed to antisemitic feelings and created the image of a dangerous and hostile neighbor. These rumors followed Jews as they migrated into Eastern Europe, where antisemitic stories about supposed Jewish plots were reinforced by the folkloric theater tradition, Christian visual arts, sermons, and even local hagiography.[7] The most striking relatively recent case is the story about the ritual murder attributed to Jews of a teenage boy named Gavriil, later canonized as St. Gavriil of Zabłudów.[8]

Yet these myths represent just one of the factors that have influenced the formation of stereotypes about Jews among the Slavic population of Central and Eastern Europe. The very situation of close contact and the inevitable interaction with the Other, the differences in religion, customs, calendar, and lifestyle called for a need to compare and interpret these differences. In a traditional culture, conformity to a particular pattern of behavior and engagement in local communal life mark the difference between "us" and "them." There appears to be a need to interpret the Other through discovering similarities and discrepancies, a kind of translation from the language of the foreign culture into our own language. The untranslatable becomes the marker of the stranger; it is the negative that becomes mythologized. In this context, as Olga Belova observes, "the identification of members of other ethnicities with demonological characters plays a significant role in the folkloric mythological mentality."[9] However, as far as one can judge from contemporary field research, folkloric ethnic and religious stereotypes are not the only factor defining interethnic relationships at the level of the neighborhood.

The stereotype of the Jew existed alongside individuals' personal experience, often contradicting it, yet it remained fixed and unchanging. For example, a Christian Slav might believe that Jews put blood in their matzo but still accept matzo from them and find it good, resolving the cognitive dissonance by reasoning that this matzo was different.[10] This confirms the idea of the weak correlation between stereotypes and personal experience.[11] At the same time, stereotypes can be elaborated on and evolve in response to external cultural, social, domestic, and other circumstances. Thus, following the Holocaust, the interethnic balance in the region radically changed. The Slavs' former ethnic neighbors were almost entirely wiped out, and the multiethnic and multicultural region became monoethnic and monocultural, which had a significant effect on the fixedness of the stereotype of the Other and its elements. Field research conducted recently in the former Pale of Settlement has shown that the basic structure of the stereotype of the Jew has been preserved, proving to be quite stubborn. However, in the absence of Jews, this stereotype has become a kind of tacit understanding and has ceased to inform people's behavior, slowly transforming into a theme for oral narratives from memory relating to a personal experience (*memorates*) and folk stories told for entertainment (*fabulates*).

Nonetheless, it is impossible to ignore the new components in this stereotype that make it evolve following the explanatory models that are characteristic of the local ethnocultural tradition. The tragedy that befell the Jews of Eastern Europe during World War II left its mark in the memory of their non-Jewish neighbors. The memory of these events has, to a certain extent, turned into folklore. Stories about the mass murder of the Jews are now passed down by people who did not witness this tragedy, and regardless of where these stories are recorded, they repeat the same fixed characteristics and details. Thus, in Belarusian and Ukrainian traditions, there are widespread stories about Jews portending a similar fate for their Slavic fellow villagers as they went to their executions. These prophecies often take the form of metaphors, such as *nami razvedut, a vami zamesiat* (they'll use us for mixing, but you will be kneaded, as with bread dough). In these stories, the Jews' submission to small convoys of men is explained by a local rabbi's call for obedience.[12] Stories about the execution of the Jews continue to be repeated, and memories of former Jewish shtetls are so alive that their present residents, even those born after the war, can point out former Jewish neighborhoods, homes, stores, and so on. Those who lived in surrounding villages recall Jewish merchants and purveyors of various goods, as well as Jewish holidays.[13]

This chapter will discuss how the residents of former shtetls and their surrounding villages account for the Holocaust today, what they see as the root of this tragedy, and how long-standing ethnocultural stereotypes about their neighbors of a different ethnicity and religion—who are not quite "one of us" but not totally "other"—affect their explanations. I analyze field materials gathered in a number of regions, primarily Belarus (the Vitebsk, Mahilyow, and Hrodna Regions), but also Russia (Smolensk Region), Poland (Podkarpackie voivodeship, formerly Przemyśl), and Latvia (Latgale). The earliest of these accounts is from 1984, and the rest are from 2009–17.[14] The informants were born between 1928 and 1963 and grew up in the localities where they were interviewed. All of them are ethnic Slavs (Belarusians, Russians, Poles) and Christians by confession (Orthodox or Roman Catholic), at least nominally. Thus, the majority of the informants either did not witness the Holocaust or were so young when the tragedy happened that it could not have affected their perspectives directly. Accordingly, their points of view derive either from their reflections on the event after the fact; the transmission of traditional knowledge; or a retelling of something they had recently seen, heard, or read.

There is no substantial difference between the stories about Jews recounted by the residents of former shtetls and by the inhabitants of villages. We are dealing here with a common tradition that is much wider in scope than our field research. The relative uniformity of opinion among informants can be seen in the field research conducted by our colleagues.[15] This can be explained by the fact that the informants' views represent not their individual interpretations based on empirical data but rather a peculiar elaboration on a mythology of World War II. This mythology serves as a conceptual framework not just for their general knowledge about ethnic neighbors but also for the personal interactions they have had with Jews and for the information they received from the older generation.

As far as I can judge, stories about the Holocaust in general and speculations about its causes in particular do not currently circulate widely for two reasons. On the one hand, they belong to a time long passed, which was witnessed only by a small number of our informants; on the other hand, there are no Jews left in the places where we conducted our field research. Jewish cemeteries are largely abandoned; houses have been rebuilt and are inhabited by local Slavic residents; memorials on the sites of Jewish massacres, though known to local residents, are rarely visited by them. Nevertheless, some background knowledge of the Holocaust is still present, and local residents can recall their former neighbors and the tragedy when an occasion for doing so arises.

As a rule, discussions of the reasons behind the mass murder of the Jews were not initiated by respondents. In the course of talking about the circumstances related to the Jews' executions—details of these murders, grave sites, and their memorialization—the interviewer would usually ask why Hitler or the Germans did not like Jews. Most people answered this question, and their answers were given either as claims based on a firm conviction or as theories the informants were not entirely sure of. In either case, the fixedness and repetition of the reasons for Hitler's antagonism given by informants across different regions point to the existence of a tradition of perceptions of the motives behind the Holocaust among Russian-speaking non-Jews. Forty-nine texts were analyzed; six contained several rationales for the same event.

In folkloric, quasihistorical texts, rationales meant to explain events or circumstances usually connect them either to a specific individual or a precedent event whose reverberations are felt in the rationale.[16] This can be observed in the case of the Holocaust as well. About half of the texts (twenty-three out of forty-nine texts containing fifty-five rationales) connect the reasons behind the Holocaust directly to the persona of Hitler. In all of these cases, informants speak of some contact between Hitler and Jews that as a rule took place in his childhood. The nature of this contact varies, but in all cases but one, according to the informants, it affected Hitler's life trajectory.

One of the more common explanations is childhood trauma. Informants reported that Hitler's stepmother, mother, or grandmother was Jewish and had a troubled relationship with him. As a result, he vowed to take revenge on the entire Jewish people when he grew up: "I was told that a Jewess abandoned him . . . she gave birth to a German, you know, Hitler. His mother was a Jewess, I heard, and abandoned him. So he grew up and he hated her ever since. He started hating her."[17] And: "His mother was a Jewess, you see, and she beat him all the time. They say, you know, that it wasn't really his mother, it was his stepmother. 'I'll get her back,' he said. Whether it's true or not, that's what people say. That, they say, is why he got so mad at them. And also because they were more cunning than him. That's what happened."[18]

The following example is illustrative of the cases where this justification is elaborated on with graphic details and attributed to Germans themselves, which is meant to make the rationale seem more plausible:

> One time, there was this German—the Germans were advancing on Russia and one of them knew how to talk our language and one time he told me all this. I remember, I was weaving on a loom, I was still little then. He started talking about how he doesn't like Jews. Germans don't like Jews. I said, "Why? They're people, too." I was, maybe, twelve at the time. "They're still people, they still don't want to die, why do you kill them?" That German said (was he a German or . . . anyway, he was dressed like the Germans), so anyway, he said, "Because his stepmother was Jewish! Hitler! And she was really bad to him. So he said, 'When I grow up and become president, I will destroy all the Jews in the world.'" I don't know if it's true or not, but that's what he said. How could they? The Germans don't like the Jews, but they're still people! We had so many of them here when the Poles were in power! And he said, "He didn't have a mother, he had a stepmother. She was a Jewess and she was bad to him. And he," he said, "went out to the garden to rip out . . . he got a stick and started hitting her flowers. She asked him, 'Why are you ripping up my flowers?' And he said, 'I'm gonna chop all of the Jews' heads off.'" That's what he said. That's what that German told us. They said that they didn't like the Jews because their most important president didn't like them. When they were advancing on Russia, they stopped over here and stayed a week in Matevchuki.[19]

These texts contain the standard folkloric figure of the evil stepmother who attempts to eliminate or oppresses her stepchild.[20] However, the role of the stepmother can be taken on by a grandmother or even a mother who abandoned the child. In some cases, the logical and expected connection between a child being mistreated and the subsequent genocide organized by him might be absent, and Hitler himself, or his wife, are ascribed Jewish origins. It is important to note that accounts that postulate that his grandmother was Jewish ("Hitler came to power and began killing Jews because his grandmother had been Jewish"[21]) or that his mother was, do not indicate the logical consequence of Hitler himself being Jewish. Instead, he is placed outside of his family and considered in isolation. The opposite is also true: if the story is that Hitler was Jewish, neither his mother nor his grandmother is brought up. Thus, if his mother or grandmother is Jewish and he is not, he is getting revenge on them by destroying their people, but if Hitler is himself a Jew, he hates his fellow Jews:

> INFORMANT: Hitler was a Jew himself. He himself... They kill the Jews, they need to destroy everything Jewish.
> INTERVIEWER: So you say Hitler was a Jew?
> INFORMANT: Well, you know, he was like a half-Jew somehow. And so that's what he ordered his men to do, he gave his orders and that was that. In Germany, they killed all the Jews right away, the ones who fled to other countries managed to survive.[22]

A second example illustrates a strategy to increase the authority of traditional knowledge by attempting to ascribe it to a book, though these references are not always reliable.[23]

> INFORMANT: Do you know how many books I've read? There: Hitler was a Jew, too.... Yes, Hitler was Jewish, too, and so he destroyed everything Jewish.[24]

However, we have no reason to completely dismiss the informants' credibility, particularly since the kinds of publications they reference do exist. For instance, accounts of Hitler or his mother being Jewish can be found in antisemitic publications such as *Voina po zakonam podlosti*, by Vladimir Chertovich. This book has many "accounts," often in the form of short, unsubstantiated theses, explaining a worldwide Jewish conspiracy and particularly Jews' plans to annihilate the Slavs. There, without references to even fake sources, the author simply states, "Hitler was Jewish on his mother's side. Göring, Goebbels—also Jews." It also says that "the Nazis were planning to kill only the Jews who did not support Zionism."[25] Similar claims are repeated by our informants: "Well, on the other hand... there are sides, people support the war... it was all financed by the Zionists in Israel. They had a good relationship with the Zionists and it was the other ones, all of these... where they're on Slavic, Eastern Orthodox lands, these Christian ones, they killed all of them."[26]

Informants who claim Hitler was Jewish usually see no contradiction and do not try to explain why someone would want to kill his own people—just the two facts are enough. However, in two cases, the informants offered explanations. These accounts apparently represent the individuals' attempts to create a logical connection. The first one goes as follows:

> INTERVIEWER: Why didn't Hitler like the Jews?
> INFORMANT: Because he was a bastard like that himself and didn't like people who were like him [*laughs*]. What's the big deal? It's . . . it's Hitler, what do you expect? It's in the past, long in the past. . . . You don't even want to remember it because it was so wrong what he did.²⁷

It is possible to see antisemitism in this example, even though on the whole, neither this informant nor any of the others exhibited even a trace of animosity toward Jews outside of repeating the fixed stereotypes described above. For this reason, "people like him" should be interpreted not as "bastards" but as "Jews."

The second text gives a more substantiated account. It underscores the fact that Hitler was a christened Jew, and it is this fact (being apostate) that led him to hate his fellow Jews.

> INTERVIEWER: They say that when the Germans were killing Jews, they knew exactly who was Jewish?
> INFORMANT: He's a fourth-generation Jew. You didn't know that? You should. Hitler was . . . his grandpa was a Jew. So write that down, he was a fourth-generation or third-generation Jew. That's a fact, one hundred percent.
> INTERVIEWER: So why did he kill Jews then?
> INFORMANT: Well, as someone (maybe Lenin) said, the ones that are, what's it called, christened, who went from Jewish to Russian, like that Volfovich [Zhirinovsky], they're even madder at them, at the Jews. Just like that . . . geez, what's his name again . . . the one in Ukraine, Ma . . . no, not Manakholny, but . . . uh . . . [*tries to remember*] he has that long last name . . . well, anyway. So he's a Jew, too, and . . . there was even a story when in Kiev someone had done something bad to a Jew. So those Jews there disowned him, but he's considered Ukrainian because . . . this is another one of those things . . . like Adolf Hitler . . . he's not the first sort (*ne pervogo razliva*). So there. Kolomoyskyi! So you . . . Jews excluded him from your special groups. You kept him out.²⁸

Hitler's wife is also sometimes said to be Jewish. Those who claim this do not, as a rule, know or concretely articulate the details of his married life: "Who knows why he attacked the Jews, God damn him. Who knows why he hated them. I thought his wife was Jewish. That's what they say. But he killed everyone and himself anyway."²⁹ In these kinds of texts, it is never claimed that there were conflicts between Hitler and his wife that grew into hatred for the entire Jewish people. It is possible that ideas about Eva Braun's nationality arise from her name; however, our informants never referred to the relatively recent DNA tests to determine Braun's ancestry. The results of these were published in 2014 and disseminated rather widely online, although it is highly unlikely they would have reached our informants.³⁰

Hitler's hatred toward the Jews is sometimes attributed to other childhood experiences, particularly to being hurt in some way, causing him either psychological or physical injury. In these kinds of accounts, we see the common stereotypes of Jews as usurers, swindlers, or even conscious evildoers striving to harm people from other ethnic or religious groups. Hitler is forced to be dependent on Jewish creditors: "He was forced to beg and borrow from these Jews . . . and his relatives, to live a miserable existence."³¹ In other versions, Jews knock out one of his eyes or castrate him:

> INTERVIEWER: Why did Hitler dislike the Jews so much?
> INFORMANT: Who knows. People said that that . . . ugh, what's his name, Hitler, had one eye. They say that a Jew knocked his other eye out. But whether that's true or not, I don't know. But that's what people said.³²

> INTERVIEWER: Why didn't Hitler like the Jews?
> INFORMANT: Well, you know, people say, but this is like rumors, it might not be true, that Jewish doctors castrated Hitler. Whether this is true or not, I don't know.
> INTERVIEWER: They castrated him?
> INFORMANT: Yes. They castrated him, so that's why he ha(ted them) . . . he couldn't stand them.³³

This final accusation against Jewish doctors is possibly related to the fear of Jewish doctors stoked by the infamous 1953 Doctors' Plot (the criminal case of the Zionist conspiracy, fabricated by the Soviet authorities in 1953 against a group of prominent Soviet Jewish doctors accused of plotting and assassinating a number of Soviet leaders).

The search for the reasons behind the genocide might be directed not toward Hitler and his biography but toward Jews themselves and the characteristics that Slavic perceptions of them are founded on.³⁴ In this version, it is not Hitler's personal animus but how the Jews were seen by the Germans in general that is to blame. At the same time, these accounts ascribe to the Germans ways of perceiving Jews that are actually common among our informants. The mass murder of their Jewish neighbors is described as overly cruel but, in general, understandable and not without its reasons. In this sense, the informants differentiate themselves from the occupiers and contrast themselves to them, but they are inclined to see the logic in the circumstances they describe.

The most common account in this vein connects the Holocaust with the crucifixion of Christ; often, informants refer to the relevant passage from the Gospels (Matt. 27:25, "His blood be on us and on our children"). "The Gospel passage became a kind of leitmotif running through all the stories, bringing together 'blood libel' and the Holocaust, as an indisputable argument for the Jews' guilt. There is a contemporary narrative about this recorded in Podolia."[35] The author, Olga Belova, a Russian anthropologist who many years studied folklore stereotypes of Jews in the Slavic environment, goes on to cite the narrative that when the Jews were crucifying Christ, they said, "His blood be on us and on our children. This meant that their children would pay for the sin of those who crucified him. This was two thousand years ago, but that was why the Germans shot all the Jews. Jews were against this (Christian) religion. They have their own Jewish religion."[36]

This motif comes up regularly across the entire region studied and, apparently, even far beyond its borders: according to another informant, "The German, the Germans, that Hitler, didn't like Jews because they betrayed the Lord, they're traitors. They, the Jews, were the ones who crucified Jesus Christ. And he, Jesus Christ, was a Jew, too. But they didn't like him because he knew everything, helped everyone, he even raised the dead and healed the sick. He walked the Earth for thirty-three years and then he was crucified. And that's why the Germans didn't like the Jews, that Hitler. He ordered them to destroy them. And so they did."[37] Thus, Nazis become Christ's avengers, reestablishing the balance of historic justice. This claim is sometimes further supported by the idea that the Germans were very religious: "It was because the Yid had betrayed the Lo[rd] ... Christ the Savior. They said where he was hiding, though you know, we don't know, we weren't there. But I do know that the Yid sold out God. And Germans really believed in God, and so they really murdered them, especially during the war."[38]

According to a number of informants, Jews themselves acknowledged this connection, they understood their "guilt" and so were prepared for this turn of events: "The Jewish elders knew that what Hitler did was revenge for their impiety and their failure to adhere to the faith of Moses, because the young people didn't have beards and *peyes* anymore, and ate *treyf* meat—that's why this retribution befell them. It had been predicted before the war."[39]

These rationales are occasionally attributed to Jews themselves. For instance, Cała presents an account recorded in 1984 in the Przemyśl (now Podkarpackie) Province in Poland about a young Jewish boy whom a Polish (Ukrainian?) family had hidden during the war. He explained the tragedy that had befallen his people: "Oftentimes, Vintliuk himself would say, 'Our Jews killed the Lord Jesus, that's why they're tormenting us.'"[40] Stories specifically about executions of Jews, the destruction of ghettos, and the submissiveness with which the victims went to their doom also often emphasize that the call to not resist issued by rabbis or other leaders came from an awareness of the fact that the Jews were being rightfully punished for the crucifixion of Christ.[41]

Another reason cited for the Germans murdering the Jews was the latter's considerable craftiness and cunning. Jews are more cunning and wise than the Germans, which made the Germans hate them:

INTERVIEWER: Why did the Germans kill Jews?
INFORMANT: Because they were . . . more cunning.[42]

A second informant adds:
INFORMANT: Well, Hitler didn't like Jews [because] they're more cunning than him.
INTERVIEWER: More cunning?
INFORMANT: Yes, they are more cunning, and they wanted to take over all of his power so that . . . but Hitler didn't like them.[43]

Sometimes, the competition between the Jews and the Germans and their battle for supremacy can be explained thus: "They're both wise and so. . . . Well, they . . . see, they hated them a lot."[44]

Informants do not always explain what the Jews' alleged cunning entails, but in a number of cases, they connect it to another important aspect of the stereotype held by Slavs: that Jews do not like to work. It is important to note that by "work," our informants always mean working the land. Occasionally, those who live in cities will specify an urban equivalent to this type of labor. Other kinds of work—primarily trade, which, as is constantly repeated, is what the Jews did—do not count as work:

INFORMANT: They didn't want to work. Nobody wanted to do simple, honest work. Jews were always off somewhere . . . doing some shakher-makher [this implies that they were not working but stealing, selling, and secretly making deals]. Buy and sell—that's the kind of thing they did. . . . They didn't like to work like our simple people, and they had to work.
INTERVIEWER: Buying and selling isn't work?

> INFORMANT: Well, it didn't used to be considered work, it's only now that every other person you meet is a salesman.
> INTERVIEWER: What used to be considered work?
> INFORMANT: Well... some kind of traditional trade, probably, yes, because... and they... they had that... they'd do leatherworking like the Tatars. That, what's it... what did they call it in their language... making leather goods.[45]

Often, selling goods itself is seen as a form of deception:

> INFORMANT: [Jews] are people who don't like work. And Germans are a hardworking people. Plus they are *oshchukantsy* [swindlers], that's how they are. They did it to gypsies, too. They didn't put gypsies in ghettos because there weren't as many; they would just shoot them where they found them. But with them [Jews], they didn't like them because they were cunning, more cunning than Hitler, probably.... And they are, you know, incapable of working. The only thing they know how to do is lie and cheat.
> INTERVIEWER: Do Jews just lie and cheat, too?
> INFORMANT: What else do they do? Not a single one of them came to work on the building site.[46]

This is a fairly widespread perception.[47]

The Germans did not just see Jews as their competition; they were afraid of their intellect, cunning, and sense of their own superiority:

> INFORMANT: Not one of them did physical labor, they all only worked with their heads. That's why Hitler didn't want... He was afraid of them, that's why he annihilated them.
> INTERVIEWER: Who annihilated them?
> INFORMANT: Hitler. Well, he wanted to kill them, all of the Jews, because they were smart. They always said, "Stone houses for us and the streets for you."[48]

According to our informants, the Jews' intellect and cunning might have been applied to taking power in Germany; that is, taking down Hitler. Thus, we can see that the theory of a Jewish conspiracy has not escaped their attention, although it must be noted that it is only specifically mentioned in three of the interviews:

> INTERVIEWER: Why didn't Hitler like the Jews?
> INFORMANT: It must have been that they wanted to kill him at that point and he...
> INTERVIEWER: The Jews wanted to kill Hitler?

INFORMANT: There was an assassination attempt.
INTERVIEWER: What did they want to do to him?
INFORMANT: They wanted to eliminate him, actually, so that he wouldn't be in power.[49]

INTERVIEWER: Why didn't the Germans like the Jews?
INFORMANT: They say they were organizing an uprising in Germany . . .
INTERVIEWER: The Jews in Germany?
INFORMANT: Yes, the Jews.
INTERVIEWER: That was why?
INFORMANT: That was why they didn't like them and killed them. I'm . . . somebody told me that—I don't remember anymore.[50]

And: "And the Germans were worried, they were just scared they would . . . get into . . . how should I say it . . . their affairs . . . into their government or wherever."[51]

The conspiracy theory also explains another fear that our informants ascribed to the Hitlerites: they killed the Jews because of the similarity of their languages. The linguistic proximity made them afraid that Jews would understand what the Germans were talking about:

> INTERVIEWER: Did Jews only live in Kriychaw or did they also live in the villages around it?
> INFORMANT: There were a lot of them, and then they were all killed in the war. The Germans hated those Yids so much. . . . They could speak their language, I don't know. That's what people say. . . . They say that Yid language is like German . . .
> INTERVIEWER: You mean the Jews could understand how the Germans spoke?
> INFORMANT: Yes, yes.[52]

Despite their apparent diversity, the explanations of the tragedy provided by the folkloric tradition all refer to a very limited number of factors. None of these explanations contains an explicit accusation that Jews were guilty of what happened to them (the closest thing to such an accusation is a reference to the episode of the crucifixion of Jesus, which has medieval origins). Implicitly, however, without justifying Hitler, the informants express some justification for what happened by trying to find a reason in the Jews themselves. Yet it would be reductive to attribute these explanations exclusively to antisemitism. In his study of an 1823 child murder case in Velizh, Russia, Eugene Avrutin answers his own question about why all the Christian residents of Velizh could claim that Jews were culpable of ritual murder in the death of the three-year-old boy: "The answer has less to do with what is often referred to as anti-Semitism or with economic rivalries (although we should be careful not to dismiss the twin factors altogether) than with cosmologies of the time. Ritual murder accusations proved profoundly durable because of their capacity to mobilize fears and express popular worldviews."[53] The explanations of the Holocaust are an illustration of the same principle.

From these materials, we can see how the attempts to rationalize the killing of the Jews, which left a significant mark on Belarusians' cultural memory, employ all available traditionally developed mechanisms for making sense of the world. Combined with individual interpretations, both ethnoreligious stereotypes and narrative clichés borrowed from traditional, quasihistorical folklore provide the cognitive tools for comprehending the horrifying tragedy within a historical logic characteristic of folkloric consciousness. Thus, the tragedy witnessed by previous generations is transmuted from personal experience into the experience of an ethnocultural community. Based on these interviews, one cannot claim that the local Slavic population of the former shtetls has ever had a sense of guilt for not intervening on behalf of Jews during the Nazi occupation and transmitted this sense of guilt to their descendants. However, there is undoubtedly some compassion for their former Jewish neighbors in the stories about the reasons for the Holocaust. In the cultural-historical context under consideration here, the dichotomy "one of us vs. the other" (*svoi vs chuzhoi*) becomes a triad, "one of us vs. stranger vs. other" (*svoi vs inoi vs chuzhoi*), whereby the Nazis become the "others," and the Jews occupy the ambiguous position of "strangers" or "our strangers" (*svoi chuzhoi*), who are perceived as foreign, peculiar, wild, and sometimes even hostile but at the same time as a part of "our" ethnocultural space. This ambiguity is reflected both in the ambivalence of the attempts to explain the reasons behind the Holocaust (Hitler is guilty vs. Jews are guilty) and in the emphasis on the peculiar character of Jews, who could foresee the impending disaster, who were aware of their tragic fate, and who were prepared to accept it without resistance.

Abbreviations

ALF   Folklore Archive of the Russian State University for the Humanities
ASC   Archive of the Sefer Center
ATU   *The Types of International Folktales: A Classification and Bibliography Based on the System of Antti Aarne and Stith Thompson*, by Hans-Jörg Uther

UMCS Marie Curie-Skłodowska University, Institute of Polish Philology, "Ethnolinguistics Archive" Lab

Notes

* This research was made possible by grant RFFI No. 17–24-01004, "The Belarussian and Russian Ethnocultural Relationship in a Transnational Context."

1. Quasthoff, "Ethnozentrische Verarbeitung von Informationen," 38. All translations, unless otherwise noted, are my own.

2. See Katz and Braly, "Racial Stereotypes of One-Hundred College Students"; Gilbert, "Stereotype Persistence and Change among College Students"; and Karlins, Coffman, and Walters, "On the Fading of Social Stereotypes."

3. Madon et al., "Ethnic and National Stereotypes," 1007.

4. Hosokawa, "A Functional Theory of Ethnic Stereotypes," 16.

5. Belova, *Etnokulturnye stereotypy v slavianskoi narodnoi traditsii*, 10–11.

6. Bremmer, *The Strange World*, 3–4; see also Strack, *The Jew and Human Sacrifice*.

7. Avrutin, *The Velizh Affair*, 25.

8. Sviatoi muchenik-mladenets Gavriil Belostkskii. See "Akatyst. Życie I męczeństwo św. Gabriela Zabłudowskiego."

9. Belova, *Etnokulturnye stereotypy*, 213.

10. See Moroz, "Evreiskii Lepel glazami selskikh zhitelei," 35–36.

11. Madon et al., "Ethnic and National Stereotypes," 97.

12. Belova, "Istorichekaiai pamiat i sovremennyi folklor."

13. See Amosova, Andreeva, and Ivanov, "Evreiskaia religiia, religioznye praktiki i sinagogi"; Bazarevich, "Evreiskoe naselenie v narodnoi traditsii g. Ushachi"; Belova, "Byt i povsednevnost v rasskazakh zhitelei Glubokogo"; Moroz, "'Evreiskii tekst' goroda Velizha"; Moroz, "Evreiskii Lepel glazami selskikh zhitelei."

14. The accounts from 1984 are published in Cała, *Wizerunek Żyda w polskiej kulturze ludowej*.

15. Buszko, "Żyd żydem"; Tokarska-Bakir, *Legendy o krwi*; see also Aleksandra Arkhipova's paper "'Hitler Didn't Like Jews because of His Grandmother': Types of Historical Belief Narratives Describing World War II and the Holocaust on the Territory of the USSR," presented at the conference Jewish Field Research 2020: Theoretical and Empirical Frameworks at Moscow Jewish Museum and Center of Tolerance, December 16–17, 2020. Videorecording https://www.youtube.com/watch?v=tBeGCd8LoBI.

16. Nicolaisen, "Place-Name Legends," 147; Sokolova, *Russkie istoricheskie predaniia*, 253.

17. "Mne hovorili, sho i͡avrėĭka kinula ... rodila nemtsa, nu ėto, Hitlera. Mat' i͡aho byla i͡avrėĭka, i͡a slyshaŭ, i brosila i͡aho. Vot on vyros, s tekh por eĭ

nezanavideŭ. Staŭ nenavidet' eĭo." ASC, M. S. Krytsky, born 1956, Liepiel, Vitebsk Region, Belarus.

18. "Matka ĭaho byla zhydoŭka, panimaesh, i bila, panimaesh, nadta ĭaho. Kazhuts' use roŭna, panimaesh, shto ne matka to ĭaho byla, a machakha ĭaho. 'ĪA sil'na,—kazaŭ,—atamshchu.'... CHy praŭda, a taki razhavor byŭ. Paėtamu, en kazhuts', razzlavaŭsĭa na ikh. I shto ĭany khitrėĭshyĭa za ĭaho. Vot u chom dzela." ASC; F. M. Marchurkevich, born 1929, Zhaludok, Shchuchyn District, Hrodna Region, Belarus.

19. Eshche nekali byl nemets, ishli ĭany na Raseĭu, nemtsy, i byl nemets adin, umel pa-nashemu havarit', i neshta tak razhavarilisĭa. ĪA pomnĭu, sho krosna tkala, ĭa ще maláĭa byla. Neshta ĭon razhavarilsĭa, shto, znachit', zhydoŭ ne lĭubit'. Ne lĭubit' zhydoŭ nemtsy. ĪA kazhu: "A chamu tak? ĪAny vsĭo ravno lĭudi." Mne hadóŭ, mozhe, dvanadtsat' bylo. "ĪAny zh vsĭo ravno lĭudi, vsĭo ravno umirat' ne khochut, na shto vy ikh b'ĭote?" A toĭ nemets kazhe (chi ĭon tam nemets, chi ĭon... no ĭon vsĭo ravno adety tak, ĭak nemtsy), tak kazhe: "Patamu shto u neho byla machekha zhydoŭka! U Hitlera! I ochen' abizhala ĭaho." To ĭon skazaŭ: "ĪAk ĭa vyrastu i budu prėzidentom, to vsekh na svete zhydoŭ vyb'ĭu!" Pravdu ĭon kazaŭ—ne praŭdu, no ĭon raskazyvaŭ! No ĭak hėto—ne lĭubĭat' nemtsy zhydoŭ, vsĭo ravno ĭany zh lĭudi! Pri palĭakakh u nas zhe ikh skol'ko tut byló! A ĭon hėto kazhe, chto kazhe: "Byla u ĭaho ne mati, a machekha. Byla zhydoŭka, ĭaho abizhala. I ĭon, kazha, pashĭol u haród rvat'... vzĭoŭ palku i pa kvétkakh biŭ, a ĭana skazala: 'Na shto rvesh' ėtye kvetki?' A ĭon skazaŭ: 'ĪA vsim zhydóm holovy postináĭu!'" Razhovor taki byŭ. Hovoril hėtat nemets, raskazyvaŭ nam. Havarĭat, ne lĭubĭat ĭany zhydoŭ, patamu shto samyĭ hlavnyĭ prėzident ne lĭubit'. ĪAk ĭany shli na Raseĭu, tak u nas stanovilis', v Motevchukakh z nedelĭu staĭali. ASC; R. M. Tsivinskaia, born 1931, Minotovichy, Shchuchyn District, Hrodna Region, Belarus.

20. ATU 403, 404, 409, 412, 432, 450, 451, 480A, 510A, 511, 567A, 592, 708, 709, 720, 780B, 781.

21. Amosova "'Vot latish so staroverom posporili...,'" 26.

22. ASC; M. M. Bolshakova, born 1929, Preili, Latvia.

23. Moroz, *Narodnaia agiografiia*, 74–82.

24. ALF; V. V. Sedunova, born 1932, Amosenki, Rosson District, Vitebsk Region, Belarus.

25. Chertovich, *Voina po zakonam podlosti*, 116.

26. ASC; S. I. Zhuchinskaia, born 1963, Beshankovichy, Vitebsk Region, Belarus.

27. ASC; V.A. Soshnev, born 1951, Beshankovichy, Vitebsk Region, Belarus.

28. ASC; K. N. Belyaeva, born 1937, Liepiel, Vitebsk Region, Belarus. This text exhibits traces of the common tendency to ascribe Jewish roots to anyone who has achieved high social standing. C.f. the theme of the world Jewish

government, the Bolshevik state as a successful realization of a Jewish conspiracy, particularly Lenin's Jewish roots, as well as the widespread conviction that Vladimir Zhirinovsky is Jewish, which derives from a statement he made at a press conference before the presidential elections in 1991 that his mother was Russian and his father was a lawyer. This informant also mentions Ihor Kolomoyskyi, who was the head of the administration of the Dnipropetrovsk Region from 2014 to 2015 and holds Israeli citizenship.

29. "KHto eho znaet, ch i͡ao on navi͡azalsi͡a na evreev, khaĭ khvoroba na eho. KHto eho znaet, chto-to ne pol i͡ubil. Da, ne li͡ubиl on evreev. U neho zh zhena tozhe evreĭka byla vrode. Hovori͡at. Nu, a vsi͡o ravno on poubивal vsekh, и sebi͡a." ASC; E. M. Degtiar, born 1928, Jewish. Liepiel, Vitebsk Region, Belarus.

30. See, for instance, https://www.inopressa.ru/article/07apr2014/repubblica/eva.

31. ASC; Anonymous, Liepiel, Vitebsk Region, Belarus.

32. "A khto ikh znaet'. Ėto kazali, што ėtyĭ . . . ikhnyĭ . . . i͡ak eho—Hitler byŭ adnahlazyĭ, dak kazhut', zhid i͡amu vybiŭ hlaz. A ti ėto pravda, ti ne. No tak havaryli." ASC; O. B. Golovko, born 1931, Sloboda, Nepalsk District, Vitebsk Region, Belarus.

33. "Nu vot havorat'—nu, ėto tak khodit' panika, mozhe, ne—chto kastryrovali Hitlera i͡avrėĭskie doktory. A ti to pravda, ti to ne. [Kastrirovali?] Da. Vot kastryrovali, i͡on za ėto nena . . . ne moh perėnosit'. Ėto tak, no i͡a ne znai͡u, ėto tochno ili netochno. Vot." ASC; V. V. Beresten, born 1936, Beshankovichy, Vitebsk Region, Belarus.

34. See Belova, *Etnokulturnye stereotypy*.

35. Belova, *Etnokulturnye stereotypy*, 113.

36. Belova, *Etnokulturnye stereotypy*, 113.

37. "No nemets, nemtsy, Hitler ėtoĭ, eŭreeŭ ne li͡ubil, i͡any kak predateli Boha, i͡any kak predateli. I͡Any zh raspi͡ali, eŭrei, Iisusa KHrista. A i͡on zhe, Iisus KHristos, tozhe byl eŭreĭ. A i͡any svoeho plemeni . . . i͡any ne li͡ubili, chto on . . . chto ŭsi͡o on znaŭ, i on pomohal ŭsi͡o, dazhe mi͡ortvykh voskreshaŭ, bol'nykh vylechivaŭ. On khodil po zi͡amle tridtsat' tri hoda, pokuli i͡any eho raspi͡ali. Vot za ėto nemtsy i ne li͡ubili, Hitler ėtoĭ. I i͡on vot prikazyval, chtob ikh istrebli i͡ali, istrebli i͡ali ėtokh. Vot tak i͡any istrebli i͡ali." ALF; A. S. Bogova, born 1947, Kholmy, Velizhsky District, Smolensk Region, Russia.

38. ALF; N. M. Efimova, born 1934, Pogorelie, Velizh District, Smolensk Region, Russia.

39. "Starsze Żydy uważali, że hitlerowskie wydarzenia, to jest kara za ich nieuczciwość, za nieutrzymanie wiary mojżeszowej, bo młodzież nie nosiła bród ani pejsów, jadła mięso trefne i dlatego przychodzi kara. To było przepowiedziane przed wojną (Radymno, woj. przemyskie, 1984 rok)." Cała, *Wizerunek Żyda w polskiej kulturze ludowej*, 162.

40. "Często Wintluk sam mówił: 'Nasze Zydy Pana Jezusa zabili i za to nas tak męczą.'" Cała, *Wizerunek Żyda w polskiej kulturze ludowej*, 171–72.

41. Belova, "Istorichekaiai pamiat i sovremennyi folklor," 284–86.

42. ASC; I. I. Orekhova, born 1931, Hlybokaye, Vitebsk Region, Belarus.

43. ASC; V. A. Dubrovskaya, Hlybokaye, Vitebsk Region, Belarus.

44. ASC; V. V. Platonchik, born 1933, Hlybokaye, Vitebsk Region, Belarus.

45. ASC; G. F. Mikhalevich, born 1949, Hlybokaye, Vitebsk Region, Belarus.

46. ASC; Y. M. Botianovskaya, born 1930, Hlybokaye, Vitebsk Region, Belarus.

47. See Cała, *Wizerunek Żyda w polskiej kulturze ludowej*, 163.

48. "Każden żyd nie parał się, ten, pracą fizyczną mocno, tylko on zawsze głową. Na, dlo tego Hitler nie chciał, bał sie ich, dlatego ich wytępił. [Kto, kto ich wytępił?] No, Hitler no jak, kciał wymordować wszystkich Żydów, bo oni, oni mieli głowy do interesów i wszystkiego. Zawsze mówili: Nasze kamienice, a wasze ulice." UMCS; Bąk Zyta, born 1942, Krasiczyn, Podkarpackie Province, Poland. This saying, which is attributed to Jews in Polish nationalist discourse, expresses how the Jews presumably felt about Poles. See, for example, http://www.klubinteligencjipolskiej.pl/2013/07/wasze-ulice-nasze-kamienice.

49. ASC; A. V. Parfenovich, born 1931, Hlybokaye, Vitebsk Region, Belarus.

50. ASC; M. K. Ziaziulia, born 1929, Hlybokaye, Vitebsk Region, Belarus.

51. ALF; R. P. Timoshchenko, born 1936, Krasnopolye, Vitebsk Region, Belarus.

52. ALF; A. V. Rubanova, born 1939, Ivanovka, Krichaw District, Mahilyow Region, Belarus.

53. Avrutin, *The Velizh Affair*, 30

HLYBOKAYE: MEMORIES OF THE SHTETL

5

The Death of the Shtetl of Hlybokaye through the Eyes of Its Teenagers

JULIA BERNSTEIN

The Visual History Archive (VHA) of the University of Southern California Shoah Foundation Institute for Visual History and Education contains several dozen accounts from former residents of Hlybokaye taken in the late 1990s.[1] After the war, these former residents spent their lives in various countries, so the video interviews conducted with them by the foundation are in a number of different languages. Twenty interviews in Russian and English provide accounts of prewar and wartime Jewish life in the town. In this chapter, I focus on several interviews with witnesses, mostly males, born between 1923 and 1932. On the eve of World War II, they were still boys or teenagers with little experience of independent existence in the adult world, a circumstance that would affect their perception of the events. After the war, they had no one to return to in Hlybokaye and had to build their adult lives elsewhere, often in other countries. As a result, their memories were formed under the influence of the social perceptions of the societies they lived in after the war. At the same time, Hlybokaye remained in their memory as a place where they had received their first knowledge of the adult world from their family stories. This group of survivors includes children of families of different occupations and social statuses who have different perspectives on prewar life in Hlybokaye and on the subsequent destruction of its Jewish community. The purpose of this project is twofold. In this chapter I follow the testimonies of several former residents of the town, trying to reconstruct a picture of the life and death of Jews in Hlybokaye from the Soviet annexation of western Belarus in September 1939 to the end of the war in 1945. In the following chapter I redirect my attention from the events themselves to the different ways they are narrated. I closely examine the testimonies of two brothers, Zalman and Don Feigelson (after immigrating to the United States, they changed their last name to Felson, and Zalman changed his first name to Stan), who largely shared the same experiences but use different narrative strategies to talk about them.

The Informants

The informants who shared their testimonies for the VHA come from diverse social and cultural backgrounds. Iakov Sukhovolskii was the adopted son of wealthy businessman Gershon (sometimes remembered as Motke) Lederman, who became head of the Judenrat (Jewish council) during the German occupation.[2] Boris Glaz was the grandson of wealthy merchant Isroil-Iosl Glaz and the son of communist sympathizer Rakhil Glaz.[3] His mother was elected an assistant judge (*narodnyi zasedatel'*) in the local Soviet court in 1939 and was shot by the Germans during the early weeks of the occupation. Reuben Youngelson was the son of a wealthy businessman;[4] Zalman Feigelson (who later changed his name to Stan Felson) was the son of a poor tradesman;[5] and Israel Chanovich was the son of Ben-Tsion Chanovich, a *shoykhet* (ritual slaughterer) and mohel (person who performs ritual circumcision).[6] Dorothy Gordon, the only woman in my selected group, was the daughter of a small shopkeeper.[7] Chanovich managed to leave the Soviet Union on the eve of the German invasion; Sukhovolskii and Glaz stayed in the Soviet Union; while Youngelson, Feigelson, and Gordon survived the Holocaust and immigrated to the United States after the war. Occasionally, but not always, the accounts of the American witnesses follow the narrative in *Memorial Book of Glubokie*, by the brothers Michael and Zvi Rajak, who owned Hlybokaye's Jewish Gymnasium until 1939.[8] Their accounts also differ from the Russian-language Wikipedia entry on the Hlybokaye ghetto.[9] The extracts from the English-language interviews with Youngelson, the Feigelson brothers, Gordon, and Chanovich are reproduced verbatim in English; the extracts from the interviews with Glaz and Sukhovolskii are given in my translation from Russian.

Hlybokaye under the Soviets, 1939–41

All informants report that the Jews in Hlybokaye breathed a sigh of relief at the arrival of the Red Army. People were much more afraid of German antisemitism than they were of the Soviets. Zalman Feigelson recalls: "We didn't have too much fear about Russian troops. They were friendly to us, we were friendly to them." His father, however, was forced to shut down his store. Like many other Hlybokaye Jews, he fell into the category of "former traders," a class that was subject to political and social discrimination by the Soviet authorities. But Jews also had the opportunity to hold positions at Soviet institutions, and he found employment at the state agency for procuring grain. Boris Glaz's mother, Rakhil, went to work on the city council. She had been sympathetic to communist ideas, and Glaz recalls that some of her friends were "members of the underground communist party of Poland. She herself was not in the party, but was always around those people. She was very well-read, generous, and sociable. She wasn't home often; she was always busy. If someone in a poor family was sick, they had no money for a doctor, that was her concern. Some unlucky guy's horse gave out, he needed to raise money to buy another—my mother was there. A poor girl needed to have a wedding—and there she was again." At first, she welcomed the arrival of the Soviet state, but "after she met the new authorities who had come from the East [pre-1939 Soviet Union], her enthusiasm cooled. When she learned the new rules in full, when the district [Communist] Party committees were formed, she entirely lost her enthusiasm for all of that but still continued working. In the election for people's judges (*narodnye sud'i*) she was elected a member of the local court (*zasedatel'*)." On the city council, she was responsible for resettling the refugees flooding the town, and "there was a family of refugees from Poland or ... Vilnius living in almost every home." From the refugees, the town learned about the Nazi persecution of Jews in German-occupied Poland. Reuben Youngelson reports: "Not in the Russian newspapers. It was in the Jewish newspapers when Poland existed. With Russians we didn't have Jewish newspapers and Russian newspapers didn't write about it."

Stories about the nationalization of family businesses are often accompanied by remembrances of renewed relations with relatives living in the pre-1939 Soviet territories. Until then, there had been almost no contact between different branches of the families living in Poland and the Soviet Union. According to Feigelson, a letter to a town fifty kilometers across the Polish-Soviet border took longer to reach its destination than a letter to San Francisco. After the arrival of the Red Army, things changed: "My mother ... hoped to see her family. She has not seen them for twenty years. One sister, Vikhna, came to visit her from Polotsk with her husband, Moshe Magid.... He was a manager of a department store in Polotsk."

It seems that, under the threat of losing everything, the Jewish merchants of Hlybokaye were striving not only to reunite their families but also to hold on to what they could of their property. Dorothy Gordon, whose father was a shop owner, recalls: "When Russians came, people who had stores grabbed whatever they could from their stores and sent it deeper into Russia to their families. And that's how they dissolved their businesses.... In Russia everything belonged to the government."

Along with the fear of losing their property and belongings, beginning in February 1940, all well-off and educated Hlybokaye residents, including Jews, felt the threat of imminent deportation. Many of them fell victim to one of the four mass deportations from western Belarus, which took place in February, April, and June of 1940 and in June of 1941. The first deportation targeted Polish military settlers and forest workers. The second deportation affected Jewish craftspeople; the third, refugees from German-occupied territories, as well as doctors, engineers, teachers, professors, lawyers, one actor, rabbis, and members of Zionist parties and the Bund. Most of the victims of the fourth deportation were family members of those who had been arrested or deported earlier.[10]

According to Feigelson: "There was a rumor that they might send ex-business people to Siberia.... Once I got some burlap bags ... shook them well to get rid of dust because we were thinking of drying bread to take with us to Siberia. Some richer Jews and Poles were sent to Siberia, but, actually, they survived."

Gordon remembers how "entire families were put on trains and sent into the depths of Russia and Siberia." Iakov Sukhovolskii, who went to school in 1940–41, recalls how "they [the Soviet secret police] would come to school and take the children directly out of class. Their parents were already there [under arrest]. This came as a total surprise to us.... Everyone was in shock." The deportations stoked hatred toward Jews among the non-Jewish population. Because the Soviet administration did not trust Poles, most government posts in Hlybokaye were given to Jews. Almost all the policemen, for instance, were Jewish. Sukhovolskii remembers that "Jewish communists actively participated in the organs [Soviet secret police]." He reflects, "When something bad happens, the anger falls on the people who do it. If a Jewish policeman comes to take someone away, people will remember this for the rest of their lives, that it was Jews who came for them."

Those who evaded deportation were forced to adapt to the new order. At first, Gershon Lederman, Sukhovolskii's adoptive father, "was asked to organize the consumers' cooperative, then he was kicked out of it, because he'd been a bourgeois.... My brother Ierukhim graduated from school and went to Lvov to enroll in the mining institute. They wouldn't take him because of his class origins."[11] Youngelson's father's business was nationalized, and his house was seized. The family was forced to rent housing. His father got a job with a very meager salary, but the family was not poor because they lived on the money they made selling their secret stash of prerevolutionary gold coins on the black market. Youngelson recalls: "I played soccer, I went ice-skating and skiing, the same thing, but the only thing was . . . they didn't want to keep me in school because my father was a capitalist. My parents looked for protection from the people who used to work for my father to help me to stay at school, so I wasn't expelled." Polish teachers disappeared from the school, "some were arrested, and a Russian administration took over." Jewish life also changed dramatically: "There were no more Jewish schools or other Jewish organizations; Jewish charities were forbidden."[12] Sukhovolskii's bar mitzvah was modest: "In 1940, I turned thirteen. My father bought me *tefillin* and a *tallis*, but there was no ceremony [before the war, over one hundred guests had been invited to his older brother's bar mitzvah]. [Jewish] holidays were celebrated quietly. My father prayed at home. A large painting of the Wailing Wall hung in the corner he always prayed in."

Feigelson muses, "I think younger people attended the synagogue less than older people, because of propaganda. The synagogues stayed open. Altogether we had eight to nine synagogues in Hlybokaye, at least five big ones." He remembers the aggressive antireligious propaganda that led to fewer younger people attending synagogue. Young people were the main target of Soviet propaganda efforts. Sukhovolskii remembers the opening of Hlybokaye's Young Pioneers' Club and the wonderful Pioneer leaders Kalikova and Hana Fisher, who lavished attention on their charges. Children spent all their time there: "We were almost never home; all the usual routines at home had changed."

Some religious people could not tolerate their children's indoctrination into Soviet atheism. At first, they were able to send their teenage sons to study in the yeshivas in Vilnius. As Israel Chanovich recalls,

> At that time, many people were escaping from western Poland. My uncle and aunt and brother and sister-in-law landed near Vilnius [they were escaping from Warsaw]. My uncle was scared to go to Hlybokaye because he was known as a messenger of the Lubavitch rabbi. . . . Three people came to get my father's advice: two people who had a Jewish school, and the *melamed*. Half-asleep, I heard my father tell them that he was planning to send me to Vilnius. "What will he do here? He'll join the Komsomol and turn into a communist." . . . I went to Vilnius; two weeks later, they closed the border. I desperately missed home even though I was with my relatives. We were all part of the Lubavitch movement—there was a small Lubavitch yeshiva in Vilnius that had been there since before the war.

Later, Chanovich and a group of his fellow yeshiva students would travel to the Japanese consulate in Kaunas. There they received transit visas, which Vice Consul Sugihara issued to Jews despite it being forbidden by his government, and managed to leave the Soviet Union.

1941: The German Invasion of the USSR

When the voice of Viacheslav Molotov announced over the town loudspeakers that the Germans had invaded the Soviet Union, eleven-year-old Berl (Boris) Glaz recalls being very upset that this meant he would no longer be able to go to Polatsk to the regional Olympiad, a school competition for which he felt he was well prepared:

> My mother took great care to make sure that my sister and I . . . knew Yiddish literature well, that we learned how to read and write, for which we had a special tutor. We would go to him twice a week for two hours to study Yiddish. . . . Before the war, they held Olympiads all across the Soviet Union: kids sang songs, recited poems and monologues. The winners were chosen to go on to the next round. I had won the district tournament, reciting a monologue from [Sholem Aleichem's] novel *Motl the Cantor's Son* in Yiddish, and I was supposed to go to Polotsk to compete in the regional Olympiad. Katz, our Jewish literature teacher, had been practicing with me every day. The trip had only been a few days away.

Soon, the retreating Soviet Army began passing through the town. Glaz tells of the panic among the escaping soldiers, town administrators, and party workers:

> We retreated in panic. There were no units. The men came alone or in small groups. Tattered, hungry. Oftentimes, unarmed. They'd come into people's homes and were more or less decent. Just asking for food and water. People fed them. Then they moved on. . . . During the very first days of the war, the district committee, city council, and police all dropped what they were doing, got into their vehicles, and abandoned the town. . . . There was no mass evacuation. The town was left without any authorities, the radio didn't work. There was no connection with the outside world.

Mobilization was announced immediately. The town was left without a government, and people began looting shops and warehouses. According to Glaz, "it was mostly the non-Jews doing the looting. I ran from warehouse to warehouse. I was in the center of it all, and I didn't see any Jews."

Sukhovolskii remembers that people began settling their accounts with Jews and that Jews were now afraid to go into the countryside for food. Many Jewish families faced a dilemma: to evacuate or to stay. He explains this vacillation among his fellow townspeople and his parents' position on evacuation thusly: "When the Soviets were in power, some people began to view the situation negatively. So some people vacillated. Some wanted to evacuate, others didn't; it depended on many factors. . . . For our family, there was no question."

For the Glaz family, the question was difficult: Rakhil Glaz understood that when the Germans came, she, as a Soviet local administration worker, would be punished. And still, she decided to stay in Hlybokaye to avoid tearing her family away from their household. "I don't want you to suffer just because I was an assistant judge," she said, according to her son.[13] After this, events unfolded "with terrifying speed.... The German motorcycles appeared on July 2nd."[14] Glaz describes his first encounter with the Wehrmacht:

> The Germans' cars didn't really stop, there was no pillaging. The German soldiers paid no attention to us at all. Then the bicycle units came. They would stop, come into the yard. We had a well, they asked for water... I remember a group of Germans came into our yard and asked for water. We brought them a bucket of water, a cup. One German said, "You drink it." Our parents did. "Give your children the water." They gave some to me and my sister. After that, they were willing to drink it themselves.... They didn't ask for anything but water. They didn't steal anything.

Sukhovolskii remembers how, during the first days after the German incursion into Hlybokaye, "Jews were afraid to go out. Then [Germans] started coming for them, grabbing people to do certain jobs. They established the *komendatura*.... Recruited a police force made up of Poles and Belarusians." Jews were ordered to wear a white band of fabric on their sleeve. Relying on people who were willing to report on others, the military authorities began "arresting Soviet activists," among them Rakhil Glaz.[15] "Several days later, they arrested completely innocent people. It was the local non-Jews reporting on them, saying 'they're communists,'" recalls Gita Geseleva.[16]

Boris Glaz remembers his mother's arrest and visiting her in jail, which was the last time he ever saw her:

> When the Germans came, people we knew from the local police warned her that she'd be arrested. She left to go to her cousin's house in Dunilavichy. Two days later, they came for her. My father said that she wasn't there, so they took him, instead. When my mother found out, she came back. Two locals [non-Jews] turned her over to the German authorities after seeing her come back to town. They let my father go. He was able to talk a policeman into letting us see her late at night. A solitary cell, August, cold; my mother came out in her gray autumn coat, full of life, and told us that she would serve a few years in a concentration camp, then come home. She forbade us to cry. I was eleven, my sister, thirteen—that was the last time I ever saw her. Those policemen told my father that she was shot with thirteen other town activists soon afterwards.

A short while later, a German civil administration headed by the *Gebietskommisar* arrived. The administration had departments that, according to Youngelson, were called "Deutschtum, Judentum and Christentum." A new system of city governance was established, and the German administration began issuing orders targeting the Jews: "With his [the *Gebietskommissar's*] arrival, the persecution became more organized.... The white armband was replaced with a yellow circle—a badge—then they said it had to be a Star of David [sewn on the left side of the chest and back]. When you ran into a German—and later, any Aryan—you had to take off your hat. Jews were not allowed to walk on the sidewalk."[17]

The order to remove one's hat when encountering an Aryan led to the death of Glaz's father's younger brother: "He was walking down the sidewalk, and he didn't take his hat off in front of a German. The German stopped him, admonished him, and shot him on the spot."[18]

With every new order, the daily life of the Jews grew more constricted and frightening. As Glaz reports:

> The decrees would be posted in the streets. There were special posts for announcements in the center of town, and on the outskirts, they'd be on the electric poles and the walls of buildings. Jews were only allowed to go to the market after noon. By then, most of the food was gone. Gold and silver had to be handed over to the authorities by all those whose names were on their list. The authorities had a list of the town's affluent Jews, and next to each wealthy Jew's last name, it said how much gold and silver they were required to give. People were allowed to keep minimal amounts of flour, sugar, and things like that, but they were required to hand over everything else. Give up everything made of wool. Failure to do so resulted in being shot. Any failure to follow these orders was punishable by death. Our neighbors were shot for not handing over all of their wheat. After the decree was issued, they loaded their wagon with grain and had wanted to try to take it somewhere.

To deal with the increasing pressures, some Jews attempted to resort to their tried and tested methods for dealing with discriminatory authorities: to become economically valuable to them. Through personal connections in the non-Jewish world, they offered their services to the municipal administration. According to Sukhovolskii, "Using the petitions, the Jews themselves attempted to organize labor for the Germans. At first, this wasn't work at the factories or workshops, as there were very few of them. It was loading and unloading jobs and fixing the roads." His adoptive father, Gershon Lederman, the future head of the Judenrat, was one of those who got this kind of work.

After one day of work and the beatings that followed, he was brought home on a stretcher.[19]

The Ghetto

At the end of September 1941, a ghetto was established in the town's poorest neighborhood.[20] Jews whose homes were outside the ghetto started looking to trade houses with non-Jews who lived inside.[21] Glaz's grandfather "had a very, very big wooden house. It was split in two parts, with a big kitchen in between them. In one half, it was my grandpa, grandma, and their unmarried children, and on the other side, it was the families of his married sons. It was a rich house with beautiful drapes, chandeliers. For Jewish holidays, all the children and their families would gather in that house. There was a huge dining room seating up to forty people." Now the whole family had to move into an old, run-down two-room house that had previously belonged to a poor Belarusian cobbler. In exchange, the Belarusian received the large, rich home of Glaz's grandfather.[22] However, the Glazes only owned part of their new house, one room measuring six square meters; the second room housed an eight-person family.

Sukhovolskii recalls the formation of the ghetto and moving to it:

> The neighborhood between Vilenskaia and Lumzhinskaia Street was designated as the ghetto. At first, it wasn't fenced off—it wasn't until 1942 when they started building a fence, and then they totally blocked it off in the second half of 1942, when they built a formidable fence with barbed wire on top. Housing ... was a problem. Those who had relatives in the ghetto would move in with them. If they didn't have relatives already living there, they needed to find people willing to take them in. ... We had only a short time to move into our new homes. ... People took what was available. You wouldn't believe how the streets looked. Furniture, home goods—all of that lay on the street because people only took the bare necessities. ... The locals stood and laughed at us. The Germans went around taking photos of how "half-humans" behaved—as they said, "Halbmensch." It was theater to them. To us, it was a grave shock.

An unnamed Jewish police force was created at the same time as the ghetto.[23] According to Youngelson, the head of this force was named Yudah Blant. Feigelson knew several Hlybokaye Jews who were in the Jewish police: "I don't remember anything negative about them. Some of them later dropped off the police and went to partisans. I tried to avoid them because, as long as I had nothing to do with them ... on account of their job, they had to be pretty cruel."

The Jewish police force was under the jurisdiction of the Judenrat, which was established around the same time. Sukhovolskii recalls the election to the Judenrat, which he was present at with his father. "One day, they said that representatives from every family had to come to Kopanitsa. The gathered Jews were to elect the Judenrat. Remarkably, the Germans showed great respect at the arrival of our rabbi, Reb Katz. They brought him a special chair and sat him in it. Everyone else stood. Candidates were nominated. I remember some names, my father was also elected. Shundl Misin, Shaul Geifer, Khaim Rubashkin, Khaim Olmer—these were respected citizens. Afterwards, all of ghetto life was organized with the help of the Judenrat."

Youngelson says that his father was also offered a seat on the Judenrat, but he refused because he did not want to serve as an instrument for forcing the ghetto's Jews into compliance. Feigelson believed that Lederman's reputation as an experienced businessman and his knowledge of German were important reasons for his appointment as head of the Judenrat. His recollections of the Judenrat are neither accusatory nor apologetic. The role of mediator between a merciless aggressor and a helpless victim left no room for humane behavior. He recalls: "The Germans, for example, would give a list of what they wanted to the Judenrat: money, gold, furniture, bicycles. Everybody knew what everybody had—this was a small town. So, the police had to go to who they thought had things and to force them to give whatever the police needed. . . . So, the Germans took our cow away right after they came to Hlybokaye." Glaz accuses the Judenrat of directly collaborating with the Germans: "When young people went off to join the partisans, the Judenrat would tell the Germans the last names of their relatives. Those people would be shot."

Sukhovolskii, whose stepfather served on the Judenrat, emphasizes the self-sacrificing attempts of the Judenrat to save as many Jews as possible and tries to indirectly refute these accusations. Speaking in the 1990s at his home in Kaliningrad, Russia, he feels the need to correct the record regarding the Hlybokaye ghetto: "Today, there is a lot of new literature. I think that everyone who remembers what happened, and finds mistakes in the literature on this subject—and I have seen such mistakes—must try to correct them. It might not be that important to our descendants, but the truth must be established. Because a history book can contain a lot of distortions. It depends on who is writing it and what the author's biases are."

When speaking of the time after the liberation of Belarus by the Soviet Army, Sukhovolskii repeatedly emphasizes that he never hid the fact that he had been in the ghetto but that, at the same time, he never told anyone about what occurred there: "The men serving with me [in the Soviet Army] knew that I'd been in the ghetto. But I didn't tell them anything else. At work, they also knew that I'd been in the ghetto." It is likely that, having survived, he preferred to distance himself from his painful past, which, at the time, could have put him in danger with the Soviet authorities. When he decided to tell the truth in his testimony to the Shoah Foundation, he confessed: "All of these years I have been living in that past. I anxiously take in everything related to it. I repent for my mistakes because I believe that I hastened the death of my parents."[24]

Sukhovolskii's story of the Judenrat begins with his recollection of one of its first meetings, which he attended with his adoptive father, Gershon Lederman: "I witnessed a discussion among these respected men—there were twelve of them—about how to go on living, what they should do. There were hotheaded ones who believed that we should not work for the Germans, that we should resist. But they ended up coming to the conclusion that the dilemma before them was either to submit to the authorities and work with them or die a beautiful [i.e., heroic] death as a community." The Judenrat came to its decision with great difficulty, their sense of responsibility for the elderly and the children winning out in the end:

> The issue was clear: in order to survive, we needed to work.... By then, we only had one little tannery, a small wool-spinning factory, a mill, and an electric station—not many enterprises. The question was where they could employ that many people. The majority of these people didn't have any special skills—they'd been traders, for instance. Teachers, doctors. These people had to quickly become accustomed to a new way of life, they had to be able to work.... They decided to make the greatest possible efforts to attract as many specialists in various fields as possible and organize different kinds of manufacturing on the weak foundation found in Hlybokaye.[25]

It was decided that they would start making linseed oil and create workshops where people would make clothes, shoes, and knit stockings. At a certain point, there was a small enterprise called Goldkreizer, where people collected medicinal plants. "Jewish girls sorted the plants and then all of this was sent off [to Germany]." They expanded the tannery.[26] Former ghetto prisoner Dorothy Gordon worked in the group of knitters:

> At one time they asked for young girls who know how to knit. And there was a lady in charge ... she was a Jewish lady, she was very, very nice. And she organized a group of girls who were knitting sweaters. I asked her if I could belong to the group because I knew how to knit.... And we stayed inside as a

group, maybe thirty girls. We had a house and we had to check in every morning at seven o'clock.... We knitted sweaters and they had to be done in five days. They were sent to the front for German soldiers. The soldiers supplied the wool from the people who lived in the villages. They used to tell us exactly how they wanted it done.... And I was very grateful because I didn't need to go outside anymore and work hard in the fields.... We called ourselves "the knitting girls."

The Judenrat arranged to feed the ghetto's needy and opened a hospital.[27] Thanks to its efforts, everyone—even minors—was able to work and therefore receive a bread ration card and an identification card. Sukhovolskii concludes that "practically everyone who wasn't working at the German warehouses, the railroad, doing loading operations, or at the meat-processing plant, which had been functioning since before the war, practically everyone else was also active and working."

In addition to looking after Hlybokaye's Jews, the Judenrat was also responsible for refugees from other towns and settlements who "had nowhere to go" after the destruction of their communities.[28] As an example of this, Sukhovolskii tells the story of the fate of the refugees from Sharkaushchyna: "Half an hour before the Germans managed to fully surround the town, Jews... set their houses on fire and ran into the forest. Some of them were shot, and those who survived were later killed by the locals. They couldn't survive in the forest under those conditions, and eventually they ended up in the Hlybokaye ghetto." He remembers that some of the refugees came "organized" because the Germans would sometimes "give Jews permits to go and gather these refugees." Sukhovolskii cannot explain the motives of the German authorities, but "for Jews hopelessly dying of hunger, this meant salvation."

By the end of 1942, by Sukhovolskii's calculations, the ghetto had two thousand Hlybokaye Jews and almost six thousand from around the region: "We had Jews from 42 cities and mestechki, including Bialystok, Vilnius, and around the entire region. In addition to our relatives, we had about fifteen people [living with us], and then the survivors arrived, and we ended up with around thirty. They came practically naked and with nothing. They also needed jobs, and they got used to life in the ghetto in hopes of *a nes*" (Yiddish for "miracle").

Feigelson speaks of the value the Judenrat placed on productivity: "They organized all kinds of factories in the houses on Vilno *gas* [street]. They were producing different things for Germans. They were trying to find all kind of jobs.... We were trying to be useful. The psychology of the Judenrat was 'you don't kill a milking cow.'"

The job twelve-year-old Zalman Feigelson and his brother Don had cutting wood was considered very good because they could go off into the forest without supervision.[29] Fifteen-year-old Reuben Youngelson carried water for German gendarmes and tended to their garden.[30] Boris Glaz's father had a deal with the Judenrat that eleven-year-old Boris could work instead of his older sister Mira. Their father was afraid to send her to work "because there were often rapes."[31] Along with everyone else, Boris cleaned the streets, loaded and unloaded grain, and cleared snow in the winter. Even though all these boys were younger than sixteen, which was the age when work became compulsory for everyone, they worked to earn their bread ration cards.

Glaz recalls the ration that each individual in the ghetto received: "Two hundred grams of unhulled oat bread and a tiny bit of grain." Getting enough food was a constant struggle, although the hunger experienced in the ghettos of larger cities like Warsaw was more severe than in Hlybokaye. Feigelson does not remember "being hungry. We used to make 'Stalin's cutlets' [cutlets of bread, onions, and bread, but no meat]. There was oil, we must have been getting some rations of oil and bread." Youngelson's family, who managed to hold on to some money in the ghetto, was able to buy food on the black market. He remembers: "In the ghetto it was black market food.... There were no stores. There was no market.... It was the Jewish people who used to smuggle some products into the ghetto, make business, make money. I am ashamed to say, there were people who became rich on the suffering of other people."

It was not often that someone could take advantage of the black market, but many came to use their children to get food for their families, as it was easier for children to get around outside the ghetto unnoticed. Feigelson remembers: "In the winter of '41 I rented a horse and a sledge and went to a friend of ours, his name was Marko.... I went to him to Gvozdovo about seven kilometers from our town. I was wearing pelts with the fur inside. I took away my Star of David and went to him. He gave me a sack of flour. So, we had flour for bread."

Glaz also brought groceries into the ghetto, given to his parents by their friends on the outside: "This was risky because if they stopped someone at the entrance to the ghetto and caught them bringing in food, he'd be punished. One time, I got through the German cordon, but then, on the inside, the Jewish policemen found a loaf of bread on me. They took me to the police station and brutally beat me. But still, I continued bringing food to my family."

Getting groceries was particularly difficult for observant Jews. Not all the food available in the ghetto was what they could eat. Thus, Feigelson's mother refused the soup that the Germans, for whom they worked, allowed her sons to take home: "I ate this food, but I think my mother still kept kosher."

According to Feigelson, religious life in the ghetto was very active: "We could not go to shul, they were all outside of the ghetto. At any one time, I bet, in fifty or a hundred houses, there were minyanim. My father continued his observance."

It was not only the unkosher food that made life in the ghetto particularly miserable for religious Jews. Quite soon, as Sukhovolskii recalls, the Germans issued a decree forbidding burials at the Jewish cemetery. And still, many people continued to live according to religious law as best they could, gathering for prayer and celebrating holidays. Glaz recalls: "People didn't celebrate the Sabbath as they had before, of course. Because people had to work that day, too. I remember very well how we made matzah at home, although it was rye. People celebrated Passover. It wasn't a happy Passover like before, but it was tradition."

No matter how difficult the circumstances were at first, it seemed like the Judenrat's strategy would help save most of Hlybokaye's Jews. According to Sukhovolskii, "Those who wanted to believed that they just needed to bide their time and then they would suddenly be saved. . . . They waited . . . for the opening of the second front." Occasionally, the Judenrat managed to go around an anti-Jewish order using their prewar connections with non-Jews. As a rule, Jews had to pay generously for their helpers' assistance, as Sukhovolskii recalls: "We had a well-known paramedic, Esei Geller, . . . Vandt, he had a store, and then two others. Out of nowhere, they were taken and shot. We didn't know where they were. People said they were in jail. One of their wives came to my father, 'Help us at least get their bodies.' . . . It required a bribe and so on . . . but they managed to get the bodies." Theirs were "the first and last burials at the Jewish cemetery. After that, people were no longer given funerals."[32]

A bribe from the Judenrat to the military or civil administration would occasionally allay a threat to the entire ghetto. Sukhovolskii speaks of one such lucky deliverance: "In May 1942, Gestapo troops in black jackets appeared in Hlybokaye. They were called 'black students' because of their uniforms. In the town, people learned of this, and there was great tumult. People knew that their arrival was connected to pogroms and executions. The Judenrat was able to make them good gifts and so on, and so they left." Speaking of the mood in the ghetto at that time, Feigelson concludes: "There was one word that all the people used to say: *iberlebn*, to survive." Hopes of survival began to fade when one day, without any particular justification, the Germans "went around people's houses, took 110 people and shot them," Sukhovolskii recalls. His grandmother and grandfather were among those executed. "This was the first blow of that kind, they took 110 people," he says. Later, they learned of a mass execution of a large group of Roma. "They were also led past the ghetto and then, suddenly, there were screams and wailing. They were also taken to the Borok [forest] . . . and shot there."[33]

This execution in the ghetto took place on March 19, 1942, around the same time that, according to Glaz and Sukhovolskii, the Germans ordered the creation of a second ghetto for elderly people: "There was a second ghetto, Staraia Kiseleika. The two ghettos were separated by a street. It had a separate fence around it. There was communication between the ghettos. People with parents there would visit them there. They [the Germans] would let them in, you didn't need anything special [a permit]. . . . The great tragedies, the soul-rending scenes that took place when these old folks were moved to the second ghetto, that was another matter."[34]

A month later, all the elderly people from the second ghetto were taken to the Borok Forest and shot. When they learned that the elderly were being taken somewhere, the boys, including Glaz, ran to watch: "Rabbi Katz sat on the wagon. He was very old and, apparently, not very healthy, he couldn't walk, his lips were moving, he was praying. His wife sat next to him." Sukhovolskii recalls these events differently. He believes that Rabbi Katz was in the group chosen to be shot during the mass execution on June 20, 1942. According to him, the population of the second ghetto was killed immediately after this execution, which only affected people from the first ghetto:

> On June 20th, there was an order that all working people and their entire families were to come out to the Sportplatz athletic field for reregistration. Some people were afraid and didn't come, so they went around the apartments and chased everyone out. Those who had proof that they worked considered themselves untouchable. One of the Gebietskommissar's assistants stepped forward. "Don't worry. Nothing bad is going to happen to you. We're just sending some of your people to work in Polotsk and Orsha." People did not really believe this. Over 4,000 had come out to the field and they started separating them . . . sending some to the left and others to the right. Those who had a *Schein* (proof of work) were sent to the right with their families, and those without *Scheins* were sent to the left. After a while, they started sending those with *Scheins* to the left, as well. Our rabbi, Reb Katz, was in that group. . . . Suddenly, right in front of us, those who remained, they put those who'd been sent to the left on their knees and started dividing them into groups. . . . These people, and there were over 2,000 of them, were taken to the Borok [forest] in groups and shot there. On the road to Borok, which led past a lake, many people threw themselves into the lake. . . . In Borok, the ditches had already been dug by non-Jews. They'd brought in peasants.

Feigelson believes that twenty-five hundred people were shot, while Glaz recalls that there were four thousand victims. The latter recalls: "We went home. Several hours later, we started hearing machine gun fire from the direction of Borok. Everyone realized what was happening." Feigelson: "There are no words to describe the fear, the anger. Just . . . it was unbelievable." Sukhovolskii remembers that after the execution everyone shut themselves up in their homes. Several days after the executions, the Jewish police announced that people could come and collect the clothing of those who had been killed. Boris Glaz's father's unmarried sister and two brothers were killed in this execution, one along with his whole family, and the other with his pregnant wife. Neither Glaz's father nor sister went, but he ran there. He "found the coats of my little cousins Isrolik and Moisey, Musya's short fur coat, Mariasha's jacket . . . I didn't take anything. I went home and told my family." Feigelson's memory about the episode with the clothes of those who had been shot includes a further detail. Because many had thought that they were going to be sent to work somewhere, they had dressed in their best clothes and hid valuables in them. After the executions, those who survived "had to find all of it."[35] Sukhovolskii describes how the belongings of the executed were processed: "The clothes of the executed were taken to warehouses next to ghetto, then Jewish women were supposed to put those clothes in order. Sometimes, a woman would come upon the bloodied shirt of her husband or son. The clothes were washed, ironed, and stockpiled. Then they were sent to Warenkauf, the store for Germans, police officers, and various German civil servants, and sold to them in accordance with their documents."

Naturally, in this horrific situation, many people, particularly the young and those without families, thought of escape. Trying to think of how he could escape, Feigelson bought from Jews who worked at the printing house "a piece of paper that you could fill in. It was stamped. Like a false passport." His mother gave him the money to buy it, a gold five-ruble Tsarist coin that they had put away "for a rainy day." But after he got the document, he realized that he would not be able to use it: "To write a name would have been easy, but I didn't know where to go. I felt safer in the ghetto. Also, although I speak Polish and Russian, my *r* is Jewish; they can tell. So, I didn't pursue it."

Some people knew of the partisans hiding in the forests. Feigelson, for instance, knew about them because when he came to work, he "read some bulletins talking about lots of partisans around Polotsk, which is ninety kilometers from our town. They said, 'thousands of partisans.' It was in German." Jewish refugees from surrounding small towns had more contacts with Belarusian peasants and through them knew and could provide information about the partisans.³⁶ According to Sukhovolskii, "At that time, it was hard to escape to the forests because there weren't that many partisans to begin with and, on top of that, they wouldn't take you without a weapon. Plus, they only took those who could fight."

The partisans were reluctant to take Jews into their ranks, particularly in the first year of the war. While widespread antisemitism played a role, there was also the consideration of the risk involved, because Jews attracted attention with their appearance and accents. Moreover, an influx of untrained civilians would decrease the military efficiency of a unit. In August 1942, the State Defense Committee issued Order No. 189 On the Objectives of the Partisan Movement, which stated that partisan "units are obligated to accept all honest Soviet citizens striving towards liberation from the fascist yoke." Order 189 opened the doors into the partisan ranks for those few Jews still alive by the late summer of 1942. In the first nine months of the war, over half of urban ghettos were destroyed, and the majority of Jews had either been murdered or had escaped from the occupied territory.³⁷ After this order was issued, partisan commanders became more willing to take Jews into their ranks.

It was not only the fear of not being accepted into a partisan brigade that kept Jews from escaping the ghetto, nor was it not knowing where to run. It was also fear for family members left behind in the ghetto, who were threatened with execution in cases like this. After Feigelson escaped the ghetto and joined the partisans, he came back to take his mother and younger brother out of the ghetto. But his family members who still remained in the ghetto were shot: "They arrested my father, aunt, cousin, and they were also shot. As punishment. And after that happened the commander of the Jewish police—Yudah Blunt—he was a neighbor of ours before the war, he spoke and said: "You see, that's what will happen to you; one member goes away, the whole family suffers." They used this type of psychology to scare people. . . . It stays with me all my life.³⁸

As the savagery toward the ghetto prisoners intensified and their hopes of surviving vanished, the number of those willing to attempt escape grew. People noticed that "the Germans had a list of ghetto residents, but no list of those who were shot."³⁹ Because of this, it was wise to escape immediately after a mass execution. After the first mass execution, there was a successful escape led by Avner Feigelman, who had at one point worked for Lederman.⁴⁰ Sukhovolskii believes that they were the first to leave like that.

Groups began escaping the ghetto with more and more frequency, and eventually, Feigelson was allowed to join one of them. He recalls:

> I had a lucky day, which was in November 1942. I came from work and happened to stand not far from [the] Judenrat, trying to hear some news. And a friend of mine came over and said, "There is a Jewish partisan in the house across the street." He didn't tell me much. I went in. His name was Friedman, I didn't know him before, he came from a different town, Postav. And he actually organized a group, and he asked me if I wanted to join. I told him I wanted to go with him, I was ready; I didn't beg, I was very determined. The way I spoke to him, I think he couldn't refuse.... He told me to come [at] eight o'clock at night to a certain spot near the fence. And I came home. I didn't discuss much. I was decided, I think. I said I made the decision and was going. Nobody could have stopped me—I didn't ask [for] the permission.

Sukhovolskii speaks of an increase in the general will to resist. He remembers how he and his brother Ierukhim joined an underground youth group that aimed to organize armed resistance. The group helped the partisans however they could: "We had hiding places where we began stockpiling weapons. We'd buy weapons . . . we'd steal boots [from the tannery], sweaters, socks, and passed them on to the partisans in the forest through those who were leaving. . . . We had two caches and a decent number of weapons."

Youngelson explains how it was possible to "stockpile weapons" in the ghetto and why it was important to have a gun if one was going to try to join the partisans: "There was a small black market for contraband weapons, rifles, guns. It was very small, but nonetheless, it existed . . . those who had weapons were very readily accepted [by the partisans]."

Sukhovolskii is certain that Lederman was aware of what his sons were doing and of their desire to leave and join the partisans: "Our father once warned us . . . that we must never think of this under any circumstances. Because we were visible, the whole ghetto was on our shoulders, it was a big risk. Once, our acquaintance Rodnitsky came to us . . . and asked my father to give me to him. He'd gotten a Tatar's passport—they'd lived in the same hamlet. . . . My father refused his offer, saying, 'What happens to everyone else is what will happen to him.'"

Despite their father's efforts to convince them otherwise, Ierukhim and Iakov decided to go when it was time for their group to leave the ghetto. Sukhovolskii recalls this moment, wiping away tears:

> I'm coming to the most difficult part. . . . There was a moment when we—I will put it like this—betrayed my father. With a group of eighteen people, we went into the forest on December 2, 1942. . . . We joined the *Mstitel'*

[Avenger] unit. We didn't have time to do anything with them, not even take the oath, nothing. We weren't there for long. Things started happening in the ghetto. They immediately arrested the relatives of two people from our group and executed two families. . . . Sometime in the middle of January, messengers came from the ghetto telling us that our father had asked that we return no matter what. So we decided to come back. This wasn't a simple matter, we practically voluntarily deserted the unit.

Iakov and Ierukhim's decision to return was strongly influenced by their acutely "negative impression" of the atmosphere of cruel mercilessness that imbued their partisan unit. Several days after the brothers joined the unit, "one of the people who came there with us, Moshenke Vainshtein, he was born in 1925, he was totally green. They captured someone and he was supposed to stand guard over him. He fell asleep at his post, the prisoner ran away, and literally the day after that he was sentenced. Moska was taken into the woods and shot. I didn't see it happen, but I saw how they carried his boots out of the woods. It was so cruel, how young he was."[41]

Before their escape, the young people thought that by risking their lives to obtain weapons and clothing for the partisans, they would earn the partisans' trust and acceptance. It turned out that these things "paid" their way in but did not buy them permanent acceptance. "We thought that everything we had sent them . . . meant something," Sukhovolskii recalls, "but all of that was fantasy."

Boris Glaz, who heard from adults about the return of Lederman's sons, recalls this episode somewhat differently. According to his version, Lederman's sons returned to the ghetto to avoid the partisans' retaliation: "There was a rumor that Lederman's sons had returned to the ghetto. Because when young people would leave to join the partisans, the Judenrat handed the names of their remaining relatives over to the Germans. Those people would be shot. When two of the sons of the head of the Judenrat joined the partisans—and their unit included children whose parents had died because they'd been reported on by that same Lederman—they were arrested [by the partisans]. They were sharp guys, though, so they escaped and came back to the ghetto."

Another survivor, M. Tsimkind, seems to refer to this episode in his testimony: "When the Germans learned that Jews had appeared in the forest [with the partisans], they forced the Judenrat to go out into the woods and hang notices asking the Jews to gather in the ghetto, saying we won't hurt you, we'll take care of you. But everyone already knew this was lies."[42]

According to Sukhovolskii, the escape of the head of the Judenrat's sons to join the partisans caused "a tremendous stir"; many feared that the entire ghetto would be destroyed as punishment. Lederman, understanding that "no good would come of all this," reported to the German authorities himself that his sons had "gone off somewhere." When the brothers returned, "everyone was relieved thinking that now everything would turn out alright," that their father would somehow punish them, but that it would not "affect everyone else." The Germans' reaction was swift: "On February 27, 1943, my father didn't come home. He'd gone out on business to the *Gebietskommissariat*, the gendarmes' headquarters (there was a special labor bureau there that organized manufacturing) . . . he talked to them (some business, gifts for some people, something like that). . . . That evening, he didn't come back, night, he was still gone, naturally, we were worried. In the morning, three Germans in civilian clothing showed up. . . . They came to our house and took my mother, me, my brother and sister."[43] They were led through the ghetto, then down Senkevich Street to the park where the Gestapo offices were located. Here, the brothers managed to run away. Remembering this, Sukhovolskii weeps: "Today, from the heights of my age, how could I have run away when my mother was still there?" Iakov made it to the Borok Forest and spent the entire day there. Ierukhim was slightly wounded and ran "right back to the ghetto. The Germans knew that he went back there." To find out what had happened, Sukhovolskii returned to the ghetto. Relatives hid the brothers at the homes of their good friends: Iakov at Khana Tsepelevich's, and Ierukhim at Asna Gindina's. Though their uncle was able to remove the bullet Ierukhim received, he could not save him: "On March 3rd, gendarmes came to the house where he had been hiding in the attic. He had a gun, he tried shooting at them. He was killed in the attic. Then our uncle took the body, and he was buried."[44]

According to Sukhovolskii, some saw the brothers' escape from the hands of the police as "practically a heroic feat; a song appeared [in the ghetto], it was called 'There were two brothers, two heroes.'" After his brother's death, the hidden weapons became his, and he left the ghetto for the second time on March 5, 1943. But now, he and four of his companions—Kasriel Fuks, Shaike Sheikhtman, Mulia (Samuil) Kats, and Moshke Zhmievsky—did not want to join the partisan unit. They had weapons from the cache and so "were able to immediately obtain food: if you're armed, you can do anything." They went off in the direction of Dzisna because all the members of their group except for Sukhovolskii were from there and knew "where the Dzisna Jews hid around there." On the way, they "came upon Ziamka Kats, Fania Fuks, and some others." From them, they learned that in the unpassable areas near Miory, on a large peat bog, "Jews from Miory, Druya, and other small towns were hiding," having organized a large family camp there. "We went there, found a guide—you could only reach it at a certain time of day, going down narrow trails.... And there was a rather large number of people there, but they were so helpless. First of all, they didn't have any weapons. So we tasked ourselves with providing supplies."[45]

The group slowly grew. The Jews in this family camp considered their main objective to be revenge. They were in no condition to undertake any major operations. They acted "without a plan, but desperately." Sukhovolskii managed to "capture and personally kill Mosalsky, the head of the Dzisna police."

The commander of the partisan unit based not far from the family camp learned of the Jewish group's activities. The central command did not approve of the existence of scattered, independent groups, but the commander did not insist on the Jewish group joining his unit. When he learned that the group remained in contact with the ghetto, he asked them to bring a doctor to his unit. Accompanied by a member of the "real partisan unit," Sukhovolskii headed off to the ghetto with an official letter from the commander. His uncle Meishe, a doctor, was still alive there. They reached Hlybokaye and got in touch with Meishe, but they were not able to convince him to leave the ghetto. The Jewish partisans later made several more trips back to the ghetto on errands for the partisans.

Liquidation of the Ghetto, August 1943

The last time Sukhovolskii came to Hlybokaye was at the request of Dovid Pintsov, who had obtained official permission from the Soviet command to organize a Jewish partisan unit. Pintsov asked Sukhovolskii to "go to the ghetto and get people out." In early August 1943, Sukhovolskii and Tsimmer, another partisan also originally from Hlybokaye, returned to the ghetto. At first, everything went according to plan. Tsimmer "took a few people and they left the ghetto," while Sukhovolskii stayed behind "to help the local youth organize resistance ... [for] when the partisans begin to liberate the ghetto." He managed to complete his mission, but "unfortunately, the course of events turned out differently":

> On August 17, 1943, fighters from the Rodionov military brigade, stationed in Sharkowshchyna, attacked the Germans, destroyed a German garrison and gendarmes from Hlybokaye and went into the forest.[46] ... On August 18, the murdered gendarmes were brought to Hlybokaye to be buried. On the evening between August 19 and 20, the ghetto was surrounded, troops came from Pastavy, where an SS unit was stationed, as well as policemen from other places. A representative came and told the Judenrat that everyone had to be

forced out. But of course, no one could take people out at that point, and at four or five in the morning, panic broke out.[47]

Glaz tells the story of this episode somewhat differently (although he stipulates that he knows it "from stories from people who knew what happened"): "[In Sharkowshchyna] there were soldiers from the Vlasov Army [Russian collaborationist formation fighting under German command], who guarded the station. Colonel or Lieutenant Colonel Rodionov was their commander. One day, there was a phone call from Sharkowshchyna to the garrison in Hlybokaye saying that they'd been attacked by partisans and needed help. The entire Hlybokaye garrison left for Sharkowshchyna; Rodionov's troops met them with gunfire. The entire Hlybokaye garrison was killed and Rodionov's soldiers went to join the partisans. The Germans got scared that the partisans would attempt to liberate Hlybokaye Jews and reinforced the security surrounding the ghetto." Glaz adds that, when he was among the partisans, he heard that "representatives from the Soviet government had come to see Vlasov and Rodionov, offering them immunity in exchange for surrender. Vlasov refused, but Rodionov agreed to go over to the side of the Soviet Union."

When shots rang out in the ghetto, Sukhovolskii had a Nagant gun and a grenade on him. Young people ran to him thinking that he had come with partisans, but in reality, the preparation for the resistance had only just begun: "Basically, nothing was ready yet." When they realized their mistake, they decided to try to escape the ghetto with Sukhovolskii. He recalls: "We ran to the fence, I threw my grenade, but they opened so much fire from the other side that there was no point in trying to break through that way. The only stone building remaining in the ghetto was Kantorovich's house; it was big with good cellars. There was a . . . hideout shelter in the basement. We went down into it hoping to stay until nightfall and try to break through in the dark." But then, once again, "events took a different course":

> They [the Germans] started burning the ghetto down. Because no one was coming out of their homes, they started flying planes over the ghetto, pouring down some flammable liquid, and setting it on fire. Everything was burning, and people were suffocating in their hideouts because the houses were made of wood. . . . Minka Kasovskaia was in one of these hideouts. She ran out with a few others and, apparently, in hopes of saving herself, she knew that Kantorovich also had a shelter, she ran toward his house. The Germans watched where she ran to, let her go, and when we opened the door for her, they ordered us all to come out.[48]

It is likely that courage and battle experience from participating in partisan military operations are what saved Sukhovolskii. The unexpected German order did not paralyze him:

> Naturally, no one moved. The German shepherds were barking. And it was so tight in there.... Then, they threw a grenade through the door. Those close to the entrance were wounded... then it was silent. A little while later, we wondered, "Why just sit here? We'll suffocate, they'll snuff us out like rats." I decided to come out. I shoved my Nagant behind my jacket lapel, and a couple other people went up with me.... We came up, and there were two Germans there and a policeman. In German, I told them, "Let me show you my papers." Then I took out my Nagant and shot at them. Seems like I got them. And I ran, across the street, and found myself in the Shuleviches' garden, which was filled with tall, overgrown potato vines. I don't know what happened to me, but once I ran into the potato vines, I fell and only came to my senses when it was dark.

Glaz had spent the previous day in the ghetto infirmary taking care of his sister, who had come down with dysentery (he recalls that "in the summer of 1943, there was a dysentery epidemic"). That evening, his father came to replace him, and this was the last time that Glaz saw either of them. That night he tried to hide from the shooting in a hideout he had discovered.[49] He saw old men in tallis and tefillin praying in one of the houses.

> They asked me, "What are you going to do?" I said I was going to try to get out.
> "You better not. We have a hideout here under the chicken coop." I went down into the hideout.... There was room for ten to fifteen people, but there were more than fifty already hiding in there. My father's cousin and his wife were down there. People started fainting from lack of oxygen. I recovered at night [and found myself] lying on the ground [outside]. I looked around and recognized the chicken coop through which I'd been lowered down. The ghetto was burning. Everything was in flames. I heard Yiddish speech coming from the attic of the barn. I managed to climb up into it. My father's cousin and two other Jews were up there. He told me that his wife had lost her mind. He noticed that I'd passed out and tossed me outside, and then went up to the attic. "We've decided to hang ourselves"—they were holding a rope—"but you should try to get out."

Glaz decided to go to the Christian Orthodox cemetery, two hundred meters from the ghetto, and from there make his way to the Belarusians he knew who could hide him. But there were many other Jews already at the cemetery, and it was surrounded by Germans and under fire. Many of the Jews were injured, and moaning, weeping, and shouting came from all around. In this chaos, Glaz's neighbor Tsale Kremer came up to him and asked if he wanted to join him in trying to escape. Smiling, Glaz tells of the miraculous deliverance:

> "I'll go with anyone just to get out of this nightmare." He led me to a young woman who didn't look Jewish, a snub-nosed blonde. She was fluent in Yiddish. Tsale was sixteen or seventeen, she was between twenty and twenty-two. It was instantly clear that she was a commander. She wasn't from Hlybokaye. She led us back into the ghetto and into a house that wasn't on fire yet. She found food and fed us. She spotted a burning building just outside of the ghetto. A crowd of Germans was standing around it watching the fire. She said that if we took the alley near the burning building and pressed ourselves to the wall, the Germans wouldn't see us because they were distracted by the fire. The fire was loud—they wouldn't hear our footsteps. After that, it would be easy to get out. She was right. We came out to the adjacent street. There was a German standing on the corner. She quietly said, "There's three of us and one of him. Let's walk straight at him." And so we went right up to him. He made no attempt to stop us. When we were in front of him, he said, "Go to the German barracks, there's only one watchman there. Get around him"—the barracks were way out on the outskirts of town—"and you will be saved." He warned us that he would shoot, but not at us. We did what he told us. When we got close to the barracks, Nekhama told us to lie down while she tracked the watchman's rounds. It later turned out that she was an experienced partisan, she served in a reconnaissance unit. She figured out the watchman's pattern, and when he turned behind a different wall, we quickly ran past the barracks and found ourselves in a field. We spent the whole night half-running, following her. We went past some villages. When it was light out again, we went into the forest. We saw a hamlet there.

It is not uncommon for informants to recall some help from Germans. As a rule, it was low-ranking soldiers who helped them. Feigelson recalls how, on the day of the first execution, "I ran into a German truck driver. His name was Franz Sillingach, he always helped us. He asked me what was wrong. I told him the whole story. He put me in the back of his truck, took me to the ghetto, stopped next to our house, and waited for me. I went in and found my parents and little brother alive. I asked Franz to take me back to tell the girls [his coworkers] that they could come down [from the attic]. Franz drove them back to the ghetto."

Youngelson recalls how, when he worked at the police station, the German who ran the kitchen would feed him. "He gave me bread to take home, and sometimes butter, and walked me back to the ghetto. At the same time, I later saw how he took part in the liquidation of the ghetto." Sukhovolskii also mentions some Germans when he describes the situation with food: "Many people worked for Germans at warehouses and so on. The Germans were all different, too; many of them were generally helpful. It was hard to bring [food] into the ghetto. One person to whom a German had given something got caught, and they almost got to punishing the German. In order to rehabilitate that German, they decided to shoot that Jew."

On the morning of August 20, Jewish policemen came to the Jews who were still left in the ghetto and told them that it was being liquidated. Youngelson remembers this visit from the police: "The Jewish police explained to us what the Germans told them. They told us that, because the front had come close, the ghetto had to be liquidated and transferred to Lublin. We understood that that was the explanation before the liquidation. Friday morning, August 19 [he probably means Friday, August 20], 1943, the ghetto was liquidated." Youngelson's father had told him many times that if there was a liquidation, he must not obey the Germans but flee. When they got to the forest and the Germans told the Jews to undress and lie down in the already-dug ditches, Youngelson's parents and sisters complied, while he jumped up and ran. He was not alone in his attempt to cheat death; many others ran beside him. He recalls:

> I wasn't alone. There were a hundred to a hundred fifty people who started to run. . . . When I came to the forest . . . there were around fifteen of us. The rest were killed or wounded. We knew that there were partisans, but we didn't know where exactly. We found them the same night. We saw the sky was red; the ghetto was burning. One of us, he was a religious person, said "Let's stand and say Kaddish." I didn't know how to say Kaddish, I didn't remember. I was listening: what they were saying, I said. We came to a house. It wasn't a village, it was a house on a piece of land. And we saw a little light in this house. We had big sticks, we didn't have guns, and started to move to the house. When we came to the house, one of the guys looked into the window . . . "Wait a minute, here is Kalman Rabinovitch, the son of one of my father's partners." They were partisans. So, we came in, they embraced us and took us to the partisan camp.

Boris Glaz also made it to the partisans. First, Nekhama led Boris and Tsale to a Pole—the liaison for the partisan unit. The partisans came later and took Nekhama and Tsale, who was capable of holding a rifle, but left Boris behind.

With the other surviving Jews gathered in the home of the liaison, they took a path that they were told to follow by the partisans, and four days later, they reached the appointed spot in the partisan-controlled zone. There, they found a family camp where people lived in dugout mud huts, which was run by Abram Isakovich Shub, a good friend of Glaz's parents. Most of the people in this camp were Jews. They owned five or six cows and a few horses that the partisans had been able to capture from the Germans, who had intended to take them to Germany. Glaz and two other boys herded them. After teaching Boris to work with horses, Shub made him his personal coachman. Partisans provided the camp with supplies. Glaz recalls the principles that the camp was founded on:

> It was organized by the Second Belarusian Brigade, who'd gathered specialists—tailors, bootmakers, metalsmiths who fixed the firearms, and even a man who knew how to make dried sausage. When the brigade was deployed somewhere else, other partisan units used the camp's services. Wounded partisans were sent there for treatment, and partisans went there to rest after particularly difficult missions. You could always repair your clothing and shoes there. You could have a bath in a good bathhouse. You could always get your hands on a bottle of homebrew. The partisans would bring us their worn-down horses and take good ones. They fixed their wagons, carts, and reins.

At first, the camp had very few weapons. After the Soviet planes started bringing in weapons, there were enough for everyone, and the unit commander gave each camp resident a rifle. Glaz remembers that when the sausage maker's turn came to receive his—he was a very old man—he asked the commander, "Tell me, did I come here to fool around with rifles or to make sausages?"

After the Red Army liberated Hlybokaye and its surroundings on July 3, 1944, Abram Isaakovich Shub, Boris Glaz, and Iakov Epshtein, another one of Boris's peers, returned to Hlybokaye. Shub took the boys in—he had a wife and a son of his own. The boys went back to school at the beginning of the school year. Then, sometime at the end of September, they learned that an orphanage was opening in Vilnius for children who had lost their parents in the war. As kind as Shub was, he could not support that many people. Glaz recalls the beginning of his life in the orphanage:

> Shub explained the situation to us and took us there on the train. At that time, he was the head of the special shop for the personnel of the Ministry of Internal Affairs in Hlybokaye. He brought us to the orphanage, which was at 12 Zhigmuntovskaia Street, on the banks of the Viliya [today Neris]. It was in a big, beautiful private home and had a little over one hundred children

living there. You could hear plenty of terrible stories.... Our teachers did not encourage us to remember those things at that time. All the teachers and other instructors were Jews. They were old teachers, we celebrated New Year together, they didn't abandon us. Often times, they would invite orphanage children into their homes, where they spoke Yiddish. The orphanage had its own Jewish school, which was very quickly shut down. The orphanage also shut down because there wasn't enough new enrollment. I only spent half a year there.

Dveira Finefter, also from Hlybokaye, remembers being at the Vilnius Jewish orphanage from 1944 to 1951. She also recalls that Vilnius Jews sent their children to the orphanage's Jewish school. Like Glaz, she has fond memories of her time at the orphanage: "Everything was in Yiddish. I was happy there. The teachers were very kind and taught us everything: how to wash our clothes, how to make our beds so that everything would be tidy. Like a mother teaches her daughter. They sang Jewish songs with us. Once [Shloyme] Mikhoels and [Binyomin] Zuskind came for a holiday party and talked to us."[50]

Glaz spent Victory Day at the orphanage. His memory of this day is one of the most dramatic episodes in his interview:

> It had been raining very hard since morning. For some reason, I found myself alone. I was sitting in Chernyakhovsky Square, crying. I'd realized that none of my relatives would ever be with me again. While it was still the war, while there was shooting—it hadn't been too long since we'd heard explosions from the direction of Königsberg; in Vilnius, the Lithuanians and Polish legionnaires were still shooting at times—I had no hope that the shooting would ever stop, and that I would live alone. It hit me that it was all over. A male private and a woman in officer's uniform came up to me; they both looked Jewish. They sat down on either side of me and asked why I was crying. I explained. They took me with them. She was an army doctor; he was a soldier who'd recovered from being wounded. They were celebrating Victory Day. They got me drunk so that I'd stop crying.

Contacts between Jews and Non-Jews

Naturally, the attitudes of Jewish survivors, when they remember their interactions with the town's non-Jews, differ depending on their personal circumstances and the postwar cultural lenses through which they view their wartime experiences. Some people remember these relationships with resentment and anger; others are amazed at the goodness of their non-Jewish neighbors. Reuben Youngelson, for instance, is confident that "non-Jews had no sympathy toward the persecuted Jews." He recalls how his Polish friend betrayed him: "I had a friend who'd eat with us, play with my soccer ball; he borrowed books from me, rode my bike, and then he joined the Polish police. He showed up to my house with his brother and took my bike and my soccer ball and my soccer shoes and my Kodak camera. I said nothing. I was grateful that they didn't kill me. He came and asked for everything politely. He said, 'You don't need them.' So I gave him everything."

Boris Glaz's experience was different. Semion Selitsa, who had often stopped by to talk to Boris's mother about politics, was good and honorable toward them. One time, he even visited the Glazes at their home in the ghetto late at night and brought them a large sack of food. Glaz marvels, "How did he manage to get in? He was a large man, two meters tall. He brought bread, potatoes." One gets the impression that in the ghetto, the Glazes had no doubts about the sympathy and support of the Poles and Belarusians who had been friends of the family. As Glaz recalls, "I'd leave for work with my father and then, oftentimes, I'd run off to visit the Belarusians and Poles I knew, my parents' close friends. They'd give me food for our entire family."

The following episode from Feigelson's account, in which he returns to Hlybokaye from the partisan unit to get his brother, covers the entire range of relationships between the non-Jews and Jews:

> I met somebody because I asked him directions. . . . The farmer gave me a hug, blessed me, promised to pray to God for me, and gave me the address of his sister who lived in Hlybokaye. When I got to Hlybokaye that day I went first to this sister. By mistake, I knocked at the next door; there was a policeman. I don't know how I found out—he was not dressed as policeman. Maybe somebody told me later. I asked him in Polish where this Mrs. Wojciechowicz lives. I was lucky I didn't say anything with *r*—that would give me out. He said, "next door," and I walked in, talked to them, but they were afraid and didn't want to help me.

Peter Smuszkowitcz, a prisoner of the Hlybokaye ghetto, tells of his encounter with a Catholic priest in the basement of a local jail. Later, Smuszkowitcz learned that the priest had ended up there for his sermons, in which "he told the locals not to participate in any violence against the Jews. He said, 'You never know what will happen to you. Don't cooperate with the Germans, don't go catching Jews.'"[51]

Conclusion

Until now, the two most comprehensive overviews of the history of the Hlybokaye ghetto remain the Rajaks' *Memorial Book* and the Russian Wikipedia article (also available in French), which differ in some respects. A scholarly history of that ghetto is still waiting to be written. Unlike the Jews in big-city ghettoes such as Minsk or Vilnius, Jews in the Hlybokaye ghetto had more contacts and communication with the non-Jewish residents of the town and with partisans in the surrounding forests. Their strategy of survival through performing useful work for the Germans allowed the ghetto to survive for a comparatively long period. The VHA's rich collection of testimonies by the survivors from this ghetto will certainly serve as an important source for this history. Individual testimonies will be critically analyzed, checked against other documentary sources, and incorporated into the historical narrative. Inevitably, the diversity of individual survivors' voices that has been preserved thanks to the recording technology will be lost. The purpose of this chapter was not merely to provide primary material for a future history of the Hlybokaye ghetto but also to complement this history by trying to construct an imaginary conversation among the survivors and preserve the multiplicity of personal perspectives on a particular episode in the history of the Holocaust.

Notes

1. The USC Shoah Foundation, Institute for Visual History and Education. The archive was founded in 1993. See https://sfi.usc.edu/vha. Each interview in the archive has an ID, and subjects can be searched by their name or ID number, and so both are listed in the article's citations.

2. Iakov Sukhovolskii (ID: 36910).

3. Boris Glaz (ID: 50428).

4. Reuben Youngelson (ID: 50602).

5. Stan Felson (ID: 33651).

6. Israel Chanovich (ID: 1229).

7. Dorothy Gordon (ID: 6428).

8. Rajak and Rajak, *Ḥurbn Glubok, Sharkoystsene, Dunilovitsh, Postov, Droye, Kazan*. A partial English translation is available at http://www.jewishgen.org/yizkor/Hlybokaye/hly009.html.

9. Wikipedia (Russian edition), s.v. "Глубокское гетто" ("Hlybokaye ghetto"), last edited on July 29, 2022, 10:09, https://tinyurl.com/yzu86vke.

10. Gross, *Revolution from Abroad*, 196–99; Litvak, "Jewish Refugees from Poland in the USSR, 1939–1946," 128–29.

11. Iakov Sukhovolskii (ID: 36910).
12. Iakov Sukhovolskii (ID: 36910).
13. Boris Glaz (ID: 50428).
14. Iakov Sukhovolskii (ID: 36910).
15. Boris Glaz (ID: 50428).
16. Gita Geseleva (ID: 13718).
17. Iakov Sukhovolskii (ID: 36910).
18. Boris Glaz (ID: 50428).
19. Iakov Sukhovolskii (ID: 36910).
20. Boris Glaz (ID: 50428).
21. Boris Glaz (ID: 50428).
22. Boris Glaz (ID: 50428).
23. Stan Felson (ID: 33651).
24. The Lederman brothers' escape to the partisans led to their parents' death.
25. Iakov Sukhovolskii (ID: 36910).
26. Iakov Sukhovolskii (ID: 36910).
27. Iakov Sukhovolskii (ID: 36910).
28. Iakov Sukhovolskii (ID: 36910).
29. Stan Felson (ID: 33651).
30. Reuben Youngelson (ID: 50602).
31. Boris Glaz (ID: 50428).
32. Iakov Sukhovolskii (ID: 36910).
33. Iakov Sukhovolskii (ID: 36910).
34. Iakov Sukhovolskii (ID: 36910).
35. Stan Felson (ID: 33651).
36. Stan Felson (ID: 33651).
37. Slepyan, "The Soviet Partisan Movement and the Holocaust," 10.
38. Stan Felson (ID: 33651).
39. Iakov Sukhovolskii (ID: 36910).
40. Iakov Sukhovolskii (ID: 36910).
41. Iakov Sukhovolskii (ID: 36910).
42. M. Tsimkind (ID: 19869).
43. Iakov Sukhovolskii (ID: 36910).
44. Iakov Sukhovolskii (ID: 36910).
45. Iakov Sukhovolskii (ID: 36910).
46. Red Army Colonel Vladimir Gil' (Rodionov) was captured in 1941, defected to the Germans, and was appointed commander of a Russian brigade under SS command. In 1943, his brigade switched sides again and on August 18, 1943, attacked the German garrison in Dokshytsy and the railway station at Krulevshchina, not far from Hlybokaye. This information is from Zhukov and Kovtun, *1-ia russkaia brigada SS "Druzhina,"* 206–26, which is not an unbiased

academic study. According to Glaz, when he was among the partisans, he heard that "representatives from the Soviet government had come to see Vlasov and Rodionov, offering them immunity in exchange for surrender. Vlasov refused, but Rodionov agreed to go over to the side of the Soviet Union."

47. Iakov Sukhovolskii (ID: 36910).
48. Iakov Sukhovolskii (ID: 36910).
49. Boris Glaz (ID: 50428).
50. Dveira Finefter (ID: 13260).
51. Peter Smuszkowitcz (ID: 3403).

6

A Family between the Ghetto and Red Army Partisans

Two Holocaust Testimonies from Hlybokaye

JULIA BERNSTEIN

Survivors' Testimonies and "The Art of Listening"

Sergei Iarov, a prominent Russian historian of the siege of Leningrad during World War II, in which the city's residents suffered greatly, asserts that to understand the depth of the pain experienced during such an upheaval, one must consider the survivors "in the full diversity of their contradictory characteristics." He suggests that a catastrophe be examined by its impact on the ethical norms of its survivors.[1] Iarov urges us to consider how people today, despite the incommensurability of their life experiences, can empathize with the moral dilemmas faced by the survivor. Addressing the issue of differences among the testimonies of Holocaust survivors with similar experiences, Hannah Pollin-Gallay remarks in her study of testimonies from Lithuania that "their differences do not call into question how the Holocaust destroyed Jewish lives, but if and how it destroyed Jewish paradigms of living."[2] This chapter presents a case study of two brothers who survived the Holocaust by escaping from the Hlybokaye ghetto to the Red Army partisans. Though their stories are similar, their testimonies highlight different aspects of their experience, reflecting their respective "paradigms of living."

It may be impossible for a contemporary person to understand the scope of the catastrophic experience of the war and the Holocaust, but one can engage more deeply and more emotionally with the subject by watching and listening to testimonies. By attending not only to the narratives but also to the emotional, ethical, and aesthetic aspects, one avoids using them only as a historical source. The medium of video enables a stronger emotional connection than a text does by engaging a fuller range of the senses. The auditory and visual features create levels of meaning that transcend the verbal content. Narrated in front of the camera for an unknown remote viewer, a video testimony uses both verbal and nonverbal forms of communication, such as gestures, changes in facial expressions, pauses, repetitions, and so on. These nonverbal elements are important for analyzing the reception of the video testimony. As I will explain, closer attention to these nonverbal features will help viewers better understand the complexity of the traumatic experience as it is being both relived and reflected on through the act of a recorded testimony.

One of the first scholars to approach the perception of the Holocaust survivors' testimonies as a specific form of aesthetic experience was American psychologist David Boder. In 1946, he visited several camps for displaced persons in the US-administered sector of Germany and recorded audio interviews with the residents. Thinking about future uses for his interview collection, Boder wrote, "It is highly probable that in time we shall develop an art of listening to authentic recordings and find new methods of appreciation of verbally reproduced narratives."[3] By "an art of listening," Boder meant the ability to appreciate and interpret the auditory nuances of survivors' speech, facilitated by the advances in sound reproduction technology. He tried to transcribe and publish recordings of selected interviews verbatim, asserting that such publication would present "the first case in world literature where use is being made of actually verbatim recorded narratives."[4] He failed, however, to convince the Jewish Publication Society of the value of his materials. In his analysis of the recorded testimonies, Boder paid close attention not only to their textual content but also to the nuances of presentation, what he described as "psychological and cultural factors," which were driving the narrative flow of the testimony.[5]

The Feigelson Family: Historical Background

The recorded testimonies of former Hlybokaye teenagers from the Visual History Archive (VHA) of the University of Southern California Shoah Foundation Institute for Visual History and Education tell the story of the destruction of Jewish Hlybokaye from a variety of perspectives, reflecting the diversity of interviewees' backgrounds and postwar experiences.[6] In one case, the backgrounds and postwar experiences were very similar, but the testimonies differ in some significant respects. The following brief case study closely examines the testimonies of the Feigelson brothers (who later changed their name to Felson): Stan (née Zalman, born 1923) and Don (born 1925), by focusing on one of the most traumatic events they experienced: the death of their mother.

I am using the Felson brothers' video interviews from the VHA Shoah Archive and Don's unpublished memoir, "Don Felson: In His Own Words" (2004), which the Felson family granted me access to. In accordance with the VHA practice, the participants discussed the key questions with their interviewers before the interview. The Felson brothers describe largely the same events, but their accounts differ in style and mode of narration. Stan's way of telling his story is personal and emotional, highlighting the ethical issues he had to face, while Don's narrative style is objective and detached and hews closely to the facts of the events. These differences in narrative mode may suggest different ways of engagement with the presumed audience, the future viewers of the VHA testimonies. This raises thought-provoking questions about preserving the memory of the Holocaust. What are these survivors trying to convey by telling their stories in front of the camera, and how do they expect their remote viewer to respond to their message? How significant is the emotional aspect of a testimony for a Holocaust researcher? How can these nonverbal aspects of a testimony be analyzed?

In their interviews, the Felson brothers sometimes refer to each other's testimonies and to the Yiddish *Memorial Book of Glebokie* by Michael and Zvi Rajak.[7] This book describes prewar Jewish life in Hlybokaye and its surroundings and also includes the names of the Jewish residents who perished in the Holocaust so that they may be remembered on their *yortsayt* (death anniversaries). The Rajak brothers, who before the war were Jewish schoolteachers in Hlybokaye, claim in the introduction that they "compiled only actual events, which are authenticated with hundreds of names and endless data."[8] Using the Rajaks' *Memorial Book* as their reference framework, Don and Stan provide their perspectives, which complement the master narrative of that account. From the beginning of Stan's testimony, the viewer feels that the emotional focus of his narrative is the story of the death of his mother, Riva-Leah Feigelson, and his younger brother Leybele. This story is particularly painful for Stan because he feels responsible for their deaths. Don focuses on the broader historical context of their life in Hlybokaye and survival among the Soviet partisans. He seems familiar with the role of guide to the culturally remote past. In his memoir, he mentions that he had shared his memories with other oral history projects before recording his testimony with the Shoah Archive.

The Felson brothers' testimonies provide some details of their mother's biography, which are important for this analysis. Riva-Leah Swerdlin was born in the eastern part of Belarus in an orthodox Lubavitch Hasidic family. Before World War I, she was betrothed to a cousin in the United States, but the war left her stranded in Hlybokaye, where she eventually married Yosef Feigelson.[9] One of her sisters lived in San Francisco, and two others remained with their parents on the Soviet side of the 1920 Soviet-Polish border. Riva-Leah corresponded with her American sister but was cut off from the Soviet part of the family. In 1935, anxious about the rise of Nazism in Germany, she asked her sister in San Francisco to save at least one of her children. On Stan's behalf, Riva-Leah made an immigration application in the regional center of Vilnius. The waiting period for an American visa was about five years, and in 1939, when eastern Poland was annexed by the Soviet Union, Stan's emigration became impossible.[10] After 1939, Yosef Feigelson lost his business and went to work for a Soviet state–owned enterprise. As Stan explains, "The Communist ideology was hard individually on business people, [but] otherwise many Jews felt relieved. They got more opportunities . . . many more jobs became available." This balanced attitude toward the Soviet regime would help Stan when he had to find a place in a Red Army partisan detachment.

In the ghetto, Riva-Leah tried again to save Stan and gave him some money to facilitate his escape, but it did not work out. In November 1942, Stan met a Jewish man who was organizing a group of around thirty people to escape the ghetto and join partisans in the forest. He left the ghetto with this group, which eventually reached the area controlled by Soviet partisans under the command of Fedor Markov. From this group, Markov selected only two young men to join the partisan group, and one of them was Stan.[11] Markov's decision was related to the politics of partisan warfare in Belarus. By mid-September of 1941, the German army had occupied the Baltic states, Belarus, and Ukraine and was rapidly advancing toward Moscow. Millions of Soviet soldiers surrendered, and thousands were wandering inside the occupied territories. The scant numbers of German troops in the rear of the rapidly advancing Wehrmacht were unable to stop the partisan movement. Many former Red Army soldiers and escapees from POW camps found shelter in the large, swampy forests of Belarus, where they tried to organize resistance. These guerrilla groups were inadequately equipped and survived by taking provisions from peasants or pilfering from their fields. Although the extermination of Jews became apparent to the Soviet leadership by the end of the summer of 1941, authorities were silent. Partisan units loyal to both the Soviet Red Army and the Polish Home Army often refused to admit Jews, who as a rule were unarmed and exhausted and could jeopardize the partisans' security by their appearance and accent. Some partisans were openly hostile to Jews, and many Jews who tried to join their units were robbed or murdered. This uncertainty about the partisans' sympathies is reflected in Stan Felson's interview. When asked about the escape options that existed before the execution of some twenty-five hundred ghetto Jews in June 1942, he replied, "Nobody actually knew where to go. . . . I read some [German] bulletins talking about lots of partisans around Polotsk, which is ninety kilometers from our town.... So, I kind of was aware about partisans.... Some younger people left, but not many."[12]

When the situation at the front line worsened for the Red Army in August 1942, the Soviet State Defense Committee issued a directive ordering partisan units to admit everyone who wanted to join them, but most partisan commanders still prioritized military objectives over humanitarian concerns and turned away unarmed and untrained Jews.[13] Stan remembers that the oath everyone had to take before being admitted to the detachment was all "about fighting," not about preserving people's lives. Because of this objective, as Stan recalls, Markov refused to admit another large group of Jewish survivors from the massacre in the shtetl of Danilavichy.

At the beginning of the summer of 1943, Stan made the dangerous journey to Hlybokaye. He met up with Don, who was working at a German hospital, and sent a message to his family pleading with them to leave the ghetto. A few days later, his mother and brothers Don and Leybele joined him, but his father refused to leave. Stan was required to return to the Markov unit, but by the time he arrived, it had already relocated, so he joined another partisan unit that came to a nearby village.[14] Fear of the partisans' antisemitism was one of Stan's reasons for joining the new and much smaller unit headed by the Jewish commissar Mayerson, who admired Stan's courage in rescuing his family. Mayerson's unit was "maybe ten people, but ... [was] supposed to grow, get larger, fight."[15] A year later, the unit had grown by four or five times. Not only was Mayerson Jewish, as Don recalled, but "somehow, we encouraged Jewish partisans to come in, and we kind of felt maybe not half, maybe forty percent Jewish." When the unit had to relocate, Stan left his mother and younger brother in the village of Lesiny, which was at that time controlled by the partisans. A short while later, the Felsons learned that the Germans had raided Lesiny. Stan walked more than sixty kilometers back to that village only to discover that Riva-Leah and Leybele had been murdered by local peasants. Shortly after, he learned of the deaths of his father and aunt, who were shot in reprisal for his mother's and brothers' flight. Stan and Don stayed with Mayerson's group until the end of the war. As former Polish citizens, the brothers left the Soviet Union for Poland and then moved to a displaced persons' camp in Germany. They contacted their aunt in San Francisco and eventually immigrated to the United States.[16]

The Brothers Tell the Story of Their Mother's Death

Following the VHA questionnaire, Stan's interview starts with questions about his family. Visibly composed, he mentions his father, then pauses, his face becoming more emotional: "He and my mother and one of my brothers perished during the Holocaust." Trying to elicit Stan's memories of his mother, the interviewer asks about his earliest recollection of her. With a distraught expression, Stan answers, "One time when I was small, I was in the house and saw tears in her eyes. She worried or something; all her family was across the border on the Russian side. She was never able to communicate with them."

Everything Stan recalls about Riva-Leah related to her unselfish caring for the family or her tragic fate. When Hlybokaye was annexed by the Soviet Union, Riva-Leah "was hopeful because she hoped to see her family" on the Soviet side. When Germans confiscated the family's only cow, "it was a tragedy" for her. With tears in his eyes, Stan explains: "She worried that [the family] will have no food." He remembers her as a sad and pure human being, and he is almost certain that, unlike the rest of the family, she observed the rules of kashruth (Jewish dietary laws) even in the ghetto.

Unlike Stan, Don does not view Riva-Leah through the lens of her martyr's death. Even when speaking of her stay in Lesiny, which led to her murder, Don keeps his informative, objective perspective: "She lived in a village and felt good. She came from that area and knew someone." While Stan depicts his mother's death primarily as a result of his self-interested decision, Don views her as an inevitable victim of the historical catastrophe: "Somehow down the line she knew that we were not going to survive otherwise." Contrary to his older brother's remorseful version, Don presents Stan's decision to leave their mother in the village as a reasonable risk, since at that time Lesiny was in partisan-controlled territory: "Zalman [Stan], having experience already, thought we should leave our mother and little brother in the village in partisan territory."

Riva-Leah's death is the emotional climax of Stan's testimony. As his narrative approaches this episode, he takes long pauses and becomes visibly distressed. Rather than speak about the murder directly, he merely states that "somebody from that village, Lesiny, betrayed my mother," but he omits the details of Riva-Leah's and Leybele's deaths and burial. These details are elucidated by Don, who recounts that it was Stan who found Riva-Leah's and Leybele's bodies and buried them in a Jewish cemetery not far from Lesiny. Whereas Don tries to rationalize the inevitability of their mother's death in those circumstances, Stan refrains from any explanation. He seems unable to force himself to recall the episode of her death and talk about it to strangers. The trauma that his mother's murder inflicted on him seems to be too deep to allow him to speak about this tragedy.

Don is committed to recounting his memories dispassionately. Educating his audience, he relies on his viewers' interest in history and their ability to absorb the information he provides into the broader narrative of the Holocaust. Stan's perspective is personal. Invoking Riva-Leah's tragic fate, he elicits an emotional response from the viewer. His perspective foregrounds the emotional, intellectual, and ethical challenges faced by a human being in the situation of war. Stan seems to be aware of the cognitive gap separating the contemporary American viewer from a Jewish teenager among Belarusian partisans in 1944. Whereas Americans today, Stan presumes, tend to treat almost every situation as a predictable outcome of their individual choices, his and his family's experiences taught him that life is unpredictable and events cannot be controlled. Having lived through the Soviet annexation, followed by the German occupation, the Jews of Belarus knew how little their individual choices mattered at a time of major historical upheaval. Discussing Riva-Leah's passive acceptance of his decision to leave her in Lesiny, Stan contrasts her fatalism with the choice-oriented mentality of his modern American audience: "If she said that it would be nice (now I am thinking) if we could go with you.... But she said nothing, we never discussed things like choices like today: what choices we have here."

By laying bare his inner struggle for viewers who have never had to face a situation anything like this, Stan Felson tries to convey the burden of the memory of the war. He is judging his past behavior using the ethical norms of contemporary American society, in which people are presumably free to make choices and are responsible for their outcomes. In the confused circumstances of 1943, leaving his mother and brother behind in Lesiny felt like a justifiable risk. In the 1990s, Stan finds his conduct morally unacceptable. He tries to replay this situation again in his testimony, blaming himself for making a wrong choice: "If I had said [to Mayerson], 'I want to take my mother and brother with me where I went,' it seems to me I could've done it." By sharing his self-recriminating reflections, he signals that for him, the emotional experience of living with the consequences of difficult wartime choices is perhaps the most traumatic part of the memory of the war.

What motivated Stan to share his self-accusing reflections with the viewers? The agonizing consequences of the difficult wartime choices are part of his memory of the war: "It haunts me all my life." Why is the viewer's empathy important to him? Reflecting on the reasons people share their self-recriminating memories or confess their guilt, Russian philosopher Anna Iampolskaia notes that our culture is predicated on the belief that the act of confession of guilt soothes the self-recrimination of the confessant.[17] Alleviation results not because the sense of guilt loses its gravity but because the very act of confession transforms the confessant's self-perception. The act of confession is perceived not as an informative message to the listener or viewer but, as Iampolskaia puts it, referring to Jacques Derrida, as an act of "making the truth."[18] Derrida asserts that the presumed presence of a benevolent listener is necessary for the confession to have a healing effect. Such a listener, according to Derrida, is the inherent addressee of the confessant's speech. What relieves the confessant's feeling of guilt is the gift of this presumed listener's mediation and forgiveness.[19] Following this logic, one can assume that Stan's motivation in revealing his self-accusation before the anonymous audience is the implicit hope that the future viewer's empathy will somehow mitigate his moral suffering.

Seeking the viewer's empathy, Stan talks about the impossibility of rationally explaining why he left his mother and brother in Lesiny. He points to the intuitive nature of this decision: "Somehow my whole life I always think why it's hard to explain but somehow I thought that in the east [Lesiny was located to the east of Mayerson's detachment's location] ... there were more partisans, it was safer." Today, Stan is puzzled by his confidence in the partisans' power and his disregard for German military strength. No matter how tempting it would have been to ascribe his decision to Mayerson's influence (as his partisan friend recommended), Stan accepts sole responsibility for it: "I wish I could blame somebody else for their destiny, but somehow that's how it was." After the war, remorse became a permanent feature of Stan's otherwise successful life in America: "Part of it was victory and part was tragedy. It stays with me all my life."

Stan never describes how he discovered the bodies of his mother and brother or how he made the risky decision to take the deceased to the Jewish cemetery. These and other lacunae in his narrative indicate the intensity of his self-recriminations. Another aspect of the narrative that indicates his psychological condition is his choice of narrative details to reflect his emotional state. He conveys his feelings and emotions through particular metonymical images. For example, he describes the abundant consumption of meat in the Markov brigade: "They had meat almost every day. They had more food than you can think of. They used to bring a sheep and cook it with potatoes and so on." This abundance of fresh meat pillaged from destitute peasants alludes to the partisans' crude and sometimes gratuitous violence and conveys Stan's anxiety and fear of that excess of violence. However, when it comes to Mayerson's partisans, the same imagery loses its threatening associations. Here, the fighters had "some meat" and only "occasionally." Obviously, Mayerson's partisans also had to commandeer food from peasants, but the amount taken was, apparently, strictly limited by their needs and therefore more permissible by Stan's ethics. The qualifier he uses repeatedly when referring to meat—"some"—indicates

Stan's sense of Mayerson's ethical moderation. Recalling his visits to his mother in Lesiny, Stan mentions the nourishment that meat provided, giving his family strength to survive, and he uses the same qualifier: "I saw them a few times over this time: when we had some meat, I took over some meat to them." Whether or not Riva-Leah ate this nonkosher meat, she cooked it for her sons the way they used to eat it back home: "I came back when she made some stew." That was their last meal together, after which Stan and Don moved on with their partisan unit to its new position.

As Stan's account approaches the episode of Riva-Lea's death, the steady flow of his narration becomes punctuated by emotional surges. His voice tapers off, his face flushes; he is at a loss for words and visibly tries to suppress his feelings of sorrow and guilt. As if to magnify the impending misfortune by contrast, Stan recalls how good he felt at Mayerson's: "I liked them, and they liked me. Maybe he [Mayerson] was impressed by what I did rescuing my family . . . [*on the verge of tears*] That was like a victory." But the "victory" descends into a tragedy. When Stan turns to his mother's doom, his voice falls: "All of a sudden we got news that in the east, where we came from, the Germans came, organized police and went on big actions against partisans. Somebody from that village Lesiny betrayed my mother." That is all Stan can tell us directly about Riva-Leah's and Leybele's murders. He never uses the word *kill* when speaking of their deaths. Rather than being informed directly, the viewers have to infer the murder and empathize to some degree with the horror Stan experienced when he learned about their deaths. Thus, it is only the combination of verbal and nonverbal expressions that allows the viewers to experience the video testimony in its fullness.

Conclusion

Like any archive of documents related to a historical event, the VHA has a particular agenda. Steven Spielberg, who started the Survivors of the Shoah Visual History Foundation, stated that the project's mission was to emphasize the theme of survival. Viewed as survival stories, Stan and Don Felson's testimonies engage the viewer differently. Whereas Don chooses to construct his testimony as a kind of case study in the broader history of the Holocaust, his brother Stan tries to convey the difficult moral dilemmas he faced to stay alive. By laying bare his unrelenting remorse for his wartime actions, Stan tells us that reckoning with the personal sense of guilt is a key part of his memory of the Holocaust. These different kinds of testimonies call for different kinds of engagement on the part of the viewer and affect viewers' perceptions in different ways. Don's detailed factual narrative enriches our knowledge of the history of the Holocaust in Belarus. By following Stan's painful confession, viewers become engaged emotionally. Here, facts play an auxiliary role, while the primary goal of this testimony is to offer the viewers a glimpse into the traumatic impact of the Holocaust on the survivor's personality. By sharing with the viewers his psychological anguish over the ethical choices he was forced to make, Stan presents this as a significant part of the trauma of the experience of the Holocaust. Incapable of fully comprehending the scope of Stan's personal tragedy, the viewers can nevertheless empathize with it through their perception as they watch Stan speak and listen to his voice. Empathy with Stan becomes what Iampolskaia calls "suffering that teaches us," deepening our understanding of our existence.[20]

Fig 6.1 The Feigelson family in the early 1930s. *Courtesy of the Felson family.*

Fig 6.2 Yehuda Yungelson at the ruins of the synagogue in Hlybokaye, 1951. *Courtesy of Deborah Rothman.*

Fig 6.3 A group of Holocaust survivors of Hlybokaye at the monument near the Borok Forest. *Courtesy of Deborah Rothman.*

Fig 6.4 A group of Holocaust survivors of Hlybokaye at the monument near the Borok Forest commemorating the anniversary of the destruction of the ghetto, 1951. *Courtesy of Deborah Rothman.*

Notes

1. Iarov, *Blokadnaia etika*, 5.
2. Pollin-Galay, *Ecologies of Witnessing*, 2.
3. Boder to Maurice Jacobs, November 13, 1948, David Pablo Boder Papers, UCLA Library, Box 21.
4. Boder to Maurice Jacobs, November 13, 1948.
5. Boder, *I Did Not Interview the Dead*, 2.
6. See chapter 5 for more details about these testimonies.
7. https://www.jewishgen.org/yizkor/Hlybokaye/Hlybokaye.html.
8. https://www.jewishgen.org/yizkor/Hlybokaye/Hlybokaye.html.
9. Don Felson (ID: 52547).
10. Don Felson (ID: 52547).
11. Stan Felson (ID: 33651).
12. Stan Felson (ID: 33651).
13. Slepyan, *Stalin's Guerrillas: Soviet Partisans in World War II*, 57.
14. Stan Felson (ID: 33651).

15. Stan Felson (ID: 33651).
16. Stan Felson (ID: 33651).
17. Iampolskaia, *Iskusstvo fenomenologii*, 176.
18. Iampolskaia, *Iskusstvo fenomenologii*, 190.
19. Iampolskaia, *Iskusstvo fenomenologii*, 191.
20. Iampolskaia, *Iskusstvo fenomenologii*, 133.

7

Daily Life in the Hlybokaye Ghetto
Photographs from the United States Holocaust Memorial Museum

IRINA KOPCHENOVA

A Jewish ghetto was established in Hlybokaye on October 22, 1941, in the neighborhood of today's Engels, Zaslonov, Krasnoarmeiskaia, Chkalov, and Krasnykh Partizan Streets. The ghetto was separated from the rest of the town by a wooden fence with barbed wire that had only one gate. A total of six thousand Jews from Hlybokaye and forty-two other settlements in its vicinity were forced into the ghetto. In early 1942, the Judenrat (Jewish council) began creating workshops and enterprises in which Jews could work and be recognized as so-called essential workers by the German occupation regime. The ghetto's population was divided into those who were deemed suitable for work in the numerous workshops and those who were considered not useful. In December 1941, forty people considered "elements of little use" were shot; on March 25, 1942, about one hundred more people were shot.

Between late May and early June of 1942, a smaller ghetto was created inside the main one for Jews deemed "of little use." On June 19, 1942, about twenty-five hundred of them were murdered in the nearby Borok Forest. Between August 18 and 19 of 1943, some Jews noticed that during the night the guard around the ghetto had been reinforced. On August 19, the Judenrat received an order to prepare the ghetto's population for deportation to Lublin, Poland. But this plan could not be realized because the Jews mounted an armed resistance. The fighting continued for two days, and the ghetto was destroyed by heavy artillery bombardment, after which it burned down.

Fig 7.1 Jewish women press Nazi military uniforms in a workshop. (USHMM Desig #483.07 W/S #08057 Museum Photo Archives CD # 0120). *Courtesy United States Holocaust Memorial Museum.*

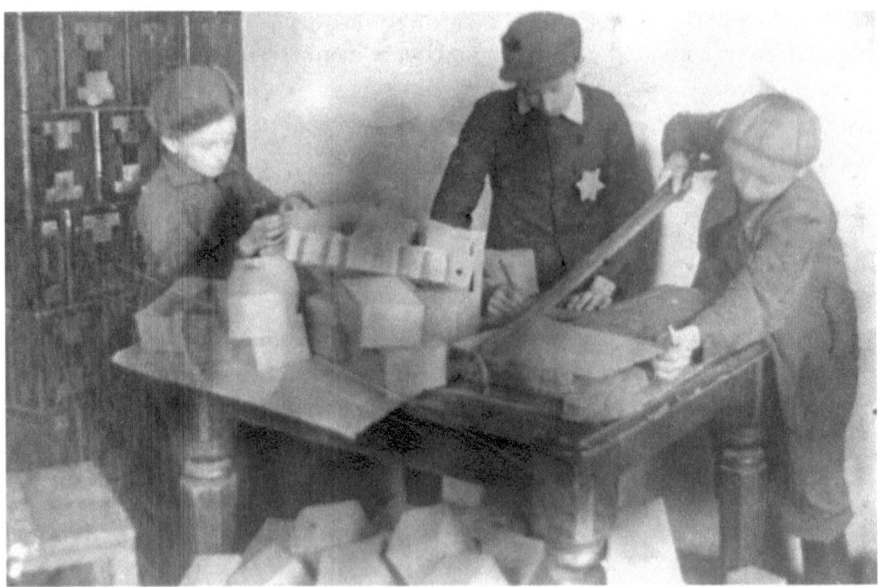

Fig 7.2 Jewish children making boxes (USHMM Desig #483.07 W/S #08059 Museum Photo Archives CD # 0120). *Courtesy United States Holocaust Memorial Museum.*

Fig 7.3 Jewish men making street signs in a workshop (USHMM Desig #483.07 W/S #08076 Museum Photo Archives CD # 0120). *Courtesy United States Holocaust Memorial Museum.*

Fig 7.4 Jewish women make shoe polish at a workshop (USHMM Desig #483.07 W/S #08086 Museum Photo Archives CD #0120). *Courtesy United States Holocaust Memorial Museum.*

Fig 7.5 Jewish men working in a tanning workshop (USHMM Desig #483.07 W/S #07954 Museum Photo Archives CD #0120). *Courtesy United States Holocaust Memorial Museum.*

Fig 7.6 Jewish men at work in a shoemaking workshop (USHMM Desig #483.07 W/S #07968 Museum Photo Archives CD #0120). *Courtesy United States Holocaust Memorial Museum.*

Fig 7.7 Jewish youth at work in a shoemaking workshop (USHMM Desig #483.07 W/S #07957 Museum Photo Archives CD # 0120). *Courtesy United States Holocaust Memorial Museum.*

Fig 7.8 A Jewish woman and a girl work in a clothing warehouse (USHMM Desig #483.07 W/S #08048 Museum Photo Archives CD #0120). *Courtesy United States Holocaust Memorial Museum.*

Fig 7.9 Jewish men working at an oil press (USHMM Desig #483.07 W/S #07886 Museum Photo Archives CD # 0508). *Courtesy United States Holocaust Memorial Museum.*

Fig 7.10 Jewish men at work in a factory producing cooking oil (USHMM Desig #483.07 W/S #07955 Museum Photo Archives CD #0120). *Courtesy United States Holocaust Memorial Museum.*

Fig 7.11 Jewish women at work producing slippers (USHMM Desig #483.07 W/S #07980 Museum Photo Archives CD #0120). *Courtesy United States Holocaust Memorial Museum.*

Fig 7.12 Jewish men and women make felt boots in a workshop (USHMM Desig #483.07 W/S #07988 Museum Photo Archives CD #0120). *Courtesy United States Holocaust Memorial Museum.*

Fig 7.13 Jewish men and women working in a plant nursery (USHMM Desig #483.07 W/S #08072 Museum Photo Archives CD #0120). *Courtesy United States Holocaust Memorial Museum.*

Fig 7.14 Jewish men and women working at a spinning mill (USHMM Desig #483.07 W/S #08082 Museum Photo Archives CD #0120). *Courtesy United States Holocaust Memorial Museum.*

Fig 7.15 Jewish men at work producing wooden shoes (USHMM Desig #483.07 W/S #07973 Museum Photo Archives CD #0120). *Courtesy United States Holocaust Memorial Museum.*

Fig 7.16 Jewish women working in a hat-making workshop (USHMM Desig #483.07 W/S #08047 Museum Photo Archives CD #0120). *Courtesy United States Holocaust Memorial Museum.*

Fig 7.17 Jewish men and women working in a print shop (USHMM Desig #483.07 W/S #08101 Museum Photo Archives CD #0508). *Courtesy United States Holocaust Memorial Museum.*

8

Representations of the Jewish Past in Today's Hlybokaye

Memory on Demand? *

MIKHAIL LURIE AND NATALIA SAVINA

Imagine a group of visitors to Hlybokaye, a small town in the Vitebsk Region in northwestern Belarus, with a particular interest in the town's Jewish past.[1] They might come away with a strong impression if they are lucky enough to go on the themed tour "A Walk through a Jewish Shtetl" created by historian Margarita Kozhenevskaya while she was working at the local museum. They might have a similarly profound experience if they arrive on the day of remembrance for the victims of the ghetto, visit three impressive memorials with an international Jewish group, attend a reception organized by the district administration, or enter the well-maintained old Jewish cemetery. At the same time, these visitors might find themselves deeply disappointed. Walking through the town, they would not see any characteristic examples of Jewish architecture, not even informational plaques on formerly Jewish buildings. They would find no stores with stylized names or cafés serving Jewish food and no souvenirs with images of Jewish Hlybokaye. If they were to visit the local museum, they would see that the town's Jewish history is mentioned in only two parts of the exhibition, one devoted to religious diversity and the other to the occupations of residents before the war.

This mindfulness about the existence of the memory of the Jewish past remained with us after concluding our field research in Hlybokaye in 2019. This memory is not something that readily emerges when one visits Hlybokaye or talks to its residents; it is fragmentary and not formulated as a more or less coherent narrative known or easily accessible to town residents and visitors. That trip was inspired by our critical reflections on how the memory of the Jewish past was presented in the collection of materials from the expedition to

Hlybokaye organized by the Sefer Center in 2015, in which one of the authors of this chapter took part.² As the editors of this collection of materials state in the summary, "After the war, Jewish life in Hlybokaye, as in other Jewish towns, has come to a halt. However, the memory of Jewish life in Hlybokaye has survived in the many stories that the town inhabitants so generously shared with participants of the expedition, for which we are very grateful."³ Our doubts were not raised by suspicions regarding the bias of the informants or the influence of their perception of researchers' focused attention on the subject of Jews.⁴ Our main concern were the questions: What do these colorful oral narratives recorded by ethnographers tell us about the forms that the memory of the Jewish past takes in Hlybokaye today, outside the controlled context of the interviews, and what don't they tell us? Does this memory remain only at the level of individual memories, or is it also present in the public sphere, and, if so, what institutions are engaged in its preservation?

During our visit to Hlybokaye, we spoke to local residents of various ages and occupations, intentionally not focusing on the subject of Jews.⁵ Among our interviewees were also local experts such as journalists, tour guides, and *kraeveds* (local history expert).⁶ We asked the informants about the town; its space; its history; the particulars of local culture; and the economic, social, and cultural developments in today's Hlybokaye. We visited the Hlybokaye Historical and Ethnographic Museum, the House of Crafts, city parks, war memorials, and other sites and institutions. We went on town and museum tours, which were organized by institutions or conducted at our request. The materials we collected as a result of these conversations and observations, the recordings of interviews from the 2015 Sefer Center expedition, and publications on local topics in the press and online served as the foundation for this chapter.

Research Context

The tradition of researching the memory of life in the shtetls of Eastern Europe before the Holocaust based on oral and written memoirs by Jews, the carriers of this memory, was established in the framework of Jewish studies. Its founders were Mark Zborowski and Elizabeth Herzog, who recorded the memories of American immigrants who had come from the mestechki of Poland and Ukraine.⁷ Scholars from St. Petersburg Jewish University and the Center for Judaica and Bible Studies at the Russian State University for the Humanities used materials collected from field expeditions during the 1990s and 2000s in former mestechki in Ukraine, focusing on folk art and architecture, Jewish cemeteries, and Jewish folklore and its comparison with Slavic folklore.⁸ The same methodology was used in Jeffrey Veidlinger's book on the life of Jews before World War II and under Romanian, Hungarian, and German occupation, which was based on nearly four hundred interviews with the elderly residents of small towns in Ukraine, Moldova, Romania, Hungary, and Slovakia.[9] The study of Jewish memory through attempts to reconstruct everyday life in the prewar shtetl and describe the discourses and cultural stereotypes surrounding it is an approach continued by the Sefer Center's projects for recording the oral histories of the non-Jewish residents of formerly Jewish towns and mestechki, which have resulted in a number of collections of articles.[10]

Reflecting on his experiences working with field expeditions and doing research using these materials on one aspect or another of Jewish culture in the past, Aleksandr Lvov contends that any approach that seeks to identify a kind of normative *Jewish* culture is limited because it does not take into account the contemporary culture of *Jews* in post-Soviet shtetls, which he considers a worthy subject in its own right.[11]

Another approach is oriented toward the constructivist paradigm. Researchers analyze contemporary memorial representations of Jews in the former Jewish mestechki and urban areas that are the result of certain intentional activities. In some cases, the context for these kinds of activities is a city's symbolic economy.[12] Responding to the demand produced by the culture industry, the urban environment and events calendar in places with formerly high concentrations of Jews may be intentionally saturated with "Jewish" content. In the 1990s, several European cities began actively cultivating their Jewish past and filling their urban space with signs of Jewish cultural presence, which generated a steady stream of interested visitors and established "Jewish-themed tourism" as a branch of the tourist industry.[13]

Eszter B. Gantner and Mátyás Kovács discuss the visible presence of Jewish culture in the form of themed festivals, guided tours, concerts, exhibitions, cafés, shops, store signs, and so on in modern-day Berlin, Kraków, Budapest, and Prague, cities whose Jewish population shrunk dramatically after World War II. Using these examples, the researchers examine situations in which a city's Jewish cultural space is constructed by non-Jewish actors for tourist consumption.[14]

Andrea Corsale and Olha Vuytsyk discuss the experience of actualizing the Jewish past in terms of cultural heritage. As they have demonstrated, one of the important factors contributing to the systematic heritagization of urban space and to the development of Jewish heritage tourism is the presence of a significant number of material objects or projects for their restoration and repurposing (as an example, they mention a project in Lviv where the ruins of the Golden Rose Synagogue have been used for the creation of a memorial space).¹⁵

Olivia Sandri argues that the structure of urban space can play a key role in these processes. For example, in Vilnius, where Jewish heritage sites are scattered throughout the city, Jewish-themed tourism is developing slowly. By contrast, in Kraków, the historic Jewish sites are largely concentrated in the Kazimierz District, which has a reputation as an "authentic Jewish place" and attracts a significant number of tourists, though some critics characterize it as a "Jewish Disneyland."¹⁶

The unique case of a Jewish population that disappeared five centuries ago, none of whose physical sites remain—though a phantom Jewish landscape and the absence of material traces have nonetheless become a site attracting tourists—is discussed by Naomi Leite in her article on Jewish Portugal.¹⁷ She describes the practices of imagining and constructing the absent Jewish presence that are created collaboratively by the tourism industry and tourists, which she calls "practices of surrogacy."

In other cases, when a town lacks active institutional forces such as a tourism industry or a resourceful Jewish community, other local residents may take initiative in constructing the image of their town as a former shtetl. This is what happened in the small towns across Podolia, where Jews were not completely exterminated during the war and a significant Jewish population remained until the 1990s. When researchers from the Petersburg Judaica Center visited these towns in the 2000s, they encountered residents who still had the cultural experience of living in a "Jewish town," a phenomenon that had otherwise seemed to have been wiped out in Europe.

Scholars studying the "local text" of Mohyliv-Podilskyi have argued that, in Ukraine, the overall perception of a town as "Jewish" in local narratives often becomes one of its defining cultural connotations. In this case, these scholars contend, "all culturally and generally significant features are inevitably denoted in the local text of the town as 'Jewish,' from the perception that in Mohyliv, a town of trade and smuggling, you can buy and sell literally anything if you just ask the Jews, to the reputation of the town's most important manufacturing enterprise as a 'yid factory.'"¹⁸

Alla Sokolova demonstrates how Podolia residents today easily take on the role of experts in local Jewish heritage, exoticizing "antique Jewish houses" while at the same time interpreting them in the local context by showing them off to Jewish tourists, researchers, and others interested in the culture and history of these places. Discursive manipulations aimed at turning "ordinary" houses into "monuments of Jewish antiquity" help draw attention to these buildings and perform a "mental reconstruction of 'the genuine Jewish townships.'"[19]

Marina Hakkarainen explains how widely circulated local stories about Jewish craftspeople who used to live in these towns are important for constructing an image of the ethnic past that is ignored in the local museum narrative: "For the external spectator, stories about age-old handicrafts and Jewish artisans, about the quality of their work and its beauty, romanticise the atmosphere of the shtetl and make it attractive to the consumer of antiquity—again, authenticity and ethnic colour on the one hand, and 'pan-European values' on the other. Thus, stories about handicrafts and artisans form a part of a general 'museumification project' for the shtetl. In this way, the Jews of small Ukrainian towns and their neighbours turn to the Jewish 'ethnic idealised past' in order to construct their own local identity."[20]

There are no Jewish families living in Hlybokaye, and the town has no tourist routes or sites that could be labeled as "Jewish."[21] How and under what circumstances can Jewish memory function in this formerly Jewish town? Who are its producers and consumers? Who interiorizes this memory, and when and how does this happen? In an attempt to answer these questions, we will examine two cases dealing with the treatment of the Jewish past in post-Soviet Hlybokaye.

The Discovery of *Green America*

Commemoration with International Participation

In the late 1980s, former Jewish residents (or their descendants) of prewar Eastern European Jewish shtetls, including Hlybokaye, began visiting their old homes in postsocialist Europe from abroad. Their main purpose was to restore and memorialize Jewish burial sites.[22] An Israeli woman named Rakhil Klebanova who was born in Hlybokaye initiated these memorial activities by contacting her fellow townspeople in other countries. Tatsiana Saulich, deputy chair of the District Executive Committee, agreed to support this initiative, despite the local government's indifference to the project.[23] An active community of emigrants from Hlybokaye and a few local Jews was formed around the energetic and farsighted bureaucrat, and all of them were highly enthusiastic about working toward their common goal.

The first order of business for this group was the rehabilitation of the old cemetery. The work was financed by participants from abroad and done by local professionals contracted to work on municipal construction projects.

After the reconstruction, the abandoned cemetery took on its present appearance. It was planted with new trees (mainly pines); the remaining tombstones were lifted off the ground and cleaned; a large plant bed, in the shape of the Star of David, was planted in the center, with fragments of broken tombstones in it; and, at the entrance, a stone memorial structure was erected with an inscription in Hebrew and Russian that translates as "May the Grace of God Be with You." Later, a metal fence was erected around the cemetery, and a plaque in three languages—Hebrew, Russian, and English—was installed on the gate, reading "Old Jewish Cemetery Destroyed by the Nazis, 1941–1945." Today the cemetery is not open to the public.

In addition to the appearance of other memorial sites in and around Hlybokaye, another visible result of the group's activity was the regular visits by Jewish groups from abroad, taking place several times a year. These were the relatives of former Hlybokaye residents, officials, and representatives of Jewish organizations, whose arrival always felt like an event in this small town.

In interviews, local informants often talked about these visits, though the depth of their knowledge varied. This is illustrated by fragments from two interviews with elderly residents of Hlybokaye, who attended memorial events. The first informant is a former staff member of the financial department of the District Executive Committee, who was by virtue of her work well acquainted with the memorial practices of the groups from abroad: "It has a special fence around it, Jews come here on the 24th, August 24th. They used to come from Leningrad but now, I don't know where they come from, someone is supposed to come from Germany . . . people come from Israel to visit this cemetery, they just hold this kind of rally here now. The District Executive Committee comes and welcomes them. Well, they take a couple of people from the District Executive Committee and they take them around the cemetery, they pray there, they have commemorations."[24] The second informant observed the memorial actions as an interested spectator. It is significant that she recalls them after telling us about two Paskhas (Russian uses the same word for Easter and Passover), calls the commemoration day of the ghetto's victims "a festival," and spontaneously displays the ethnocultural stereotypes that were of interest to the interviewers:

> Inf.: [after the story about the Orthodox Easter and Jewish Paskha] Let me tell you more. We have this festival, in August, sometime in the beginning of August they come . . . here we have a monument, we had a ghetto here, you understand, it was here, along Zaslonov and Chkalov Streets, there was a ghetto here. And they always come, and they pray in an interesting way.[25]

Int.: How?

Inf.: Not like in our way, in a Jewish way.... And this Pelsina Regina L'vovna [local physics teacher] translated it for us into Russian. It's all... they pray like our Lord's Prayer but they have different words, but she said, "It's the Lord's Prayer." It's interesting, very interesting indeed.[26]

In conversations with younger locals ("ordinary residents" who have no special knowledge of local matters or are even completely oblivious to them), we would often hear about visiting Jews' memorial activities, albeit in a condensed form and expressed with a clear lack of confidence in their knowledge. After a story about the ghetto, the young woman who owned the hotel where we stayed mentioned the Jewish cemetery, which "miraculously survived": "Well, as far as I know, people come here and look after it a bit, too, they see to it.... And I even know that there are some, like, organizations from Israel involved in that. But I can't say anything for sure because I might be mistaken."[27]

A maid at the hotel who could not tell us about the fate of the town during the war reacted immediately to what we said about the cemetery "being in decent shape." "Yes, they do a little bit around there, too. Before, there was no one looking after it.... Today, lots of their relatives come and.... They have a special day they do it... it has some kind of significance, and delegations come, too."[28]

For the members of memorial "delegations" and the few independent visitors who come to Hlybokaye out of an interest in their own genealogy, the Jewish cemetery is a tangible manifestation of family and national history, but the town residents perceive it in the reflected light of the commemorative rituals they observe. For the visitors, it is a foreign site of their own memory, whereas, for the locals, it is their own site of foreign memory.[29]

Folk Toponymy as a Historical Source and a Guide for Action

The rehabilitation of the Jewish cemetery and the steady interest in this site have generated a stable historical narrative about it. A new name for the Jewish cemetery has appeared in the repertoire of local history experts, who present it as an ironic old folk name, Green America. Its source is the eponymous story by Leontiy Rakovskiy, a native of Hlybokaye, published in Leningrad in 1927 in a collection also called *Zelionaia Amerika (Green America)*.[30] The story was republished in 2000 as a fifty-page book containing another story called "Chasy" ("The Clock"). The publisher of this edition was Moscow author Anton Sobolevskiy, whose last name is one of the most renowned in Hlybokaye.[31] In the introduction, written in Belarusian, Sobolevskiy spells out the book's purpose: "To acquaint twenty-first-century Hlybokaye residents with the part of their history tied to the town's Jewish population from the beginning of the twentieth century."³²

In discussions about the Jewish cemetery, the name *Green America* functions not as a place name but as an interpretive descriptor. The epithet *green* indicates that, before the war, the cemetery was densely covered in trees. The metaphorical image of America is interpreted in two ways: first, as a place where people do not return from, because Jews who immigrated to America remained there permanently and never came back—just as it is impossible to come back from the cemetery. "The local Jews called this place 'Green America.' This name carries a strong flavor of Jewish humor—laughter through tears. People used to emigrate to America in search of a better life, never to return. A place you can't return from, a cemetery, was thus called America in Hlybokaye."³³

Secondly, Green America is interpreted as an alternative to those who were not lucky enough to leave: many Jews dreamed of leaving Hlybokaye for America, but the majority only managed to make it as far as the local cemetery. "We have this Jewish cemetery . . . it was called Green America—people dreamt of getting to America but, as a rule, ended up in that cemetery, Green America, instead."³⁴

In addition to the beautiful name and no less beautiful legend, the modern narrative of the Jewish cemetery includes a number of unvarying compositional elements. We will examine three demonstrably similar examples: passages from the book *Kilometry evreiskoi istorii* (*Kilometers of Jewish History*), by the editor of the international Jewish journal *Mishpokha*, Arkadi Shulman, and excerpts from two interviews, one with the aforementioned Tatsiana Saulich, and another with a former local journalist who wrote about the Jewish cemetery and visiting Jews.

> Green America stopped being green during the war. The Germans cut down the trees, used the *matseives* to build roads or as building foundations. This [cemetery's destruction] went on until the beginning of the 1980s. Then they decided to build a house here and make a foundation using the stones from the cemetery. They made up the blueprints. But luckily, people came out who said that you can't build on a cemetery, for many reasons, including sanitation rules.³⁵

> This Green America—it really used to be a Green America—it was a very beautiful cemetery, old, green, lots of vegetation. And when the Germans came, they were the ones who destroyed it all, completely. And then when, in the 1980s, members of the Jewish community returned here for the first time,

people who'd moved away from here, native residents, the first thing they did was go to the cemetery, and when they saw the state it was in.... And across the street, there's a market, that's how I told you about that part of it, that it was the Germans, not even our people, no, it was the Germans who toppled everything over in there, cut everything down, destroyed the trees, there was no fence. And our people carried on just the same: when someone comes to market, they'd tie their horse [to a tombstone]. And people did whatever they wanted at that cemetery. And so they [Jews] came and when they saw it, the first thing that occurred to them, of course, was to get this cemetery back in order.[36]

They [the Germans] took all the precious stones to Germany. Cut down all the trees. And they'd send the trees by trainloads, there used to be so many here, this high... giant pines, tall, long, very valuable lumber. Germans took it all. Then they poured some kind of poison over this ground, on this ground, I even remember, I was about 15, so nothing could grow here. So it was just the dirt here. Nothing at all. Things didn't start growing again until maybe the 1970s. People started letting their cows graze here.... And then in 1974 Klebanova started up with all that Jewish stuff.[37] That's when they built that synagogue.[38]

These three excerpts reconstruct the cemetery's history with a similar narrative arc that goes from a golden age, through destruction and forgetting, to rebirth. A beautiful cemetery of historical value is defaced, and the labors of the Hlybokaye emigrants are aimed at restoring its lost identity, significance, and status in the urban space. The toponym itself or, more precisely, the word *green*, describing the cemetery's appearance before its destruction, serves as the starting point for the unfolding of this plot structure, which Arkadi Shulman rhetorically plays with in his quote "Green America stopped being green."[39]

In some cases, even the statements about the cemetery by the few elderly locals who lived through the prewar and wartime periods clearly reflect elements from the stereotypical narratives like those quoted above:

Informant: There was a Jewish cemetery near the bazaar, you know where the market.
Interviewer: Yes.
Informant: There is ... there are tombstones there, yes. Before the war, beautiful, centuries-old pines grew there, in that cemetery, it was full of them, with little graves between them. As soon as the Germans came, they cut down all the pines and sent them to Germany.[40]

In this long interview, a local woman born in 1937 told many stories and shared details from her memories of the time of the German occupation. Even so, the imagery of "beautiful, centuries-old pines" that "Germans . . . cut down . . . and sent . . . to Germany" should not be seen as a verbalization of the informant's personal impressions from her childhood but as a story marked by the influence of present-day texts.

The publisher of Rakovskiy's stories directly addresses Lev Artur Simonovich, a former Hlybokaye resident and one of the main sponsors of the rehabilitation of the cemetery, "And for Artur Lev, we hope that his efforts succeed in getting a pine grove planted at the Jewish cemetery in remembrance of Green America."[41] In these words of encouragement to the foreign philanthropist, as well as in other conversations about the modern-day greening of the Jewish cemetery, references to Rakovskiy's story render it a precedent text in relation to both the newly recovered name and the old cemetery's newly minted image. "When Rakhil Klebanova started up that whole business with the reconstruction, when they were reconstructing the cemetery with other Hlybokaye Jews, they also planted a lot of trees. It turned out that it had once been a green, well, that it'd been Green America. So there had always been trees there. They wanted it to be as green as it had been in the past."[42] Thus, the movement to reconstruct the Jewish cemetery inspired the publication of a book that put a concise toponym into modern-day circulation. Green America simultaneously refers to the "correct" pre–World War II past of this local Jewish site and hints at its "corrected" present-day state. This movement also triggered the creation of the persistent historical narrative about the cemetery from the times of Green America to today, and this narrative in turn has determined the practical and symbolic activity around the cemetery.

Although the colorful tale about the old "folk" name of the Jewish cemetery currently circulates only among the small group of Hlybokaye's intelligentsia, and its sphere of functioning is apparently limited to guided tours, newspaper articles, and thematic conversations and interviews with interested visitors, the narrative about the difficult fate of Green America is also, to some extent, known more widely among the townspeople.

Ekaterina Melnikova examines the phenomenon of "strangers' cemeteries" in a study based on the materials from her fieldwork in the Northern Ladoga Region and on the Karelian Isthmus. The author pays special attention to the phenomenon of "emotionalization" of the old Finnish cemeteries by contemporary residents (descendants of Soviet settlers who replaced former Finnish residents after these territories had been annexed by the Soviet Union after World War II). "'Shame,' 'guilt' and 'pity' have become the most effective instruments for the symbolic transformation of the recently useless 'past' into a highly valued and estimable heritage in the region."[43] All the differences among the situations with the "strangers' cemeteries" in the former Finnish territories and in former Jewish shtetls notwithstanding, a similar phenomenon is taking place in Hlybokaye: one need only think of the recurrent expressions of "regret" about the Jewish cemetery that was destroyed by the Nazis and neglected by the local residents and authorities during the postwar Soviet period. Presumably, this "shift of empathy" has also affected the stability, popularity, and replicability of the stereotypical narrative about the Jewish cemetery and its history.

The Famous Townsman Eliezer Ben-Yehuda

On the Initiative of Kraeved Henadz' Plavinski

A bust of Eliezer Ben-Yehuda, the renowned Zionist credited with the revival of the spoken Hebrew language, was installed in Hlybokaye in 2012 along with seven similar monuments, composing the Alley of Famous Townspeople. The plaque on the bust reads: "Eliezer Ben-Yehuda, the creator of modern Hebrew." At that time, Ben-Yehuda was a new, unassimilated figure, not previously included in the local pantheon of prominent historic and cultural figures.

Eliezer Ben-Yehuda came to the attention of the local intelligentsia and authorities as a famous figure with ties to Hlybokaye several years before the installation of the monument, which was a result of the efforts of the kraeved Henadz' Plavinski. Plavinski became interested in researching and popularizing Hlybokaye's history during the 1990s, and his interpretations of historical narratives, remarkable for their originality and complex plots, were published in the local press and presented in public talks. He also often spoke with visiting researchers.[44] Plavinski advocated for the local "canonization" of two historical figures who were very different in many respects, including their respective ties to Hlybokaye: Jozef Korsak (the owner of part of Hlybokaye's land in the seventeenth century and "fundator") and Eliezer Ben-Yehuda.

In 2008, Plavinski proposed the installation of a memorial plaque to the famous Jewish cultural figure. He sent official inquiries to the local administration, collected signatures, and published articles about his efforts in newspapers. His initiative, however, was not supported by the administration, in part because almost nothing was known about the time Ben-Yehuda spent in Hlybokaye. Creating the Alley of Famous Townspeople became an opportunity for Plavinski to realize his personal project of memorializing Ben-Yehuda in Hlybokaye. Some of the people we spoke to derided his enthusiasm, even though they acknowledged that Plavinski's triumph in getting the monument installed was impressive since it was done single-handedly: "It is in large part due to his efforts that we have a monument to Ben-Yehuda. He simply wouldn't leave our authorities alone until they understood that they needed to do it," and

Fig 8.1 Monument of Eliezer Ben-Yehuda in Hlybokaye, July 2015. *Courtesy SEFER Center for University Teaching of Jewish Civilization.*

"In order to finally get him to leave them alone, they went ahead and put it up. Not just a plaque on a building, but a real monument."

Plavinski gave the following reasons why the creator of modern Hebrew ought to be considered a townsman by today's locals. Eliezer Ben-Yehuda, born Eliezer Itzhak Perlman, was born not far from Hlybokaye, in the mestechko of Luzhki. As a teenager, he lived with his uncle in Hlybokaye where he studied for two years. Both of Ben-Yehuda's wives were from Hlybokaye: he met his first wife while living at his uncle's house. She taught him French and Russian, and they later moved to Jerusalem. When his first wife died, Ben-Yehuda, following Jewish custom, married her younger sister, who became his assistant. These are the three key points of the narrative, which are presented in different combinations depending on the audience and the guide's own interest, to visitors who tour the Alley of Famous Townspeople.

The first two of the following quotations come from guides who lead tours almost exclusively for primary and middle-school children in Hlybokaye. The final quote is from a walk around town conducted for us by a kraeved who is rather well known and considered an authority by the Hlybokaye intelligentsia.

> The main street in Jerusalem is named after this man. That is where he is buried. Eliezer Perlman, born in 1858 in Luzhki, which was then part of the Disna Povet, this was part of our region. And so, friends, he goes to school in Polatsk. Back then, people spoke Yiddish. Do you know about Yiddish? You don't? Well, and then, after that, he went to a college in Paris to study to become a doctor. But then he got sick. So he came back to Hlybokaye, got married to one of our local girls, Deborah Jonas, and they left for Palestine. But in Palestine, he didn't work as a doctor, but instead, he began to revive the Hebrew language. Hebrew was an ancient language, which Jews had spoken long ago, and it had been lost. But, little by little, guys, he recreated this language from bits and pieces.[45]

> He wasn't a resident of Hlybokaye, of course, but he was important. He had two wives from Hlybokaye. And his mother-in-law. And so he's considered a resident of Hlybokaye. He is famous for founding the modern Jewish language that people speak today.[46]

> This is the man who resurrected Hebrew. He wasn't born here. There's a mestechko about thirty kilometers away from here, Luzhki. That's where he's from, they still have the ruins of the synagogue where he studied. But his two wives, who were ... sisters, they were from Hlybokaye. And he lived here, too, for about a year and a half, and then he left for Palestine. And when one of his wives died, he married her sister. But those sisters were from Hlybokaye.[47]

These quotations vary greatly in terms of depth of information but also the tone used by the tour guides when presenting Ben-Yehuda as a local.

Some kraeveds see Ben-Yehuda's connection to the town as highly fragmentary and/or insufficiently documented and therefore an exaggeration (which does not reflect negatively on their opinion of the monument to him). For his part, Plavinski uses a variety of arguments to demonstrate the depth and significance of this connection for Ben-Yehuda and for Hlybokaye. Various texts written by Plavinski present several lines of argument. First of all, he highlights the key role that Hlybokaye played in Ben-Yehuda's development by bestowing on him its characteristic local energy: "He lived here . . . well, for about two years, but it was more for him . . . what Hlybokaye formed. . . . Without Hlybokaye, there would not have been a Ben-Yehuda. This . . . well, this man—he performed a miracle; the soil of Hlybokaye gave Eliezer such power that he was able to perform a miracle: Jews once again began to speak Hebrew at home, on the street, when declaring their love."[48]

Secondly, Plavinski presents Eliezer Ben-Yehuda's efforts to resurrect Hebrew as a magnificent example of serving one's nation, something that is particularly relevant in Belarus, where the question of the national language is one of the sore spots in public discourse: "He was a pioneer in formulating and realizing a national idea: Our Land, Our Language. Language is the cement that turns a population into a nation. Lazar of Luzhki, the Hlybokaye resident, is a living reminder for Belarusians of how important it is to value their language."[49]

Thirdly, appealing not to Ben-Yehuda the man but to his bust, Plavinski "reads" national character traits and foresight about the future fate of the Jewish people into his imagined person (which was possibly the sculptor's intention): "Well, it looks like him . . . I mean, the sculptor did a good job. . . . The monument was made, I'll tell you how . . . well. In a subtle way, it makes a lot of sense as Jewish . . . like he was . . . modest. It's really sufficient . . . he was very self-sufficient and so is the monument and look, he's looking down like, 'How terrifying our history is . . .' He regrets this, but with pride."[50]

Thus Plavinski rhetorically inscribes the figure of Eliezer Ben-Yehuda simultaneously into three contexts: the local (Hlybokaye), the national (Belarus), and the Jewish, and with this, he argues for the appropriateness and significance of his memorialization.

Among Other Local Brands

Magdalena Waligórska has studied Henadz' Plavinski's initiative and the installation of the bust of Ben-Yehuda and a number of other initiatives connected with the revitalization of Jewish heritage and other Jewish-related commemorative projects in many other Belarusian cities.[51] Interpreting these initiatives in the political context of modern-day Belarus, Waligórska concludes that Jewish heritage has lately been used by both the authorities and opposition figures as an important element in shaping the national narrative: "Framing the Jewish past as part of the national historical narrative, activists, public historians, and authorities instrumentalize Belarus's history of multiculturalism to advance their competing visions of what constitutes the Belarusian national identity."[52] Following this logic, she sees the decision by the local authorities in Hlybokaye to install the bust of Ben-Yehuda alongside other famous townsmen as a political gesture of a piece with the federal policy of positioning Belarus as a country sharing the European values of tolerance and respect toward ethnic and religious minorities.

Waligórska's proposed interpretation of the memorialization of Jews in Belarus seems fairly convincing. But if we shift the perspective from the national to the local level, we see the installation of a monument to a famous Zionist in a former Jewish mestechko as an act of municipal management.

In the 2010s, the local government, headed by the chairman of the District Executive Committee, Oleg Morkhat, conducted an intensive local branding campaign and a transformation of the urban space. In less than ten years, the small town center has gained more than forty new sculptural objects, as well as a large festival with international ambitions; local residents speak about these changes with some irony. Among other things, two local products became associated with the Hlybokaye brands: local cherries and Baron Munchausen. The slogan "Hlybokaye: The Cherry Capital of Belarus" was coined to promote the town's brand, and as part of this effort, Hlybokaye has been holding an annual cherry festival since 2013. The image of the fictional literary character Baron Munchausen also became a local symbol after some journalists discovered a grave with the names of Ferdinand and Wilhelmina Munchausen at the old Koptevka cemetery.

All recent campaigns for creating and promoting new Hlybokaye municipal brands share a single schema with three components: (1) a (quasi)historical individual and the justification for his relationship to the town or district; (2) a physical manifestation in the town space, such as a sculpture; (3) mass public events with performative elements. In the case of the "cherry capital," the plant breeder Boleslaw Lapyr, who developed a special variety of cherries adapted to local conditions, was used as the appropriate historical figure. A bust of Lapyr was installed at the Residence of the Cherry Queen, and a sculpted image of the cherry was placed on the main street of the town. With Munchausen, who was also commemorated with a monument, the performative aspect entails the participation of this mascot in the public events around the cherry festival. Its main event is a parade through the town center led by costumed figures including the Cherry Queen and her companion, Baron von Munchausen.

The idea of introducing Ben-Yehuda into the pantheon of locally significant figures preceded the period of active town branding and appeared in a different context. Implementing this idea first took the form of individual activism and did not gain recognition for some time. However, once this initiative was finally approved by the authorities, the municipal branding was conducted using all the mechanisms as described above. A possible explanation for why Plavinski's project was eventually supported by the local authorities is that the brand of the "famous townsman Ben-Yehuda" is aimed at a specific foreign (Jewish) consumer rather than local residents or tourists in general.

The opening of the Alley with the bust of Eliezer Ben-Yehuda was followed by a number of events aimed at fleshing out the narrative of the newly acknowledged townsman and converting the installation of the bust into an event. Two years later, in 2014, a memorial stone with a plaque was installed in Ben-Yehuda's home village of Luzhki in the Hlybokaye District. After the opening ceremony in Luzhki, its participants traveled to see the bust of Ben-Yehuda in Hlybokaye. Both events were attended by Ben-Yehuda's great-grandson, the Israeli ambassador to the Republic of Belarus, the first secretary of the Israeli Embassy, the lead representative of the Jewish Agency in Belarus, and about twenty other people.[53] The delegation was treated with all the same pomp and solemnity as occurred at other local public ceremonies. In addition to the town's leading figures, also in attendance were the actors from Hlybokaye's folklore theater in Belarusian national costumes, who offered the guests bread and salt, and girls from the drum ensemble in Hussar dolman jackets and busby hats. In late August 2017, a group of Israelis who had come for the traditional day of remembrance honoring the people killed in the Hlybokaye ghetto visited the bust of Ben-Yehuda among other places in the town and had their photo taken with it.[54]

Thus, the brand of "famous townsman Ben-Yehuda" reaches its consumer via a "dedicated lane" of connections with Jewish organizations similar to the "direct-to-consumer brand" marketing strategy, in which a product is aimed at a particular group of consumers.

Ben-Yehuda as a Convenient Other

The approach to branding that emphasizes local specificity may explain why this monument honoring a renowned local Jew was erected. The selection of figures for the Alley of Famous Townspeople, which was apparently not undertaken lightly (the list of candidates was discussed with not only local but also regional authorities), was complicated by current political and ideological factors. For today's authorities, Belarusian nationalist figures are politically problematic, while, for the opposition intelligentsia, it is precisely these figures who are the most worthy of commemoration from among their compatriots. The Hlybokaye kraeved mentioned above spoke of this situation: "It was hard to get in there [into the Alley]. If you dig deeper, almost everyone is a nationalist around here."[55] We do not know whether the selection process included a debate, but writer and historian Vaclau Lastouski also entered the pantheon of commemorative busts for his contribution to the development of Belarusian as a literary language. According to the plaque under the bust, "Vaclau Lastouski was a social and political figure, writer, historian, and ethnographer." The inscription does not mention that Lastouski was also the first leader of the Belarusian National Republic, founded in 1918, and was consequently arrested by the Soviet government and shot in 1938. It is also silent about his death, and only those who know the town well would mention it when giving informal tours. We can suppose that Ben-Yehuda, who had been so insistently promoted by Plavinski, was also accepted by the authorities because he made a fitting counterpart to Lastouski. The presence of an "other," a Jewish nationalist, creates a good international background for their own, the Belarusian nationalist, and, considering the parallels between their major achievements as described on their plaques, it deflects attention from the purely political to Lastouski's linguistic accomplishments.

The creator of modern Hebrew is noticeably different from the other figures whose busts are included in the Alley. Among the famous townspeople, Ben-Yehuda is the only one whose actions worth commemorating were performed outside of this territory and outside of any national context that this territory might associate itself with, whether it be the Grand Duchy of Lithuania, the Polish-Lithuanian Commonwealth, prewar Poland, the Soviet Union, or the modern Republic of Belarus. However, the collective memory of the "historical" presence of Jews in the town apparently turned out to be sufficient grounds for including this "other" hero in the local pantheon.

Since the installation of the bust, no one in the town other than the tireless enthusiast and originator of the idea, Henadz' Plavinski, has taken on the task of popularizing the image of Ben-Yehuda in local knowledge. Among the locals—except for kraeveds, journalists, and those who work in the culture and tourism industries, as well as some members of the municipal government—knowledge about the renowned creator of modern Hebrew as a former resident and even of his statue in the town is rare and cannot compare with the popularity of new brands or other symbols of the town that have existed for years. Thus, in our conversations with locals of various ages and occupations, there were numerous mentions of famous townsmen like Soviet aerospace engineer Pavel Sukhoi and Yazep Drazdovich, "the Belarusian da Vinci," while "renowned townsman" Ben-Yehuda did not come up even once.[56]

In the local context of contemporary Hlybokaye, the Jewish figure turned out to be a rather successful source for targeted branding. It is attractive to an external target audience that local authorities are interested in him, but, at the same time, his inclusion in the pantheon causes no political controversy or public pushback, due to both his absolute marginality in comparison with the mainstream municipal symbols and the fact that the subject of Jews, whether consciously or unconsciously, is seen in Hlybokaye as organic to the place.

Memory on Demand

As we have tried to demonstrate, the image of the Jewish past is being actively constructed by several different individuals and institutions and variously articulated in the urban space. One might expect that this would lead to the internalization of the emerging narratives and images by contemporary residents of Hlybokaye and to the formation of a cohesive layer of local memory. However, our field research has convinced us that this has not happened in Hlybokaye. For example, Margarita Kozhenevskaya, who has given several lectures about Hlybokaye's Jewish past for schoolchildren and adults, told us that both groups lacked basic knowledge about the Jewish layer of local history. Both groups showed the greatest surprise and liveliest response to the stories about the Jewish etymologies of well-known sites and buildings in town. Even the cemetery with its unequivocal sign on the gates was not familiar to either group, not by far.

In general, discrete, selected elements of the Jewish past are constructed or articulated in certain situations, where there appears to be a demand for a subject or image from this past or, rather, its representation. We tried to demonstrate this mechanism in the two case studies above, which represent only a small number of all cases and situations known to us in which the memory of Hlybokaye's Jewish past is brought to the surface. A key role in this process is played by individuals, groups, and institutions that are the sources of ideas, initiatives, and/or direct activity. Such actors take on the role of "agents of memory," according to the definition of this function given by Paloma Aguilar.[57]

In some cases, the agents of memory themselves formulate the demand. Such are the researchers who came to Hlybokaye to study the epigraphy on the Jewish tombstones and elderly residents' memories of Jews; former natives of prewar Hlybokaye and their descendants currently living abroad, who initiated the project to restore the cemetery and create a memorial for the victims of the ghetto; engineer Henadz' Plavinski, who moved to Hlybokaye and became interested in local history, discovering Ben-Yehuda as a townsman for himself and others; and historian Margarita Kozhenevskaya, a native resident who studies the history of the Hlybokaye Jews out of scholarly interest. In other cases, the initiatives of the agents of memory presuppose interested parties from outside the town. This is the case with Tatsiana Saulich, the only representative of the local administration who supported the memorial initiative of the former residents and became their contact person and facilitator in Hlybokaye. Today, municipal authorities organize memorial rallies and other themed events for visiting Jewish delegations, and tour guides and other experts in local history include Jewish sites and subjects in their tours depending on visitor interest.

The emerging representations of the Jewish past fall in line with the initial demand even in cases when they are not created directly "on demand." In this regard, the narratives about the Jewish cemetery and the commemorative activities of its visitors are even more telling than the reconstruction itself. In all their various concrete realizations, these narratives' typical content structure and pragmatics are predetermined by the dynamics around the reconstruction of the cemetery and the public attention devoted to these dynamics. Another illustration is provided by the monument to Ben-Yehuda, which, despite Plavinski's persistent advocacy and enthusiasm, appeared only when the local authorities saw an appropriate context in the form of the Alley of Famous Townspeople constructed as part of an intensive campaign of city branding. Perhaps an even more important consideration was the presumed target audience of official Jewish delegations. These factors helped determine the optimal form for this commemorative sign in the form of a bust rather than a memorial plaque.

Thus, separate representations of the Jewish past have been appearing in modern-day Hlybokaye. Among them are official and vernacular narratives, municipal sites, cemeteries and memorials tied to commemorative practices, elements of the museum exhibit, fragments of town tours, and so on. In the space of local knowledge, these sites of Jewish memory remain as separate little islands, each of which emerged of its own accord and which together do not make up a unified archipelago.

It is telling that the few initiatives to produce a more or less coherent narrative about Jewish Hlybokaye for tourists have not yet been successful or had a noticeable impact. The tour titled "A Walk through a Jewish Shtetl" mentioned at the beginning of this chapter was, according to Margarita Kozhenevskaya, conducted only about ten times over two years. In June 2020, officials in Belarus and Israel inaugurated a new tourist route called "Paradise Lost: Life and Catastrophe in the Belarusian Shtetls" that passes through three districts in the Vitebsk Region. On this occasion, a memorial sign was erected in the center of Hlybokaye on the site where the main synagogue and Jewish community buildings once stood.[58] The stone memorial may be the first step in the systematic "heritagization" of Hlybokaye's urban space, but no other new objects, whether associated with the announced tourist route or independent of it, have appeared in the town.

Not only individual enthusiasts and large international organizations but also, as we know from other cases, local Jewish communities or larger Jewish organizations, the tourist business, and cultural and political institutions on the municipal level and beyond can also act as agents of memory that formulate a demand for an overarching narrative about the local Jewish past. But the case of Hlybokaye is remarkable because the parties that came closest to this role were visiting researchers, members of the 2015 expedition who contributed to the collected volume *Hlybokaye: Memory of a Jewish Shtetl*. This can be explained by the fact that the research methodology used by many of the members was intended to be an "experiment in the reconstruction of the 'Jewish history'" of a place (creating a documented map of the town's preserved and lost Jewish buildings and structures, family-name lists of former property owners, historical panoramas of Hlybokaye during various periods, and re-creating parts of traditional culture related to the Jews of prewar Hlybokaye).[59] In creating reconstructions of past historical and cultural realities, historians and folklorists were motivated by their scholarly interests and methods rather than by any institutional commission or social demand, and the results of their work had no impact on Hlybokaye. Apart from this group, nobody seems to be interested in promoting the image of today's Hlybokaye as a former Jewish shtetl.[60]

In many contemporary studies of the memory of twentieth-century Jewish history (most of which deal with the Holocaust), researchers discuss the *politics of memory*. They focus on analyzing the intentions, rhetoric, and actions of its different participants on the national and local levels who "work" with Jewish memory in the areas of politics, culture, and education.[61] This kind of approach is characteristic of studies of traumatic or contested memory, but for Hlybokaye, the Jewish past of the town is a topic that is ideologically and emotionally neutral. If one can speak at all of a particular politics of memory regarding the Jewish past in today's Hlybokaye, one could say that the town's authorities and the cultural elite have no strategy of their own but are ready to cooperate in response to an outside demand if this suits their interests.

At the same time, in the context of local culture and history, the Jewish component is not small, accidental, or made up, and this fact is acknowledged by certain groups and individuals to various degrees. Kraeveds bestow the idea of the significant place and role of Jews in the life of Hlybokaye before the middle of the twentieth century with the status of "objective historical knowledge." This is based on a multitude of facts known to these experts, but for the majority of present-day residents, the historical Jewish character of their town is understood only in terms of stereotypes. For example, they perceive the town's bustling commercial activity among these residents as a sign of the influence of the Jewish past ("the Pale of Settlement actually ran through here . . . so that itself forms some kind of . . . maybe that's why we're so enterprising here, because in all of us,"[62] and "And what about Jews? They don't work the land, they're big, you know—bankers, shops, and all that. And to this day, I don't know why, maybe because it's our heritage. Everyone who visits notices that there's a lot of stores for such a small town"[63]). This partly self-deprecating, partly self-congratulatory line of reasoning was one of the most noticeable common points in our conversations with locals and would come up not only in conversations about Jews but also in other contexts.[64]

It is apparently this combination of ideological neutrality and marginal significance attached to the historical Jewish character of the town that conditions, on one hand, the secondary nature of the Jewish theme in local knowledge and the benevolently indifferent attitude to it and, on the other hand, the occasional demand for the memory of the Jewish past in today's Hlybokaye, which neither allows the Jewish past to take on any great importance nor to entirely disappear.

Fig 8.2 View of Hlybokaye from the Bell Tower of the Church of the Nativity of the Most Holy Mother of God. The historical photograph features the view of the town from the same position before World War II. *Courtesy SEFER Center for University Teaching of Jewish Civilization.*

Notes

* We would like to express our sincere gratitude to the residents of Hlybokaye, who warmly talked to us, and to the Sefer Center for University Teaching of Jewish Civilization, for kindly providing access to the field materials.

1. At the beginning of the twentieth century, Hlybokaye belonged to Poland as a *miasteczko* (historically developed type of settlement in the Polish–Lithuanian Commonwealth with a significant proportion of the Jewish population) in the Wilno Voivodeship. On the eve of the German invasion of the Soviet Union, Jews constituted about half of the town's population. During the Nazi occupation, there were about ten thousand inmates in Hlybokaye's Jewish ghetto. After the war, the few Jewish survivors left for Israel, Europe, or North America, and new residents have since moved to the town from surrounding villages and more remote areas of Belarus, attracted by new industries. The current population of the city is around nineteen thousand people (according to 2019 data). More on the demographics of Hlybokaye in Rajak and Rajak, *Memorial Book of Glebokie*; Mochalova, "Glubokoe—stranitsy istorii"; Sorkina, "Mestechko Glubokoe i ego zhiteli"; and Kozhenevskaya, "Evreiskaia obshchina mestechka Glubokoe."

2. One of the authors of this chapter took part in the field research organized by the Sefer Center for University Teaching of Jewish Civilization in 2015. See Savina, "Zametki o lokal'nom tekste Glubokogo."

3. Belova and Kopchenova, Summary, *Glubokoe: Pamiat' o evreiskom mestechke*, 372.

4. For an analysis of a case like this, see Petrov, "Na menia vsio govoriat."

5. Exceptions to this were the interviews with Tatsiana Saulich and Margarita Kozhenevskaya, whom we spoke to as experts whose professional work was related to the Jews of the region.

6. This word is important for the discussion of local cultural processes. A kraeved (local history expert or local historian) is an amateur researcher who studies the history, culture, and nature of his or her village, town, district, or region and popularizes this knowledge. The discipline of *kraevedenie*, literally, "learning about a territory," is a practice that began in Russia and other Slavic countries at the beginning of the twentieth century as a movement to study one's locale or region. As a rule, kraeveds are seen as authoritative local experts.

7. See Zborowski and Herzog, *Life Is with People: The Culture of the Shtetl*.

8. For examples of work focused on folk art and architecture, see Sokolova, "Architectural Space of the Shtetl" and Sokolova, "The Podolian Shtetl as Architectural Phenomenon." On Jewish cemeteries, see Dvorkin, "Staroe evreiskoe kladbishche v Medzhibozhe," Nosonovsky, "Ob epitafiyakh evreyskikh nadgrobii Pravoberezhnoy Ukrainy," and Nosonovsky, *Evreiskie epigraficheskie pamiatniki Vostochnoi Evropy*. On comparing folklore, see Amosova and Nikolaeva, "Sny

ob umershikh v evreiskoi i slavyanskoi traditsiiakh" and Kaspina, "The Dybbuk and the Ikota."

9. See Veidlinger, *In the Shadow of the Shtetl*, based on material in the AHEYM Archive, Indiana University, Bloomington.

10. See Kopchenova, *Zheludok: Pamiat' o evreiskom mestechke*; Kopchenova, *Glubokoe: Pamiat' o evreiskom mestechke*; Amosova, *Lepel': Pamiat' o evreiskom mestechke*.

11. Lvov, "Shtetl v XXI."

12. Zukin, *The Cultures of Cities*.

13. Sandri, "City Heritage Tourism without Heirs."

14. Gantner and Kovács, "The Constructed Jew."

15. Corsale and Vuytsyk, "Jewish Heritage Tourism." The concept of heritagization has been used in the past two decades in research on political and social aspects of local heritage and tourism as an analytical tool for conceptualizing the process of assigning, formally or informally, the status of cultural heritage and value to various material and nonmaterial objects. As a result of this process, "objects and places are transformed from functional 'things' into objects of display and exhibition" (Harrison, *Heritage: Critical Approaches*, 69; see also Walsh, *The Representation of the Past*).

16. Sandri, "City Heritage Tourism without Heirs."

17. Leite, "Materializing Absence."

18. Alekseevsky et al., "Slovar' lokal'nogo teksta kak metod opisaniia gorodskoi kul'turnoi traditsii," 198. See also Alekseevsky, Lurie, and Senkina, "Materialy k 'Slovariu lokal'nogo teksta Mogileva-Podol'skogo."

19. Sokolova, "Jewish Sights."

20. Hakkarainen, "A Town Recalls Its Past," 30.

21. Although Hlybokaye is actively positioning itself as an attractive and popular tourist destination, the former Jewish mestechko has not been used in creating this image. See Julia Barilo, "7 gorodov i mestechek v Belarusi, kotorye smogli sebia podat' i privlech' turistov" ("Seven Towns and Mestechki of Belarus That Could Present Themselves and Attract Tourists"), *Planeta Belarus*, May 10, 2019, https://planetabelarus.by/publications/7-gorodov-i-mestechek-v-belarusi-kotorye-smogli- sebya-podat-i-privlech-turistov/?sphrase_id=17835; Tatiana Matveeva, "'Belorusskaia Veneciia': Piat' prichin posetit' gorod Glubokoe" ("Belarusian Venice": Five Reasons to Visit Hlybokaye"), Novosti, TUT.by, https://web.archive.org/web/20210117034641/https://news.tut.by/kaleidoscope/454963.html.

22. Arkadi Zeltser, the author of a book about the memorial activities of Soviet Jews, sees perestroika as one of the most significant stages in the general process of memorialization, which he connects in part with the activities of two groups of Leningrad Jews, the Leningrad Holocaust Research Group (Leningradskaia

gruppa issledovaniia Katastrofy) and the Center for the Study and Presentation of the East European Diaspora, which collected data about the mass executions of Jews by shooting, maintained the already-existing memorial complexes, and created new ones in Russia, Belarus, and Ukraine. See Zeltser, *Unwelcome Memory*, 323–36.

23. Chair of the District Executive Committee is the highest position in the district executive branch. The chair makes most decisions with the first secretary of the Regional Committee of the Communist Party of the USSR (District Committee). During both the Soviet period and today, the municipal administration is subordinated to that of the district.

24. The informant is a female district financial department worker (born 1923) interviewed in 2015. Sefer Center Field Archive.

25. Hereafter, the abbreviations "Inf." and "Int." stand for "Informant" and "Interviewer," respectively.

26. The informant is a female veterinarian (born 1946) interviewed in 2015. Sefer Center Field Archive.

27. The informant is a female hotel owner (born 1990) interviewed in 2019.

28. The informant is a female maid (born 1980) interviewed in 2019.

29. Researchers use different terms to refer to this type of tourism: *ancestral tourism, genealogy tourism, nostalgia tourism, personal heritage tourism, roots tourism*. See Birtwistle, "Genealogy Tourism"; McCain and Ray, "Legacy Tourism."

30. Leontiy Rakovskiy left Hlybokaye to pursue a higher education, first in Kiev in 1915, then in Petrograd (Leningrad) in 1922. *Green America* was the first collection of his stories about life in Belarusian mestechki. From the beginning of the 1930s to the end of his life, Rakovskiy wrote primarily historical fiction. His most famous novels are *Generalissimus Suvorov* (1938–46), *Admiral Ushakov* (1952), and *Kutuzov* (1960). Rakovskiy's early stories and novellas were never republished during the Soviet era.

31. Anton Sobolevskiy is the grandson of Aleksandr Sobolevskiy (1886–1983)—a famous Hlybokaye teacher and local history expert who founded and ran an underground intelligence cell during World War II—and a nephew of Yuri Sobolevskiy (1923–2002), founder of the Belarussian school of geotechnology and development engineer of the Minsk metro. A sculpture of Aleksandr Sobolevskiy holding a book in front of town symbols is known as the "monument to grandpa *kraeved*." There is a bust of Yuri Sobolevskiy in the Alley of Famous Townspeople (*Alleia znamenitykh zemliakov*) and a street named after him. In his introduction, Sobolevskiy wrote that his great-grandfather worked with Rakovskiy's father on the city council, and on the book's flyleaf, he placed a photograph of the Sobolevskiy family from 1910.

32. Sobolevskiy, introduction to Rakovskiy Leontiy, *Zelionaia Amerika* (Minsk, 2000), 3.

33. Arkadi Shulman, "Zelenaia Amerika: Iz knigi 'Kilometry evreiskoj istorii'" ("Green America: From the Book *Kilometers of Jewish History*"), *Mishpokha: Mezhdunarodnyi evreiskii zhurnal*, http://mishpoha.org/pamyat/260-zeljonaya-amerika.

34. "Cherry Capital" Hlybokaye town tour, conducted as part of the annual Belarusian Tour, led by professional tour guides, 2019.

35. Shulman, "Zelenaia Amerika."

36. Interview with Tatsiana Saulich, 2019.

37. The informant was mistaken or misspoke regarding the date: most likely, she meant a later date.

38. The informant is a female journalist (born 1946) interviewed in 2015. Sefer Center Field Archive. There is no synagogue at the cemetery and no plans to construct one; she is probably referring to the stone structure at the entrance.

39. Shulman, "Zelenaia Amerika."

40. The informant is an unskilled female worker (born 1937) interviewed in 2015. Sefer Center Field Archive.

41. Sobolevskiy, introduction to *Zelionaia Amerika*, 3.

42. Interview with Margarita Kozhenevskaya (born 1988), former researcher at the Hlybokaye Historical and Ethnographic Museum, 2019.

43. Melnikova, "Finskie kladbishcha v Rossii," 12.

44. Henadz' Plavinski's position on Ben-Yehuda is taken from his publication on WESTKI.info: naviny paunochnaj Belarusi i Vil'ni, a news portal for northwestern Belarus and Belarusian Vilnius "Glybocki panteon pamyaci" ("Hlybokaye pantheon of memory"), January 31, 2013, accessed June 13, 2020, http://www.westki.info/blogs/14242/glybocki-panteon-pamyaci?taxonomy_vocabulary_2_tid=All&taxonomy_vocabulary_4_tid=All&page=4 (by the time this article was published, Westki.info no longer existed). See also interviews with Plavinski conducted by Magdalena Waligórska in 2013 (for fragments, see Waligórska, "Ben-Yehudah—The Belorussian Hero" and Waligórska, "Jewish Heritage") and Olga Belova in 2015, during the Sefer Center expedition.

45. "Cherry Capital" Hlybokaye town tour, a quest and tour organized as part of the Belarusian Tour Guide Fest by a professional tour guide, 2019.

46. "Hlybokaye Connoisseur" Hlybokaye town tour, a quest and tour organized as part of the Belarusian Tour Guide Fest by a kraeved, 2019.

47. Quoted from a conversation during a casual, unofficial walking tour through Hlybokaye with a kraeved and journalist, 2019.

48. Plavinsky, "Glybocki panteon pamyaci."

49. Plavinsky, "Glybocki panteon pamyaci." As another kraeved said, the rhetoric surrounding the figure of Ben-Yehuda as an exemplary native son who revived the national vernacular is now widely accepted: "Well, he is also a good example for Belarusians who . . . well, for example rebirth of the language. . . . For

Belarusians... not everything is lost, a lot can be brought back—well, that's how they usually present it." (Quoted from a conversation during a casual, unofficial walking tour through Hlybokaye with a kraeved and journalist, 2019.)

50. Interview with Henadz' Plavinski, born 1938, kraeved, local columnist, in 2015. Sefer Center Field Archive.

51. The two other cases investigated by Waligórska were the foundation of the Museum of Jewish History and Culture of Belarus in Minsk, spearheaded by Inna Gerasimova, scholar of Jewish history and public activist, and the creation of the private museum of Belarusian heritage in Hermanovichi as well as the organization of exhibitions on the Holocaust by Ada Raĭchonak.

52. Waligórska, "Jewish Heritage," 351.

53. See "Pamyat' sozdatelia sovremennogo ivrita Eliezera Ben-Iegudy pochtili v Belorussii" ("Respects to the Memory of Eliezer Ben Yehuda, the Creator of Contemporary Hebrew, Were Paid in Belarus"), Jewish.ru: global'nyj evrejskij onlajn-centr, September 12, 2014, https://jewish.ru/ru/news/articles/168897/; Eleonora Khrizman, "Ben Ieuda vernulsia v Luzhki" ("Ben Yehuda Returned to Luzhki"), Zhurnal «Isrageo», September 12, 2014, http://www.isrageo.com/2014/09/12/benehydalujki/.

54. Diana Bernikovich, "Bol'shaya delegatsiia iz Izrailia posetila Glubokskii raion" ("A Big Delegation from Israel Visited Hlybokaye District"), Vitebskie vesti, August 29, 2017, http://vitvesti.by/obshestvo/bolshaia-delegatciia-iz-izrailia-posetila-glubokskii-raion.html.

55. Quoted from a conversation during a casual, unofficial walking tour through Hlybokaye with a kraeved and journalist, 2019.

56. The reputation of Soviet aerospace engineer Pavel Sukhoi as a famous townsman was formed long before the appearance of the Alley with his bust and is actively promoted to this day. In 1985, a memorial museum dedicated to Sukhoi was established at one of the town's schools, and in 2012, this school was named in his honor. At various times, there have been three different Su brand airplanes installed in the town: at the town entrance, in front of the school, and in the town park. Yazep Drazdovich was a primitivist artist, writer, and ethnographer who became known for his *maliavanki*, wall rugs illustrated with fairy-tale and cosmic scenes. There is a children's art school named after him.

57. Aguilar, "Agents of Memory."

58. Andrey Pankrat, "V Glubokom otkryt pamyatnyi znak na meste, gde kogda-to razmeshchalsia sinagogal'nyi kompleks evrejskoj obshchiny" ("Memorial Sign Unveiled in Hlybokaye on the Site of the Former Synagogue Complex of the Jewish Community"). Vestnik Glybochiny, June 18, 2020, http://vg-gazeta.by/2020/06/18/в-глубоком-открыт-памятный-знак-на-мес/?jmophlfcjmgdbiek.

59. For a map of the town's Jewish structures, see Kozhenevskaya, "Karta Glubokogo"; for lists of the names of former property owners, see Kozhenevskaya, "Spisok domovladel'tsev" and Kozhenevskaya, "Spisok vladel'tsev promyshlennykh i torgovykh predpriyatii"; for panoramic drawings of Hlybokaye during different periods, see Kozhenevskaya, "Evreiskaia obshchina mestechka Glubokoe" and Sorkina, "Mestechko Glubokoe i ego zhiteli"; and for re-creating parts of traditional culture related to Jews of prewar Hlybokaye, see Belova, "Byt i povsednevnost v rasskazakh zhitelei Glubokogo" and Moroz, "'Stol'ko istorii v etikh stenakh...'"

60. To be fair, one should mention memoirs by former Jewish residents of Hlybokaye that reconstruct prewar Jewish life, such as the *Memorial Book of Glebokie* by the brothers Rajak, particularly the chapters "The Destruction of Globokie" and "To the Story of Globokie" (Rajak and Rajak, *Memorial Book of Glebokie*), and the memoir "My Shtetl Glebokie" by Sirka Shapiro in Israel Rudnitski's *Vilner zamlbukh* (Rudnitski, *Vilner zamlbukh*, 139–40). But these documents, as well as the project that gave rise to their production, were created many decades ago and have even less connection to the situation with Jewish memory in today's Hlybokaye than do the abovementioned studies by the Sefer Center.

61. See, for example, Levin, Lenz, and Seeberg, *The Holocaust as Active Memory* and Hansen-Glucklich, *Holocaust Memory Reframed*.

62. The informant is a female hotel owner (born 1990) interviewed in 2019.

63. The informant is a male doctor (born 1978) interviewed in 2019.

64. This ironic stance can also be seen in Vodolazhskaya, *Igra v goroda*, 61–62.

APPENDIX

The Shtetl of Zhaludok: A Memoir

MIRON MORDUKHOVICH

Miron Mordukhovich and his daughter Margarita Trofimova, 2000.
Credit: Margarita Trofimova.

Miron Mordukhovich was born in 1929 in the town of Zhaludok, at that time part of Poland. He survived the war in the Soviet interior and later studied architecture at the Latvian State University in Riga. From 1954 until his death in 2015, he lived in the city of Lipetsk, Russia, where he worked as the chief architect at the city civil engineering department. His memoirs are the only literary source about Jewish life in Zhaludok before the Holocaust. The editors are grateful to Mr. Mordukhovich and his family for the opportunity to publish his memoirs.

The region from which our forefathers came was situated between the cities of Hrodna and Lida along the Neman River and included the shtetlekh of Shchuchyn, Zhaludok, Razhanka, Vasilishki, Astryna, Belitsa, and Orlia. In each of these towns, the Jews made up sixty to ninety percent of the total population. They were densely concentrated in the town center and along the main streets. The Christian population, consisting primarily of Catholics, was also densely settled, but on the outskirts of the town and, consequently, near the agriculturally rich hinterlands.

Located approximately fifteen to twenty kilometers apart, these towns had populations of about two to three thousand people each. The towns appeared some time in the Middle Ages during the time of the great migration of Jews from Western to Eastern Europe, to Polish and Lithuanian lands, where they were granted the right to engage in trade and handicrafts and were protected from violence by royal decree. The towns arose at the intersection of roads, at river crossings, and, in many cases, on the lands of the Polish nobility. As discussed below, such was the story of Zhaludok.

The Social Composition of the Population

As in all shtetlekh, Zhaludok was heterogeneous in its social composition. Approximately 2,500 people lived here, more than two thousand of them Jews. The greater part of the population was middle class, although there were also people of means and other very wealthy elites, as well as many poor and destitute people. Families were traditionally large, with ten to twelve children each, half usually dying in childbirth. An average of five or six children was thus considered normal. In the twentieth century, with increasing material and cultural prosperity and decreasing infant mortality, the birth rate fell starkly, so that in my generation, families generally had two or three children. As the children grew up, they began to help their parents, thereby entering their family traditions of commerce and handicrafts. Professions were passed down from father to son.

The highest stratum of society consisted of wealthy and well-known members of the town's most prominent families. These were merchants, shopkeepers, doctors, and other members of the intelligentsia. They were responsible for the town's basic needs, maintaining its synagogue and its schools and charities. They were the guardians of the town's peace and order.

The religious elite, consisting of the rabbi (*rov*) and the cantor (*khazn*), were also among this class. The town had two doctors: a Polish one, by the name of Pan Jelski, and a Jewish one, named Erdman. The town also had a family of dentists, the Olshteyns, as well as three pharmacies, and a local bank, where Shmuel Levin served as its long-time director.

The teachers at the town's two schools—a traditional Jewish school taught in Yiddish and a Hebraist school taught in *Ivrit* (Modern Hebrew)—were highly respected. They were few in number and lived in great modesty, but were committed to their work of bringing culture and knowledge to the community.

A second important social class was made up of small-scale merchants, workshop owners, and craftsmen practicing various trades, of whom there were a great many in the town. All of them earned their daily bread through hard work and made an average income.

Around the perimeter of the market square, where manufactured goods were traded, there were shops that sold textiles, ironwork, grain, and animal feed. There were several small grocers' stands, which sold so-called "colonial goods" of all kinds, from chocolate and *landrin* (caramel lollipops) to herring pickled in barrels. There were many butchers' stands. However, meat was usually sold on credit and delivered directly to customers' homes, so the butchers could rid themselves of their highly perishable merchandise as quickly as possible.

Bakery owners—who kept the town and the surrounding villages supplied with bread, rolls, and bagels—lived well, as did the proprietors of the town's taverns, beer halls, and pastry shops, where residents could drink, eat, and play pool. There were also several barbershops, where the townsmen could have their hair and beards trimmed. More often, however, men would pass the hours here chatting about town gossip and news. The town also had several repair shops, where bicycles, locks, Singer sewing machines, and Primus stoves—that miracle of culinary equipment—could all be fixed.

But most people in the town worked as tailors and shoemakers of different kinds—such as shoe clickers, who prepared the leather parts for footwear—as well as saddle makers, bricklayers, carpenters, roofers, stove makers, coopers, potters, and even a chimney sweep, who wore a traditional outfit. Of particular note was the guild of blacksmiths, all of whom were related to each other. There were five or six smithies in the town where sickles and scythes were forged, wheels and carts crafted, and horses shod. These were strong, hard-working people who performed miracles with iron with the help of the forge, an anvil, and a hammer.

A third social class consisted of petty traders, peddlers who wandered from village to village on skinny horses, engaging in small-time business. They bought chickens, eggs, grain, wool, and hides from peasants, often in exchange for thread, buttons, mirrors, and dishes. In town, these goods were then resold to larger merchants who processed, sorted, packed, and transported them by cart to Hrodna, Vilnius, and other cities. The town also had warehouses for storing grain, underground storage for eggs—where they were sorted and covered with lime—and several primitive workshops for processing raw skins and hides. There was even a small mechanical wool mill in the town. Almost all the town's houses had their own vegetable gardens, and some had fruit orchards. Some families, especially those with children, kept a cow or a goat and raised chickens. In the fall, they would buy and fatten geese for their lard and feathers. All this helped them survive under difficult economic conditions.

As to the overall economic situation in the town, it would be fair to say that, excepting a small wealthy class, life was hard and those who toiled could barely make ends meet. These people lived without any amenities, in small, cramped wooden houses, and with only the most primitive furniture. Since the poor were not able to pay taxes, it often happened that an "executor" (as the tax collector was then called) would come to appraise a family's furniture or repossess their horse. Tragedy was usually avoided, however, because the townspeople always knew about the official's visit beforehand and so hid their valuables and took the horse out of the barn. Drama was thus deferred until the executor's next visit.

But there was still a small group of people in the town who stood on the lowest level of society. These were poor people with large numbers of children who earned small and inconsistent incomes. In such families, there was constant need. They lived from hand to mouth and dressed in rags. They survived thanks to the charity of others and not infrequently begged for alms.

In addition to local poor people, there were also wandering beggars, who went begging from village to village. The shtetl had a room—in truth, it was more like a kennel—where these unfortunates stayed overnight while visiting the town. There were also many mentally ill people in the town, known to all by their names and habits. Some of these people were very amusing and delighted the town's boys with their unusual antics and strange ways of speaking.

All Jewish affairs in the town were managed under the supervision of the *kehilah*, an elected body of wealthy and respected people. This body preserved order and looked after the moral well-being of its citizens, oversaw the expenditures associated with public amenities and charity, resolved disputes, and helped the poorest in the community. Under its jurisdiction were the town's synagogues, a cemetery, a bathhouse, and various guilds and societies.

The *gmina* was the headquarters of the municipal authorities, where the town's administrative affairs were managed. In its courtyard there was even a prison, in the form of a stone barn with small windows, although it was almost always empty. Next to the *gmina* there was a post office with a uniformed postman. There was a small police station in town—known in Polish as a *posterunek*—with a few police officers. Their main job was to keep the town's streets orderly and clean. They would issue a citation for disorderly conduct or if the front yard of a home was in an unsanitary state. No Jews were employed by these state institutions or the police; they were not accepted there, nor did they seek those positions for themselves.

Despite the harsh living conditions of the prewar years, the shtetl developed and grew undisturbed. The established social hierarchy was accepted as though it had been created from on high by God Himself. There was no envy or malice. The majority accepted their fate dutifully. There were no major disputes or clashes between people. There was no theft, drunkenness, or debauchery. Fights between neighbors or relatives broke out only occasionally, usually over a piece of land, a fence, or the division of property in an inheritance.

A common misfortune for all Jews was the antisemitism of the prewar years. This manifested itself in graffiti that students from the town's Polish school wrote in chalk on the walls. Inscriptions such as "Yids to Palestine!" or "Beilis was a Yid!" were perceived as an inevitable nuisance and everyone was used to seeing them.[1]

Although there were no pogroms, simple fights did break out between the town's young Jewish men and the Christian peasants from nearby villages. Whether young or old, the Jews felt constant danger and anxiety, fear and insecurity, and this had a tangible impact on how they conducted their day-to-day lives.

The Natural and Urban Landscape

The shtetl of Zhaludok once belonged to Count Czetwertyński's family, some members of which were still living on their family estate up to 1939. They built the town according to a clear plan, whose structure remains apparent to the present day. In the center was the town market plaza, in the shape of a regular ellipse. Along its perimeter were one- or two-story stone houses. On the first floor there were shops, with living quarters located on the second floor or in the attic. In the center of the market square was a large two-story building with shops on the ground floor divided by an arch that was known in Polish as a *brama* (gate). Streets radiated out from the center in all directions, leading out to neighboring towns. The names of the streets reflected where they led. Thus, the most beautiful street was *Dvornaia ulitsa*, which led to the *dvor*, or nobleman's estate. *Vilenskaia* went in the direction of Vilnius, while *Orlianskaia* and

Субботняя прогулка

Поездка на станцию

Top, Sabbath stroll. *Bottom*, Ride to the railway station. Drawings by Miron Mordukhovich. *Courtesy Margarita Trofimova.*

Belitskaia led to Orlia and Belitsa, respectively. There was a Catholic church, a *kościół*, located on *Kostel'naia ulitsa*. "Deaf Street"—*Glukhaia ulitsa*—was so called because it was a dead end. This was a short street where the peasants lived and it resembled a village path. Several smaller side streets connected these larger radial arteries.

Along the narrow pathways were densely packed wooden homes of a rather miserable appearance, many of which had thatched roofs and were devoid of front gardens or any greenery whatsoever. In the courtyards were barns and other sorts of storerooms. Every ten houses or so had a well, usually in a form of a square log structure operated by a wooden crank, but there were also several for which a shadoof, or well sweep, was used.

In the early years of the twentieth century, the town was always deep in mud. The streets became impassable in the spring and autumn due to the waterlogged soil. Significant improvements were made in the 1930s, under Polish rule. All the streets were paved with cobblestones, and concrete sidewalks and drainage ditches were built.

In 1937, a small steam-driven electrical power station was built in the town. Everyone went to look at this "construction of the century." Electricity was brought into the homes of the town's most affluent residents. I remember that winter night when the streetlamps flashed for the first time, and the entire town strolled around until late at night, admiring the unprecedented spectacle. During these years, the first buses appeared on the Lida-Vasilishki line, which passed through Zhaludok and Shchuchyn. The first cars appeared in the early 30s. These belonged to the count's family. The boys would run after them until they disappeared in clouds of dust.

The town itself was very picturesque, situated on a small hill among fields, forests, and meadows. According to legend, the name Zhaludok comes from the Polish word *żołądź*, or acorn, which could be found in large quantities in the region's many oak forests. The swampy banks of a small river, the Zhaludianka, looped around the town. Its shores and meadows were frequented by white storks. Known in Polish as *bociany*, these were large, beautiful birds that meandered gracefully, searching for frogs. Their cheerful squawking could often be heard on sunny spring days.

At the end of Orlianskaia Street, there was a large, dense forest of coniferous and deciduous trees, stretching out for several kilometers along the road to Orlia. It was called the Lapishki Forest and it belonged to the count's family. Their carriages, bearing elegant passengers, would ride smoothly among the forest's hidden trails. In the summertime, children would noisily gather wild berries at the edge of the forest, never venturing inside. The dark and thick woods terrified our children deep into their souls. It was much more pleasant to visit the small coniferous forest at the end of Vilenskaia Street, where people went to relax on Saturdays during the summer. Not far from there was the Jewish cemetery, which was ringed by a ditch. Underneath the pine trees, traditional Jewish tombstones lay, made from finely cut stones with oval tops and engraved with Hebrew inscriptions. There were several recent tombstones of polished granite. The town's wealthiest citizens built small crypts out of brick.

On the other side of the street there was a slaughterhouse and an area surrounded by a wooden fence that served as the horse market. Horses were sold here several times a year, an event that brought together peasants, landowners, Jews, and Roma. We boys were fascinated by these dealings: the horses were made to run in circles, prodded, and examined, while the men haggled and argued until they lost their voices. But in the summertime the area was also used as a soccer field. The matches between our local aces and the teams from other shtetlekh became an important event for the town.

For centuries, the main mode of transportation was the cart, known in Polish as a *fura*. Among Jews, these were made very simply, with braided willow branches. They carried goods, travelling from village to town, and, on market days especially, took passengers to the train station in Skribaŭtsy.

Vehicles from the count's estate were distinguished by their finer quality. Here there were large trucks, small gig carts for foresters or managers, and heavy carriages with lanterns on either side, drawn by teams of four horses.

In the final years before the war, bicycles and even a few semi-motorcycles appeared. These were something like a modern motor bike. Only the wealthy could afford them. The same could be said of battery-powered radios. Families would gather together to listen to the radio, to political news broadcasts from Europe, especially as the war approached, or to joyful music and songs in Yiddish broadcast from Moscow and Minsk. And so, on the eve of Second World War, life in the shtetl continued quietly and peacefully, with all its joys and sorrows, all its idiosyncrasies and particularities, and without a thought or a worry as to the horrible catastrophe that would come to pass just a few years later.

Way of Life and Language

The main language spoken in the town was Yiddish. It was spoken at home, on the street, and in the synagogue. Many non-Jews in the town spoke Yiddish quite fluently and almost everyone understood the language. Hebrew was the language of religion, poetry, and literature. Although all prayer was recited in Hebrew, only a very small number of people, mainly religious functionaries and highly cultured Jews, could understand this ancient language. At the beginning of the twentieth century, due to an emerging self-awareness among the Jews and the growth of socialist ideas, many abandoned Hebrew, preferring the Yiddish language, which was spoken by ordinary people and used as a literary language by Sholem Aleichem, Mendele Moykher Sforim, and Avrom Reisen. All the left-wing newspapers were written in Yiddish, including *Folkstsaytung* ("The People's Newspaper"), *Haynt* ("Today"), *Der Emes* ("The Truth"), *Vilner tog* ("The Vilna Day"), and others. Most men in the town could read Hebrew characters and many subscribed to newspapers and bought books.

Knowledge of other languages was much less common. The merchants and artisans who had a connection to village life knew Polish, Russian, and "goyish" [Belarusian]. There was a large number of villages near the town where Belarusians lived, although the word "Belarusian" was then unknown in Poland. Villages in which the majority of residents were Orthodox were called "Russian." In Russian, the priest here was known as a *pop* and the church as a *tserkov*. Villages where the majority was Catholic were called "Polish," and the people considered themselves Poles. Here a priest was called a *ksiądz* and the church, *kościół*. Polish villages spoke Polish, Russian villages spoke Belarusian. There was constant hostility between Polish and Russian villages, and Russian villages were oppressed by, and often found themselves in opposition to, the authorities. The Jews, therefore, more often preferred to deal with Russian villages, where they were welcomed with kindness. In Polish villages, on the other hand, they could be verbally or even physically attacked. Few people thus spoke proper Polish or Russian. Rather, the vast majority of people spoke "goyish," a mix of bad Belarusian and Polish, the language of the peasantry.

At the end of the nineteenth century, all the town's Jews were religious, regularly attending synagogue and observing customs and holidays. Conversion to Christianity or becoming completely non-religious was very rare. At the beginning of the twentieth century, under the influence of the changes wrought by the revolutions and other cultural trends, young people abruptly abandoned religious observance, although there was no mass assimilation in the small towns. In the 1930s, about which I am writing, things were still going in the old way, and although many became atheists, the Sabbath was still kept and holidays were still observed, the rite of circumcision and bar mitzvah were still strictly performed, and a connection to the history and fate of the Jewish people was maintained.

Atheism and assimilation were to come later, with the rise of the Soviets. That is when the patriarchal way of life, which had persisted for four centuries, began to collapse. Over the centuries, this patriarchal way of life cohered around many different things: religion and the commandments, the struggle for subsistence and the fear of death, the attraction to science and creativity, as well as the inherent ingenuity found in folksongs, humor, and faith in the coming of the Messiah.

And the thread that ran through all aspects of Jewish life was the synagogue.

The Synagogues

Along the side of the market square, in a kind of alcove, there were two synagogues, known as the old one and the new one, as was customary in small towns. They stood next to each other at a right angle, creating a common courtyard where worshippers stepped out during breaks to have a rest, chat, and get some fresh air. In the mid-1930s, one dark, autumn night, the new synagogue burnt down on account of a fallen candle, but its brick walls remained unharmed, and soon it was reborn in a more contemporary form. It had a beautiful façade with semi-circular windows and many fine architectural details. Inside, it was rather ascetic: clean white walls, a balcony for women, and a platform in the center (*bimah*) for reciting the Torah, as well as a lavishly-ornamented altar (*oren-kodesh*), where the Torah scrolls were kept in their velvet sheaths.

On Shabbat and holidays, Jews would go to the synagogue alone or with their families, dressed in their finest. Men carried their *talis-zekl*, a bag with their *tallis* and *siddurim* (prayer books). In the synagogue (*bes-medresh*), everyone had their own place at the prayer stands (*stender*). Prayers were chanted individually and as a congregation, and at certain intervals, everyone would say *omen*. Unlike Christian places of worship, the synagogue would be rather noisy, as everyone would be praying in their own manner, often while swaying and bowing, and sometimes singing, as well. Between prayers, people talked about everyday affairs, *parnose* (earnings/profits), the price of oats, and news about the town and the world.

Holiday prayer services were especially festive because many people came and the *khazn* (cantor) would lift his voice, reaching the highest notes of the Jewish prayer melodies, and this singing deeply touched the hearts of the simple and poor. The synagogue wasn't just a place for prayer. It took the place of a community center, where people could meet, talk, and solve important town problems. It was where young people met and had dates, and the little ones, while the adults attended to holy duties, would run around the courtyard, playing and having fun.

After prayers, people would slowly part ways and go home, where festive dinners awaited them with challah, gefilte fish, and traditional *cholnt* (a special dish with meat, potatoes and prunes, braised overnight in a Russian oven). Often

Synagogue in Zhaludok (RG 120 Poland 6421 Zoludek). *Courtesy YIVO Archives Institute for Jewish Research, New York.*

times, there would be *tsimes*, *kugel*, and other Jewish dishes, in addition to the obligatory vodka or glass of wine.

The synagogue remains there to this day, although in a radically altered form. It is now the village club, with a lobby added on that has ruined the façade. The remains of the old architecture can only be seen on the eastern wall, with a distinct niche where the altar used to be.

Former synagogue (now House of Culture), 2012. *Credit: Sefer.*

Customs

Many religious and ritualistic customs, accompanying Jews from birth to death, were tied to the synagogue. In good weather, the official part of weddings would take place in the courtyard in front of the building. That was where the *khupe*, a canopy of rectangular cloth stretched over four poles held up by adolescents, was placed. The bride and groom stood under the *khupe*, and the rabbi would read the marriage contract, as parents, witnesses, relatives, and just friends who had come by to get a look at the wedding stood by. The young people drank from a glass of wine and broke the glass, the accompanying prayers were chanted, and with that, the *khupe* was considered done and a new family formed. This ritual was required of all Jews, even atheists, because without a religious ceremony, they would not be issued the requisite documents and their marriage would not be considered valid.

But it wasn't always cheerful in the noisy courtyard. Funeral processions also passed through it. Jewish funerary rituals were mournful ceremonies that were essentially different from Christian ones: the dead would be sewn into a white cloth shroud and the body laid out on the floor, surrounded by candles. Relatives sat on the floor around it. On the day of the burial, someone from the *khevra kadisha* (funerary association) would walk through the streets of the town and, with a monotonous cry, call the citizens to take part in the funeral. The body would be placed on a stretcher and four men would carry it to the cemetery. The women wailed aloud in lamentation. People weren't buried in coffins but rather nailed-together wood enclosures. Pottery fragments and pine branches were placed on the body so that it would be easier for it to rise when the Messiah came. Jews do not have wakes. The close relatives sit on the floor at home for seven days, "sitting shive," without shaving or washing, and the son or another younger man recites the Kaddish (memorial prayer).

The synagogue was also a place for all kinds of local and itinerant preachers. The poor and afflicted slept there, as well as people who found themselves in difficult situations.

The *shames* (beadle) and *shoykhet* (ritual slaughterer), who was permitted to slaughter livestock and poultry for a certain fee, were associated with the synagogue. Chicken that hadn't gone through the *shoykhet* was considered *treyf*. This was because Jews were categorically forbidden from consuming blood. Even an egg with a bloody spot was supposed to be thrown away. There are many laws and customs related to *treyf* meat, meat and dairy, fasts, and other restrictions. The laws governing what is *treyf* and what is kosher were serious restrictions on what could be eaten, but people were accustomed to them, having observed them from childhood, and ended up taking them for granted.

The Fire Brigade

The fire department stood next to the synagogue. As in all other towns, the fire brigade was a special source of pride. Young and old, people from all social backgrounds, volunteered to be part of it. In their uniform jackets, bronze helmets—polished until they sparkled—and broad belts with little axes hanging from the side, they looked positively heroic, and the boys admired them and dreamed of becoming one of them.

All of the fire-fighting machinery stood in their large and clean shed, which had a stone floor. This was made up of: a giant, black German machine, "the black pump," a harness for four horses, and a pump that eight men had trouble working, four on each side. There were also two smaller hand pumps on carts, but they were not particularly revered. All of this was overshadowed at the end of the 1930s with the acquisition of a *motorówka*—a very powerful motor-powered pump. Watching this machine at work filled boys with a righteous awe. Usually, no one could get it to start for a long time, then suddenly, something would finally combust, it would give out a terrifying, deafening roar, and then, shrouded in blue smoke, it would begin running with its monotonous motion to the general amazement of the crowd of gawkers who always surrounded the fire brigade trainings.

Fires happened occasionally. Drawing by Miron Mordukhovich. *Courtesy Margarita Trofimova.*

The trainings usually took place in the field behind the synagogue. The firemen would form columns, change formations, march, and then they would begin their training exercises with ladders and fire hooks; they would unwind the hoses and connect them in complicated configurations; commands were shouted, motors revved, and everything was very precise and decorous.

During actual fires, which happened several times a year, things would turn out quite differently. At the pealing of a bell, which was later replaced by an air siren, the volunteer firemen, cobblers and tailors, would run from their homes, tear off their work aprons, put on their helmets and broad belts as they ran, rushing to get to the fire shed. Ordinary town folk hurried over on their horses, hastily harnessing them into the pumps and two-wheeled carts with buckets of water. Thus prepared, the entire brigade moved headlong toward the fire. The "black pump" was rolled out ceremoniously, loudly banging over the cobblestones, and firemen with ladders and fire hooks ran alongside it, as did adults, boys, and dogs.

Usually, by the time they got there, the house would be just about done burning down: thatch roofs burn fast. Now, the fire hooks would be used to push aside still-burning logs, walls would be broken down, everything would be sprayed with a weak stream of water from the hose, and, most importantly, the surrounding buildings would be saved. After each fire, discussions would go on for days about who had distinguished themselves with daring and courage, who had been incompetent and fumbling, and the other sad and sometimes funny things that come with a fire.

But the true pillar of the fire brigade was its brass band with its kapellmeister Herzl Shifmanovich, a musically gifted man and good organizer.

In the summer, the trainings and parades were rather frequent, and when the brass band marched down the streets of the town with the entire fire brigade behind them, in uniform, it made quite an impression on us boys, and all of us dreamed of becoming firemen. Afterwards, playing in our courtyards, we would imitate all of their commands and formations in minute detail, copying our heroes.

The Catholic Church and the Mill

On the hill at the end of Church Street (*Kostel'naia ulitsa*) there was a Catholic church with its typical architecture, columns, and a pediment with three amazing reliefs of saints. The grounds were surrounded by a fence made of large stones, and there was a bell-tower on one corner of the building whose bells would be rung on holidays.

The Catholic church had its own life, attracting Catholics from all around the area. The priest and his assistants stayed on church grounds, not interfering with the affairs of the town, although the priest was well-regarded and welcomed. Jews avoided this place and practically never crossed the threshold of the church.

The second important Catholic shrine was at the end of Belitskaia Street. It was a fenced-in area with three crosses and the figure of the Crucifixion. Once a year, in the summer, there would be a procession from the church to the three crosses. It was a very picturesque sight, with banners, standards, icons, and lanterns. A great many people took part, walking and singing and wearing festive clothing. On this day, the town stood still out of respect for this other religion.

Often times, Polish Christian funeral processions from surrounding villages would pass down the town streets, and these also followed long-standing traditions: a cross with a crucified figure would be carried in front, followed by black banners with emblems of death—skulls and crossbones; the members of the procession carried lanterns and other things and were followed by a wagon with a coffin covered in flowers and, finally, relatives singing mournful psalms.

Below the church was the watermill. It stood on a strong stone foundation at the edge of a pond next to a wide artificial reservoir overgrown with white willows and alders. When the gates were raised, the water noisily rushed at the wheel, and the mill would slowly begin to turn. The stone threshers would be set in motion, its mechanisms and sieves would begin to shake and drone, and hot flour would fill the hoppers set out to receive it. The mill always smelled like flour dust, and the people who worked there were covered in flour, running around and dragging sacks, everyone talking about how well-fed they would be in the coming winter.

It was especially loud and cheerful further downriver. The water ran fast and spun, making whirlpools. On these rare days, the boys and young men would be very happy—they swam, dove, crisscrossed the water hole from side to side and from end to end, happy beyond measure. But then, after several hours, the water supply would be exhausted, the gates would close, and stillness would once again reign over the mill, except for an occasional fish jumping out of the water and noisily splashing back in.

In addition to the water hole and the mill, there were two other places where both adults and children swam in the summer. It was especially noisy at the Olesnik, a small river that ran past Orlianskaia Street. The banks were overgrown, thick with cattails, the bottom was swampy, and the water a little muddy, but what a joy it was to run across the wet field through the tall and fragrant grasses in a big gang bursting with shouts and laughter, then jump into the cool water of the Olesnik.

How fun it was for children from poor families, since it was free, accessible, and the same for everyone.

The Estate

The estate of Count Czetwertyński had a special place in the life of the town. It was about a kilometer from the town, down a road lined with ancient trees that turned into a shady alley right in front of the estate, with a massive gate at the end. After that, there was no path. You could see the magnificent lawn through the gate with its flowerbeds and dark green decorative trees. Beyond the courtyard, there was the two-story mansion, a *palats*, with its ornate architecture, red tile roof, and imposing porch. Behind these gates, the count and his family led their quiet and mysterious life. It was with amazement rather than envy that the town boys watched the little aristocrat children, all dressed up, playing on their lawn.

Only the count lived on the estate full time; his sons and daughters stayed in Warsaw and Paris and only visited during summer and winter vacations. They would come through the town, down its narrow, impoverished streets,

Графское имение

Возвращение с охоты

Top, Count Czetwertyński's mansion. *Bottom*, Return from the hunt. Drawings by Miron Mordukhovich. *Courtesy Margarita Trofimova.*

in noisy, cheerful cavalcades of dozens of carriages, men and women on horseback, wagons full of provisions, trailed by jaegers and hunters. This entire company would go out hunting in the count's forests. Several days later, they would come back that way again but now with their trophies, their wagons laden with the boars, deer, and chamois that they had shot. Sometimes, they'd get wolves. We were so impressed by the young aristocrats, their appearance and manner, and we understood that this was their lot in life, their fate, while ours was this poor town street.

To the right of the grand palace stood a more modest building, though it also had white balustrades and balconies. This was the home of Slawinski, who ran the estate, and his family.

Behind those buildings was their beautiful park, then a pond that had a mysterious green island in the middle with a gazebo. Behind the pond was the farm, which included barns, stables, storehouses, and the homes of the numerous servants. Next to the pond, on one side, there was a watermill, and on the other, a small distillery. Both buildings were made of red brick and quarry stone. Until a few years ago, you could see their ruins from the road. Jews and simple folk were discouraged from going any further into the estate—that could earn them a beating from the count's servants. However, on Saturdays, the town Jews would walk down the road and the alley to the count's gates and back, relishing their leisure time, the beautiful views of the green fields, and the surface of the pond, with its big golden carp—this miraculous, blessed world that was so calm and peaceful in the mid-1930s. No one could have guessed that just a few years later, a horrifying tragedy would befall the town, the count's estate, and all the lands on the banks of the Neman.

The Market

The market, which in Zaludok was held on Mondays, deserves its own special description. It was a noisy, crowded, and colorful spectacle, with peasants and merchants from all around the district and the surrounding towns. It took place on the round market plaza. In the center, there were collapsible tables for the tradesmen who sold textiles, pre-made clothing, linens, and so on. Several people, shouting loudly, sold winter hats, caps, and brimmed hats. They would stick a small hat on the large head of an unexpecting peasant, shove a mirror in his face, compliment him left and right, shouting and begging, until the muzhik finally gave in and paid for his purchase. The dry goods dealers arranged their merchandise on the small tables under the overhang: candy, glazed *prianiki* shaped like animals, birds, and people. They sold every kind of toy and their

Top, At the water mill. *Bottom,* The Jewish cemetery. Drawings by Miron Mordukhovich. *Courtesy Margarita Trofimova.*

Каждый понедельник на площади располагалась ярмарка

Monday fair. Drawings by Miron Mordukhovich. *Courtesy Margarita Trofimova.*

famous tilting dolls. It was noisiest next to the potters because their goods had to be knocked on to test the quality of the dishware.

People sold farm equipment: the blacksmiths brought their sickles, scythes, spades, wagon wheels, and entire wagons; harness makers sold yokes and harnesses. Close to a hundred wagons fit on the square, unharnessed horses in feedbags calmly chewing their oats, while in the wagons, all kinds of livestock bayed, baa'd, and clucked: chickens, ducks, geese, sheep, piglets. Jews walked between the carts touching the goods, bargaining, laughing, and getting angry, walking away and coming back, until the duck they wanted was finally handed over to them in a woven willow basket. There was a constant wall of noise on the square interrupted by individuals sounds: sometimes the barrel organ would start up, sometimes the blind man would sing his mournful song next to the gate. Magicians appeared on the square; acrobats laid out their mats and performed their tricks, rolling up into balls and tapping themselves on the head with their feet. It was all very entertaining, and peasants reluctantly tossed their coppers into the mugs acrobats held in their teeth. What didn't they sell at that market! By lunch, trade would die down and after lunch, the market would close. The stands would be taken apart, profits counted, and goods packed away into carts and covered in tarps. The peasants, on their way home, would stop by the tavern to have a shot of vodka chased by a mug of beer, with a bite of their own provisions. And then, having watered their horses at the well, they would head back to their villages. Then the sweepers came out on the square and cleaned the horse dung, straw, vegetables peels, and paper off of the cobblestones, making the square presentable again until the following Monday.

On the next day, the whole market brotherhood set off to Shchuchyn, where the market day was Tuesday, then Vasilishki, then Ostryn, and so on all week long. The tailors and cobblers, milliners and shopkeepers all had high hopes for these markets, where, if they managed to sell just one of their not very elegant items, they could at least afford to feed themselves the next day.

Schools

There were three schools in the small town: a government-run Polish school going up to seventh grade and two private Jewish ones—one taught in Yiddish and the other in Hebrew. They were called the Yiddish school (*yidishe shul*) and the Hebrew school (*hebreishe shul*). The former, named after Dr. Szabad, was more secular and supported the Bund and socialist ideas; the latter was religious, and its students were taught the Torah and other holy books.[2] The intellectuals and those who considered themselves liberals—merchants and some craftsmen—enrolled their children in the Yiddish school. The Hebrew school was attended by children from religious families who believed that their children needed first to learn how to properly worship God and the Torah, and then everything else. This school supported Zionism, the Palestine idea, and learning Hebrew. Some children took vows to speak only Hebrew or Polish everywhere—in school, on the street, and at home—and this led to conflict because everyone spoke Yiddish but only a handful of people knew Hebrew. People like this were seen as fanatics, and the idea of emigrating to Palestine seemed like an impossible fantasy.

The schools had to be paid for, and tuition was based on parents' income: students from poor families paid only a nominal fee. Still, if the fees were not paid, the children would be sent home, although this happened rarely.

The teaching staff was small, just a few people, but most of them were very passionate about their subject, like the teacher Wolczkowski, who was long remembered by the town's residents.

Usually, children went to school for four or five years, with the ones who did best transferring to the Polish school to complete seven grades. Very few then went on to high schools or vocational schools in other towns, most often Vilnius.

The two Jewish school were in constant competition for students and especially eager to attract those from rich families. It was truly a battle for minds and social and political influence in the town.

Having a secular school where children were taught literature, math, natural science, and history represented significant progress. As recently as the beginning of the twentieth century, children—mostly boys—had only attended cheders where barely literate rabbis only taught holy laws with a bit of arithmetic and writing in Yiddish on the side. Schools in the modern sense only appeared in the towns after World War I, and ones where classes were taught in Yiddish were few and far between: in our district, we only had them in Zhaludok, Dzyatlava, and the larger towns of Lida, Slonim, and Vawkavysk.

For a Jewish child, school was more than just where he or she learned to read. This is where they learned art and culture. The schools put on children's plays, published handwritten magazines, acting as lively and welcoming second homes, especially for children from large, poor families.

A special feature of small towns was the yearning for theater among the intellectuals and cultured craftsmen, and since professional troupes did not travel to such places, people would create their own folk theaters, drawing on the enthusiasm of local art lovers. The production of a play would be an important event in the small town's life in which people invested a great deal of time and painstaking effort. Everything began with choosing a repertoire and performers, and then surmounting all technical and financial hurdles. Our town had a collective of amateur actors, accompanists, prompters, and a stage crew. On average, they would put on about one play a year. The repertoire included plays from famous playwrights and Jewish writers; sometimes they also put on revues with various numbers and musical pieces. Everyone was a volunteer, working for free, donating their own time and energy to the theater. There was competition for playing starring roles, and participating in a play was considered prestigious.

My father was in charge of the technical side: he painted and installed the stage sets, did the lighting and sound effects, and operated the curtain. Sometimes, the sets would be quite elaborate: for a musical number from Goethe's poem "Erlkönig," a rider sat on a life-sized mock horse; during a storm in Ibsen's *Peer Gynt*, a "sea" raged onstage, with roars of thunder and flashes of lightning; the children's play *Bum and Spintop* featured a forest with fresh-cut pines, where it snowed cotton balls and a fairy castle's windows shone brightly.[3] It's important to remember that this all took place before the town had electricity. The stage was lit with kerosene lamps, and my father did his lightning tricks with a powerful electric flashlight shining through colored paper.

Costumes were collected from around the whole town. For children's plays, people would start sewing and gluing six months out, making armor and costumes, using colored paper, foil, beads, and other odds and ends.

A special group sold tickets a few days before the play. The money usually went toward the school or charity.

In the final days before the show, it was the talk of the town. People discussed arguments among actors, who refused to go on stage, who was replaced due to illness, the accompanist suddenly leaving town, a prompter losing their voice. And then it would be opening night, and people would pour into the 200-seat town assembly hall. Ushers, maintaining order, would seat people according to their tickets. The most prominent citizens with the most expensive tickets sat in the front rows. The poor sat in the last rows, on tall benches, like chickens on their roosts. Everyone was in their best clothes, munching on apples and candies. People came as families, chatting and laughing. There was no ventilation, so it was very hot and stuffy in the auditorium. And then the bell rang, silence fell, and slowly, the curtains parted.

On the stage, we see the interior of a fishing hut. In the center of the room, in a blue light, there is an old, gray-haired woman from a Swedish village delivering a sorrowful, heart-rending monologue in Yiddish. And although everyone knows this actress is just Elka, who isn't a fisherwoman, but the wife of Nokhum the blacksmith, all the women start to cry, and the men, usually so stoic, lower their heads so that no one can see the tears sparkling in their eyes. Oh, the incredible power of art!

After the play, people in the town discussed the characters and performers they liked, learned the songs, and often sang them among friends and family.

The plays often touched on social issues, such as when the song "Auf der Kanone," about the Spanish Civil War, was sung in one of the revues.[4] Very discreetly, some plays raised the topic of Soviet Russia, singing the praises of the good life that Jews enjoyed in Birobidzhan. There was often a policeman in the audience making sure there wasn't any Bolshevik sedition, red flags, and so on. And everything was always veiled enough that the guardian of the peace would leave happy and satisfied.

Musical revues with songs, dances, and poetry were especially popular.

On the eve of the war, they put on the children's play *Bum and Spintop*, which was a favorite among the locals, who would remember it for the rest of their lives. People prepared for over six months: several dozen children took part, magical costumes were made for them, as well as lavish decorations, and there were many songs and dance numbers. It was a veritable festival of children's art. And all the participants' hearts were in it; no one was forced—much to the contrary, since participating in a play was a great honor that had to be earned. These were happy moments in the lives of both the children and adults.

The terrible tragedy is that almost everyone who appeared in the play would remain children forevermore, finding their premature deaths in the terrible grave at the edge of the town. Only three are alive today: Chana Shifmanovich, Zelik Smolensky, and myself.

Holidays

All week long, people sweat and toiled for their daily bread, but then, when Saturday came, the day of rest set aside by God, even the poorest Jew was like a king in his humble home.

He'd await this day eating like a pauper: black bread, potatoes with herring brine—which you could get for free at the shop—cabbage, rutabagas, turnips, covered in sunflower oil. But on Saturday, there would always be challah—which women said the blessing over—cholent and kugel, matzah ball soup, tsimes, and other delicious food. After lunch, everyone would rest, and toward evening, they would go out to sit with the neighbors on a bench near their houses and talk about life, politics, prices, horses, and other everyday affairs and concerns.

But there were also many religious holidays turned into folk holidays, each one special and different in its character and customs.

On Hanukkah, people would light Hanukkah candles on their windowsills, where they glowed against the dark glass, reminding us of events from the ancient past. Children played with spintops and received Hanukkah money. It was nice making latkes and eating them in large groups at the table.

On Sukkot, the fall holiday, people built huts, covering them with ordinary fir and pine branches instead of palm leaves, and held meals in them. Guests went from house to house with palm leaves and a fruit that's like a lemon (lulev and esreg), delivering blessings.

On Shvues, the festival of spring, there was a cult of greenery, and homes and apartments were decorated with young shoots and greens.

On Purim, they read the tale of Mordechai and Esther in the synagogues, with King Artaxerxes and evil Haman. They put on plays based on this Bible story, cursed Haman, and at home, they would bake Homentashen, triangular pastries filled with sweet poppy seeds.

But the king of all holidays was Passover, or Pesach. Everyone dreamed of it, young and old, rich and poor, religious and agnostic. It was a week of rest, fun, and pleasure. Children were especially excited about the eve of the holiday (Erev Pesach). After a long and cold winter, people would open their windows and doors, whitewash the ceilings, paint the walls, clean and organize everything. In the courtyards, there were bonfires where people burned everything they didn't need and *homets* [leftovers of leaven bread], meanwhile "koshering" their pots and pans. It got very warm, the sun soaked the awakening earth, nature came back to life, and light filled the soul.

The most important moment would come when the boxes of Passover dishes were taken down from the attic. What didn't we have? There were porcelain soup tureens and silver ladles, beautiful tableware sets for six, cupronickel spoons and forks, and of course, shot glasses, wine glasses, and water glasses with drawings and inscriptions on Passover themes. I had a shot glass made of blue glass in the shape of a little keg, and every year, I would impatiently await reuniting with it when it emerged from the depths of the dark crate where it had spent an entire year in confinement, in order to sparkle and wink at me with its blue cut-crystal eyes on this wonderful holiday.

About a month earlier, the teams of bakers that prepared the matzah would begin their work. A day before Passover, people got rid of their *homets*, everything that was leavened, and hid it or took it out to the barn, and then, for a whole week, matzah and things made of matzah ruled the kitchen. Dinners were very filling and delicious: meat bouillons with matzah balls, all kinds of meat, fish, fruit. Everyday, people drank wine labeled "Kosher for Passover" at dinner. Many families, including ours, made "mead" from honey, hops, and other ingredients. It would ferment for a few weeks then drip through paper filters for a long time so that by the beginning of the holiday this delicious, sweet, slightly alcoholic, amber liquid would be ready.

In every religious home, in the evening, they would hold a Seder with its famous rituals and reading of the Haggadah, singing, and prayer; and people would put a glass of wine in their doorway for Elijah the Prophet (Eliyohu-hanovi).

The holiday would end when the week was out, life would return to normal, and the Passover dishes would be packed back up in their crates until the next year. There was a summer of work ahead with its own pleasures and difficulties, and after that, Rosh Hashanah, the joyous new year celebration.

Leisure

What did the shtetl Jews do to relax in the summer? Many different things, of course, depending on what they could afford. If you look at it from a modern environmental point of view, the air in our region, infused with the pine forests and wet meadows, was already wholesome, like spa air. It would have been hard to find a better place for a vacation. Still, people believed that we lived in a city and that in the summer, it was important to go to the country, to a summer house. The rich went to Zakopane, a famous Polish resort in the Carpathians; people with less money went to Druskinikai or, worst case, to villages on the shores of the Neman. But the overwhelming majority went nowhere and took no vacations. People worked day and night, striving and toiling, in order to provide the best lives they could for their families.

But in the summer, on Saturdays, all the townspeople would head to the nearest pine forest, into our famous evergreens, and give themselves over to rest. The forest was not very dense, it was clean, with large pines and with crows always crying in their crowns. People would bring the whole family, hang hammocks made from simple and sturdy cloth between the trees, lay out their provisions, and relax. People lay around, read, napped, visited with each other, chatted, argued, and... ate. Under those pines, in that monotonous murmur of pine needles and cawing crows, the people's appetite was whetted. Entire bags of provisions would be devoured, an especially popular dish being cold sorrel soup with sour cream, but also beets, cold meat patties and chicken legs, lekakh, and strudel, everything swallowed down with cold tea and compote, and then, people would lie back down. Sometimes, groups would gather and sing. The children ran around playing and going wild, their souls rejoicing. In the field, the young men played soccer, which had come into fashion even in small towns.

The woods emptied out toward evening as people returned to their homes with empty bags, rested and relieved, ready to get back on the wheel of hard work again the next day.

Who would ever have imagined that only a few years later these people would be brought here, to the edge of the pine forest, to be dumped into a single, giant, terrifying pit?

Those woods are gone now. They chopped down the old trees and undergrowth rising along its edge. All that's left are the very old pines in the Jewish cemetery, which is also abandoned, the old tombstones toppled, many of them carried off for the foundations of new houses. Just a little while longer, and there will be no traces left of the quiet and happy life that people once led here.

The only challenge to this silence is a small cement obelisk in memory of the 2,000 Jews from Zhaludok and Orlia who perished here.

Political Parties and Other Movements

The small town had its own movements, societies, and parties. It was divided not only according to which school a family's children attended. There were also people who were more to the left and those who were more to the right.

The Kholuts Zionist Youth organization had quite a few members, young people who supported the idea of creating a Jewish homeland in Palestine. They had their own association, as well as preparatory courses and camps where they studied, learned the skills of a trade, and prepared to move to Palestine.

Many took advantage of what this group offered even though moving to British-Arab Palestine did not promise any material advantages and was associated with difficulty and deprivation. But the idea was very powerful, since it was founded on the postulates of socialism and communalism. The Zionist Youth had their own slogans, songs, and a powerful faith in the future. Only a handful actually left, but they would become the pioneers who mastered the harsh soil of the fruitless land Erets-Yisrael.

Another, more extremist Zionist organization was Betar, which attracted many young men, more with its army-like organization and almost military uniform than its ideas. Their leader, [Vladimir] Jabotinsky, called for decisive action, which was very unpopular with the moderate among our community. These Zionists were very incendiary and stirred up scandals and fights, and their brown uniforms reminded people of [Nazi] stormtroopers.

The legal leftist organizations were allied with the Bund, the Jewish social-democratic party. They had their own trade union that lobbied for workers' rights. They fought for the eight-hour workday, better conditions for hired laborers, and so on.

The Communist Party was forbidden and so it operated underground. The town administration knew that there were those who sympathized with communist ideas and friends of the Soviet Union among the citizenry. These people were put on police lists and secretly watched, but as they never engaged in any serious activity, no one was ever arrested. One could be put in jail for hiding forbidden literature, distributing leaflets, owning a red flag, or celebrating May 1. Many town residents spent several years in jail for their underground activity. The majority of the craftsmen secretly sympathized with communism and spoke warmly of the Soviet Union, where labor, freedom, and justice reigned.

My father and his friends were committed Soviet supporters and read everything they could get their hands on about life in Russia. They were impressed with Soviet achievements, the Jewish republic of Birobidzhan, and the great leaders Stalin, Molotov, Voroshilov, and, of course, Kaganovich.[5] Where else could a Jew, the son of a worker, become the fourth-most-important figure in the government, the right-hand man to Comrade Stalin, the leader and teacher of all nations.

In the evenings, they would listen to forbidden broadcasts from Minsk in which they spoke Yiddish and sang Jewish songs. They would lock the door and read Yiddish translations of Sholokhov's *Quiet Flows the Don* and *The Tilled Soil* and read over and over Gorky's *Mother*, a lodestar for many who dreamed of revolution.

In our family, they talked about the good fortune of several acquaintances who managed to get across the border and relocate to Russia. What happened to them afterwards was a mystery, since there was no way to communicate with Russia, but what did that matter? The important thing was that they were OVER THERE, which meant they were boundlessly happy . . .

Oh, blessed naiveté! All of them found themselves in the Gulag in 1937 and only a few survived to die their own deaths.

My father would tell me about the amazing Soviet nation, where all people were equal, there were no rich and poor, everything was just, and there was friendship among different nationalities and, most importantly, not even a hint of antisemitism. That was something we felt very strongly in Poland. It wasn't too noticeable on the level of everyday life in a small town, but the propaganda in newspapers, antisemitic leaflets, nationalist parties, the [separate] benches on the left side for Jewish students, and discrimination in trade and culture—all of this came down on us in a dirty torrent, and Polish schoolchildren wrote antisemitic slogans on the walls of the houses in chalk, such as "Yids to Palestine," "Beilis," and other things of that nature.[6]

Antisemitism swept many nations. In Germany, they attacked Jewish stores and expelled masses of Jews from the country.

This was why the Soviet Union seemed so attractive—though, on occasion, rumor did reach us that terror reigned there, that people were shot without trial and sent to Siberia, and there were even photos published of the repressed. In our family and the families of our friends, however, people did not believe any of this and said that these were just stories spread by the enemies of the Soviet state.

My Family

At the end of the nineteenth century, Jewish families were known for having many children. Each family would have ten to twelve, or more. It was common for half of them to die in infancy, and the rest, surviving illness and epidemics, would grow up and start their own families.

My father's father, Perets [Morkhudovich], had twelve children, five of whom made it to adulthood: three from his first wife and two from his second, who was named Esther. I don't remember my grandparents, since they all died before I was born and there were no photographs or documents saying who they were or where they came from. But many generations had lived in Zhaludok and left behind a big family with many branches scattered throughout the surrounding towns.

My uncle Shloyme Morkhudovich was married to Ene, and they lived in Zhaludok, sold fruit, and had a small store on the market square. His nickname was "the Swede," and all of his children inherited this nickname and were also known as "the Swedes." Shloyme and Ene had six kids: Khashka, Mikhl, Etka, Moyshe, Beyle, and Shmuel. Khashka married Ruven Borovsky, and they had two sons, Shmulik and Perets. They lived in Zhaludok. Mikhl Morkhudovich was married to Keyle; they lived in Shchuchyn and had two kids. Etka and her husband lived in Ostryn; Moyshe and his wife and kids lived in Zhaludok; Beile, her husband, Moishe Toker, and their little daughter lived in Zhaludok; and Shmuel, the youngest, was a bachelor. After the war, only Shmuel was left of this large family. He married a Russian woman in Russia, has a daughter named Galina and a granddaughter. He currently lives in the Rostov Region, in Kamensk, and is retired. When he dies, this branch of the family tree will essentially be broken off.

My other uncle, Moishe Morkhudovich, emigrated to America in 1905, got married, and started a large fruit company. He had two sons about whom nothing is known. After the war, they answered a letter from my father saying that my uncle had died in 1942, hinted at offering help, and never wrote us again. Our father didn't write them, either, because in those years it was dangerous to have any kind of correspondence with people in other countries. My American uncle had been very religious and he changed his last name, taking a new, better-sounding one, calling himself Morris Cohen.

In 1913, Moishe had wanted to bring his half-brother (my father) over, but then World War I broke out and the trip fell through. After the war, in 1920, when Moishe learned that his brother was now a godless Bolshevik, he sent him an angry letter and cut off all ties. Only in 1939, when I got very sick, did my uncle send us 200 dollars, which was a lot of money, but we were not able to use it.

Frume Morkhudovich, my father's older half-sister (from my grandfather's first marriage), lived in Zhaludok. Her husband, Faivel, died in 1935, and she moved in with us. She had no children and was a very unhappy and weepy old lady with a difficult personality. As far as I can remember, she was at war with her older brother Shloyme and his family. When the war began, all of our relatives made up so they could lie down in the mass grave together, in each other's arms.

The second branch of the Morkhudoviches included my father, Velvl, and his older sister, Sore-Gitl—the children of Perets's second wife.

When their mother died, Velvl was just a little boy and Sore-Gitl took her place for him. She supported and raised him—he studied at the cheder and even completed two grades of school. Because he knew how to read and write in Russian and Yiddish, he was considered educated. And he really was a very cultured person: he was good at drawing, sought interesting people for conversation, and was friends with people from the intelligentsia.

Sore-Gitl married Faivish Zavadsky and moved to Rozhanka. They had a little shop and tiny coaching inn whose chief amenity was a large stable where people could put their horses. Often times, on market days, my aunt would come to our house with her big, ugly husband (one of his eyes was white). She always gave me cheap treats, hugged and kissed me, and I remember the kindness that exuded from her little body, wrapped in a shawl as she climbed out of their cart. They had three children. Their eldest daughter was Dveyrke, who moved to Palestine in 1933 with her husband, Moshe Katz. Their eldest son, Tevye, was tall, strong, and silent, just like his father, and worked as a woodworker in Orlia and Zatsepich. Then came Kadesh, who was the same age as our Perl, very cheerful and sharp, a cobbler in Rozhanka.

Before the war, in 1935, I visited my aunt. For a long time, she had wanted me to come and live with her. I was mostly excited to go to Rozhanka because of the train that passed beyond the edge of the town. And so the day came and I went to Rozhanka with my aunt and uncle on their wagon. Maybe as soon as the very next day I would get to see a real train rushing down the tracks. None of my friends had ever seen a train, either. When the wagon got a good distance away from the town and darkness fell, I began to feel sad, and I wanted to cry, but I was embarrassed—I was a boy, after all. Then, in the big, unfamiliar house in Rozhanka I got even sadder. My aunt didn't know how to distract me from my sad thoughts. I kept thinking of home, where right then they were eating dinner without me, and about the cat, who was probably looking for me, and the tears just fell from my eyes on their own. What a person is willing to go through for a chance to see a real train!

On the next day, in the evening, we went to the railroad. This was the most popular form of entertainment in Rozhanka—to go and watch the train. Entire families went and stood in large groups at the crossing, waiting. The train didn't come for a very long time, and I started to worry that maybe it wouldn't come at all. But finally, a black dot with white smoke over it appeared on the horizon beyond the woods. It began to grow and grow, and you could see the steam engine with its giant smokestack. It flew ahead at full steam, puffing out clouds of smoke. We stepped further back from the rails. It was so close now, we could hear the thundering of its wheels and see its green train cars. Then suddenly something giant, metal, and thundering flashed past us with its enormous wheels, something spinning and clanging, whistling steam, spouting smoke, and in the window, the laughing face of the driver. Then it was car after car after car after car, people waving their handkerchiefs from the windows, and we waved back, smiling and wishing them a good journey. The final car thundered by with a red light on its end, and then, instantly, it got quiet, just the rails still humming. The train disappeared quickly, and I stood there amazed and couldn't believe that it even happened. We had to hurry, hurry home so I could draw everything I could remember while it was still fresh in my mind. What a vision! What power!

The next time I went to Rozhanka was 57 years later. It was in 1993, when I went with Yoav, the American grandson of my aunt Sore-Gitl, to visit the town of his ancestors. Rozhanka was unrecognizable. Jews don't live there anymore, the old synagogue is in ruins, and old people showed us the place where Sore-Gitl Zavadsky's house had once stood. Going past it on the train from Hrodna to Moscow, I saw that crossing again, but there was no one there watching the passing train, no one waving a handkerchief. The times had completely, utterly changed, and so had the people. The distant and warm memory of my first train lived on only in my heart.

On my mother's side, all my male relatives were blacksmiths. My grandfather, Meyer-Yankl Toker, had been a blacksmith, as had all of his brothers and even my great-grandfather. Three of my grandfather's sons became blacksmiths, too: my uncles Elchik (Elya), Meyshke, and Khaim-Berl. In addition to them, there were Nokhum-Zelik, Leia, and Rakhil (my mother).

My eldest uncle, Elya Toker, was short, strong, and broad-shouldered, with a small beard and curly hair. He was married to Beylka, and they had three children: Moshe, Mirche, and Hadaske. The last two girls were friends with my sister, our houses were practically next to each other, and our families were very close.

In his younger days, my uncle had been a blacksmith, but he slowly transitioned to selling textiles; he was also a driver, making deliveries to Vilnius on his wagon, and grew vegetables. The backbone of their household was a strong horse and a milk cow. In the autumn, they would buy geese to fatten, butcher them, and sell the meat, fat, and down. In the summer, they sold cucumbers by the bagful, going out to sell them in villages beyond the Neman, where they didn't grow well. He would often take me with him on his trips. It was so wonderful when my uncle would get drowsy and let me take the reins and drive. With the sweat of his back, he saved up, sold his horse, and, together with a doctor and a banker, bought a real truck. Then my uncle and his son Moshe started transporting goods—not on a wagon, but in a truck. The two of them drove all around Poland and would have probably gotten rich if it hadn't been for an accident in the beginning of 1939: the truck was destroyed by a fire, along with all of its cargo, which meant total ruin. But then World War II broke out, and after that the Soviets came [to Poland], and all debts were dissolved.

My uncle Nokhum-Zelik lived in Ostryn and had a family, but I don't remember them well.

My mother's older sister, Leyka (Leya), was married to Yankl Remz and lived in Vasilishki. She had two children: a son named Zalmen and a daughter named Mira. My aunt was a very energetic and smart woman, as far as I can remember. She had diabetes but nonetheless ran the household and a textile store herself. She would often come to Zhaludok for the markets and always stayed with us.

Uncle Meyshke also lived in Vasilishki. He was short, completely kindhearted, and very myopic. He had a small shop selling metal goods. He had two children, a daughter named Sore and a son named Berl, who was my age. In 1939, I visited them and I remember their small town very well. I was quickly sent home from there on August 20, 1939, when the Polish army began mobilizing. War was just around the corner.

The youngest Toker, Khaim-Berl, lived in Zhaludok, near us, in my grandfather's old house with his wife, Sore-Leia, and two sons, Meyer and Dovidka, both younger than me. My uncle's smithy, which had belonged to my grandfather, was behind our house and I visited it often. I knew the process of forging metal backwards and forwards, how a simple metal rod, passed through the forge and worked on the anvil, could become an elegant sickle or the metal ring of a wheel. In the smithy, they shoed horses and made scythes, sickles, horseshoes, hoops, and other things. The forge made its monotonous hum for days at a time and was surrounded by soot, coals, and the sound of hissing water from red-hot metal. Occasionally, you would hear the ringing of the mallet and sledge hammer. I liked all of this, and most likely I would have become a blacksmith, but fate had a different, a completely different, plan.

At home, from dawn to midnight, you could hear the whirr of two Singer sewing machines, as my mother and a helper or two sewed linens, shirts, pajamas, and bedding for the whole town, which provided a decent living for our family.

My father worked with Shleymo Dubchanksy sewing women's coats and jackets—they were ladies' tailors. They didn't have much work, because in the 1930s everyone had started buying readymade clothes, which were cheaper and more elegant. Many professionals could not compete with the stores that sold readymade clothes and went out of business. My father's workshop turned into a clubhouse. In the middle of the large room, there was a big table that was always covered in patterns and materials, a gas lamp hung from the ceiling, a mannequin stood in the corner shaped like a woman's torso, and on the benches and chairs there were usually a few friends. They talked about politics, discussed local news, told jokes, argued, bantered, laughed. The regulars included Nokhum-Velvke Graishevsky, a world class sign-painter, practically an artist, a wit and a joker. Berl Lipshovich, a purveyor [buyer of agricultural produce and other goods from peasants] would come around, as would Velvke Zernitsky, a tailor, and many, many others. You could always hear something interesting there and have a good laugh at town mores.

But my father and mother's closest friends were the Volchkovskys, the teacher Shimen and his wife Sara, who ran a small shop. We went to their house practically every Saturday, and their children Chana and Neyka were like my own siblings. They always had treats on their table: white sunflower seeds and hard candies. They talked business and politics, read newspapers and literature, took strolls down Dvornaya Street.

My sister, Perl, was good friends with our girl cousins and other girls from school. I had two groups of friends: one was my school friends, children from rich

A tailor and in the smithy. Drawings by Miron Mordukhovich. *Courtesy Margarita Trofimova.*

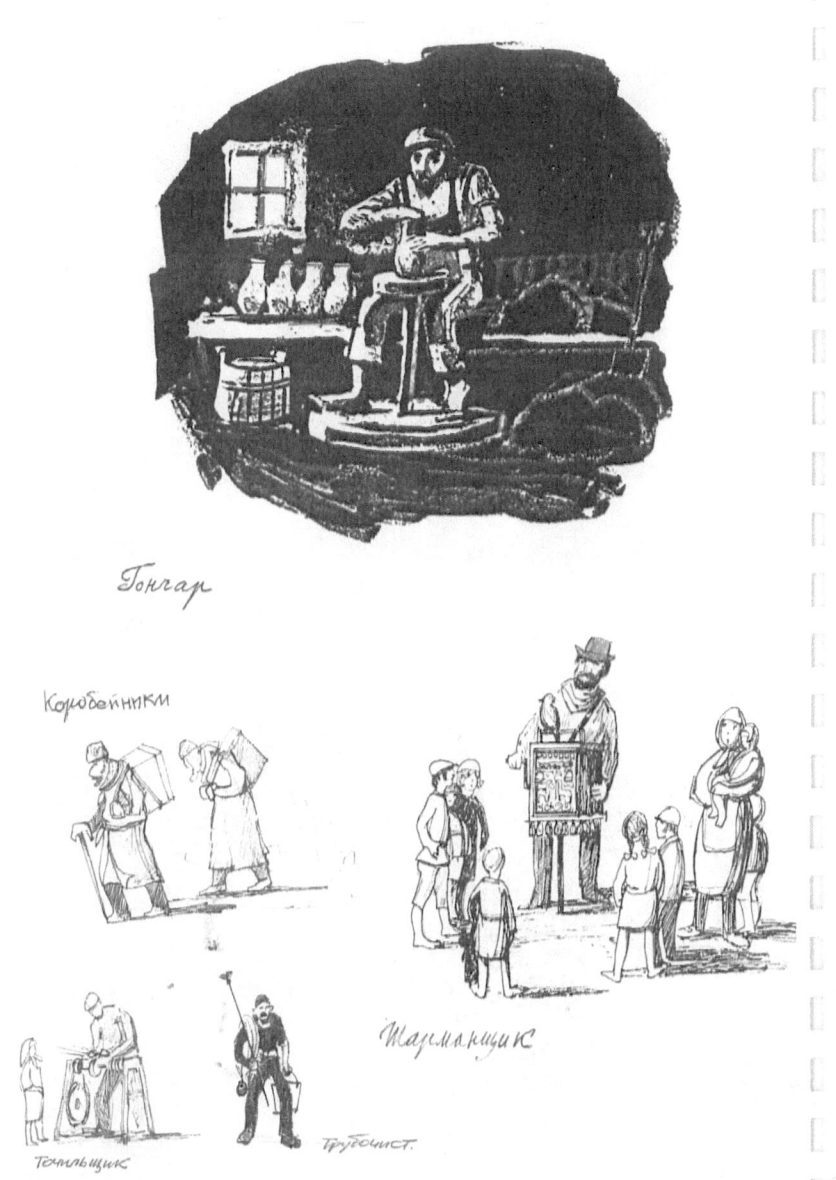

Potter, peddlers, organ-grinder, knife sharpener, chimney sweep. Drawings by Miron Mordukhovich. *Courtesy Margarita Trofimova.*

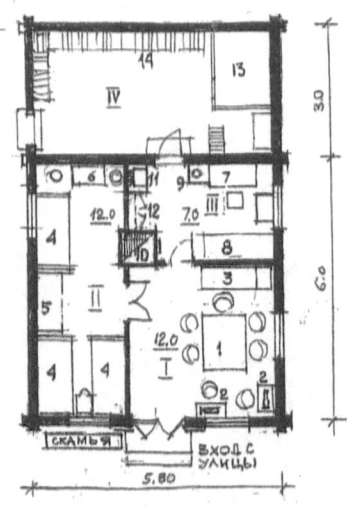

Our house in the 1950s. Drawings by Miron Mordukhovich. *Courtesy Margarita Trofimova.*

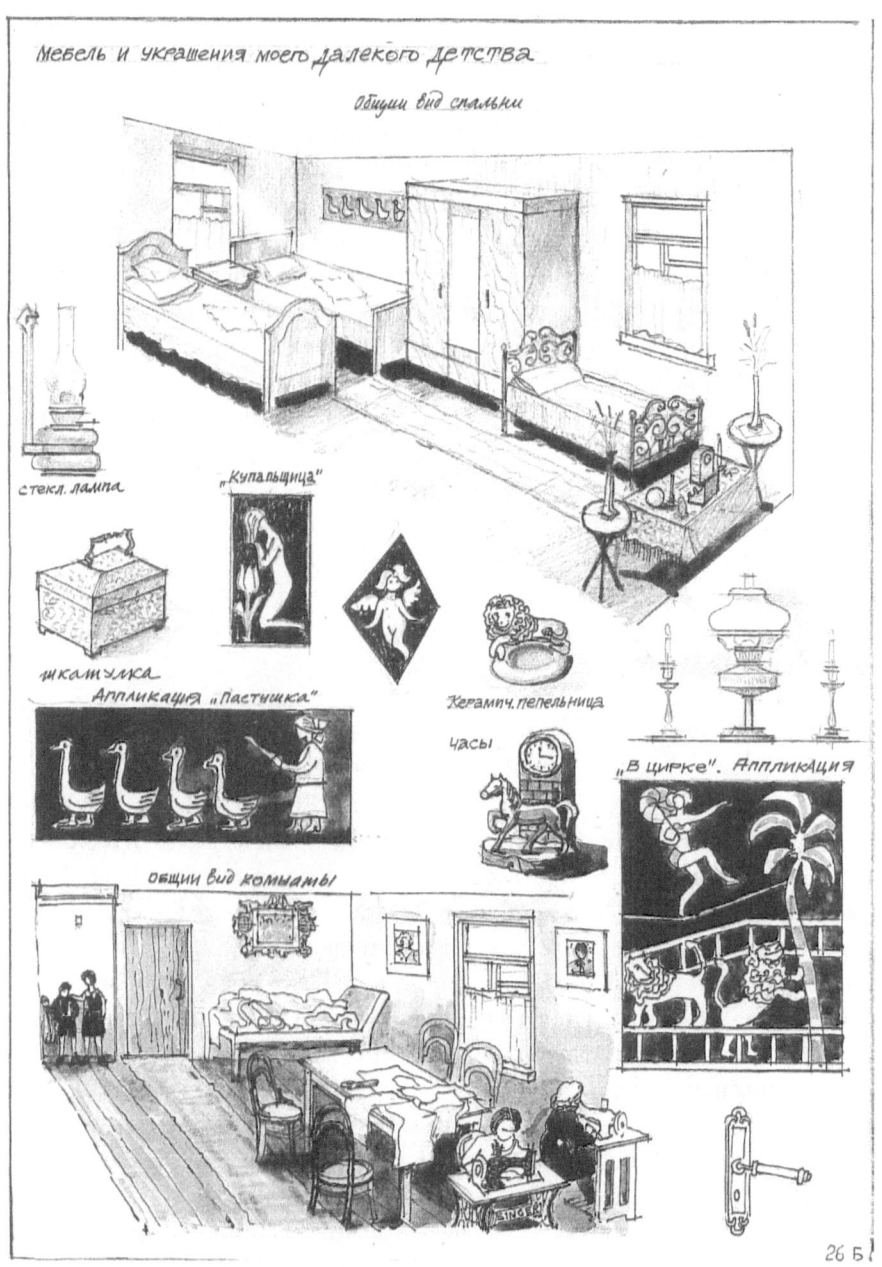

Inside my childhood house. Drawings by Miron Mordukhovich. *Courtesy Margarita Trofimova.*

families who lived on the market square, and the other included kids from the neighborhood, children of craftsmen and the poor. We played the same games that all children around the world play: we were firemen, policemen, and robbers; we played hopscotch and hide and seek; we ran, shouted, and laughed. In the evening, after a hot summer day, we would gather around on some porch and tell scary stories about demons, mermaids, *malakhaichiki*, vampires, and other monsters that terrified children.[7]

Our entire extended family that stayed under the German occupation died in horrible torment in the mass graves on the edge of the town in 1942. By a stroke of luck, my immediate family—myself, Polya [Perl], and our parents—were the only local members of our family to survive. Other survivors were Dveirke Katz, who lived in Palestine, and her three sons, who lived with their families in the USA. Shmuel Mordukhovich, who lives in Russia, also survived, as did Uncle Yankl Remz from Vasilishki. He was arrested before the war for speculation, given five years, and sent to Siberia. This saved him. After the war, he moved to Poland, then on to Israel, where he soon died.

My cousin Moshe Toker did not return from the Polish war. He was taken prisoner, and in 1940 we'd even sent him packages. Nobody knows where he ended his life's journey, in which death camp.

The Beginning of World War II, 1939

The year 1939 was an anxious one throughout Europe. Austria had fallen, Czechoslovakia was annexed, and Poland was next in line. German diplomacy grew increasingly aggressive, demanding that Poland cede the lands in the Poznan region and the "corridor" around Danzig. There were frenetic preparations for war and secret diplomatic visits attempting to create an anti-Hitler coalition between England, France, and the USSR to come to the defense of Poland. War was in the air, but people didn't want to believe it; they hoped that the politicians would find a way to check Hitler's appetite.

That summer was full of anxiety. Everywhere, there was talk of war—speculation, conjecture—and it all came down to the same thing: Russia would not allow Poland to be attacked, it was not in its interest; and in general, just and kind Russia would not abandon us in our time of need; plus, why would it want to have a border with fascist Germany? Talks between England, France, and Russia had already begun, and everyone was expecting them to come to a speedy conclusion, when suddenly, in August, like a bolt from the blue—the Ribbentrop-Molotov Non-Aggression Pact. Everyone was shocked, especially Papa's friends. Imagine! The communists who ran the government of our just Russia were shaking hands with the most evil enemy of humanity, the fascists. It was enough to make one lose his mind. Many made malicious jokes: "Looks like those communists of yours are friends with Hitler now." It was both embarrassing and terrifying. Poland was doomed. Now, there was nothing to stand in the way of a German invasion.

World War II began on September 1. A week earlier, Poland began mobilizing. The town went into mourning: many of the young men were drafted into the army, but also, by an inexplicable logic, middle-aged men were conscripted, as well. The goodbyes were hard because people knew that this war would be horrifying and end in defeat. My cousin Moshe Toker, whose wife had just given birth to a daughter, was drafted into the army. Even though everyone realized that war would break out any day, they secretly cherished the hope that somehow we would be spared this bitter fate. We weren't.

From the very first days, we began receiving alarming news. The Germans had instantly taken charge and advanced across all fronts. In a week, they had gotten to Warsaw and a bloody battle for the city began. The Poles fought desperately, but they were greatly outnumbered: the fate of the city and of Poland had already been decided.

The little town was in shock. What to do? Where to run?

People decided that the men should go east and break through to Russia and the women and children should stay put. Everyone's nerves were stretched to their breaking point. One evening, at the end of our street, a man appeared on a two-wheel cart who was not wearing a Polish uniform, and those who saw him decided that he was a German and ran through the streets shouting that the Germans were right outside of the town. Everyone, big and small, grabbed their already packed bags and set off running down Vilna Street. After running for a kilometer, they stopped and looked around. There were no Germans in sight. It turned out that the man who was taken for a German was really just a forester. And people started laughing at themselves, and at others, at our cowardice and panic and our shtetl Jews' fate. People went home and began to await what would come to them. Where can you run from yourself?

One morning, a rumor circulated that someone had heard on the radio that the Red Army had crossed the border and was coming to the rescue of its brother nation, the Belarusian people—in other words, us. It was hard to believe. It couldn't be. It was too good to be true. But the rumors grew more and more persistent. Warsaw had fallen, by all accounts, and the Germans should be here by now, but for some reason, they weren't. So maybe it was true, after all?

Sore told my mother, "Rokhke, pinch me, I think I'm dreaming." But it wasn't a dream. On September 17, the Red Army crossed the border and came to our rescue. We thought we were saved.

Two twin-engine planes came and landed on the landing strip in our field. Right before the war, they had started building this airstrip on the count's land. Hundreds of wagons had carried in earth, diggers evened out the surface, and it was nearly completed. But no airplanes had ever landed on it. And here, there were suddenly two, and French ones at that. They had come from Lithuania for the count's family. And they flew away a few hours later, taking the young lords with them. For some reason, the old count stayed behind. He was there when the Reds came, and a few days later he was arrested and taken away somewhere. People said to Siberia.

We were anxiously waiting for the Red Army. For several days, the boys and young men stood guard on the edge of town hoping to meet the Soviet troops. There were rumors that they were already in Lida, in Baranovichy, just not here yet.

Suddenly, an army unit appeared on the estate. We were running toward them, when suddenly, to our horror, we realized that they were Poles. They were very hostile, and we quickly realized that we had to run. And truly, they weren't an army anymore, they were a Polish gang. The Poles chased everyone into their homes, took several hostages, and demanded money, valuables, and bicycles. Everyone gave them everything and they went back to the estate. In the evening there was a shootout between them and several fighters from among the leftists. It was Dubrovnik and his brother who hid in the forest and started shooting at the gang. We were almost hit while running out of our house in a panic. In the morning, they said the gang had been run out of town. During lunchtime, an airplane with red stars flew low over the town. After lunch, a lightweight truck with soldiers arrived. They ordered us to organize a guard and said that the troops would come the next day. We still couldn't believe it. Now, people were afraid of Polish gangs that terrorized the towns and killed communists. In Skidel, some young people had taken the Poles for Reds and come out to meet them with red flags. They were caught, tortured, and violently murdered. After the arrival of the Red Army, their mutilated bodies were honorably buried on the square, as heroes, in a common grave.

The policemen had run away, and now the former underground ran the police. My father also patrolled the town with a big rifle, though without any bullets. The next day, the town was awakened by a loud rumbling. Tanks were going down our streets. Real tanks. They stopped in the town center, and everyone came out to see them, smiling, weeping from joy, giving the tank drivers apples. Now, we really were saved. The infantry, with a wagon train, followed the tanks. The soldiers made camp in the field behind the synagogue. They rested and ate, and we tried talking to them. They were so simple and so kind, we shared tobacco, and people brought them fruit. People were especially surprised by the little shaggy horses from the wagon train, which they said were a Siberian breed.

The town came under Soviet rule. All of the former leftists formed the new city council, including my father. They held a dinner at my father's workshop, where there was a lot of vodka and food and about twenty people, "all friends" of the Soviet regime, but they didn't start for a long time, awaiting the *Politruk*, the political educator. Finally he came, accompanied by a handful of army men. It turned out he was Jewish. There was a gold star on his sleeve (the sign of a *Politruk*). Everyone looked at him warmly, and he raised his glass and gave a speech about brotherly nations, freedom, and friendship, and about the teacher and leader Comrade Stalin. Everyone shouted hurrah, drank, embraced, and kissed from joy. Then, there were speeches in Russian and Yiddish, they started tossing the *Politruk* and everyone who had come with him [in the air]. They parted singing songs, including "The Internationale."

We hadn't expected to be this lucky. The Germans were just about to arrive and reduce us to slavery, when suddenly, in the nick of time, there was this miracle! The Red Army came and we became citizens of the great Soviet nation that we had dreamed of!

Oh, what a future awaited us! What happiness!

The Soviets

It was a marvelous, golden autumn. On the day Western Belarus became part of the USSR, there was a brilliant demonstration. A tribune was assembled on the square in front of the synagogue. A lot of people came, many of whom gave passionate speeches, not reading from pieces of paper, but speaking from their hearts. The orchestra played "The Internationale" and the entire square sang along. Suddenly, a cavalcade appeared—it was peasants on horseback in national costume with sheaves of rye arriving in town to the greet the Soviet regime. On that day, everyone, even the rich and religious Jews, celebrated their grand transformation into Soviet citizens. Soon enough, they would see what this really meant, understand, and be horrified, but in those first days, it was total euphoria, as people would say today.

My father worked at the count's estate, nationalizing the count's library, which was being moved into a recently organized club open to all. It was interesting at the club: people gave lectures, there were games like chess, and the library opened. The army unit took over the count's estate and people were not allowed to go there. The count's property was seized and, little by little, pilfered by the new bosses who had arrived from the East.

My father went to work as the administrative manager of the hospital. It seemed like being a tailor was not the right thing to do anymore, and many tailors and cobblers sought new occupations. The Hebraist school was shut down and merged with the Yiddish school. The former Betarists quieted down, hiding away their brown shirts. The Soviets started admitting people into the Komsomol and were very selective, looking closely into everyone's background to make sure that no one from the bourgeoisie was admitted. People started reporting on what other people had done under Polish rule. Now the Poles were more silent than water and lower than grass. They were no longer writing "Beilis" on the walls. Jews were the masters of the situation now. The Jewish girls strolled with the Russians, "Easterners," as people called them, and the NKVD (People's Commissariat for Internal Affairs) began its operations. The arrests began. People were taken at total random and no one could understand why. There were especially many Poles [among those who were arrested].

One day, a long convoy went down our street. The wagons were full of frightened women and children, accompanied by policemen. These were the loggers' families, and they said they were taking them to Siberia because they were enemies of the Soviet regime. I felt sorry for them; it was very hard to believe that these poor people were enemies. But since they were being taken away, that's how it had to be: the regime was fair, it didn't punish innocents—that's what my father said. They took several rich men and arrested a rabbi. All of them were given long sentences and sent to Siberian camps. The irony of fate! They ended up being the ones who survived and, after the war, went to Israel.

Meanwhile, the Soviet regime continued its interference in town affairs. To the great disappointment of the former Reds, they were completely ignored. In fact, they had to hide the fact that they had belonged to the Polish Labor Party, because it had been excluded from the Comintern, and having been part of it could quickly land you in the torture chamber of the NKVD. A lot of "Easterners" arrived to take leadership roles, while the local "bosses" were forced to return to their former occupations. My father once again became a tailor, clearly disillusioned by the new authorities, as were the rest of his friends. They couldn't understand: were these immoral, simple-minded, thieving people really the foundation of a communist society? They grabbed and seized everything they could get their hands on and sent it back East, especially the property of the arrested wealthy. All privately owned stores and shops were shut down.

Former bakery owners now worked as employees at the businesses seized from them, and the cobblers and tailors and other specialists were gathered into cooperatives. The authorities created a District Industrial Facility (Raipromkombinat). Many goods vanished, [black] bread was distributed through a list, and white bread disappeared altogether. But the village was still strong, and peasants brought cheap goods to exchange for the new Soviet money.

In 1940, construction began on the airport, the foundation for which had already been laid when the Poles were in power. But now it was going to be very big, and new technology was being used for its construction: giant caterpillar tractors pulled huge platforms down our narrow streets, a sight formerly unseen and unheard of. But even stranger were the columns of prisoners who were marched through the town daily. So many of them! Ahead of them, to the sides, and in the rear, they were accompanied by convoy soldiers with guns, guarding this dark mass of criminals, enemies of the Soviet state, but people were still sure this was just.

In the autumn, the twin-motor bomber planes landed in the aerodrome, and the town was filled with army pilots whom the girls would make eyes at. It became very prestigious to know a pilot, and only the most outgoing and good-looking could pull this off.

The town was transformed. In order to house the soldiers, the army commandeered rooms in people's homes. A commission went from house to house determining where pilots would be given rooms, and it turned out that for the most part they were placed with the wealthy, who had nicer homes and larger apartments. Those rich people were so lucky! I fretted and worried that we would be left out. What if we didn't get a pilot? But everything worked out and we got our own lieutenant, Pyotr Kozlov, big, smiling, and clearly goodhearted. We gave him the bigger of our two rooms, and the five of us moved into the little bedroom which was not more than 12 square meters. But we were happy! What wouldn't we do for a guest like that? When he arrived with his small suitcase, we held a celebratory lunch, and since he was very shy about eating, he drank more—he drank an entire teapot of beer and got truly drunk. Again, my father was shocked: here was an army pilot, a lieutenant, but he drank like a regular muzhik. Then his wife, Klava, and their son, Shurik, came from the Urals, dressed very modestly but in big, fluffy fur hats, which was very unusual in our part of the world. Klava had a temper, while Pyotr was big and guileless, and because he often went for the bottle, fighting began to break out behind the wooden divider in our formerly quiet home. People even said that Klava beat Pyotr. It was beyond anyone's comprehension how this fragile woman could batter one of Stalin's falcons. It was the shame of the entire Red

Army. I had a new friend in Shurik, who was younger and smaller than me, but in terms of his personality, he'd gotten a lot from his mother: he was a smart aleck and troublemaker. Shurik naturally spoke Russian, and very quickly I learned this language, which I really liked. The disgusting hissing of Polish could not compare, I thought, and after all, Russian was the future language of all humanity.

Soon, Pyotr crashed somewhere near Smolensk, and even before that, Klava and Shurik had left him to go back to the Urals, and we got our big room back. Now no one wanted to give up the room, not even to the Red Army.

All day long, we'd watch the planes take off and land. This was a powerful spectacle, and it made us feel like we were behind a stone wall that was protecting us.

One day, we had an unexpected visit from my mother's cousin, who had left our town with the Red Army in 1920 and about whom no one had heard anything for 20 years. All that time, he had been living in Minsk, working as a blacksmith, and when he got a pass, he finally returned home to see his family, about whom he also knew nothing. After seeing him, Mama said that he had bought up a lot of butter, lard, and textiles and was taking it all to Minsk, where there were major shortages. We couldn't understand: why wasn't there any butter in the capital of the Belarusian Soviet Socialist Republic? He came to our house late one night, looked around, as though he was afraid of being watched, then locked himself in the bedroom with my father, where they conversed in whispers. The things he told my father were enough to make your hair stand on end: the trials, the camps, the executions, the all-powerful NKVD, which could arrest anyone and no one would know where that person went.

You had to sit tight, stay quiet, say nothing to no one, and not try to become a boss, because they were the ones who were put away the most often. He talked about mutual friends who were no longer alive or had been sent to camps in Siberia.

My father was astounded by what he revealed but still had his doubts. He couldn't believe that innocent people were imprisoned. He insisted, "Look at our Party, our army, our wonderful Politburo." Portraits of Comrade Stalin, best friend of Soviet children, were hung in every classroom. They printed colorful posters with Stalin on top and all of the members of the Politburo below him: handsome Voroshilov with graying temples and big gold stars on his buttonholes; noble Molotov in his pince-nez; Kalinin, All-Soviet elder with an intellectual's goatee and a cane; then, the fourth in line, Stalin's close friend and associate Lazar Moiseevich Kaganovich, People's Commissar of the Railways—and a Jew. Where else could you see this, what other country in the world could have a Jew in such a powerful position?

No, there wasn't a nation in the world that was better than the land of Soviets. That's what I thought, as a boy, and that's what my father thought, too, as did millions of other intelligent, farsighted adults.

With the appearance of the pilots came the need for a soldiers' club. Soon, the synagogue was nationalized and turned into the House of the Red Army. Atheists and young people welcomed this, but for believers, it came as a harsh blow. Now, they had to gather in the small, old building, the number of congregants fell sharply, and belief in God was quickly vanishing. Nobody openly objected to this display of power, because by then everyone had realized that it was better to keep your mouth shut if you didn't want to end up in NKVD headquarters. We boys were thrilled: now, every evening, they played movies about heroes at the border, secret agents, and brave communists.

There were a lot of movies about the Far East, about the treacherous Japanese, who would always be defeated at the end of the movie. The ticket collector at the door was the old synagogue beadle (shames) transformed into a Soviet worker. When the screenings were for pilots only, he would lift his chin with a beard, roll his eyes back, and chant, as though speaking from the pulpit, but in Russian, "Today ish for soldiersh only, no shitizens allowed." The boys would get mad, call him a convert, and try to sneak in.

The school was now for everyone and took over two buildings. Russian was taught very intensively. It was difficult, but everyone worked very hard to learn it. They introduced a seven-day week and the only day off was now Sunday. This angered the Jewish schoolchildren terribly, for it was strange to go to school on Saturday, on a [Jewish] holiday. We went on strike and didn't go to school one Saturday. The teachers and parents got scared. No way! An uprising at the school? We were cajoled, threatened, and finally defeated when they said that they wouldn't allow protesters to join the Young Pioneers. Soon the Young Pioneer organization really did come to our town. People were accepted into it selectively: first the older kids, then the younger grades, regardless of class background. I was upset because I felt that, as a member of the proletariat, I belonged and should have been accepted among the first of the Pioneers.

Kids ceremoniously donned their red ties and pronounced a solemn oath, and with that, we were happy. Now, all kinds and a great number of pins gleamed from our shirts: MOPR (the society for the defense of Revolutionary political prisoners); Osoaviakhim (the society for the support of aviation and chemistry); BGTO (a beautiful pin on chains, with an acronym that stood for "Be Prepared for Labor and Defense"); "The Voroshilov Shooter"; and many others.

We began rehearsing a play in Yiddish about heroic Young Pioneer Pavlik Morozov, who had reported his father to the authorities for being a traitor.

Former Jewish residents of Zhaludok at the mass grave. 1980. *Credit: Margarita Trofimova.*

Pavlik was killed by kulaks, and now, on his grave, Young Pioneers from around the world—black, white, yellow, whatever—pronounced their solemn oath. The play was a flop.

This was vulgar pandering to the Party system. After it, there were no more plays. Everything had changed. The Jews were no longer united, there was no more community with its town problems, people were no longer brought together by their common nationality, they no longer empathized with each other and helped each other out of difficult situations. In shockingly short order, the worst of humanity emerged: fear, conformity, envy, corruption, and [betrayal in the form of] denunciations. People began to chase after power and prestige, high-ranking positions, and proximity to the administration, the Party, and even the NKVD, which people were terrified of. Very quickly, we'd turned into true Soviet people.

Elections were held for the Supreme Soviets of the USSR and BSSR. People prepared as though it was a major holiday: they decorated the agit-offices, hung posters and banners with slogans everywhere, and gave agitational lectures. [Sergey Osipovich] Pritytsky, a well-known Belarusian underground revolutionary, had been nominated to the Supreme Soviet of the USSR, and Olga Nenartovich, a young, illiterate farm-hand, had been nominated to the Supreme Soviet of the BSSR and thus to run the country. People laughed to themselves but said nothing aloud. They had learned to keep their mouths shut, and on election day, they happily and unanimously marched to the polling stations to demonstrate their loyalty to the party, the state, and the greatest leader of all time and nations, Comrade Stalin.

The summer of 1941 finally arrived, and with it, the long-awaited summer vacation. The Young Pioneers organized a paramilitary unit, and we spent whole days marching, singing war songs, and preparing to defend our country.

Once again, there were whispers of war. People secretly listened to a broadcast from London that said that Germany would attack the USSR the following Tuesday. People were thrown into panic, but then came an announcement from TASS about the friendly relations between our countries. All the rumors, it said, had been invented by the British, who wanted to drive a wedge between Germany and the USSR. People were quiet and happy once more.

I already had a ticket to a Young Pioneer's Camp near Hrdona, on the very border, for July 1. We had actually wanted a ticket for June 1, but hadn't managed to get it.... My star was already protecting me.

We swam in the river, jumping naked into the cool water. The sun shone down on us mercilessly—it was hot and humid.

On Saturday, we watched a new movie, *Valery Chkalov*. We were calm and happy, with a long summer ahead of us ...

... And 12 hours left before the outbreak of war.

Notes

1. This is a reference to the notorious Beilis trial in Kiev in 1911–13, in which a Jew named Mendel Beilis was accused of murdering a Christian boy for ritual purposes; Beilis was acquitted by a jury and immigrated to America.

2. Tsemakh Szabad (1868–1935) was a prominent physician, educator, and community leader in Vilnius.

3. *Bum and Spintop* is a children's play by Russian author Nikolai Shkliar (1878–1952), translated into Yiddish by Mendel Elkin (1874–1962) as *Bum un Dreydl* (1921).

4. Song by German poet Franz von Dingelstedt (1814–81).

5. Within the Soviet political structure, Birobidzhan, or the Jewish Autonomous Region (oblast'), did not have the same status as a republic or autonomous republic.

6. In the late 1930s, Jewish students at Polish universities were forced to sit on specially designated benches separate from Catholic students.

7. *Malakhaichiki* are probably demonological characters named after *malakhai*, a type of head covering.

BIBLIOGRAPHY

Archives

Cambridge, MA, Harvard University, Widener Library, Harvard Project on the Soviet Social System. https://iiif.lib.harvard.edu/manifests/view/drs:5356479$63i.
Hrodna, National Historical Archive of Belarus (NIAB).
Jerusalem, Central Archive of the History of the Jewish People (CAHJP).
Los Angeles, CA, University of California (UCLA), Charles E. Young Research Library, Department of Special Collections, David Pablo Boder Papers.
Lublin, Marie Curie-Skłodowska University (UMCS), Institute of Polish Philology, Ethnolinguistics Archive Lab.
Minsk, Belarusian State Archives of Literature and Arts (BDAMLM).
Minsk, National Archives of the Republic of Belarus (NARB).
Moscow, Russian State University for the Humanities, Folklore Archive (ALF).
Moscow, State Archive of the Russian Federation (GARF).
St. Petersburg, Archive of the Petersburg Judaica Center.
Vilnius, Lithuanian State Historical Archives (LGIA).
Vitebsk, State Archives of the Vitebsk Region (GAVO).

Online Archives and Catalogs

Association of Jewish Refugees, Refugee Voices: The Testimony Archive of the Association of Jewish Refugees. https://www.ajrrefugeevoices.org.uk/.
Azrieli Foundation, Holocaust Survivor Memoirs Program. https://memoirs.azrielifoundation.org/.
Indiana University Bloomington, Archives of Historical and Ethnographic Yiddish Memories (AHEYM). https://libraries.indiana.edu/aheym-project.

POLIN Museum of the History of Polish Jews, Virtual Shtetl. https://sztetl.org
.pl/en/.
Sefer Center for University Teaching of Jewish Civilization, Sefer Field Research Archive (ASC). http://sfira.ru/.
University of Southern California, USC Shoah Foundation, Institute for Visual History and Education, Visual History Archive (VHA). https://vhaonline.usc.edu/login.

Other Primary Sources

Bat, Luba. *Through Tears and Laughter*. Accessed September 17, 2020. http://cpsa.info/pruzany/luba_bat.htm.

Kulbak, Moyshe. *The Zelmenyaners: A Family Saga*. Translated by Hillel Halkin. New Haven, CT: Yale University Press, 2013.

Materialy dlia geografii i statistiki Rosii, sobrannye ofitserami Generalnogo shtaba: Minskaia guberniia, V 2-x chastiakh [Materials for the geography and statistics of Russia, collected by officers from the General Staff: Minsk Guberniia, in 2 parts]. Part 2, Compiled by Lieutenant Colonel I. Zelensky. St. Petersburg: Voennaia tipografiia, 1864.

"Materialy, otnosiashchiesia do novogo obshchestvennogo ustroistva v gorodakh imperii (gorodovoe polozhenie 16 iunia 1870)" [Materials related to the new social order in imperial cities (municipal statutes as of June 16, 1870)]. St. Petersburg, 1879.

Rajak, Michael, and Zvi Rajak. *Ḥurbn Gluboḳ, Sharḳoystsene, Duniloviṭsh, Posṭoṿ, Droye, Ḳazan*. Buenos Aires: Landslayt fareyn fun Sharḳoystsene, Duniloviṭsh, Posṭoṿ, Gluboḳ un umgegnṭ in Argenṭine, 1956.

———. *Memorial Book of Glebokie: A Translation into English of Khurbn Glubok by M. & Z. Rajak Which Was Originally Published in 1956 in Yiddish in Buenos Aires by the Former Residents' Association in Argentina*. Translated by Eliat Gordin Levitan. Canton, [NY?]: Kendall Taylor, 1994. https://www.jewishgen.org/yizkor/Hlybokaye/Hlybokaye.html.

Rakovskiy, Leontiy. *Zelionaia Amerika: Povesti i rasskazy* [Green America: Novels and stories]. Leningrad: Priboi, 1927.

Rudnitski, Israel, ed. *Vilner zamlbukh/Measef vilna*. Tel Aviv: Igud yotsey vilna, 1974.

Shneour, Zalman. *Shklover yidn: Novelen*. Vilnius: B. Kletskin, n.d.

Shulman, Arkady. "Zelenaia Amerika: Iz knigi 'Kilometry evreiskoj istorii'" [Green America: from the book "Kilometers of Jewish History"]. *Mishpokha: Mezhdunarodnyi evrejskii zhurnal*. Accessed August 19, 2020. http://mishpoha.org/pamyat/260-zeljonaya-amerika.

Sobolevskiy, Anton. Introduction (Ustup) to *Zelionaia Amerika*, by Rakovskiy Leontiy. Minsk, 2000.

Sviatoi muchenik-mladenets Gavriil Belostokskii (Zabludovskii). Zhitie I istoricheskii ocherk. Sluzhba. Akafist [The saint child martyr Gavriil of Bialystok (Zabludow). Vita and historical overview. Liturgy. Akathist]. Kharkiv, 2003.

Zalesskii, I. L. "'M-ko Uzda,' Materialy po demografii i ekonomicheskomu polozheniiu evreiskogo naseleniia SSSR" ['The town of Uzda': Materials on the demographics and economic situation among the Jewish population of the USSR], no. 8 (June 1930), 64.

Secondary Sources

Aguilar, Paloma. "Agents of Memory: Spanish Civil War Veterans and Disabled Soldiers." In *War and Remembrance in the Twentieth Century (Studies in the Social and Cultural History of Modern Warfare)*, edited by Jay Winter and Emmanuel Sivan, 84–103. Cambridge: Cambridge University Press, 1999.

Alekseevsky, Mikhail, Mikhail Lurie, and Anna Senkina. "Materialy k 'Slovariu lokal'nogo teksta Mogileva-Podol'skogo'" [Materials to the lexicon of the local text of Mohyliv-Podilskyi]. *Antropologicheskii forum* 8 (2008): 419–42.

Alekseevsky, Mikhail, Anna Zherdeva, Mikhail Lurie, and Anna Senkina. "Slovar' lokal'nogo teksta kak metod opisaniia gorodskoi kul'turnoi traditsii (na primere Mogileva-Podol'skogo)" [The lexicon of the local text as a description method for the local urban tradition (case of Mohyliv-Podilskyi)]. In *Shtetl, XXI vek: Polevye issledovaniia* [Shtetl, 21st century: Field research], 186–215, edited by Valeri A. Dymshits, Aleksandr L. Lvov, and Alla Sokolova. St. Petersburg: European University at St. Petersburg, 2008.

Alexandrowicz, Stanislaw. *Studia z dziejów miasteczek Wielkiego Księstwa Litewskiego*. [Studies on the history of towns of the Grand Duchy of Lithuania]. Toruń: Wydawnictwo Naukowe Uniwersytetu Mikołaja Kopernika, 2011.

Alroi, Gur. *Ha-mahpekha ha-shkeyta:ha-hagira ha-yehudit me-ha'imperiyah ha-rusit 1875–1924*. [Quiet revolution: Jewish emigration from the Russian Empire, 1875–1924] Jerusalem: The Zalman Shazar Center for Jewish History, 2008.

Altshuler, Mordechai. *Hayevsektsiya bivrit hamo'atsot, 1918—1930: Bein leumiut lekomunizm* [The Jewish section in the Soviet Union, 1918–1930: Between nationalism and communism]. Tel Aviv: Sifriyat po'alim, 1980.

———. *Soviet Jewry on the Eve of the Holocaust: A Social and Demographic Profile*. Jerusalem: Center for Research of East European Jewry, Hebrew University of Jerusalem, 1998.

Amosova, Svetlana, ed. *Lepel': Pamiat' o evreiskom mestechke* [Liepiel: Memory of a Jewish shtetl]. Moscow: Sefer, 2015.

———. "Nekotorye osobennosti kalendarnykh prazdnikov u evreev v Latgalii" [On some particular elements of the calendar festivals of Jews in Latgalia]. In *Utrachennoe sosedstvo: Evrei v kulturnoi pamiati zhitelei Latgalii; Chast' II* [The lost neighbors: Jews in the cultural memory of Latgalians, Part 2], 2, 27–39, edited by Svetlana Amosova. Moscow: Sefer, 2016.

———, ed. *Utrachennoe sosedstvo: Evrei v kulturnoi pamiati zhitelei Latgalii; Materialy ekspeditsii 2011–2012* [The lost neighbors: Jews in the cultural memory of Latgalians; materials from a 2011–2012 expedition]. Moscow: Sefer, 2013.

———, ed. *Utrachennoe sosedstvo: Evrei v kulturnoi pamiati zhitelei Latgalii; Chast' II* [The lost neighbors: Jews in the cultural memory of Latgalians, part 2]. Moscow: Sefer, 2016.

———. "'Vot latish so staroverom posporili . . .' (Rasskazy o mezhetnicheskikh ontnosheniia v Latgalii v mezhvoenyi period)" ['A Latvian and an old believer got to arguing . . .' (Stories of inter-ethnic relations in Latgale in the interwar period)]. *Zhivaya starina* 3 (2016): 24–27.

Amosova, Svetlana, Yulia Andreeva, and Vladislav Ivanov. "Evreiskaia religiia, religioznye praktiki i sinagogi v rasskazakh starozhilov Latgalii" [The Jewish religion, religious practices, and synagogues in the stories of the Latgalian elderly]. In *Utrachennoe sosedstvo: Evrei v kulturnoi pamiati zhitelei Latgalii; Materialy ekspeditsii 2011–2012* [The lost neighbors: Jews in the cultural memory of Latgalians; materials from a 2011–2012 expedition], 78–131, edited by Svetlana Amosova. Moscow: Sefer, 2013.

Amosova, Svetlana, and Svetlana Nikolaeva. "Sny ob umershikh v evreiskoi i slavyanskoi traditsiiakh (na materiale ekspeditsii v g. Tul`chin (Vinnitskaya obl., Ukraina) i g. Balta (Odesskaia obl., Ukraina)" [Dreams about the dead in the Jewish and Slavic traditions (On the materials from the expeditions to Tulchyn and Balta, Odessa region, Ukraine)]. In *Sny` i videniia v slavyanskoj i evreiskoi kul`turnoj traditsii*, 93–114, edited by Olga Belova, Viktoria Mochalova, Vladimir Petrukhin, and Liudmila Chulkova. Moscow: Sefer, 2006.

Augé, Marc. *Non-Places: Introduction to an Anthropology of Supermodernity.* Translated by John Howe. London: Verso, 1995.

Avrutin, Eugene. *The Velizh Affair: Blood Libel in a Russian Town.* New York: Oxford University Press, 2018.

Bazarevich, Anna. "Evreiskoe naselenie v narodnoi traditsii g. Ushachi i okrestnostei: Etnokonfessionalye stereotypy" [The Jews in folk traditions in the town of Ushachi and its surrounding villages: Ethno-religious stereotypes]. In *Lepel': Pamiat' o evreiskom mestechke* [Liepiel: Memory of a Jewish shtetl], 35–52, edited by Svetlana Amosova. Moscow: Sefer, 2015.

Belarusy. Vol. 4, *Vytoki i ėtnichnae razvitstsio.* Minsk: Institut mastatstvaznaŭstva, ėtnahrafii i fal'kloru, 2001.

Belova, Olga. "Byt i povsednevnost v rasskazakh zhitelei Glubokogo" [Domesticity and everyday life in the stories of Hlybokaye residents]. In *Glubokoe: Pamiat' o evreiskom mestechke* [Hlybokaye: Memory of a Jewish Shtetl], 177–220, edited by Irina Kopchenova. Moscow: Sefer, 2017.

———. *Etnokulturnye stereotypy v slavianskoi narodnoi traditsii* [Ethnocultural stereotypes in the Slavic folk tradition]. Moscow: Indrik, 2005.

———. "Evrei glazami slavian (Po materialam traditsionnoi narodnoi kultury)" [Jews through the eyes of Slavs (based on traditional folk cultural sources)]. *Vestnik Evreiiskogo universiteta v Moskve* 3, no. 13 (1996): 110–19. http://jhistory.nfurman.com/lessons9/folklor.htm.

———. "Evreiskoe kladbishche v rasskazakh zhitelei Lepelia i okrestnostei" [The Jewish cemetery in the stories of the residents of Lepel and its surrounding area]. In *Lepel': Pamiat' o evreiskom mestechke* [Liepiel: Memory of a Jewish Shtetl], 92–114, edited by Svetlana Amosova. Moscow: Sefer, 2015.

———. "Istorichekaiai pamiat i sovremennyi folklor (na primere narodnykh rasskazov iz byvshikh evreiskikh mestechek polsko-ukrainsko-belorusskogo pogranichia)" [Historical memory and contemporary folklore: The case of folk stories about former Jewish shtetls in the border regions between Poland, Ukraine, and Belarus]. In *Historia mówiona w świetle nauk humanistycznych i społecznych,* [Oral history in the light of the humanities and social sciences] 283–97, edited by Stanisława Niebrzegowska-Bartmińska, Joanna Szadura, and Mirosław Szumiło. Lublin: UMCS, 2014.

———, ed. *Kontakty i konflikty v slavianskoi i evreiskoi kulturnoi traditsii* [Contact and conflicts in Slavic and Jewish cultural tradition]. Moscow: Sefer Center, 2017.

Belova, Olga, and Irina Kopchenova. Preface (Predislovie) to Irina Kopchenova, ed. *Glubokoe: Pamiat' o evreiskom mestechke* [Hlybokaye: Memory of a Jewish shtetl]. Moscow: Sefer, 2017, 7–16.

Bessonov, Peter. *Belorusskie pesni, s podrobnym opisaniem ikh tvorchestva i iazyka, s ocherkami narodnogo obriada, obychaia i vsego byta* [Belarussian songs, with a detailed description of their art and language and sketches on national rites, customs, and way of life]. Moscow: Tipografiia Bakhmeteva na Sretenke, 1871.

Biale, David, David Assaf, Benjamin Brown, Uriel Gellman, Samuel Heilman, Moshe Rosman, Gadi Sagiv, and Marcin Wodziński. *Hasidism: A New History.* Princeton, NJ: Princeton University Press, 2020.

Birtwistle, Moira. "Genealogy Tourism—The Scottish Market Opportunities." In *Niche Tourism,* 73–86, edited by Marina Novelli. London: Routledge, 2011.

Boder, David. *I Did Not Interview the Dead.* Urbana: University of Illinois Press, 1949.

Bokhan, Yuri. "Miastėchki viarkhoŭiaŭ Vilii i niomanskaĭ Biarėziny ŭ XV – XVIII st. (pa arkhealahichnykh i pis'movykh krynitsakh)." [Towns of the upper Viliya and Nyoman Biarezina in the 15th through 18th centuries (according to the written sources)]. PhD diss., Minsk, 1994.

Bremmer, Jan N., ed. *The Strange World of Human Sacrifice.* Leuven: Peeters, 2007.

Brutskus, Boris. *Statistika evreiskogo naseleniia: Razpredelenie po territorii, demograficheskie i kulturnye priznaki evreiskogo naseleniia po dannym perepisi 1897*

[Statistics on the Jewish population: Territorial distribution, and demographic and cultural characteristics, from the data collected in the 1897 census]. St. Petersburg: Sever, 1909.

Buszko, Paweł. *"Żyd żydem." Wizerunek Żyda w kulturze ludowej podlaskich prawosławnych Białorusinów. Miasteczko Orla.* ["Jew as a Jew." Image of the Jew in the folk culture of Orthodox Belarusians in Podlasie. The town of Orla]. Warsaw: Instytut sławistyki PAN, Fundacja sławistuczna, Wydawnictwo Agade Bis: 2012.

Cała, Alina. *Wizerunek Żyda w polskiej kulturze ludowej* [Image of the Jew in Polish folk culture]. Warsaw: Oficyna naykowa, 2005.

Charkiewicz, Jarosław, ed. *Akatyst. Życie i męczeństwo św. Gabriela Zabłudowskiego.* [Akathist. Life and martyrdom of St. Gabriel Zabludowski]. Białystok: Parafia Prawosławna św. Mikołaja Cudotwórcy w Białymstoku, 2012.

Chertovich, Vladimir. *Voina po zakonam podlosti* [A war fought according to the laws of ignobility]. Minsk: Pravoslavnaiia initsiativa, 1999.

Chkolnikova, Elina. "The Transformation of the Shtetl in the USSR in the 1930s." *Jews in Russia and Eastern Europe* 52, no. 1 (Summer 2004): 93–100.

Corsale, Andrea, and Olha Vuytsyk. "Jewish Heritage Tourism between Memories and Strategies: Different Approaches from Lviv, Ukraine." *Current Issues in Tourism* 21, no. 5 (2015): 583–98.

Di shtetlekh fun vssr in rekonstruktivn period. Minsk: Belarusian Academy of Sciences, 1932.

Dvorkin, Ilya. "Staroe evreiskoe kladbishche v Medzhibozhe" [The old Jewish cemetery in Medzhybizh]. In *Istoriia evreev na Ukraine i v Belorussii: Ekspeditsii, pamiatniki, nakhodki* [History of the Jews in Ukraine and Belarus: Expeditions, monuments, discoveries], 185–213, edited by Veniamin Lukin, Boris Khaimovich, and Valeri Dymshits. St. Petersburg: St. Petersburg Jewish University, 1994.

Dymshits, Valeri. "Evreiskoe kladbishche: Mesto kuda ne khodiat" [Jewish cemetery: A site that is not visited]. In *Shtetl, XXI vek: Polevye issledovaniia* [Shtetl, 21st century: Field research], 135–58, edited by Valeri A. Dymshits, Aleksandr L. Lvov, and Alla Sokolova. St. Petersburg: European University at St. Petersburg.

Dymshits, Valeri A., Aleksandr L. Lvov, and Alla Sokolova, eds. *Shtetl, XXI vek: Polevye issledovaniia* [Shtetl, 21st century: Field research]. St. Petersburg: European University at St. Petersburg, 2008.

Estraikh, Gennady. "The Soviet Shtetl in the 1920s." *Polin* 17 (2004).

Estraikh, Gennady, and Mikhail Krutikov, eds. *The Shtetl: Image and Reality; Papers of the Second Mendel Friedman International Conference on Yiddish*. Oxford: Legenda, 2000.

Ėtnahrafīi͡a Belarusi: Ėntsyklapedyīi͡a. Minsk: BelSE, 1989.

Fishman, David. *Russia's First Modern Jews: The Jews of Shklov*. New York: New York University Press, 1996.

Gantner, Eszter B., and Mátyás Kovács. "The Constructed Jew: A Pragmatic Approach for Defining a Collective Central European Image of Jews." In *Jewish Space in Central and Eastern Europe: Day-to-Day History*, edited by Jurgita Šiaučiūnaite-Verbickienė and Larisa Lempertienė, 211–224. Newcastle, UK: Cambridge Scholars, 2007.

Gatagova, Liudmila S., L. P. Kosheleva, and L. A. Rogovaya, eds. *TsK RKP(b) i natsionalnyi vopros. Kniga 1, 1918–1933* [The Central Committee of the Russian Communist Party of Bolsheviks and the question of nationalities, book 1]. Moscow: Rosspen, 2005.

Gavrilenko, Kirill. "Blagotvoritelnost v evreiskoi pogrebalnoi obriadnosti na territorii Zapadnoi Belarusi (1921–1939 gg.)" [Philanthropy in Jewish funeral customs in Western Belarus (1921–1939)]. In *Glubokoe: Pamiat' o evreiskom mestechke* [Hlybokaye: Memory of a Jewish shtetl], 121–40, edited by Irina Kopchenova. Moscow: Sefer, 2017.

Gekht, Marina, and Viktor Andrushkevich. "Rasskazy o evreiskikh prazdnikakh" [Stories about Jewish festivals]. In *Utrachennoe sosedstvo: Evrei v kulturnoi pamiati zhitelei Latgalii; Materialy ekspeditsii 2011–2012* [The lost neighbors: Jews in the cultural memory of Latgalians; materials from a 2011–2012 expedition], 177–90, edited by Svetlana Amosova. Moscow: Sefer, 2013.

Gilbert, G. M. "Stereotype Persistence and Change among College Students." *Journal of Abnormal and Social Psychology* 46, no. 2 (1951): 245–54.

Gindin, Maksim. "Detstvo v Ozarichakh" [A childhood in Ozarichy]. *Vestnik evreiskogo universiteta v Moskve* 17, no. 1 (1998): 219–48.

Gitelman, Zvi. *Jewish Nationality and Soviet Politics: The Jewish Sections of the CPSU, 1917–1930*. Princeton, NJ: Princeton University Press, 1972.

―――. "Thinking about Being Jewish in Russia and Ukraine." In *Jewish Life after the USSR*, 49–60, edited by Zvi Gitelman. Bloomington: Indiana University Press, 2003.

Goldberg, Silvia Anna. *Crossing the Jabbok: Illness and Death in Askenazi Judaism in Sixteenth- through Nineteenth-Century Prague*. Berkeley: University of California Press, 1996.

Goluboff, Sascha. "Obshchiny traura: pogrebalnye plachi gorskikh evreev v sele Krasnaia Sloboda (Azerbaĭdzhan) i v internete" [Communities of mourning: Funeral laments of mountain Jews in the Village of Krasnaia Sloboda (Azerbaijan) and on the internet]. *Gosudarstvo, religiia, tserkov' v Rossii i za rubezhom* 3 (2015): 31–64.

Gross, Jan T. *Revolution from Abroad: The Soviet Conquest of Poland's Western Ukraine and Western Belorussia*. Princeton, NJ: Princeton University Press, 1988.

Haberer, Erich E. *Jews and Revolution in Nineteenth-Century Russia*. Cambridge: Cambridge University Press, 2004.

Hakkarainen, Marina. "A Town Recalls Its Past: Narratives about Jewish Craftsmen and Handicrafts." *East European Jewish Affairs* 38, no. 1 (2008): 21–33.

Hansen-Glucklich, Jennifer. *Holocaust Memory Reframed: Museums and the Challenges of Representation*. New Brunswick, NJ: Rutgers University Press, 2014.

Harrison, Rodney. *Heritage: Critical Approaches*. Milton Park, Abingdon, Oxon, UK: Routledge, 2013.

Haumann, Heiko. *Historia Żydów w Europie Środkowej i Wschodniej* [History of the Jews in Central and Eastern Europe]. Warsaw: Adamantan, 2000.

Hedemann, Otton. *Głębokie: szkic dziejów* [Hlybokaye: A historical sketch]. Vilnius: Oddział Polskiego Towarzystwa Krajoznawczego, 1935.

Hershnboym, Y. *Shtshedrin: A shtetl in rekonstruktivn period*. [Shchedryn: A shtetl in the period of reconstruction]. Minsk: Vaisrusishe visnshaft-akademie, 1931.

Herzog, Marvin. *The Yiddish Language in Northern Poland: Its Geography and History*. Bloomington: Indiana University, 1965.

Hosokawa, Fumiko. "A Functional Theory of Ethnic Stereotypes." *Humboldt Journal of Social Relations* 7, no. 2 (Spring/Summer 1980): 15–30.

Hrakhoŭski, Siarhei. "Miastèchka, miastèchka ... Èlehiia." [Miastechki, miastechki ... An elegy"]. *Polymia* 2 (1992).

Hundert, Gershon David. *Jews in a Private Polish Town: The Case of Opatów in the Eighteenth Century*. Baltimore: Johns Hopkins University Press, 1991.

Hurkoŭ, U. "Miastèchka." In *Ètnahrafiia Belarusi: Èntsyklapedyia*. Minsk, BelSE, 1989.

Iampolskaia, Anna. *Iskusstvo fenomenologii* [The art of phenomenology]. Moscow: Ripol klassik, 2018.

IAnush, I. "Liepiel." In *Èntsyklapedyia historyi Belarusi*, vol. 4. BelEN, 1997.

Iarov, Sergei. *Blokadnaia etika: Predstavleniia o morali v Leningrade v 1941–1942 gg* [Siege ethics: The concepts of morality in Leningrad, 1941–1942]. Moscow: Tsetnrpoligraf, 2012.

Jelski, Alexander. "Kleck." In *Słownik geograficzny Królestwa Polskiego i innych krajów słowiańskich* [Geographical dictionary of the Kingdom of Poland and other Slavic lands], vol. 4. Warsaw, 1883.

Kaganovich, Albert. *The Long Life and Swift Death of Jewish Rechitsa: A Community in Belarus, 1625–2000*. Madison: University of Wisconsin Press, 2013.

Kaganovitch, Moshe. *Der yidisher onteyl in der partizaner bavegung fun Sovet Rusland* [Jewish participation in the partisan movement in Soviet Russia]. Rome: Central Historical Commission at the Union of Partisans, 1948.

Kantor, Yakov. *Natsionalnoe stroitelstvo sredi evreev v SSSR* [Nation-building among Jews in the USSR]. Moscow: Vlast' sovetov, 1934.

Karlins, Marvin, Thomas L. Coffman, and Gary Walters. "On the Fading of Social Stereotypes: Studies in Three Generations of College Students." *Journal of Personality and Social Psychology* 13, no. 1 (1969): 1–16.

Karpachev, Afroim. "Sotsialno-ekonomicheskoe razvitie gorodov Belorussii vo vtoroi polovine XVII-XVIII veka" [The Socioeconomic development of cities in Belarus from the second half of the seventeenth through the eighteenth century]. PhD diss. Minsk: Akademiia nauk BSSR, 1970.

Karpekin, Konstantin. "'Oni zhili v etom gorode...': Ocherki istorii lepelskikh evreev v 1840–1930s gg" [They lived here...: Sketches of the history of Liepiel Jews from the 1840s through the 1930s]. In *Lepel': Pamiat' o evreiskom mestechke* [Liepiel: Memory of a Jewish shtetl], 13–28, edited by Svetlana Amosova, Moscow: Sefer, 2015.

Kaspina, Maria. "The Dybbuk and the Ikota: Similarities and Differences in the Jewish and Slavic Traditions about Possessions of an Evil Spirit." *East European Jewish Affairs* 38, no. 1 (2008): 35–43.

Kassow, Samuel D. "Community and Identity in the Interwar Shtetl." In *The Jews of Poland between the Two Wars*, 198–220, edited by Yisrael Gutman, Khone Shmeruk, Ezra Mendelsohn, and Jehuda Reinharz. Hanover, NH: University Press of New England, 1989.

———. *YIVO Encyclopedia of Jews in Eastern Europe*. https://yivoencyclopedia.org/article.aspx/Shtetl, s.v. "shtetl."

Katsenelenbogen, Uriah. "Litvakes." In *Lite*, vol. 1, 307–91, edited by Mendel Sudarsky and Uriah Katsenelenbogen. New York: Jewish-Lithuanian Cultural Society, 1951.

Katz, Daniel, and Kenneth Braly. "Racial Stereotypes of One-Hundred College Students." *Journal of Abnormal and Social Psychology* 28 (1933): 280–90.

Katz, Dovid. *Lithuanian Jewish Culture*. Vilnius: Baltos Lankos, 2010.

———. *Litvish: An Atlas of Northeastern Yiddish*. Last modified June 2, 2020. http://www.dovidkatz.net/WebAtlas/AtlasSamples.htm.

Katz, Jacob. *Tradition and Crisis: Jewish Society at the End of the Middle Ages*. Syracuse, NY: Syracuse University Press, 2000.

Katz, Steven T., ed. *The Shtetl: New Evaluations*. New York: New York University Press, 2007.

Kharik, Izi. "Lider," in *Zamlbikher* 8 (1952), 35–36.

———. *Mit layb un lebn* [With body and life]. Minsk: Melukhe farlag fun vaysrusland, 1928.

———. *Ot poliusa k poliusu* [From Pole to Pole]. Moscow: Khudozhestvennaia literatura, 1971.

Klier, John D. "The Pogrom Paradigm in Russian History." In *Pogroms: Anti-Jewish Violence in Modern Russian History*, 13–38, edited by John D. Klier and Shlomo Lambroza. Cambridge: Cambridge University Press, 1992.

———. *Russia Gathers Her Jews: The Origins of the "Jewish Question" in Russia, 1772–1825*. Dekalb: Northern Illinois University Press, 1986.

———. "What Exactly Was a Shtetl?" In *The Shtetl: Image and Reality*, 23–35, edited by Gennady Estraikh and Mikhail Krutikov. Oxford: Legenda, 2000.

Kniazeva, V. "Miadzel." In *Ėntsyklapedyĭa historyi Belarusi*, vol. 5. Minsk: BelEN, 1999.

Konstantinov, Viacheslav. *Evreiskoe naselenie byvshego SSSR v XX veke* [The Jewish population of the Former USSR in the 20th century]. Jerusalem: LIRA, 2007.

Kopchenova, Irina, ed. *Glubokoe: Pamiat' o evreiskom mestechke* [Hlybokaye: Memory of a Jewish shtetl]. Moscow: Sefer, 2017.

———. *Zheludok: Pamiat' o evreiskom mestechke* [Zhaludok: Memory of a Jewish shtetl]. Moscow: Sefer, 2013.

Kopysskii, Zinovii. *Ekonomicheskoe razvitie gorodov Belorussii v XVI- pervoi polovine XVII v* [Economic development in Belarusian towns from the 16th through the first half of the 17th century]. Minsk: Nauka i tekhnika, 1966.

———. *Sotsialno-politicheskoe razvitie gorodov Belorussii v XVI—pervoi polovine XVII v* [Sociopolitical development in Belarusian cities from the 16th through the first half of the 17th century]. Minsk: Nauka i tekhnika, 1975.

Kotik, Yekhezkel, David Assaf, and Margaret Birnstein. *Journey to a Nineteenth-Century Shtetl: The Memoirs of Yekhezkel Kotik*. Detroit: Wayne State University Press, 2002.

Kotler, Igar. "Yaureiskiya myastechki w Belarusi w chase nepa" [Jewish towns in Belarus in the period of the new economic policy]. *Belarusika* 4 (1995): 103–104.

Kozhenevskaya, Margarita. "Evreiskaia obshchina mestechka Glubokoe v kontse XIX–nachale XX vekov na stranitsakh arkhivnykh dokumentov" [The Jewish community of Hlybokaye in the late 19th–early 20th century in archival documents]. In *Glubokoe: Pamiat' o evreiskom mestechke* [Hlybokaye: Memory of a Jewish shtetl], 91–100, edited by Irina Kopchenova. Moscow: Sefer, 2017.

———. "Karta Glubokogo s raspolozheniem evreyskikh ob"ektov" [Map of Hlybokaye with the location of Jewish sites]. In *Glubokoe: Pamiat' o evreiskom mestechke* [Hlybokaye: Memory of a Jewish shtetl], 9, edited by Irina Kopchenova. Moscow: Sefer, 2017.

———. "Spisok domovladel'tsev mestechka Glubokoe za 1921 god" [List of Hlybokaye homeowners for 1921]. In *Glubokoe: Pamiat' o evreiskom mestechke* [Hlybokaye: Memory of a Jewish shtetl], 317–336, edited by Irina Kopchenova. Moscow: Sefer, 2017.

———. "Spisok vladel'tsev promyshlennykh i torgovykh predpriyatii v mestechke Glubokoe (1923 g.)" [List of the owners of industrial and commercial enterprises in Hlybokaye in 1923]. In *Glubokoe: Pamiat' o evreiskom mestechke* [Hlybokaye: Memory of a Jewish shtetl], 337–46, edited by Irina Kopchenova. Moscow: Sefer, 2017.

Krutikov, Mikhail. "Shtetl mezhdu fantaziei i realnostiu" [The shtetl: Between fantasy and reality]. *Novoe literaturnoe obozrenie* 102 (2010). http://magazines.russ.ru/nlo/2010/102/k10.html.

Kupriyanov, Pavel. "Istoricheskii personazh kak lokal'nyj brend, ili Skazochnaia istoriia Dunyashi Streshnevoi" [A historical character as a local brand, or, the fairy-tale story of Dunyasha Streshneva]. In *Voobrazhaemaia territoriia: ot lokal'noj identichnosti do brenda*, 107–33, edited by Nikita Petrov and Maria Akhmetova. Moscow: Neolit, 2018.

Lakotka, Aliaksandr. *Natsyĭanal'nyĭa rysy belaruskaĭ arkhitėktury* [National features of Belarusian architecture]. Minsk: Uradzhaĭ, 1999.

Le Foll, Claire. "The Missing Pogroms of Belorussia, 1881–1882: Conditions and Motives of an Absence of Violence." In *Anti-Jewish Violence: Rethinking the Pogrom in East European History*, 159–73, edited by Jonathan L. Dekel-Chen. Bloomington: Indiana University Press, 2011.

Leite, Naomi. "Materializing Absence: Tourists, Surrogates, and the Making of Jewish Portugal." In *Things That Move: Material Worlds of Tourism and Travel* (Conference Proceedings). Leeds, UK: Centre for Tourism and Cultural Change, Leeds Metropolitan University, 2007.

Levin, Irene, Claudia Lenz, and Marie Louise Seeberg. *The Holocaust as Active Memory: The Past in the Present*. London: Taylor and Francis, 2013.

Levin, Shmarya. *Childhood in Exile*. London: Routledge, 1939.

Levin, Vladimir, and Darius Staliunas. "Lite on the Jewish Mental Maps." In *Spatial Concepts of Lithuania in the Long Nineteenth Century*, 312–70, edited by Darius Staliunas. Brighton, MA: Academic Studies, 2016.

Litvak, Yosef. "Jewish Refugees from Poland in the USSR, 1939–1946." In *Bitter Legacy: Confronting the Holocaust in the USSR*, 123–50, edited by Norman Davies and Antony Polonsky. Bloomington: Indiana University Press, 1997.

Liuty, Anatoly. *Sotsialno-ekonomicheskoe razvitie gorodov Belorussii v kontse XVIII—pervoi polovine XIX v* [The socioeconomic development of cities in Belarus from the end of the 18th through the 19th century]. Minsk: Nauka i tekhnika, 1987.

Lukin, Veniamin, Boris Khaimovich, and Valeri Dymshits, eds. *Istoriia evreev na Ukraine i v Belorussii: Ekspeditsii, pamiatniki, nakhodki* [History of the Jews in Ukraine and Belarus: Expeditions, monuments, discoveries]. St. Petersburg: St. Petersburg Jewish University, 1994.

Lurie, Ilia, ed. *Istoriia evreiskogo naroda v Rossii*, vol. 2. Moscow: Mosty kultury/Gerashim, 2012.

Lvov, Aleksandr. "Mezhetnicheskie otnosheniia: Ugoshchenie matsoi i 'krovavyi navet'" [Interethnic relations: Sharing matzah and "blood libel"]. In *Shtetl, XXI vek: Polevye issledovaniia* [Shtetl, 21st century: Field research], 65–82, edited by Valeri A. Dymshits, Aleksandr L. Lvov, and Alla Sokolova. St. Petersburg: European University at St. Petersburg, 2008.

———. "Shtetl v XXI v. i etnografiia postsovetskogo evreistva" [The shtetl in the twenty-first century and the ethnography of post-Soviet Jewry]. In *Shtetl, XXI vek: Polevye issledovaniia* [Shtetl, 21st century: Field research], 186–215, edited by Valeri A. Dymshits, Aleksandr L. Lvov, and Alla

Sokolova. St. Petersburg: European University at St. Petersburg, 2008Dymshits, Lvov, and Sokolova, *Shtetl, XXI vek*, 9–26.

Madon, Stephanie, Max Guyll, Kathy Aboufadel, Eulices Montiel, Alison Smith, Polly Palumbo, and Lee Jussim. "Ethnic and National Stereotypes: The Princeton Trilogy Revisited and Revised." *Personality and Social Psychology Bulletin* 27, no. 8 (August 2001): 996–1010.

Martin, Terry. *The Affirmative Action Empire: Nations and Nationalism in the Soviet Union, 1923–1939*. Ithaca, NY: Cornell University Press, 2001.

Mastianica, Olga. "Between Ethnographic Belarus and the Reestablishment of the Grand Duchy of Lithuania: How Belarusian Nationalism Created Its 'National Territory' at the Beginning of the Twentieth Century." In *Spatial Concepts of Lithuania in the Long Nineteenth Century*, 279–311, edited by Darius Staliunas. Brighton, MA: Academic Studies, 2016.

McCain, Gary, and Nina M. Ray. "Legacy Tourism: The Search for Personal Meaning in Heritage Travel." *Tourism Management* 24, no. 6 (2003): 713–17.

Melnikova, Ekaterina, ed. "Finskie kladbishcha v Rossii: Kross-granichnye gruppy pamiati i novyi moral'nyi poriadok [Finnish cemeteries in Russia: Cross-border groups of memory and the new moral order]. *Antropologicheskii forum* 43 (2019): 11–40.

———. *Granitsa i liudi: Vospominaniia sovetskikh pereselentsev Priladozhskoi Karelii: sbornik materialov* [The border and dwellers: Memories of the Soviet migrants of the northern Ladoga region and Karelian Isthmus]. St. Petersburg: EUSP, 2005.

"Mestechko." *Elektronnaia evreiskaia entsiklopediia* [Russian Jewish encyclopedia]. World Ort, 1990. http://eleven.co.il/jewish-history/new-age-16-18-centuries/12737/.

Metelskakia, N. "Mir evreiskikh mestechek Belarusi vchera i segodniia. Problemy izucheniia" [The world of Jewish mestechki in Belarus yesterday and today: Issues in research]. In *Dubnovskie chtenie: Materialy 1-i Mezhdunarodnoi nauchnoi konfer. "Nasledie S.Dubnogo i izuchenie istorii evreev v stranakh SNG i Baltii"* [The Dubna readings: Texts from the 1st International Scholarly Conference "The legacy of the shtetl of Dubna and studying the history of the Jews in former Soviet Republics and the Baltics"], edited by Innokenty P. Gerasimov and Genrikh Rutman. Minsk: 2001.

Mikhedko, Valentin. "Vlast, revoliutsiia i pogromy v Belarusi v nachale XX v." [Power, revolution, and pogroms in Belarus in the beginning of the 20th century]. *Tsaytshrift* 8, no. 3 (2013): 20–34.

Miron, Dan. *The Image of the Shtetl and Other Studies of Modern Jewish Literary Imagination*. Syracuse, NY: Syracuse University Press, 2000.

Mochalova, Viktoria. "Glubokoe—stranitsy istorii" [Hlybokaye: Pages from history]. In *Glubokoe: Pamiat' o evreiskom mestechke* [Hlybokaye: Memory of a Jewish shtetl], 23–48, edited by Irina Kopchenova. Moscow: Sefer, 2017.

Moroz, Andrei. "Evreiskii Lepel glazami selskikh zhitelei" [Jewish Liepiel through the eyes of the villagers]. In *Lepel': Pamiat' o evreiskom mestechke* [Liepiel: Memory of a Jewish shtetl], 35–52, edited by Svetlana Amosova. Moscow: Sefer, 2015.

———. "'Evreiskii tekst' goroda Velizha" [The 'Jewish text' of the town of Velizh]. In *Krug zhizni v slavianskoi i evreiskoi kulturnoi traditsii*, 385–95, edited by Olga Belova. Moscow: Sefer, 2014.

———. *Narodnaia agiografiia: Istochniki, siuzhety, obrazy* [Folk hagiography: Sources, narratives, images]. Moscow: Forum-Neolit, 2017.

———. "'Stol'ko istorii v etikh stenakh . . .': Istoriia Glubokogo cherez prizmu istorii odnogo doma" ['So much history inside these walls . . .': The history of Hlybokaye through the prism of the history of one house]. In *Glubokoe: Pamiat' o evreiskom mestechke* [Hlybokaye: Memory of a Jewish shtetl], 265–74, edited by Irina Kopchenova. Moscow: Sefer, 2017.

Moshchuk, Anatoly. "Bor'ba s antisemitizmom v Zapadnoi Belarusi v praktike pol'skogo Bunda (1921–1939)" [The battle with antisemitism in Western Belarus in practice by the Polish Bund, 1921–1939]. *Tsaytshrift* 9, no. 4 (2014): 111–18.

Mstislavsky, S. "Evrei v Mogilevskoi gubernii: Istoriko-statisticheskii ocherk" [Jews in the Mohilyow guberniia: A historico-statistical outline]. *Voskhod* 6, no. 9 (1886): 1–10, second pagination.

Nathans, Benjamin. *Beyond the Pale: The Jewish Encounter with Late Imperial Russia*. Berkeley: University of California Press, 2004.

Nicolaisen, Wilhelm Fritz Hermann. "Place-Name Legends: An Onomastic Mythology." *Folklore* 87, no. 2 (1976): 146–59.

Nora, Pierre. "Between Memory and History: Les Lieux De Mémoire." *Representations* 26 (1989): 7–24.

Nosonovsky, Mikhail. *Evreiskie epigraficheskie pamiatniki Vostochnoi Evropy* [Hebrew epigraphic monuments from East Europe]. Boston: Trafford, 2002.

———. "Ob epitafiyakh evreyskikh nadgrobii Pravoberezhnoy Ukrainy," [Jewish epitaphs in the Right-Bank Ukraine] in *Istoriia evreev na Ukraine i v Belorussii* [History of Jewis in Ukraine and Belarus], 107–199, edited by Valerii Dymshits et al. St. Petersburg: Peterburgskii Evreiskii Universitet, 1994.

Oktyabr (newspaper), February 20, 1929.

Paperna, Abram. "Iz Nikolaevskoi epokhi. Vospominaniia" [From the Nicholas I era: A memoir]. In *Perezhitoe. Sbornik, posviashchennyi obshchestvennoi i kulturnoi istorii evreev v Rossii* [Lived experience: Materials on the social and cultural history of Jews in Russia], 2:10–96. St. Petersburg, 1910.

Pazdniakoŭ, V. "Kletsk." In *Ėntsyklapedyi͡a historyi Belarusi* [Encyclopedia of the history of Belarus], vol. 4. BelEN, 1997.

Petrov, Nikita. "Na menia vsio govoriat: 'Ty na iavreiku pohozha!': Individual'noe interv'u v sisteme znanii o traditsii" [They all say about me: You look Jewish!: Individual interview in the system of knowledge about tradition].

In *Lepel': Pamiat' o evreiskom mestechke* [Liepiel: Memory of a Jewish shtetl], 68–80, edited by Svetlana Amosova. Moscow: Sefer, 2015.

Petrovsky-Shtern, Yohanan. *The Golden Age Shtetl: A New History of Jewish Life in Eastern Europe*. Princeton, NJ: Princeton University Press, 2014.

Pi͡atkevich, Chaslaŭ. *Rėchytskae Palesse* [Rechytsa Palesse]. Edited by U. A. Vasilevich. Minsk: Belaruski knihazbor, 2004.

Pinchuk, Ben-Cion. "The Eastern European Shtetl and Its Place in Jewish History." *Revue des études juives* 164, no. 1 (2005): 187–212.

———. "How Jewish Was the Shtetl?" *Polin* 17 (2004): 109–18.

Pinkus, Benjamin. *The Jews of the Soviet Union: The History of a National Minority*. Cambridge: Cambridge University Press, 1988.

Pivovarchik, Sergey, and Inna Sorkina. "Istoricheskii ocherk evreiskoi obshchiny Zheludka" [A historical sketch of the Jewish community of Zhaludok]. In *Zheludok: Pamiat' o evreiskom mestechke* [Zhaludok: Memory of a Jewish shtetl], 17–38, edited by Irina Kopchenova. Moscow: Sefer, 2013.

Polonsky, Antony. *Dzieje Żydów w Polsce i Rosji* [The history of the Jews in Poland and Russia]. Warsaw: PWN, 2014.

Pollin-Galay, Hannah. *Ecologies of Witnessing: Language, Place, and Holocaust Testimony*. New Haven, CT: Yale University Press, 2018.

Quasthoff, Uta. "Ethnozentrische Verarbeitung von Informationen: Zur Ambivalenz der Funktion von Stereotypen in der interkulturellen Kommunikation" [Ethnocentric information processing: On the ambivalent function of stereotypes in intercultural communication]. In *Wie verstehen wir Fremdes? Aspekte zur Klärung von Verstehensprozessen*, 37–62, edited by Petra Matusche. Munich: Goethe-Institut, 1989.

Rabinowitsch, Wolf Zeev. *Lithuanian Hasidism*. New York: Schocken, 1971.

Reles, Hirsh. *Evreiski sovetskie pisateli Belorussii* [Soviet Jewish writers of Belarus]. Minsk: Dmitri Kolas, 2006.

Romanovm, Evdokim. *Belorusskii sbornik*. Vol. 4, *Skazki kosmogonicheskie i kulturnye* [Belarussian anthology. Vol. 4, Cosmogonic and cultural fairy tales]. Vitebsk, Belarus: Tipo-Litografiia G. A. Malkina, 1891.

Romanovsky, Daniel. "The Soviet Person as a Bystander of the Holocaust: The Case of Eastern Belarussia." In *Nazi Europe and the Final Solution*, 276–306, edited by David Bankier and Israel Gutman. New York: Berghahn, 2009.

Rosenthal, Herman. "Lithuania." In *Jewish Encyclopedia*, vol. 8. New York: Funk and Wagnalls, 1904.

Roskies, David G., and Diane K Roskies. *The Shtetl Book: An Introduction to East European Jewish Life and Lore*. New York: Ktav, 1975.

Rosman, Moshe J. *The Lords' Jews: Jews and Magnates in the Polish-Lithuanian Commonwealth*. Cambridge, MA: Harvard Ukrainian Institute and Harvard Center for Jewish Studies, 1990.

Rozenblat, Evgenii, and Irina Elenskaia. "Dinamika chislennosti i rasseleniia belorusskikh evreev v XX veke" [Dynamics of the population and dispersion of Belarusian Jews in the 20th century]. *Diaspory* 4 (2002): 27–52.

Sabaleŭskaia, Volha. "Habrëĭska-khrystsiianski dyialoh u Harodni ŭ XIX—pachatku XX st." [Jewish-Christian dialogue in Hrodna in the 19th–early 20th centuries]. *ARCHE* 1–2 (88–89), 2010.

Saganovich, Geandz. *Neviadomaia voina: 1634–1667* [An unknown war: 1634–1667]. Minsk: Navuka i tekhnika, 1995.

Samjakin, I. P., ed. *Statut Vialikaha kniastva Litoŭskaha 1588 hoda* [The Statute of the Grand Duchy of Lithuania]. Minsk: BelSE, 1989.

Sandri, Olivia. "City Heritage Tourism without Heirs: A Comparative Study of Jewish-Themed Tourism in Krakow and Vilnius. *Cybergeo: European Journal of Geography* (2013). https://journals.openedition.org/cybergeo/25934.

Savina, Natalia. "Zametki o lokal'nom tekste Glubokogo" [Notes on the local text of Hlybokaye]. In *Glubokoe: Pamiat' o evreiskom mestechke* [Hlybokaye: Memory of a Jewish shtetl], 153–76, edited by Irina Kopchenova. Moscow: Sefer, 2017.

Selemenev, Viacheslav, and Arkadi Zeltser. "Kolyshki—A Shtetl in the Late 1930s." *Jews in Eastern Europe* 45, no. 2 (2001): 48–72.

———. "The Liquidation of Yiddish Schools in Belorussia and the Jewish Reaction." *Jews in Eastern Europe* 41, no. 1 (2000): 74–111.

Senderovich, Sasha. Introduction to *The Zelmenyaners: A Family Saga*, by Moyshe Kulbak. Translated by Hillel Halkin. New Haven, CT: Yale University Press, 2013.

Shandler, Jeffrey. *Shtetl: A Vernacular Intellectual History*. New Brunswick, NJ: Rutgers University Press, 2014.

Shkolnikova, Elina. "Transformatsiia evreiskogo mestechka v SSSR v 1930e gody." *Seriia prepintov i reprintov*, vypusk 26 (Moscow: Obshchestvo evreiskoe nasledie, 1998). http://jhist.org/lessons_09/1930.htm.

Shmeruk, Khone. "Hakibuts hayehudi vehahityashvut hehaklayit hayehudit bebelorusia hasovietit (1918–1932)" [Jewish society and Jewish agricultural settlement in Soviet Belarus (1918–1932)]. PhD diss., Hebrew University of Jerusalem, 1961.

Shneer, David. *Yiddish and the Creation of Jewish Culture, 1918–1930*. Cambridge: Cambridge University Press, 2004.

Shprit, Andrei. "Mogilevsky pogrom 1654 g. i religioznaia politika russkikh vlastei v period russko-polskoi voiny 1654–1667 gg" [The 1654 Mahilyow pogrom and the religious policies of the Russian government during the Russo-Polish War, 1654–1667]. In *Kontakty i konflikty v slavianskoi i evreiskoi kulturnoi traditsii* [Contact and conflicts in Slavic and Jewish cultural tradition], 112–38, edited by Olga Belova. Moscow: Sefer Center, 2017.

Shternshis, Anna. *Soviet and Kosher: Jewish Popular Culture in the Soviet Union, 1923–1939*. Bloomington: Indiana University Press, 2006.

Shybeka, Zakhar. *Harady Belarusi (60-i͡a hh. XIX - pachatak XX stahoddzi͡aŭ)* [Belarusian towns (From the 1860s to the early 1900s)]. Minsk: ĖŭroForum, 1997.

Sirotiner. "Iz zhizni 'Vozdukhotresta': Evreisokoe naselenie mestechka Sirotino" [From the life of the 'air trust': The Jewish population of the shtetl of Sirotino]. In *Evreiskoe mestechko v revoliutsi* [The Jewish town in the revolution], 89–120*i*, edited by V. G. Tan-Bogoraz. Moscow: Gosudarstvennoe izdatelstvo, 1926.

S. L. (name unknown), "Aktsiznyy otkup i evrei-posredniki v Minskoi gubernii" [Liquor tax concessions and Jewish middlemen in the Minsk guberniia]. *Trudy imperatorskogo Volnogo ekonomicheskogo obshchestva* [Proceedings of the Imperial Free Economic Society] 4 (November 1860): 279–89.

Slepyan, Kenneth. "The Soviet Partisan Movement and the Holocaust." *Holocaust and Genocide Studies* 14, no. 1 (Spring 2000): 1–27.

———. *Stalin's Guerrillas: Soviet Partisans in World War II*. Lawrence: University Press of Kansas, 2006.

Sloin, Andrew. *The Jewish Revolution in Belorussia: Economy, Race and Bolshevik Power*. Bloomington: Indiana University Press, 2017.

Słownik geograficzny Królestwa Polskiego [Geographical dictionary of the Kingdom of Poland], vol. 14. Warsaw, 1895.

Smali͡anchuk, Ales'. "Litvaki i belaruski͡ia i͡aŭrėi: mestsa ŭ ai͡chynnaĭ history" [Litvaks and Belarusian Jews: Place in local history]. *Belarus' u XX stahoddzi* [Belarus in the 20th century] 3 (2004), 219–224. http://mb.s5x.org/homoliber.org/ru/xx/xx030120.html.

Smilovitsky, Leonid. "A Belorussian Border Shtetl in the 1920s and 1930s: The Case of Turov." *Jews in Russia and Eastern Europe* 50, no. 1 (Summer 2003): 109–37.

———. "Antisemitism in the Soviet Partisan Movement: The Case of Belarussia." *Holocaust and Genocide Studies* 20, no. 2 (Fall 2006): 207–34.

———. *Evrei v Turove: Istoriia evreiskogo mestechka Mozyrskogo Polesia* [Jews in Turov: The history of a shtetl in the Mozyr Paliessie]. Self-published, 2008.

———. *Jewish Life in Belarus: The Final Decade of the Stalin Regime, 1944–1953*. Budapest: Central European University Press, 2014.

Snyder, Timothy. *The Reconstruction of Nations: Poland, Ukraine, Lithuania, Belarus, 1569–1999*. New Haven, CT: Yale University Press, 2004.

Sobolevskaia, Olga. "Iudei v belorusskikh vladeniiakh Radzivillov v kontse XVIII-nachale XIX vv" [Jews on Radziwill Belarusian lands from the end of the 18th to the beginning of the 19th century]. *Tsaytshrift* 6, no. 1 (2011): 22–40.

Sokolova, Alla. "Architectural Space of the Shtetl—Street—House: Jewish Homes in the Shtetls of Eastern Podolia." *Trumah: Zeitschrift der Hochschule fur Judische Studien* 7 (1998): 35–85.

―――. "Jewish Sights: Exoticization of Places and Objects as a Way of Presenting Local 'Jewish Antiquity' by the Inhabitants of Little Towns." In *Jewish Space in Central and Eastern Europe: Day-to-Day History*, 261–80, edited by Jurgita Šiaučiūnaite-Verbickienė and Larisa Lempertienė. Newcastle, UK: Cambridge Scholars, 2007.

―――. "The Podolian Shtetl as Architectural Phenomenon." In *The Shtetl: Image and Reality; Papers of the Second Mendel Friedman International Conference on Yiddish*, 36–79, edited by Gennady Estraikh and Mikhail Krutikov. Oxford: Legenda, 2000.

Solokova, Vera. *Russkie istoricheskie predaniia* [The historical legends of Russia]. Moscow: Nauka, 1970.

Sorkina, Inna. "Evrei i vladeltsy mestechkek Belarusi: Praktika vzaimootnoshenii (XVIII–XIX vv.)" [Jews and town owners in Belarus: Interaction practices, 18th–19th centuries]. In *Materialy XIX Ezhegodnoi Mezhdunarodnoi Mezhdistsiplinarnoi konferentsii po iudaike* [Proceedings of the 19th annual international interdisciplinary Jewish Studies conference], Academic Series 42, 3:244–61. Moscow: Sefer, 2012.

―――. "Mestechko Glubokoe i ego zhiteli na fone epokhi: XVIII–pervaia tret XX v" [Hlybokaye and its residents from the 18th century through the 1930s]. In *Glubokoe: Pamiat' o evreiskom mestechke* [Hlybokaye: Memory of a Jewish shtetl, 121–40], 49–90, edited by Irina Kopchenova. Moscow: Sefer, 2017.

―――. *Mīastėchki Belarusi ŭ kantsy XVIII–pershaĭ palove XIX st* [Towns of Belarus, Late 18th–First Half of the 19th Century]. Vilnius: Eŭrapeĭski humanitarny universitėt [European University for the Humanities], 2010.

―――. "'Ours' or 'Foreign'? The Attitude of Belarusians toward Jews in the Beginning of the 20th Century." *Belarusian Review*, special Jewish issue (2016): 13–22.

―――. "Pereseleniia evreiskogo naseleniia iz selskoi mestnosti v goroda i mestechki Belarusi v kontse XVIII-XIX vv" [Migration of the Jewish population from rural settlements to towns and mestechki from the end of the eighteenth through the nineteenth century]. In *Materialy XIII Ezhegodnoi Mezhdunarodnoi Mezhdistsiplinarnoi konferentsii po iudaike* [Proceedings of the 13th annual international interdisciplinary Jewish Studies conference], 350–65. Moscow: Sefer, 2006.

―――. "The Revolt in the Name of Freedom: The Fight of Small Town Dwellers for Lost Freedom and Land in 18th–19th Centuries." In *The Revolt in the Name of Freedom: Forgotten Belarusian Gene*, 28–35, edited by Piotr Rudkoŭski and Kaciaryna Kolb. Warsaw: Elipsa, 2013.

―――. "Shlīakhetskiīa rėzidėntsyi i mīastėchki Belarusi: Z historyi ŭzaemadzeīannīa (kanets XVIII–pershaīa palova XIX st.)" [Szlachta residences and miasteczki of Belarus: History of interaction (late 18th–first half of the 19th century)]. In *El'skiīa chytanni: matėryīaly kanferėntsyi*

"SHliakhetskaia kul'tura Belarusi XIX–pachatku XX st.," edited by L. I. Doŭnar, 104–23. Minsk, 2013.

Staliunas, Darius. "Anti-Jewish Disturbances in the North-Western Provinces in the Early 1880s." *East European Jewish Affairs* 34, no. 2 (Winter 2004): 119–38.

Stampfer, Shaul. "East European Jewish Migration to the United States." In *Migration across Time and Nations*, edited by Ira Glazier and Luigi De Rosa. New York: Holmes and Meier, 1986.

———. "Gidul ha-okhlusiyah ve-hagira be-Yahadut Poli-Lita be-et ha-hadasha" [Population growth and migration of Polish-Lithuanian Jewry in the modern age]. In *Kiyum va-Shever: Yehudei Polin-Lita le-doroteihem* [Existence and destruction: Generations of Jews of Poland], edited by Israel Bartal and Israel Gutman. Jerusalem, 1997.

———. "Patterns of Internal Jewish Migration in the Russian Empire." In *Jews and Jewish Life in Russia and the Soviet Union*, 28–45, edited by Yaacov Ro'i. London: Routledge, 1995.

Strack, Hermann L. *The Jew and Human Sacrifice; Human Blood and Jewish Ritual, an Historical and Sociological Inquiry*. New York: Bloch, 1909.

Teller, Adam. "The Legal Status of the Jews on the Magnate Estates of Poland-Lithuania in the 18th Century." *Gal-Ed* 15–16 (1997): 41–63.

———. *Money, Power and Influence in Eighteenth-Century Lithuania: The Jews on the Radziwiłł Estates*. Stanford, CA: Stanford University Press, 2016.

Tereshina, Daria. "'Mnogie evrei . . . oni vse zanimalis torgovlei': Vospominaniia o evreiskikh lavkah i brodiachikh torgovtsakh dovoennoi Latgalii" [A lot of Jews. . . . they were all merchants: Memories of Jewish stores and wandering salesmen in prewar Latgale]. In Amosova, *Utrachenoe sosedstvo: Evrei v kulturnoi pamiati zhitelei Latgalii*; Materialy ekspeditsii 2011–2012 [The lost neighbors: Jews in the cultural memory of Latgalians; materials from a 2011–2012 expedition]. Moscow: Sefer, 2013, 36–77.

Tokarska-Bakir, Joanna. *Legendy o krwi. Antropologia przesądu*. [Legends about blood. Anthropology of a prejudice]. Warsaw: Wydawnictwo W. A. B. 2008.

Uther, Hans-Jörg, ed. *The Types of International Folktales: A Classification and Bibliography, Based on the System of Antti Aarne and Stith Thompson*. Generally referred to as the "ATU Catalogue." 3 vols. Helsinki: Academia Scientiarum Fennica, 2004.

Veidlinger, Jeffrey. "Everyday Life and the Shtetl: A Historiography." In *Jewish Education in Eastern Europe*, edited by Eliyana R. Adler and Antony Polonsky. Special issue, *Polin* 30 (2018): 381–96.

———. *In the Shadow of the Shtetl: Small-Town Jewish Life in Soviet Ukraine*. Bloomington: Indiana University Press, 2013.

Vodolazhskaya, Tatsiana, ed. *Igra v goroda: Po materialam ekspeditsii v malye goroda Belarusi* [City name game: Materials from the expeditions to small towns of Belarus]. Minsk: Logvinov, 2009.

Voiteshchik, Anna. "Shtetl kak sotsiokulturnyi fenomen severo-vostochnykh voevodstv II Rechi Politoi v 1912–1939" [The Shtetl as a sociocultural phenomenon in the northeastern voivodeship of the 2nd Polish-Lithuanian Commonwealth, 1921–1939]. In *Sodruzhestvo nauk. Baranovichy 2011: Materialy VII Mezhdunarod. Nauch.-prakt- konf. Molodykh issledovatelei*, part 2. Baranovichy, Belarus: Baranovichy State University, 2011.

Waligórska, Magdalena. "Ben-Yehudah—The Belorussian Hero: Jewish Heritage and the New Belorussian National Identity Project." *Perspectives: The Magazine of the Association for Jewish Studies* (Spring 2014): 46–47. http://perspectives.ajsnet.org/the-land-issue-spring-2014/ben-yehudah-the-belorussian-hero-jewish-heritage-and-the-new-belorussian-national-identity-project/.

———. "Jewish Heritage and the New Belarusian National Identity Project." *East European Politics and Societies and Cultures* 30, no. 2 (2016): 332–59.

Walsh, Kevin. *The Representation of the Past: Museums and Heritage in the Post Modern World*. London: Routledge, 1992.

Weissler, Chava. *Voices of the Matriarchs: Listening to the Prayers of Early Modern Jewish Women*. Boston: Beacon, 1999.

Więcławska, Katarzyna. *Zmartwychwstałe miasteczko . . . Literackie oblicza sztetl* [The resurrected town: The literary faces of the shtetl]. Lublin, Poland: UMCS, 2005.

Wodziński, Marcin. *A Historical Atlas of Hasidism*. Princeton, NJ: Princeton University Press, 2018.

Yalen, Deborah. "On the Social-Economic Front: The Polemics of Shtetl Research during the Stalin Revolution." *Science in Context* 20, no. 2 (2007): 239–301.

———. Review of *Shtetl, XXI vek: Polevye issledovaniia* [Shtetl, 21st century: Field research], edited by Valeri A. Dymshits, Aleksandr L. Lvov, and Alla Sokolova. St. Petersburg: European University at St. Petersburg, 2008, *East European Jewish Affairs* 40, no. 2 (2010): 176–82.

Yasinskaia, Maria. "Obraz inoetnicheskogo i inokonfessionalnogo soseda v narrativakh zhiteli byvshego mestechka Beshenkovici" [Images of neighbors of a different ethnicity and religion in the narratives of the residents of the former mestechko of Beshankovichy]. In *Kontakty i konflikty v slavianskoi i evreiskoi kulturnoi traditsii* [Contact and conflicts in Slavic and Jewish cultural tradition], 315–32, edited by Olga Belova. Moscow: Sefer Center, 2017.

Zamoiskii, Andrei. *Transformatsiia mestechek Sovetskoi Belorussii 1918–1939* [The transformation of the shtetls in Soviet Belarus, 1918–1939]. Minsk: I. P. Logvinov, 2013.

Zborowski, Mark, and Elizabeth Herzog. *Life Is with People: The Culture of the Shtetl*. New York: Schocken, 1952.

———. *Life Is with People: The Jewish Little-Town of Eastern Europe*. 2nd ed. New York: International Universities Press, 1952.

Zeltser, Arkadi. *Evrei sovetskoi provintsii: Vitebsk i mestechki 1917–1941* [Jews of the Soviet countryside: Vitebsk and surrounding shtetls, 1917–1941]. Moscow: Rosspen, 2006.

———. "Shinuim demografiim vehevratiim-kalkaliim bekerev hayehudim mithilat milhemet ha'olam harishona vead lesof shnot hashloshim shel hamea haesrim." [Demographic and socioeconomic changes among Jews from the beginning of World War I to the end of the 1930s]. In *Toldot yehudei rusia mimehapekhot 1917 ad nefilat brit hamo'atsot*, 93–97, edited by Michael Beizer. Jerusalem: Merkaz Shazar, 2015.

———. *Unwelcome Memory: Holocaust Monuments in the Soviet Union*. Jerusalem: Yad Vashem, 2018.

Zhukov, Dmitri, and Ivan Kovtun. *1-ia russkaia brigada SS "Druzhina"* [The first Russian SS-brigade "Druzhina"]. Moscow: Veche, 2010.

Zukin, Sharon. *The Cultures of Cities*. Cambridge, MA: Blackwell, 1995.

EDITORS AND CONTRIBUTORS

Irina Kopchenova is educational programs coordinator at the Sefer Center and a Junior Research Fellow at the Institute of Slavic Studies of the Russian Academy of Sciences in Moscow. She has edited *The Shtetl of Hlybokaye in Contemporary Cultural Memory* (2017) and *Jews on the Map of Lithuania: The Case of Biržai* (2015).

Mikhail Krutikov, a scholar of Yiddish literature and Jewish culture in Eastern Europe, has authored four books, most recently *Der Nister's Soviet Years: Yiddish Writer as Witness to the People* (2019). He is Professor of Slavic Languages and Literatures and Preston R. Tisch Professor of Judaic Studies at the University of Michigan, Ann Arbor.

Svetlana Amosova, folklorist and anthropologist specializing in Slavic and Jewish traditional culture, has written more than fifty articles and edited *Jews of Borderlands: Smolensk Region* (2018). She is Head of the Research Center at the Jewish Museum and Tolerance Center in Moscow and Research Fellow at the Institute for Slavic Studies at the Russian Academy of Sciences.

Julia Bernstein, independent scholar, specializes in the oral history of the Holocaust and has authored several articles.

Samuel D. Kassow, scholar of Russian, Polish, and East European Jewish history, is the author of several books, including *Students Professors and the State in Tsarist Russia: 1884–1917* (1989) and *Who Will Write Our History: Rediscovering a Hidden Archive from the Warsaw Ghetto* (2007), which was adapted into a documentary film in 2018. He is the Charles H. Northam Professor of History at Trinity College, Hartford, Connecticut.

Mikhail Lurie, folklorist and anthropologist, specializes in the construction of local knowledge and identities, ethnography of cultural life, modern children's folklore, urban songs of the 20th century, and the history of Russian folkloristics. He is Professor in the Department of Anthropology at the European University in St. Petersburg and the scientific director of several applied urban anthropological projects.

Andrei B. Moroz is a folklorist and anthropologist specializing in Slavic traditional culture, ritualism, and mythology. He has authored *Folk Hagiography: Oral and Bookish Basis of the Folklore Cult of Saints* (Moscow, 2016) and is Professor at the Higher School of Economics University in Moscow.

Natalia Savina is a cultural anthropologist specializing in urban and rural studies, anthropology of tourism, urban-to-rural migration, folklore branding, and rural cultural entrepreneurship.

Ina Sorkina, a scholar specializing in the history of shtetls in Belarus, Jewish heritage preservation, and tourism, has authored *Miastechki of Belarus at the End of 18th – First Half of 19th Century* (2010). She is a Research Fellow at the University of Warsaw.

Arkady Zeltser, a historian of the Holocaust and Soviet Jewry, has authored and edited several books, including *Unwelcome Memory: Holocaust Monuments in the Soviet Union* (2018). He is the Director of the Moshe Mirilashvili Center for Research on the Holocaust in the Soviet Union at Yad Vashem, Jerusalem.

INDEX

abortion, 55
Abramovitsh, Sholem Yankev (Mendele Moykher-Sforim), 8
acculturation, 2, 7, 16
activism, 186; activists, 13, 69, 185, 196n51; community, 79, 84; Jewish, 65; Soviet, 68, 121
Agrarian Reform (1557), 29
agriculture, 61, 200; agricultural colonies, 15, 55, 63; agricultural modernization, 9; agricultural products, 28, 30, 64, 231. *See also* farms
Aguilar, Paloma, 188
AHEYM (Archives of Historical and Ethnographic Yiddish Memories), 17
Aksenfeld, Yisroel, 8
alcohol. *See* liquor
Aleichem, Sholem, 120, 207
Alexander II, 7
Alley of Famous Townspeople, 181, 183, 187, 189, 194n31
annexation, 236; Russian, 42; Soviet, 3, 115, 131, 149, 151, 152, 180
anthropology, 32; anthropologists, 17, 20

anti-imperial uprisings, 2, 9, 36
antisemitism, 3, 4, 17, 43, 44, 45, 96, 102, 107, 116, 131, 203, 226–27; antisemitic publications, 101; of partisans, 150
arenda (lease-holding), 5
assimilation, 2, 7, 16, 39, 59, 181, 207
atheism, 207, 210, 243; Soviet, 119
Austria, 7, 236
autonomy, Jewish, 8, 9, 32, 34, 44; Jewish Autonomous Region, 55, 246n5
Avrutin, Eugene, 107
Azarychy, 71

Babruysk, 2, 55
Babylonia, 4
Baltic states, 149
banquets, 12–13, 69, 84, 85, 90
bar mitzvahs, 119, 207
beggars, 202
Beilis, Mendel, 203, 227, 240, 245n1
Belarusian Academy of Sciences, 19
Belarusian Central Committee, 59
Belarusian National Republic, 187
Belarusian Soviet Socialist Republic (BSSR), 2, 45, 58, 244, 245

Belarusian State University, 19
Belarusization, 57, 58
Belova, Olga, 96, 97, 104
Ben-Yehuda, Eliezer, 181, *182*, 183–84, 185, 186, 187, 188, 189, 195n44, 195n49
Berdichev, 8
Berlin, 173
Bessarabia, 5, 41, 77, 89
Betar, 225, 240
betrayal, 3, 132, 142, 151, 154, 244
bikur kholim (society for caring for the ill), 37
Birobidzhan, 15, 55, 222, 226, 246n5
birth rate, 36, 55, 56, 200
black market, 15, 62, 64, 118, 127, 132
Boder, David, 147
Bolshevism, 45, 51, 71, 110n28, 222, 228
borderlands, 44; Polish-Belarusian, 17; Russo-Belarusian, 2, 76, 77, 78, 88, 91
border zone, 64
Borok Forest, 129–30, 134, *156*, *157*, 159
bourgeoisie, 45, 51, 118, 240; bourgeois society, 39
boycotts, 14
Braly, Kenneth, 95
branding, town, 185, 186, 188, 189
Braslaw, 30
bread ration cards, 126, 127
Bryansk Region, 76, 77, 78, 79, 83, 87, 88
Budapest, 173
Bukovina, 5
Bund, the, 2, 118, 219, 226; Bundism, 2, 10, 65
burials, 12, 78, 128, 151, 175, 210; burial rituals, 76; burial society (*khevra kadisha*), 12, 13, 67, 68, 69, 90, 210; Christian, 85. *See also* funerals; graves

Cała, Alina, 17
cantors, 200, 208
Carmelites, 6, 41; Carmelite monastery, 29, 30
castles, 6, 28, 30
Catherine II, 7, 42
Catholics, 1, 41, 200, 207, 213, 246n6; Catholic churches, 1, 30, 205, 213; Catholic priests, 44, 142; Greek Catholics, 19, 29, 32; Roman Catholics, 19, 29, 32, 98
cemeteries, 138, 195n38; Christian, 71, 137; epigraphic examination of, 17, 18, 19; and food, 80–81, 84, 87–88, 90; Hlybokaye, 19, 188; Jewish, 19, 77, 78, 80, 81, 83, 85, 89, 93n25, 99, 128, 151, 153, 171, 172, 177, 178, 179, 180, 181, 189, 206, 211, *217*, 225; Koptevka, 185; prayers at, 16, 79–80, 82, 89; rehabilitation of, 175–76, 177, 179, 180, 189; Roslavl, 77, 78, 79, 83; Russian, 71; in shtetls, 8; "strangers' cemeteries," 180; Surazh, 83–84; upkeep of, 79, 82, 86; visiting, 76, 77, 79, 80, 81, 82, 83, 84, 85, 86–87, 88, 89–90, 91, 92n9, 92n17, 176; Zhaludok, 19, 202. *See also* burials; graves
Center for Judaica and Bible Studies, 172
Center for the Study and Presentation of the East European Diaspora, 193n22
Central Asia, 4
Central Yiddish School Organization, 14
charity, 9, 202, 221; charity packages, 82

Charter to the Gentry (1785), 31
Chashniki, 20, 33, 59, 67
Chavusy, 30, 55, 59
Chertovich, Vladimir, 101
Christianity, 19, 32, 97, 104, 207, 208, 210; Baptists, 3; Calvinists, 32; Christian Church, 96; Christians, 5, 6, 79, 84, 93n26, 96, 98, 101, 107, 200, 203, 245n1; and Jews, 19; Lutherans, 32. *See also* Catholics; Orthodoxy
churches, 6, 30, 69, *191*, 207; Catholic, 1, 30, 205, 213; Orthodox, 1, 30. *See also* Catholics, Catholic churches; Orthodoxy, Orthodox churches
class, social, 50, 116, 118, 200, 201, 202, 243; *balebatim* (middle class), 11, 14, 200; class conflict, 16; *sheyne yidn* (well-to-do), 11, 14
Coffman, Thomas L., 95
collectivization, 15, 16
commerce, 37, 200
communalism, 5, 12, 13, 86, 97, 225; communal affairs, 12, 13; communal functions, 8; communal gatherings, 82, 83, 85; communal governance, 9
communication, 95, 129, 143, 151, 226; nonverbal, 147; verbal, 147
communism, 17, 70, 116, 117, 149, 226, 240; Communist Party, 15, 67, 117, 194n23, 226; communists, 11, 15, 68, 118, 119, 121, 236–37, 238, 243
conformity, 97, 244
Corsale, Andrea, 173
Cossacks, 6, 34, 43
Cossack War (1648–51), 33
Council of People's Commissars, 59
Council of the Four Lands, 8
craftspeople, 9, 28, 30, 50, 61, 62, 63, 64, 68, 69, 118, 175. *See also* handicrafts

credit, 62, 68, 201; credit cooperatives, 62; creditors, 62, 103; free loan societies, 14; microcredit, 14
Crimea, 55
cultural heritage, 173, 193n15
customs, Jewish, 18, 20, 46, 51, 67, 96, 183, 207, 210, 211; and cemetery visits, 80–81, 84, 85, 86, 88, 90, 91; and days of remembrance, 82; everyday, 68; holiday, 70, 223; Russian, 80; Slavic, 96, 97
Czechoslovakia, 236
Czetwertyński family, 203; Count Czetwertyński, 203, 214, *215*

day of remembrance, 76, 77–78, 79, 81, 82, 84, 85, 88, 90, 91, 92n9, 171, 186; Jewish Radunitsa, 76, 78, 83. *See also* Lag ba-Omer
deportation, 3, 64, 118, 159
Derrida, Jacques, 153
Dik, Ayzik Meyer, 13
disloyalty, 60, 64; disloyal groups, 54, 64
district councils, 8
District Executive Committee, 175, 176, 185, 194n23
District Party, 57
diversity, 14, 45, 146, 147; ethnic, 19, 32, 44; occupational, 4, 60; religious, 19, 32, 171
doctors, 60, 103, 118, 125, 135, 141, 183, 200, 230
Doctors' Plot (1953), 103
Drazdovich, Yazep, 188, 196n56
Dubrowna, 30, 59, 60, 64, 68
dziady, 91
Dzisna, 134, 135

education, 11, 12, 15, 18, 42, 45, 54, 57, 59, 64, 67, 95, 118, 190; elementary, 11; higher, 16, 53, 54, 60, 194n30; Jewish, 2, 8, 11, 71; primary, 15; religious, 12, 67, 72; secular, 72. *See also* schools
eggs, 81, 84, 201, 211; dyed, 86, 87–88, 91, 93
electricity, 122, 125, 205, 221
Elkin, Mendel, 245n3
emigration, 9, 14, 17, 39, 44, 82, 149, 178, 220, 228; emigrants, 175, 179
empathy, 146, 154, 181, 244; of viewer, 152, 153, 155
Engelking, Anna, 17
England, 236
estates, 9, 29, 31, 35, 36, 54, 203, 206, 214, 216, 238, 239–40; ducal, 28; feudal, 28; private, 28, 34
ethnicity, 27, 33, 52, 54, 57, 60, 68, 72, 76, 78, 80, 90, 95, 97, 98, 99; ethnic affiliation, 17; ethnic communities, 46; ethnic composition, 56, 71; ethnic groups, 57, 60, 95, 103; ethnic institutions, 61, 65; ethnic past, 175; ethnic policies, 52, 57, 58, 59, 60, 61; ethnic traditions, 56, 60; ethnic values, 55; interethnic relations, 95, 96, 97; multiethnicity, 37, 97. *See also* diversity, ethnic; minorities, ethnic
ethnography, 18, 32, 46n1, 91; ethnographers, 18, 172, 187, 196n56; ethnographic studies, 19, 20, 23
Europe, 5, 17, 42, 96, 173, 174, 175, 185, 192n1, 206, 236; Central, 44, 97; Eastern, 1, 4, 5, 9, 10, 13, 32, 36, 42, 44, 95, 96, 97, 98, 172, 175, 200; Western, 9, 28, 200
Evsektsiia (Jewish section of the Communist Party), 15, 16

executions, 98, 99, 105, 128, 130, 131, 133, 138, 242; mass, 81, 82, 83, 86, 92n17, 128–29, 130, 131, 149

factories, 13, 60, 61, 62, 63, 64, 68, 122, 125, 126, *166*, 174; factory-made goods, 9, 61, 62
falvark system, 28
farms, 28, 57, 216; collective, 15, 16, 45, 61, 64; Gentile, 11. *See also* agriculture
fascism, 131, 236, 237
films, 14
fire departments, 85, 211
Fishman, David, 42
Five-Year Plans, 16
folklore, 1, 5, 18, 19, 46n1, 98, 104, 108, 172, 186
folk stories, 97
France, 7, 236
funerals, 69, 128; Christian, 213; funeral processions, 210, 213. *See also* burials

Galicia, 12
Gantner, Eszter B., 173
gender, 33, 37, 55; gender roles, 13
genealogy, 177. *See also* tourism, genealogy
Gentiles, 4, 6, 10, 11, 16
Gerasimova, Inna, 196n51
Germans, 3, 116, 127, 130, 134, 135, 137, 138, 139, 144n46, 150, 154, 178–80, 237, 239; and ghettos, 129, 131, 133, 136, 143; and Jews, 99, 100, 102, 103–105, 106, 107, 126, 128, 139, 140, 142. *See also* Germany
Germany, 4, 7, 125, 140, 147, 150, 176, 179, 180, 245; fascist, 236; German occupation, 3, 108, 116, 152, 159,

173, 179, 192n1, 236; invasion of Hlybokaye, 121, 123, 124, 125, 136, 151; invasion of Soviet Union, 120; and Jews, 101, 106, 107, 227; Nazi, 71, 149. *See also* Germans; Nazism; Poland, German-occupied

ghettos, 106; destruction of, 105, 131, 133, 136, 137, 139, *157,* 159; escape from, 131, 132, 133, 146, 149, 150; ghetto prisoners, 125, 127, 131, 142, 192n1; Hlybokaye, 3, 22, 116, 123–25, 126, 127, 128–29, 130, 132, 134–36, 137, 138–39, 142–43, 151, 159, 177, 186; urban, 131, 143; victims of, 149, 171, 176, 189

Gil' (Rodionov), Vladimir, 144n46

Gilbert, G. M., 95

Gitelman, Zvi, 18, 91

Goebbels, Joseph, 101

Goldberg, Sylvie Anne, 89

Goluboff, Sascha, 90

Göring, Hermann, 101

Gorky, Maxim, 226

gossip, 70, 71, 201

graves, 77, 78, 79, 80, 81, 83, 84, 85–86, 87, 88, 89, 93, 99, 179, 185, 244; mass graves, 78, 81, 82, 83, 84, 85, 86, 222, 228, 236, 238. *See also* burials

Great Northern War (1700–21), 6, 33, 36

Great Terror, 61, 65

Green America, 177, 178, 179, 180; *Green America* book, 177, 194n30

Grodno. *See* Hrodna

guilt, 108, 154, 180; confession of, 152–53; Jews', 104, 107; survivors', 3

Hakkarainen, Marina, 175

handicrafts, 175, 200

Hanukkah, 67, 223

Haradok, 30, 59, 71

Hasidism, 1, 12, 32, 41–42; Chabad sect, 1, 2, 12, 42; Karlin sect, 1, 12; Lubavitch, 12, 119, 148; Northern, 41; Slonim sect, 1, 12; Southern, 41; Stolin sect, 1, 12, 42

Haskalah (Enlightenment) movement, 2, 42, 50

Hebrew language, 2, 58, 176, 181, 183, 184, 187, 206–207. *See also* schools, Hebrew

heritagization, 173, 190, 193n15

Herzog, Elizabeth, 16, 172

historians, 20, 22, 39, 42, 47n19, 81, 146, 171, 185, 187, 189, 190, 192n6

Hitler, Adolf, 3, 236, 237; attitude toward Jews, 99, 103, 104, 105, 106, 107, 108; Jewish ancestry, 100–102

Hlybokaye, 19, *21,* 29, 32, 41, 125, 135, 138, 140, 141, 142, 144n46, 150, 156, *157,* 171, 177, *182,* 184, 186, 187, 190, 193n21, 194nn30–31, 197n60; development of, 30; diversity in, 19, 32; and German occupation, 124, 128; ghetto, 3, 22, 116, 124, 126, 127, 142, 143, 146, 159, 192n1; history, 181, 192n1; and Jews, 19–20, 23, 36, 41, 44, 46, 46n1, 115, 116, 117, 118, 119, 121, 123, 126, 128, 136, 147, 159. 171–72, 175, 178, 180, 181, 188–89, 190, 191; liberation of, 140; prewar life, 115, 148, 188, 190; residents, 32, 41, 46, 115, 118, 147, 148, 176, 179, 180, 183, 184, 185, 188; shtetl, 1, 6, 12, 175; and Soviet annexation, 151, 175. *See also* Hlybokaye Historical and Ethnographic Museum

Hlybokaye Historical and Ethnographic Museum, 172

holidays, 6, 53, 78, 86, 87, 88, 141, 207, 208, 213, 244; folk, 223; Jewish, 13, 14, 67, 68, 69, 78, 79, 82, 83, 84, 98, 119, 123, 128, 243; national, 77; religious, 67, 68, 69. *See also* customs, holiday; Hanukkah; Lag ba-Omer, 90; Passover; Purim; Rosh Hashanah; Shvues; Simkhas Toyre; Sukkot
Holocaust, 45, 97, 98, 99, 104, 108, 143, 146, 196n51; beginning of, 9, 12, 17; history of, 154, 155, 190; memorials, 81, 83, 84; memory of, 148, 154; narratives of, 152; and shtetls, 16, 17, 20, 72; survivors, 116, 146, 147, 148, 155, *156, 157*; trauma of, 10, 155; victims, 17, 78, 81, 83, 84, 91, 148, 151. *See also* Survivors of the Shoah Visual History Foundation
House of Crafts, 172
Hrodna, 13, 29, 37, 46n1, 200, 202, 229; Hrodna gubernia, 31, 40, *41,* 42, 43; Hrodna Region, 19, 98
Hundert, Gershon David, 39
Hungary, 5, 17, 173

Iampolskaia, Anna, 152–53, 155
Iarov, Sergei, 146
identification cards, 126
identity, 96, 179; Belarusian, 185; cultural, 14; Jewish, 18, 72, 91, 175; markers of, 17, 66
immigration, 30, 115, 116, 149, 150, 172, 178, 245n1
industrialization, 2, 39, 51, 65
Institute of Slavic Studies, 18; Center for Slavo-Judaica, 44, 46
intelligentsia, 187; Hlybokaye, 180, 181, 183; Jewish, 2; Zhaludok, 200, 228
internationalization, 60, 61

International Women's Day, 69
interviews, 20, 22, 46, 78, 81, 82, 85, 86, 98, 99, 108, 116, 141, 148, 149, 150, 151, 172, 173, 176, 178, 179, 180; audio, 147; of shtetl residents, 17, 18; video, 115
Iraq, 4
Islam, 19. *See also* Muslims
Israel, 4, 38, 79, 80, 90, 101, 176, 192n1, 236, 240; Israeli organizations, 177; Israelis, 175, 186, 189
Italy, 4

Jabotinsky, Vladimir, 225
Jesus Christ, 104, 105
Jewish Autonomous Region, 55, 246n5
Jewish Publication Society, 147
John II Casimir Vasa, 40
Joint Distribution Committee, 14
Judaica Interdepartmental Center (European University at St. Petersburg), 17, 174
Judaism, 19; Soviet, 91. *See also* antisemitism; cemeteries, Jewish; Christianity, and Jews; customs, Jewish; day of remembrance, Jewish Radunitsa; education, Jewish; Hasidism; holidays, Jewish; identity, Jewish; kashruth (Jewish dietary laws); schools, Jewish
Judenrat (Jewish council), 3, 116, 122, 124, 125, 126–27, 128, 132, 133, 135, 159

Kaganovich, Lazar Moiseevich, 226, 242
kahal (community leadership), 8–9, 35, 36
Kalinin, Mikhail, 242
Kalyshki (Kolyshki), 60, 64, 65, 69

Index

Karlins, Marvin, 95
kashruth (Jewish dietary laws), 68, 151. *See also* kosher food
Katz, Daniel, 95
Katz, Dovid, 17
Kaunas, 119
kehilah (elected body of wealthy people), 9, 202
Kharik, Izi, 52, 61, 71
khevres (voluntary associations), 8, 12, 13, 14, 15; artisans' associations, 14. *See also* burials, burial society
Kholuts Zionist Youth, 225
Klebanova, Rakhil, 175, 179, 180
Kletsk, 30, 32, 36, 41
Klier, John, 33
Kobryń, 42
Kolomoyskyi, Ihor, 102, 110n28
Korsak, Jozef, 29, 30, 181
kosher food, 15, 68, 69, 72, 127, 154, 211, 223, 224. *See also* kashruth
Kovács, Mátyás, 173
Kozhenevskaya, Margarita, 171, 188, 189
kraeveds (local history experts), 172, 181, 183, 184, 187, 190, 192n6, 194n31, 195n49
Kraków, 173, 174
Kulbak, Moyshe, 2, 52, 61, 62, 63, 67, 71

labor, 105, 122, 226; agricultural, 51; collective, 45; craft, 69; labor bureau, 134; labor market, 44, 63; physical, 63, 106. *See also* serfdom; workers
Ladislaus IV Vasa, 32
Lag ba-Omer, 78, 79, 82, 83, 85, 86, 87–88, 90–91, 91n6, 93n26
landowners, 28, 30–31, 36, 45, 206; jurisdiction of, 34; relationship with Jews, 5, 35. *See also* Poland, Polish landowners
landsmanshaftn, 5, 10, 69
Lapishki Forest, 205
Lapyr, Boleslaw, 185
Lastouski, Vaclau, 187
Latvia, 18, 60, 64, 98
Leite, Naomi, 174
Lenin, Vladimir, 15, 102, 110n28
Leningrad, 9, 16, 18, 59, 146, 176, 177, 194n30
Leningrad Holocaust Research Group, 193n22
Levin, Shmarya, 88, 93n26
Levin, Vladimir, 2
Lida, 42, 200, 205, 220, 238
Liepiel, 30, 37, 46, 46n1, 59, 69, 70, 76, 77, 78, 81, 83
Liozna, 42
liquor, 5, 7, 31, 62, 84, 85, 224
lishentsy (disenfranchised people), 15, 16, 54–55, 64
Lite, 1, 2
literacy, 51, 66, 74n53, 220, 245
literature, 18, 147, 206, 220, 226, 231; Hebrew, 2; novels, 71, 120, 194n30; on shtetl, 32; Yiddish, 2, 11, 13, 120
Lithuania, 9, 146, 200, 238; Grand Duchy of Lithuania, 1, 27, 187; Grand Duchy of Lithuania Statute (1588), 28; Lithuanian-Belarusian region, 37, 41; Lithuanian language, 1; Lithuanian Republic, 2; Lithuanians, 32, 141; Lithuanian shtetls, 18, 33; present-day, 1, 5. *See also* Lite; Polish-Lithuanian Commonwealth
Litvaks, 1, 2
Lodz, 2, 9
Lublin, 139, 159; Union of Lublin, 5
Lurie, Ilia, 39

Lvov, Aleksandr, 173

Magdeburg rights, 30, 32
Magidson, Iakov Markovich, 78
magnates, 31, 34, 35
Mahilyow/Mogilev, 34, 37, 55, 59; gubernia, 37, 40, *41*, 60, 77; Region, 59, 76, 78, 88, 98
Makowski, Tomasz, 40
markets, 4, 5, 28, 30, 122, 127, 179, 216, 219, 230; market days, 6, 10, 11, 206, 219, 228; marketplaces, 6, 11, 28; market squares, 6, 10, 201, 203, 208, 216, 227, 236; market towns, 5, 6, 7, 15; Russian, 14; weekly, 28, 32; Western European, 28
Markov, Fedor, 149, 150, 153
marriage, 12, 67, 82, 210; marriage laws, 55; mixed, 55, 78, 85
Marx, Karl, 70; Marxism, 50
matzo, 15, 68, 82, 91, 97; making of, 67, 96
Mayerson (Jewish commissar), 150, 152, 153–54
Melnikova, Ekaterina, 180
Memorial Book of Glebokie, 116, 143, 148, 197n60,143
memorials, 4, 86, 89, 99, 171, 173, 174, 181, 184, 185, 186, 189, 190, 193n22, 196n56; for Holocaust victims, 17, 81, 83, 84, 91; memorial activities, 175, 176, 177, 193n22; memorial days, 90, 93; memorial food, 88; memorial practices, 80, 81, 88, 90, 176; war memorials, 172
merchants, 4, 7, 15, 51, 54, 62–63, 98, 117, 200, 201, 202, 207, 216, 219; Christian, 5; itinerant, 28; official, 63; private, 62, 40, 41
meshchane (townsmen), 7

meshchanskoe obshchestvo (town council), 7
miastechko/miastechka, 27–28, 31, 34, 35, 37, 38, 43, 45, 46, 72, 77, 78, 83, 87, 88, 91, 126, 172, 183, 194n30; BSSR, 45; development of, 28–29, 30, 32, 39–40, 43, 46; economies of, 28; effect of military conflicts, 33; Jewish residents, 33, 34, 36, 37–38, 40–41, 42, 44, 45, 82, 173, 185, 193n21; network of, 28, 31, 39; owners of, 35; Polish, 33, 38, 43–44; population, 40, 41, 56; status of, 30–31
Middle Ages, 200
migration, 52, 53, 55; to cities, 15, 53, 54; in-migration, 2; Jewish, 5, 56, 200; mass, 52, 55, 59; out-migration, 10, 57. *See also* emigration; immigration
mikvah (ritual bath), 6, 8, 51, 68, 69
Ministry of Internal Affairs, 31, 140
minorities, 44, 57, 64; ethnic, 57, 185; Jews as minority group, 37, 38, 55, 61; minority rights, 60; religious, 185
Minsk, 2, 3, 22, 37, 42, 46n1, 53, 61, 143, 194n31, 196n51, 206, 226, 242; Minsk gubernia, 40, *41*, 42
Minsk Yiddish Theater, 4
Mir, 41, 42
Misnagdim movement, 32, 42
modernity, 2, 52
modernization, 28, 39, 43, 50, 51, 63, 71; processes of, 45, 52, 70
Mogilev. *See* Mahilyow/Mogilev
Moldova, 17, 18, 173
Molotov, Viacheslav, 120, 226, 242
Molotov-Ribbentrop Pact, 3, 236
Montefiore, Moses, 66
Morkhat, Oleg, 185
mortality rate, 36, 200

Moscow, 9, 16, 18, 34, 53, 55, 56, 59, 61, 149, 206, 229; Muscovites, 6, 34
Moscow Center for University Teaching of Jewish Civilization. *See* Sefer Center
mourning, 90, 210, 237
Moykher-Sforim, Mendele. *See* Abramovitsh, Sholem Yankev
multiculturalism, 19, 45, 46, 97, 185
Museum of Jewish History and Culture of Belarus, 196n51
museums, 171, 172, 175, 189, 196n51, 196n56
Muslims, 32; Tatar, 41

narratives, 76, 104, 108, 143, 146, 151, 152, 153, 155, 171, 178, 183, 186, 188, 189, 190; historical, 177, 180, 181, 185; local, 174, 175; narrative flow, 147; narrative mode, 148; narrative strategies, 22, 116; national, 185; oral, 97, 172; reproduced, 147; stereotypical, 179, 181
nationalism: Belarusian, 2, 14, 43, 187; Jewish, 59, 60, 187; Polish, 2, 112n48; Ukrainian, 2
nationalization, 239, 243; of businesses, 117, 118
Nazism, 149; Nazi rule, 3, 108, 192n1; Nazis, 101, 104, 108, 117, 160, 176, 181, 225
Neman river, 19, 40, 200, 216, 224, 230
newspapers, 14, 53, 68, 70, 117, 180, 181, 226, 231; left-wing, 207
Nicholas I, 9
nicknames, 11, 67, 227
NKVD (People's Commissariat for Internal Affairs), 70, 240, 242, 243, 244
nobility, 1, 6, 31, 42, 203; Polish, 5, 7, 9, 200; Polish Lithuanian, 28

norms, 52, 67; American, 152; shtetl, 12, 71; Soviet, 66; of survivors, 146
North America, 192n1

occupations, 60, 62, 63, 72, 96, 115, 172, 188, 240; of Jews, 45, 71, 171; official, 64, 65; of shtetl residents, 4–5, 11
October Revolution, 43, 69
Odessa, 9, 83
Olympiads, 120
oral history, 17, 18, 46, 46n1, 148, 173
Oral Law, 12
Order No. 189 On the Objectives of the Partisan Movement (1942), 131
Orla, 225, 228
Orsha, 129
ORT (Society for Handicraft and Agricultural Work), 61
Orthodoxy, 1, 30, 77, 93, 98, 137, 176, 207; Eastern Orthodox, 32, 34, 41, 101; Greek Orthodox, 19; Orthodox churches, 1, 30; Russian Orthodox, 78, 81, 84
Other, the, 95, 97, 108

Pale of Settlement, 7, 18, 37, 43, 45, 97, 191
Palesie Region, 40, 42, 55–56, 66
Palestine, 44, 183, 203, 220, 225, 227, 228, 236
Paperna, Abram, 38
Parents' Saturdays, 76
partisans, 81, 123, 124, 130–31, 132, 133, 136, 137, 138, 139–40, 143, 152, 153; Jewish, 132, 135, 150; partisan camps, 139; partisan commanders, 3, 131; partisan territory, 151; partisan units, 131, 133, 134, 135, 139, 140, 142, 149, 150, 154; Red Army, 146, 149; Soviet, 3, 148, 149
Parychy, 56

Passover, 12, 15, 67, 68, 82, 91, 91n6, 128, 176, 223–24
passports, 53, 130, 132
Pastavy, 135
paupers, 15; pauperization, 44
peasants, 1, 2, 9, 10, 15, 28, 30, 37, 50, 51, 56–57, 64, 129, 130, 149, 150, 153, 201, 205, 206, 216, 219, 231, 239, 241; Christian, 203; former, 65; peasant languages, 1, 58, 207; peasant villages, 6; and relationship with Jews, 5, 6, 7, 9, 10, 41
perestroika, 193n22
persecution: of Belarusians, 14; of Jews, 5, 14, 15, 117, 122, 142
Petersburg Judaica Center. *See* Judaica Interdepartmental Center
Petrovsky-Shtern, Yohanan, 39
Pinchuk, Ben-Cion, 37, 39
Pinsk, 2, 42
Plavinski, Henadz', 181, 183, 184, 186, 187, 189, 195n44
Podolia, 12, 77, 85, 88, 89, 104, 174
pogroms, 2, 14, 34, 43, 128, 203
Poland, 2, 9, 20, 32, 98, 105, 150, 159, 172, 192n1, 199, 207, 226, 230, 236–37; borders of, 3, 17, 45, 64, 117, 149; central, 3; communist party, 117; Congress Poland, 7, 9, 12; eastern, 149; First Partition, 6; German-occupied, 117; interwar, 2, 10, 14, 44; and Jews, 5, 6, 13, 14, 17; northeastern, 1; northwestern, 43; Polish army, 230; Polish authorities, 43, 44; Polish Belarus, 3, 9, 10, 11, 12, 14; Polish culture, 1; Polish economy, 5, 43; Polish gangs, 238; Polish government, 44; Polish Home Army, 149; Polish Labor Party, 240; Polish landowners, 9; Polish lands, 200; Polish language, 1, 44, 58, 60, 130, 142, 203, 205, 206, 207, 220, 242; Polish law, 9; Polish pogroms, 2; Polish police, 142; Polish Republic, 2; Polish residents, 32, 118, 119, 142, 150, 227; Polish rule, 205, 240; Polish taxes, 14; Polish villages, 207; prewar, 187; Soviet invasion of, 3; wars of, 6, 236; western, 119. See also *miastechko/miastechka*, Polish; nobility, Polish; Polish-Lithuanian Commonwealth; schools, Polish
Polatsk, 117, 120, 129, 130, 149, 183; Polatsk voivodeship, 29, 33
police, 120, 121, 124, 134, 135, 137, 142, 154, 203, 222, 236, 238, 240; bribery of, 8; Jewish, 118, 123, 127, 130, 131, 139; police agencies, 43; police lists, 226; secret, 118
Polish-Lithuanian Commonwealth, 5, 7, 28, 29, 33, 34, 35, 36, 38, 39, 187, 192n1
Pollin-Gallay, Hannah, 146
Polonsky, Antony, 39, 44
Polotsk. *See* Polatsk
POW camps, 149
Prague, 173
prayer, 80, 83, 84, 86, 89, 128, 206, 208, 210, 224; collective, 79, 82; individual, 13; Kaddish, 79, 84, 88, 92n9, 139, 211; Lord's Prayer, 177; prayer books, 208; quorums, 12, 13
Presidium of the Supreme Soviet of the BSSR, 45
prisons, 202; prisoners, 34, 133, 236, 241, 242, 243. *See also* ghettos, ghetto prisoners
production cooperatives, 63
propaganda, 54, 119, 226; antireligious, 119
Prussia, 7

Pruzhany, 11
Purim, 13, 223

rabbis, 35, 37, 44, 65, 67, 68, 70, 84, 87, 93n26, 98, 105, 118, 119, 200, 210, 220, 240
radios, 53, 70, 120, 206, 237
Radziwill family, 29, 32, 34–35, 36, 41; Prince Radziwill, 36
railroads, 2, 8, 9, 39, 61, 85, 126, 229
Rajak, Michael, 116, 143, 148
Rajak, Zvi, 116, 143, 148
Rakovskiy, Leontiy, 177, 180, 194nn30–31
Red Army, 116, 117, 140, 149, 150, 237, 238, 239, 242, 243
refugees, 117, 118, 126, 130
registration, residential, 53
Reisen, Avrom, 207
religion, 8, 11, 32, 33, 34, 39, 68, 96, 97, 98, 104, 119, 206, 208, 213, 223, 224, 228, 239; antireligious policies, 51, 67, 68, 69, 70; antireligious propaganda, 119; religiosity, 71, 72; religious buildings, 70; religious centers, 30; religious circles, 70; religious experience, 13; religious functionaries, 15, 206; religious groups, 33, 103; religious institutions, 5, 9, 29, 31, 72; religious items, 69; religious law, 128; religious life, 35, 45, 68, 69, 72, 128; religious observance, 18, 207; religious pluralism, 27, 44; religious practices, 18, 69, 72; religious rights, 69; religious services, 12, 15; religious societies, 51; religious traditions, 13, 20, 46, 56, 69, 70, 210. *See also* Christianity; diversity, religious; education, religious; holidays, religious; Islam; Judaism; minorities, religious; rituals, religious; schools, religious; stereotypes, religious
remorse, 151, 153, 154
repression, 51, 61, 227; anti-Jewish, 43; repressive policies, 34, 64, 65, 68
Ribbentrop-Molotov Non-Aggression Pact. *See* Molotov-Ribbentrop Pact
rituals, 28, 50, 72, 81, 96, 116, 210; funerary, 210; religious, 12; of remembrance, 18, 76, 88, 177; ritual murder, 97, 108, 245n1; ritual slaughter, 9, 72, 116, 211; wedding, 210
Roma, 19, 32, 128, 206; gypsies, 106
Romania, 17, 173
Rosh Hashanah, 90, 224
Rossman, Moshe, 39
rumors, 70, 71, 96, 103, 118, 133, 227, 237, 238, 245
Russia, 4, 7, 18, 34, 76, 78, 98, 100, 107, 117–18, 124, 192n6, 193n22, 199, 226, 227, 236–37; anti-Russian revolts, 9; Russian administration, 119; Russian borders, 77, 151; Russian census, 8, 19, 37; Russian Civil War, 43; Russian courts, 8; Russian culture, 2, 59; Russian discourse, 20; Russian Empire, 7, 22, 30, 35, 37, 39, 52; Russian Federation, 77; Russian government, 7, 31, 36, 38, 39, 43; Russian Jews, 7, 8, 10, 39, 42, 61, 222; Russian language, 27, 51, 52, 58–59, 64, 66, 79, 84, 87, 92n9, 99, 115, 116, 130, 176, 177, 183, 207, 228, 239, 242, 243; Russian laws, 7; Russian military, 7, 116, 136, 144n46; Russian politics, 51; Russian Revolution, 2, 13, 51;

Russia (cont.)
  Russian rule, 2, 7; Russians, 2, 7, 18, 57, 81, 92n17, 98, 102, 110n28, 240; Russian senate, 7; Russian traditions, 91, 93n25; Russian villages, 207; Russian writers, 4; tsarist Russia, 13. *See also* annexation, Russian; cemeteries, Russian; markets, Russian; Orthodoxy, Russian Orthodox; Russian Academy of Sciences; Russian State University for the Humanities; Russia-Polish Lithuanian Commonwealth war; schools, Russian; Soviet Union
Russian Academy of Sciences, 19
Russian State University for the Humanities, 172
Russia-Polish Lithuanian Commonwealth war (1654–1667), 33, 36
Ruzhany, 31
Rzeczpospolita. *See* Polish-Lithuanian Commonwealth

Sabbath, 6, 10, 12, 14, 68, 128, 204, 207
Sandri, Olivia, 174
Sapieha, Cazimir Lev, 31
Saulich, Tatsiana, 175, 178, 189, 192n5
schools, 8, 18, 42, 59, 61, 118, 119, 140, 183, 196n56, 200, 221, 225, 228, 231, 243; Belarusian, 58, 59, 74n53; ethnic, 59; Hebrew, 201, 219–20, 240; high schools, 220; Jewish, 6, 60, 65, 82, 119, 141, 201, 220; Polish, 14, 44, 203, 219, 220, 246n6; religious, 15, 67; Russian, 11, 16, 58, 59, 66, 71; schoolchildren, 53, 54, 67, 183, 188, 227, 243; schoolteachers, 148, 201; secular, 220; Soviet, 67; tuition, 220; yeshivas, 42,

119; Yiddish, 11, 14, 16, 57, 58, 59–60, 219–20, 240; vocational, 220; Zionist Tarbut, 14. *See also* education
Second Belarusian Brigade, 140
secularization, 14, 51, 71
Seder, 224
Sefer Center, 17, 20, 44, 46, 46n1, 76, 173; Sefer expeditions, 18, 19, *21*, 82, 172
self-accusation, 152, 153
self-definition, 95
self-governance, 30, 39
self-image, 95
Senate Decree (October 26, 1810), 31
serfdom, 9, 30, 36, 39
Shchadryn, 59, 63–64, 69
Shchuchyn, 200, 205, 219, 227
Shkliar, Nikolai, 245n3
Shklow, 30, 42, 77
Shneour, Zalman, 77
Sholokhov, Mikhail, 226
Shulman, Arkadi, 178, 179
Shvues, 223
Siberia, 118, 227, 236, 238, 239, 240, 242
Simkhas Toyre, 13
Simonovich, Lev Artur, 180
Slavic population, 20, 96, 97, 98, 99, 108; and perceptions of Jews, 103, 104; Slavic countries, 192n6; Slavic folklore, 172; Slavic language, 4, 27; Slavic traditions, 76, 80, 81, 91. *See also* customs, Slavic; Institute of Slavic Studies, Center for Slavo-Judaica
Slonim, 42, 220
Slovakia, 17, 173
Slutsk, 42, 55
Smilavichy, 41
Smilovitsky, Leonid, 81
Smolensk, 79, 88, 89, 92, 242;

Smolensk Region, 76, 77, 78, 82, 83, 87, 88, 98
Sobolevskaia, Olga, 35
Sobolevskiy, Aleksandr, 194n31
Sobolevskiy, Anton, 177, 194n31
Sobolevskiy, Yuri, 194n31
socialism, 39, 45, 70, 207, 219, 225; socialists, 16
social mobility, 16, 45
social welfare, 8, 9
Sokolova, Alla, 174
Soviet-Polish war (1920), 43
soviets (councils), 60, 61; Belarusian, 58, 60; ethnic, 60; Jewish, 57–58, 60, 65
Soviet State Defense Committee, 131, 150
Soviet Union, 3, 16, 22, 52, 116, 117, 119–20, 136, 144n46, 150, 187, 192n1, 226, 227; and Jews, 2, 4, 17, 18; Soviets, 207, 230, 240, 243; Sovietization, 20, 46. *See also* activism, Soviet; annexation, Soviet; atheism, Soviet; Germany, invasion of Soviet Union; norms, Soviet; partisans, Soviet; Poland, Soviet invasion of; Russia; schools, Soviet
Spain, 4
Spielberg, Steven, 154
Stalin, Joseph, 15, 51, 57, 70, 127, 226, 239, 241, 242, 245
Staliunas, Darias, 2
Stampfer, Shaul, 36
Star of David, 122, 127, 176
status, social, 5, 8, 11, 35, 52, 53, 55, 57, 58, 62, 63, 115
stereotypes: cultural, 173, 176; ethnic, 60, 65, 95, 96, 97–98, 108, 176; of Jews, 96, 97, 102, 103, 104, 105, 191; and personal experience, 95, 97; religious, 97, 108

St. Petersburg, 17, 42
St. Petersburg Jewish University, 172
Sukhoi, Pavel, 188, 196n56
Sukkot, 223
Surazh, 82–83, 84, 85, 86, 88, 93n20
survivors, 3–4, 22, 115, 126, 133, 141, 143, 146, 150, 192n1, 236. *See also* Holocaust, survivors
Survivors of the Shoah Visual History Foundation, 154
synagogues, 4, 6, 8, 9, 12, 13, 21, 36, 37, 51, 69, 70, 190, 195n38, 200, 202, 206, 208, 209–10, 211, 212, 223, 239, 243; attendance, 10, 14, 67, 68, 119, 207, 208; building of, 69–70, 179; closures of, 15, 68, 69; ruins of, 156, 173, 183, 229; visits to, 76; women's sections, 13
Szabad, Tsemakh, 245n2

Talmud, 12, 70, 90; Talmudic learning, 42
Tatars, 19, 32, 46, 60, 106, 132. *See also* Muslims, Tatar
taxes, 9, 15, 51, 54, 68, 202; *chynsh* (cash tax), 28; state, 63; tax assessor, 29; tax collectors, 35, 202; tax exemptions, 30; tax inspectors, 62–63; tax policy, 52. *See also* Poland, Polish taxes
technology, 53, 71, 143, 147, 241
tefillin, 89, 137
Teller, Adam, 34, 39
testimonies, 3, 22, 115, 116, 125, 133, 143, 146, 148, 152, 154, 155; recorded, 147; testimonial sources, 19, 20; video, 147, 154
theater, 42, 123; amateur, 10, 14; folkloric, 97, 186, 220, 221. *See also* Minsk Yiddish Theater
Tisha be-Av, 77, 78, 90, 91
Torah, the, 12, 42, 69, 70, 208, 219, 220

tourism, 18; genealogy, 194n29; heritage, 173, 193n15, 194n29; Jewish-themed, 173–74

trade, 29, 34, 37, 41, 42, 44, 105, 200, 219, 227; free, 34; illegal, 64; licensed, 51, 63; nonlicensed, 62; private, 51, 67; trade centers, 28, 30, 43, 174; traded goods, 28, 30, 62, 201; traders, 15, 116, 125, 201, 216; trade unions, 226; traditional, 63, 64, 106; unsanctioned, 65

Treaty of Riga, 43

Troitsa (Trinity Sunday), 76

Trotskyism, 65

tsarist government, 13, 30, 31, 36, 51

Tsene-rene (Yiddish adaptation of the Pentateuch), 13

Ukraine, 2, 5, 7, 8, 9, 149, 172, 173, 193n22; and Jews, 6, 12, 14, 15, 17, 41, 43, 55, 174, 175; northern, 1; Ukrainians, 14, 102, 105; Ukrainian shtetls, 15, 18, 33, 38; Ukrainian traditions, 98

unemployment, 15, 52, 62, 63

Union of Lublin (1569), 5

United States, 7, 9, 116, 148, 150

University of Southern California Shoah Foundation Institute for Visual History and Education, 20, 22, 125, 143n1; Visual History Archive (VHA), 22, 115, 116, 143, 147, 148

urbanization, 14, 39, 51, 52, 71

Ushachy, 20, 30

vehicles, 120, 206; bicycles, 121, 124, 201, 206, 238; carriages, 205, 206, 216; cars, 121; carts, 10, 140, 201, 202, 206, 211, 212, 219, 228, 237; motorcycles, 121, 206; trucks, 138, 206, 230, 238

Veidlinger, Jeffrey, 17, 173

Victory Day, 83, 92, 141

Vileyka, 30

Vilna/Vilnius, 42, 44, 117, 119, 126, 140, 141, 143, 149, 174, 202, 203, 220, 230, 245n2; Vilna gubernia, 37, 40, *41*, 42, 43; Vilna voivodeship, 29, 31, 192n1

violence, 33, 153; anti-Jewish, 43, 142, 200

Vitebsk, 22, 55, 67; Vitebsk district, 58; Vitebsk gubernia, 37, 40, *41*, 42; Vitebsk Region, 19, 20, 54, 59, 60, 76, 78, 81, 83, 98, 171, 190; Vitebsk voivodeship, 33

von Dingelstedt, Franz, 245n4

Voroshilov, Kliment, 225, 242

Vuytsyk, Olha, 173

Waligórska, Magdalena, 17, 184–85, 196n51

Walters, Gary, 95

Warsaw, 2, 9, 13, 119, 127, 214, 237

weapons, 131, 132, 133, 134, 135, 140

weddings, 13, 117, 210

Wehrmacht, 121, 149

westernization, 28

Wilno voivodeship. *See* Vilna/Vilnius, Vilna voivodeship

workers, 50, 60, 63, 64, 65, 71, 138, 226, 243; essential, 159; factory, 61; forest, 118; government, 57, 69, 121; hired, 63, 64, 67; party, 120; service, 15; white-collar, 15; workers' rights, 226. *See also* labor; occupations

workshops, 68, 122, 125, 159, *160–64*, *167*, *169*, 201, 202, 231, 239

World War I, 3, 12, 43, 228; postwar period, 2, 11, 220; prewar period, 148, 173

World War II, 3, 80, 92n11, 98, 99, 194n31, 230, 237; postwar period, 16, 46, 173, 180, 220; prewar period, 12, 17, 19, 20, 46, 60, 115, 173, 180, *191*, 206

Yanka Kupala State University of Hrodna, 19
Yevsektsiya, 67, 68
Yiddish: culture, 72; dialects, 91; language, 1, 3, 8, 13, 15, 16, 52, 57–58, 59, 66, 67, 88, 89, 120, 126, 137, 138, 141, 183, 206, 207, 220, 221, 226, 228, 239, 243, 245n3; as marker of difference, 4; pronunciation, 9; status as official language, 2, 58, 60; Yiddish speakers, 17, 50, 58, 66, 206; Yiddish traditions, 44; Yiddish writers, 10, 52, 61, 77. *See also* AHEYM; Central Yiddish School Organization; literature, Yiddish; Minsk Yiddish Theater; schools, Yiddish

Yom Kippur, 89–90
yortsayt (death anniversaries), 66, 76, 87, 148
Young Pioneers' Club, 119, 243–44, 245

Zborowski, Mark, 16, 172
Zhaludok, 10, 15, 19, 20, *21*, 23, 37, 44, 46, 46n1, 199–200, 203, 205, *209*, 220, 225, 227, 228, 230, 231, *244*
Zhirinovsky, Vladimir, 102, 110n28
Zhyrovichy, 29, 40, 41; Zhyrovichy Monastery, 41
Zionism, 2, 15, 39, 65, 101, 103, 118, 220, 225; Zionists, 16, 101, 181, 185, 225; Zionist youth movements, 10. *See also* schools, Zionist Tarbut
Zorich, Semyon, 42

For Indiana University Press
Tony Brewer, Artist and Book Designer
Brian Carroll, Rights Manager
Gary Dunham, Acquisitions Editor and Director
Anna Francis, Assistant Acquisitions Editor
Brenna Hosman, Production Coordinator
Katie Huggins, Production Manager
Nancy Lightfoot, Project Editor and Manager
Dan Pyle, Online Publishing Manager
Pamela Rude, Senior Artist and Book Designer
Stephen Williams, Marketing and Publicity Manager

www.ingramcontent.com/pod-product-compliance
Lightning Source LLC
Chambersburg PA
CBHW021347300426
44114CB00012B/1121